A PRACTITIONER'S HANDBOOK FOR INSTITUTIONAL EFFECTIVENESS AND STUDENT OUTCOMES ASSESSMENT IMPLEMENTATION

THIRD EDITION

By the same author

The Departmental Guide and Record Book for Student Outcomes Assessment and Institutional Effectiveness

Assessment Case Studies: Common Issues in Implementation with Various Approaches to Resolution

A PRACTITIONER'S HANDBOOK FOR INSTITUTIONAL EFFECTIVENESS AND STUDENT OUTCOMES ASSESSMENT IMPLEMENTATION

THIRD EDITION

by James O. Nichols

Director, University Planning and Institutional Research
The University of Mississippi

Resource Sections by

Sheri Blessing, *University of Kansas*
Gale W. Bridger, *Louisiana State University, Shreveport*
Harriott Calhoun, *Jefferson State Junior College*
Eliot S. Elfner, *St. Norbert College*
Mary R. Kinnick, *Portland State University*
Marsha V. Krotseng, *State College and University Systems of West Virginia*
Gary R. Pike, *University of Missouri, Columbia*
Linda K. Pratt, *North Carolina Central University*
Gloria W. Raines, *Louisiana State University, Shreveport*
Donald J. Reichard, *University of North Carolina, Greensboro*
Brenda Hyde Rogers, *Durham Technical Community College*
Bobby H. Sharp, *Appalachian State University*
Heidi A. Tickle, *The University of Mississippi*
R. Dan Walleri, *Mt. Hood Community College*
Lori A. Wolff, *The University of Mississippi*
Michael Yost, *Trinity University*

AGATHON PRESS
NEW YORK

© 1989, 1991, 1995 by Agathon Press
100 Newfield Avenue
Edison, NJ 08837

Library of Congress Cataloging-in Publication Data

Nichols, James O. (James Oliver), 1941-
A practitioner's handbook for institutional effectiveness and
student outcomes assessment implementation / by James O.
Nichols ; resource sections by Sheri Blessing ... [et al.]. -- 3rd ed.
    p. cm.
Includes bibliographical references and index.
ISBN 0-87586-113-x
1. Universities and colleges--United States--Evaluation.
2. Universities and college--United States--Accreditation.
I. Title.
LB2331.63.N54 1995
378.73--DC20   95-40857
                                                        CIP

Printed in the United States

Contents

Preface and Acknowledgments   ix

CHAPTER ONE
Explaining the Handbook's Use in Institutional Effectiveness and Outcomes
Assessment Implementation   1

CHAPTER TWO
Overview of the Institutional Effectiveness Implementation Model:
Its Assumptions, Basis, and Execution   13

CHAPTER THREE
Building the Necessary Foundation for Institutional Effectiveness: The First Year   23
  Resource Sections
  Developing the Expanded Statement of Institutional Purpose (Michael Yost)   30

  Attitudinal Surveys in Institutional Effectiveness
  (Gloria W. Raines, Gale W. Bridger, and Lori A. Wolff)   43

  Cognitive Assessment Instruments: Availability and Utilization
  (Marsha V. Krotseng and Gary R. Pike)   60

  Assessment of Behavioral Change and Performance
  (Mary R. Kinnick and R. Dan Walleri)   86

  Assessment-Related Information from Institutional Data Systems
  (Bobby H. Sharp and Sheri Blessing)   107

  Assessment Planning (James O. Nichols)   123

CHAPTER FOUR
Detailed Design at the Departmental Level   138
  Resource Sections
  Statements of Outcomes/Objectives and Assessment at the Departmental Level
  (Linda K. Pratt)   146

  Setting and Evaluating Intended Educational (Instructional) Outcomes
  (Brenda Hyde Rogers)   157

  Assessment in General Education (Heidi A. Tickle)   172

  Setting and Evaluating Objectives and Outcomes in Nonacademic Units
  (Donald J. Reichard)   186

  Assessment and Continuous Quality Improvement (Eliot S. Elfner)   205

CHAPTER FIVE
Initial Implementation   215
  Resource Section
  Implementing Institutional Effectiveness at Two-Year Colleges
  (Harriott Calhoun)   223

v

CHAPTER SIX
Establishment of the Annual Institutional Effectiveness Cycle and Closing the Loop   236

CHAPTER SEVEN
Maintaining Institutional Effectiveness Operations
Over an Extended Period of Time   251

APPENDIX A
Our University Expanded Statement of Institutional Purpose   255

APPENDIX B
Your Community College Expanded Statement of Institutional Purpose   263

APPENDIX C
Ole Miss Expanded Statement of Institutional Purpose   265

APPENDIX D
Outline of Twelve-Month Sequence of Events for Preparation of
Expanded Statement of Institutional Purpose   267

APPENDIX E
Executive Summary of the Program Review Process of the Division of Student
Affairs at the University of North Carolina at Greensboro   270

Index   276

List of Figures

1. The Institutional Effectiveness Paradigm   8
2. The Institutional Effectiveness Implementation Team   15
3. A Generic Model for Implementation of Institutional Effectiveness and Effectiveness and Assessment Activities in Higher Education   18
4. The First Year of a Generic Model for Implementation of Institutional Effectiveness and Assessment Activities in Higher Education   25
5. Relationship and Key Linkages between Expanded Statement of Institutional Purpose, Intended Outcomes or Objectives, and Evaluation of Institutional Effectiveness   26
6. Components of the Expanded Statement of Institutional Purpose   31
7. Organization of Institutional Goals and Departmental/Program Outcomes or Objectives and Assessment   40
8. Assessment Using Institutional Information Systems   109
9. Format for Identifying Existing Assessment Data   127
10. Assessment Planning Conceptual Matrix   130
11. Assessment Planning Detailed Documentation   131
12. The Second Year of a Generic Model for Implementation of Institutional Effectiveness and Assessment Activities in Higher Education   139
13. Undergraduate English Program—Example of Linkage between Expanded Statement of Institutional Purpose and Departmental/Program Intended Outcomes/Objectives at Our University   141
14. Undergraduate English Program—Example of Linkage between Expanded Statement of Institutional Purpose, Departmental/Program Intended Outcomes/Objectives, Assessment Criteria and Procedures at Our University   144
15. Career Services Center—Example of Linkage between Expanded Statement of Institutional Purpose, Departmental/Program Intended Outcomes/Objectives, and Assessment Criteria and Procedures at Our University   193

16. Continuous Quality Improvement—Creating a CQI Culture · 209

17. The Third Year of a Generic Model for Implementation of Institutional Effectiveness and Assessment Activities in Higher Education · 216

18. Developmental Education—Example of Linkage between Expanded Statement of Institutional Purpose, Departmental/Program Intended Outcomes/Objectives, and Assessment Criteria at Your Community College · 227

19. Your Community College Automotive Technology Program—Example of Linkage between Expanded Statement of Institutional Purpose, Departmental/Program Intended Outcomes/Objectives, and Assessment Criteria and Procedures · 231

20. Your Community CollegeTransfer Program—Example of Linkage between Expanded Statement of Institutional Purpose, Departmental/Program Intended Outcomes/Objectives, and Assessment Criteria and Procedures · 233

21. The Final Year of a Generic Model for Implementation of Institutional Effectiveness and Assessment Activities in Higher Education · 237

22. Undergraduate English Program—Example of Linkage between Expanded Statement of Institutional Purpose, Departmental/Program Intended Outcomes/Objectives, Assessment Criteria and Procedures, Results, and Use of Results at Our University · 244

23. Accounting Degree Program—Example of Linkage between Expanded Statement of Institutional Purpose, Departmental/Program Intended Outcomes/Objectives, Assessment Criteria and Procedures, Results, and Use of Results at Our University · 245

24. Career Services Center—Example of Linkage between Expanded Statement of Institutional Purpose, Departmental/Program Intended Outcomes/Objectives, Assessment Criteria and Procedures, Results, and Use of Results at Our University · 246

25. Developmental Education—Example of Linkage between Expanded Statement of Institutional Purpose, Departmental/Program Intended Outcomes/Objectives, Assessment Criteria and Procedures, Results, and Use of Results at Our University · 247

26. Your Community College Automotive Technology Program—Example of Linkage between Expanded Statement of Institutional Purpose, Departmental/Program Intended Outcomes/Objectives, Assessment Criteria and Procedures, Results, and Use of Results at Our University · 249

27. Your Community College Transfer Program—Example of Linkage between Expanded Statement of Institutional Purpose, Departmental/Program Intended Outcomes/Objectives, Assessment Criteria and Procedures, Results, and Use of Results at Our University · 250

28. Annual Institutional Effectiveness Cycle Applied to an Academic Year Sequence (Early Semester) · 251

To Karen, the light of my life for over thirty years and the loving heart of our family.

Preface and Acknowledgments

When the first edition of this book was published in 1989 under the title *Institutional Effectiveness and Outcomes Assessment Implementation on Campus: A Practitioner's Handbook*, it was clear that assessment of student outcomes and institutional effectiveness was already a significant movement in higher education. By the second edition, published in 1991, the movement had grown in influence, as evidenced by the increasing interest of the federal government, the activities of regional and professional accreditation associations, and the concerns expressed by governors and state legislatures. Nevertheless, this trend is still relatively new to many institutions that are implementing a program of institutional effectiveness and educational outcomes assessment and are faced with the problem of how to put relatively theoretical assessment concepts into a clearly manageable procedural form. Institutions beginning the process will particularly benefit from this third edition because it reflects the growing record of successful implementation on other campuses.

As was suggested in the Preface to the first edition of this book, the search for an implementation model is complicated by several factors. Originally institutions with national reputations in student outcomes or institutional effectiveness were often described as (a) unique, (b) being led by a Chief Executive Officer with a particularly keen interest in the subject, or (c) financially benefiting from implementation through their state funding formula and therefore able to invest heavily in the implementation process itself. Because these institutions were unique, their models of implementation seemed irreplicable, which left more traditional two-year and four-year institutions "reinventing the wheel" of outcomes assessment or institutional effectiveness implementation.

The search for an implementation model or plan is further complicated by the difficulty of adapting another institution's actions to the campus environment and the position of a number of accrediting associations. Institutional effectiveness or outcomes assessment, more than many of the processes in higher education, must be tuned to each particular campus environment. Trying to plug in procedures used at another institution is often unsuccessful. The single piece of advice most often cited by contributors to *Assessment Case Studies* was to adapt the implementation process to the institution and not to attempt to change the institution to fit the implementation model.

Regional and professional accrediting associations have been among the leaders in the spread of outcomes assessment or institutional effectiveness implementation. However, these accreditation bodies, while willing to set criteria for implementation results, have been in most cases understandably reluctant to specify **how** these mandates are to be met for fear of being accused of being prescriptive regarding internal institutional operations.

In the summer of 1987, the undersigned primary author and a number of colleagues who had led successful outcomes assessment implementation on their own campuses, had played major roles in the authorship of accreditation association documents concerning outcomes assessment or institutional effectiveness, had pilot-tested accreditation association requirements concerning the subject, had served on accreditation teams with individual responsibility for outcomes assessment, had consulted widely in the field, or were then actively involved in the implementation activities, decided to pool their knowledge and experience in an effort to propose a general model for implementation of institutional effectiveness and outcomes assessment.

It was determined that the implementation model to be delineated in the first edition of this book should:

- Outline a general sequence of events leading toward genuine and comprehensive campus implementation of institutional effectiveness or outcomes assessment;
- Be adaptable to virtually every type of institutional circumstance;
- Require as small an amount of additional funding as possible by the institution;
- Be supported by detailed review of practice or literature in the field at the critical points of implementation.

By 1991, it was apparent to the primary author and his colleagues that the original circumstances leading to the development of the initial publication still existed, but that rapid developments in the field could usefully be incorporated into a second edition. It was determined that in addition to the very substantial updating of a number of the original resource sections, this second edition would (a) be more generic in tone, (b) include more examples of and a specific Resource Section concerning implementation at two-year colleges, (c) add coverage of performance and behavioral means of assessment of intended instructional (educational) outcomes, and (d) address assessment in nonacademic areas.

This third edition of *A Practitioner's Handbook,* which has been expanded in both depth and breadth of coverage, is a logical extension of the practical orientation of the first two editions. Because the field of assessment has matured since the second edition, this current publication includes examples and commentary through the use of assessment results to improve academic programming and administrative services. Such information concerning "closing the loop" was unavailable during earlier editions. Additionally, this third edition has been expanded in breadth to now include separate resource sections regarding assessment planning, assessment in general education, as well as the relationship between institutional effectiveness or educational outcomes assessment, and the quality improvement movement known otherwise as TQM (i.e., Total Quality Management) or more commonly within higher education as CQI (i.e., Continuous Quality Improvement).

The pages that follow were designed to meet the original criteria as well as those established for the subsequent editions. *A Practitioner's Handbook* is divided into three basic sections. Chapters One and Two explain the *Handbook's* use and offer an overview of the institutional effectiveness or outcomes assessment implementation model. Chapters Three through Seven deal with the specific sequence of events or activities suggested during the course of working toward comprehensive institutional implementation. These chapters are supported by twelve Resource Sections covering in greater depth more specific technical aspects of implementation, including tests, surveys, and other aspects of instrumentation that have advanced substantially even during the preparation of this edition. Finally the third section of the *Handbook* offers specific examples of institutional Statements of Purpose and other types of specific institutional guidance in implementation. Readers of earlier editions will want to note that the examples of expected educational outcomes and means of assessment and criteria previously contained in this third section of *A Practitioner's Handbook* have been moved to Appendix B in *Assessment Case Studies*, where the number of instructional examples has been increased by tenfold over previous editions. Overall, the *Handbook* is intended to provide the practical guidance needed for implementation as well as specific examples of that implementation.

It is important to understand that the field continues to grow rapidly, and with each passing year the experience base of institutions that have successfully implemented outcomes assessment or institutional effectiveness operations increases at a faster rate. Accordingly, no publication in this area can remain definitive over a period of years. Nevertheless, we have attempted to again provide substantially more information than was available at the time of the first and second editions and trust this new version will be a useful tool for its intended audience.

ACKNOWLEDGMENTS

I am indebted collectively and individually to the Resource Section authors whose biographical sketches follow, both for the quality and promptness of their submissions as well as for their suggestions guiding the general refinement of *A Practitioner's Handbook*.

Sheri Blessing, while working on a Ph.D. in Higher Education Administration, is the Assistant Director of Counseling and Psychological Services at the University of Kansas. Her primary responsibilities include national standardized testing, psychological testing, test scoring, and other data analysis and research activities. She has worked with Institutional Research at the University of Kansas Medical Center and East Carolina University.

Gail W. Bridger is Interim Dean of Education and Professor of Education at Louisiana State University in Shreveport, Louisiana. She formerly served as the chief planning and evaluation officer and coordinated the institutional research function as Associate Vice Chancellor for Academic Affairs. Having served as president of the Louisiana Association for Institutional Research, Bridger remains active in the field as a member of the Southern Association of Colleges and Schools visiting committees.

Harriott Calhoun is the Director of Institutional Research at Jefferson State Community College in Birmingham, Alabama, and is the secretary of the Southern Association of Institutional Research. She has been an active member of the institutional research community by serving on and chairing committees in state, regional, and national associations, making presentations, and serving on visiting committees for the Southern Association of Colleges and Schools.

Eliot S. Elfner serves the North Central Association Commission on Institutions of Higher Education as a Consultant/Evaluator, participating on and chairing accreditation visits, and as a member of review committee appeals for NCA. He has been a frequent presenter at NCA-CIHE Annual Conferences and recently participated in the NCA Regional Conferences and Spring Seminars on Student Academic Achievement. He is a member of the Business Faculty at St. Norbert College. His research and publications include articles on student outcomes in higher education, and he is currently completing a full-length work on CQI tentatively entitled *Continuous Quality Improvement in Higher Education.* The book will be published by Agathon Press in 1996.

Mary R. Kinnick is a Professor and Chairperson of the Department of Education Policy, Foundations and Administrative Studies in the School of Education at Portland State University in Portland, Oregon. She is a former Director of Institutional Research at Portland State University and served as president of the Pacific Northwest Association for Institutional Research and Planning. Kinnick focuses on educational access, assessment and evaluation, and developing learning communities in post-secondary education.

Marsha V. Krotseng is Director of Research and Information Systems for the State College and University Systems of West Virginia where she monitors state policy issues and is involved in accountability efforts for the chancellors and governing boards. She is a member of West Virginia's statewide higher education assessment committee and works with the state's public higher education institutions in helping to identify and obtain meaningful quantitative measures of student outcomes and institutional effectiveness. She is a past forum chair for the Association for Institutional Research and has authored numerous articles and presentations for professional organizations.

Gary R. Pike is the Director of Student Life Studies at the University of Missouri in Columbia, Missouri. He directs the design and implementation of a variety of research and evaluation projects intended to promote campus-wide understanding of the nature and quality of the student experience. Further interests include research design and measurement theory as it relates to outcomes assessment, and quantitative research on factors influencing student learning and development.

Linda K. Pratt is the Associate Vice Chancellor for Academic Affairs for Research, Evaluation and Planning at North Carolina Central University in Durham, North Carolina, where she coordinates and monitors the planning system and oversees institutional research, assessment, academic and administrative computing, and telecommunication activities. Pratt served at the National Laboratory for Higher Education and was president of the Southern Association for Institutional Research.

Gloria W. Raines is Vice Chancellor for Student Affairs at Louisiana State University in Shreveport. As Director of Research and Data Processing and then Vice President for Instructional Services at Valencia Community College, Raines was responsible for institutional research, management information systems and planning, programming, and budgeting. She completed a concentration in planning as part of her doctoral work, and has been actively involved in planning and evaluation activities throughout her career.

Donald J. Reichard is the Associate Vice Chancellor for Institutional Planning and Research and Adjunct Associate Professor of Higher Education at the University of North Carolina in Greensboro. He has served as a research associate with the Southern Regional Education Board and as a president of the Association for Institutional Research.

Brenda Hyde Rogers is the Dean of Institutional Research and Information Resources at Durham Technical Community College in Durham, North Carolina. She worked as Associate Director of the Office of Research, Evaluation and Planning at North Carolina Central University and as the Assistant Director of the Office of Institutional Research at North Carolina State University.

Bobby H. Sharp is the Director of Institutional Research and Planning at Appalachian State University in Boone, North Carolina, where he also holds an academic appointment in the Department of Leadership and Educational Studies. Sharp was previously an Associate Director of University Planning and Institutional Research at the University of Mississippi and a Director of Institutional Research at Mississippi University for Women.

Heidi A. Tickle is a Graduate Assistant in the Office of University Planning and Institutional Research at the University of Mississippi in Oxford, where she is pursuing a Doctoral Degree in Educational Leadership. She holds a Bachelor of Arts in Psychology and German and a Masters of Educational Psychology with an emphasis in counseling. Most recently, she co-authored a paper on performance funding in the United States, which was presented at the annual 1994 conference of the Australasian Association for Institutional Research in New Zealand.

R. Dan Walleri is the Director of Research, Planning, and Computer Services at Mt. Hood Community College in Oregon. He is a past president of the National Council for Research and Planning, a past president of the Pacific Northwest Association for Institutional Research and Planning, and an active member of the Association for Institutional Research. He has authored/co-authored articles on student outcomes, assessment, and institutional effectiveness.

Lori A. Wolff is an Institutional Research Associate and Assistant Professor of Educational Research and Statistics at the University of Mississippi. She is affiliated with both the national and regional (Southern) Association for Institutional Research, as well as the American Statistical Association. While at the University of Mississippi, Wolff has worked extensively with surveys in addition to teaching and serving on numerous committees, including the University Assessment Committee and the Undergraduate Experience Task Force.

Michael Yost has been at Trinity University, San Antonio, Texas, since 1971, and is currently Assistant to the President, Director of Institutional Research, and a tenured professor. He has earned Bachelor's and Master's degrees in the sciences and a doctorate in research design, methodology, and applied statistics. Dr. Yost is experienced in the development, implementation, and evaluation of educational and institutional programs statistical analysis, and computer applications. He has published more than 150 articles and chapters dealing with methodological and statistical applications. He has also made numerous professional presentations in the United States and in Europe and is presently a consultant to several universities and a number of corporations and law firms.

In addition to these Resource Section authors, there is another group of individuals without whose work this publication would have been impossible. These are the staff members within the Office of University Planning and Institutional Research (UPIR) at The University of Mississippi. They include Ms. Harolyn Merritt, who spent countless hours assisting in the preparation of the manuscript, as well as Ms. Katherine Adams and Ms. Heidi Tickle, who were of invaluable help in editing the work. Ms. Tickle, a graduate assistant in UPIR, also prepared the subject index at the close of the publication.

Institutional effectiveness and outcomes assessment implementation is as dynamic a field as currently exists in higher education. Suggested practices today are being improved almost overnight in the light of further experience and improved instrumentation. Nonetheless, this third edition represents the most current and up-to-date material and suggestions available to a number of us in the field. It is respectfully offered for your consideration and use.

October, 1995
James O. Nichols
Oxford, Mississippi

The author gratefully acknowledges the support of the University of Mississippi in the preparation of this volume.

Endorsement of this publication has neither been sought nor received from any professional or regional accrediting association.

JAMES O. NICHOLS has been Director of University Planning and Institutional Research and Assistant Professor of Higher Education at the University of Mississippi since 1979. He has been active in the field of Institutional Research, Planning, and Assessment and has served at a series of progressively more comprehensive institutions since 1971. During that time, he has also served in leadership capacities in state, regional, and national professional associations. Since 1986, his primary professional interests have been centered in institutional effectiveness and assessment of student academic achievement. In that regard, he has played a substantive role in the publication of regional accrediting association guidance concerning this subject; presented international, national, regional, and state level seminars and workshops concerning institutional effectiveness implementation; worked as a consultant on outcomes assessment implementation with more than 100 institutions from two-year colleges to comprehensive research universities; and founded Institutional Effectiveness Associates, a private consulting firm.

He received his Ph.D. in Higher Education from the University of Toledo in 1971. In addition to this third edition of *A Practitioner's Handbook for Institutional Effectiveness and Student Outcomes Assessment Implementation*, he is the author of *The Departmental Guide and Record Book for Implementation of Student Outcomes Assessment and Institutional Effectiveness*, and *Assessment Case Studies: Common Issues in Implementation with Various Campus Approaches to Resolution*. These three publications are intended to provide comprehensive guidance as well as practical examples of institutional effectiveness or student outcomes assessment implementation.

CHAPTER ONE

Explaining the Handbook's Use in Institutional Effectiveness and Outcomes Assessment Implementation

What can be expected from this publication?

The purpose of this *Handbook* is to provide a "cookbook" for the individual or group of persons on a college or university campus who have been given responsibility by the institution's chief executive officer (CEO) for implementation of institutional effectiveness or outcomes assessment activities. As any good cook will admit, there is more than one way to prepare a stew, and that adage also holds true regarding institutional effectiveness and outcomes assessment activities. Presented in this *Handbook* is one recipe that the author and his associates recommend as a starting point for implementation (cooking) activities. Individual cooks (practitioners) on each campus will naturally want to season or adapt this recipe to the taste (environment) of their own clientele (campus). There is no implication that the methodology proposed is the only manner through which such activities should be implemented.

How does this *Handbook* relate to other publications in the field?

Even in its third edition, this document remains different in a number of ways from others that have been published in the field. First, it focuses almost exclusively on the *how* of institutional effectiveness or outcomes assessment rather than the *why*. For a variety of reasons—ranging from the perceived intrinsic value of the assessment of student educational outcomes (as a means for refinement of the educational process) to the more pragmatic reality of external forces (accrediting agencies, state governmental agencies, etc.) requiring such actions—most institutions across the country have already answered the why question and are now seeking to determine how best to implement such assessment procedures. If your institution has not answered the why question in a clearly affirmative manner (for one reason or another), close this publication and devote your time to an activity that promises to be more productive. Unless an institution is clearly committed to institutional effectiveness or outcomes assessment at the beginning of implementation, much energy will be expended with little genuine hope for meaningful impact on actual campus operations.

Second, this document attempts to be decidedly more practical than theoretical in its approach to the subject. Even when describing *how*, professional educators frequently slip into the glories of the cognitive and affective domains and other educational jargon. This document will touch on such concepts strictly in laypersons' terms and move quickly to the more pragmatic means through which these concepts may be implemented on each campus.

This is a **handbook** rather than a scholarly work. In the body of the text, only sufficient references to credit primary sources will be found. However, in the resource sections amplifying the body of the text, sufficient references to provide additional guidance concerning the various subjects are provided. For those interested in pursuing the subject of institutional effectiveness and outcomes assessment past the level of this document into a more scholarly treatment, the publication *Assessment in Accreditation* (1989), by John Folger and John Harris, is recommended as a further primary source. For those interested in the impact of implementation on over 115 different campuses, *Making a Difference* (1993) by Trudy Banta and Associates is suggested.

The *Handbook* does have a direct relationship to two other publications from Agathon Press, *Assessment Case Studies* (1995) and *The Departmental Guide* (1995). *The Departmental Guide* is designed for the busy departmental administrator and in about 80 pages contains the minimum information and guidance necessary to facilitate implementation at that level. It is cross-referenced to this *Handbook*'s resource sections at key points where its reader may want more in-depth coverage of the topic. *Assessment Case Studies* (1995) supports both levels of implementation (i.e., institutional and departmental) as it relates the experiences of 11 institutions (from two-year colleges to major research universities) in dealing with common issues encountered in implementation. These three publications (i.e., this *Handbook*, *The Departmental Guide*, and *Assessment Case Studies*) constitute the structure, technical information, guidance (at the institutional and departmental levels), and report of experiences needed to support implementation on campuses.

For what audience is this handbook intended?

The *Handbook* is directed at the level of the practitioner rather than the chief executive officer (CEO). Although the support of the chief executive officer is absolutely essential to successful implementation, that support should have been gained in answering, "Why do this?" Also, the content of this document will be more detailed than one can reasonably expect a CEO to take time to digest. Undoubtedly, the practitioner or group whom the chief executive officer has appointed to implement such activities will want to brief the CEO or explain to him or her the general outline of the implementation model developed; however, this explanation should remain quite general unless details are requested or are necessary to insure the CEO's support.

The proposed activities described lead toward long-term implementation of institutional effectiveness and outcomes assessment activities and not to a "quick fix" to the subject. Properly implemented, institutional effectiveness will take between three and four years to become fully operational through comprehensively "closing the loop" and using assessment data to improve programs. Although clear progress in specific activities required for full implementation of institutional effectiveness can occur rather quickly, the urge to "do something quick and dirty" within a few months to satisfy an external agency will (in all likelihood) produce "something" so obviously superficial that it undermines the institution's opportunity for genuine progress toward substantive implementation over the longer period.

Finally, this *Handbook* describes a set of procedures for implementing institutional effectiveness, a concept that includes the assessment of educational outcomes. However, institutional effectiveness extends beyond that important activity by placing the assessment of student or educational outcomes as the focal point of an institution's commitment toward accomplishment of its statement of purpose, as well as improving student learning.

The "assessment" movement, which has swept through most of higher education, is frequently focused at the departmental level singularly within the academic components of an institution. These isolated departmental assessment activities often seek to determine what students are learning in an effort to improve instructional methods or curricula. On some campuses, the results of the assessment of student outcomes or learning are compared to a departmental or program statement of expected or intended educational (instructional) outcomes. Although such assessment activities are laudable in their own right, in many instances they lack institutional-level commitment, and their continuation over an extended period of time is often questionable.

Institutional effectiveness, as described in more detail later in this chapter, provides a second unit of analysis (in addition to the academic program) at the institutional level and incorporates assessment activities throughout the institution's instructional, research, and public service functions as well as its administrative and educational support components. Provision of this second unit of analysis at the institutional level is accomplished by linkage of departmental statements of intended educational (instructional), research, and service outcomes as well as administrative objectives with an expanded statement of institutional purpose or mission. Verification that the institution's statement of purpose is being accomplished can be ascertained only through assessment results, which indicate that departmental/program intended outcomes (educational, research, and service) or objectives (administrative) are being accomplished. In this process, all components of the institution have a direct or indirect role to play in supporting or furthering accomplishment of the statement of purpose.

In summary, this document can be described as:

1. Focusing primarily on the *how* in assessment and assuming that the question *why* has been answered;
2. Emphasizing the practical implementation of institutional effectiveness activities;
3. Constituting a handbook rather than a scholarly work;
4. Being intended for the practitioner-level institutional user;
5. Describing a long-term program of genuine implementation, rather than a "quick fix"; and

6. Including student/educational outcomes assessment within an overall program of institutional effectiveness.

Past and future development of the assessment (institutional effectiveness) movement

The movement toward assessment (and then institutional effectiveness) on a national basis began in the early 1980s when various national commissions or committees completed a series of studies, which included the following:

- *To Strengthen Quality in Higher Education*: Summary recommendations of the national commission on higher education issues (1982);
- *A Nation at Risk*: The imperative for educational reform (Bennett, 1983);
- *To Reclaim a Legacy*: A report on the humanities in higher education (Bennett, 1984); and,
- *Involvement in Learning*: Realizing the Potential of American Higher Education (NIE, 1984).

Each of these national commissions or committees called for a renaissance in American higher education and the development of "excellence," particularly in undergraduate education. Most of these studies also included some reference to "assessment" of undergraduate learning as a component of a program for enhancement of students' achievement.

While over ten years has past since most of the references listed above called for reshaping higher education, the belief that higher education is not completely servicing the needs of our country remains strong today. This past year in the publication *An American Imperative: Higher Expectations for Higher Education* (1993, p. 1), the authors, a distinguished panel of representatives from the public as well as the higher education community, held that:

> A disturbing and dangerous mismatch exists between what American society needs of higher education and what it is receiving. Nowhere is the mismatch more dangerous than in the quality of undergraduate preparation provided on many campuses. The American imperative for the 21st century is that society must hold higher education to much higher expectations or risk national decline.

The development of the assessment movement over the last ten years has been traced by numerous authors (including Banta, 1993, et al.). Its relationship to the federal government's interest in the subject, the resultant regional accreditation emphasis on student outcomes assessment, and the accountability focused action of most states is well documented. But what of the future of the assessment movement?

It is the "best of times and worst of times" for the future of student/educational outcomes assessment in the United States. There is a strong national consensus about the need for quality assessment through student outcomes assessment. As noted by the American Council on Education in the *Higher Education & National Affairs Journal* (June, 1994), a meeting on higher education accreditation reform attended by federal and state officials as well as higher education representatives at the Wingspread conference center resulted in an overall consensus that the assurance of quality in colleges and universities should, in fact, focus on the outcomes of undergraduate education.

> Even some consensuses regarding intended student outcomes are beginning to emerge. Participants in the conference on higher education accreditation referenced above agreed that when assessing the quality in colleges and universities, assessments should probe into the characteristics of its graduates. Examples of characteristics examined are: (a) technical competence in a given field; (b) high-level communications, computational, and information skills that enable ongoing learning; (c) ability to function in a global community, including knowledge of cultural and economic contexts as well as foreign language skills; (d) ability to define problems, gather and evaluate related information, and develop solutions; (e) range of attitudes and dispositions, including flexibility and adaptability, ease with diversity, initiative, motivation and persistence, teamwork, ethics and personal integrity, and creativity and resourcefulness; (f) and ability to deploy all of the above to address specific problems in complex, real-world settings.

Between this example and the limited guidance prescribed by *The National Educational Goals* (1991), "The proportion of college graduates who demonstrate an advanced ability to think critically, communicate effectively, and solve problems will increase substantially" (p. 5), there exists a clear indication that student outcomes assessment is "here to stay."

The "worst of times" is illustrated by the continuing lack of confidence expressed by Congress and many states regarding higher education's ability to provide the necessary quality assurances to the public through its own voluntary means (e.g., regional accreditation). The debate concerning the role of regional accreditation in assuring the public of the quality of institutional offerings which surrounded the reauthorization of the Higher Education Act in 1992 (i.e., the establishment of state postsecondary review entities) and the heavy emphasis on student outcomes in the statute, all weakened the regional accreditation process and, thereby, higher education's claim to self-regulation.

Robert Atwell, president of the American Council on Education, stated in August 1994 that, "If we don't fix accreditation, someone else—most likely the federal government—will try to do the job instead." While the federal government does not seem to be actively seeking to take control of the quality assurance function in higher education, there is no doubt that it will do so if regional accreditation policies are not strengthened. The assistant secretary of education, David Longanecker, speaking at the conference on higher education accreditation at Wingspread, indicated that federal and state agencies need not pursue quality assurance through regulatory tactics if accrediting bodies guaranteed that institutions met the outlined standards.

The movement to reassert self-regulation and quality assurance by the higher education community is, as of this writing, focused in the work of the temporary National Policy Board (NPB), founded by the regional accrediting agencies in 1993 after the disbanding of the Council on Postsecondary Accreditation (COPA), to design a new national accrediting body. In 1994 NPB distributed a set of proposed common accreditation requirements, heavily oriented toward outcomes assessment and institutional effectiveness, for comments by regional accrediting associations. Ongoing discussions at NPB and with a panel of college and university presidents represent the cutting edge of this set of issues as this publication goes to press (NPB, 1995).

What then of the future assessment movement?

The question is not whether the student/educational outcomes assessment effort will continue to expand, but by whom will this expansion be guided. Will the changes being discussed by the regional accrediting agencies which strengthens student outcomes assessment be considered adequate for the quality assurance function? Will the federal government extend its control to include student outcomes assessment requirements for all institutions? Will states become more frustrated with what many perceive as an anemic set of quality assurance policies and institute their own regulations as an excuse to reduce institutional appropriated support? Any one, and perhaps all of the above, may transpire during the near future. But one result seems assured: student/educational outcomes assessment will endure as a topic of institutional, regional, and national concern through the end of the 20th century.

The difference between "institutional effectiveness" and "outcomes assessment"

Among the earliest national leaders responding to the call for increased assessment activities was the Commission on Colleges of the Southern Association of Colleges and Schools (SACS), which in 1985 passed a major change in its accrediting procedures in which outcomes assessment (or in SACS's terms, "institutional effectiveness") was identified on an equal basis with institutional processes in the commission's *Criteria for Accreditation*. SACS consciously chose the term **institutional effectiveness** both to avoid the term **outcomes**, which many member institutions felt had become jargon-laden and acquired undesirable connotations of "measuring everything that moves," and to indicate that the concept described was broader than assessment activities solely within an institution's academic departments.

The author and his associates have also chosen to utilize the term institutional effectiveness for the *Handbook*. This choice has been based on the belief that while student/educational outcomes assessment should be the central and most visible focus of the assessment movement, the longer-term success of that movement is contingent upon its integration into and support at the institutional level on each campus. In addition, the term institutional effectiveness is more descriptive and inclusive of the identification of institutional and departmental programmatic intentions than is the term **outcomes assessment**.

Although substantial diversity in the approaches to student outcomes assessment requirements by the various regional accrediting associations remains current, the associations are currently engaged through the NPB in a coordinated effort to establish an outcomes assessment component which will be similar if not identical across all regions. As this reformulation or reconceptualization takes place, it is entirely possible (some would say probable) that the product will tie in both the existing requirements for "appropriate purposes" and "demonstration that each institution is accomplishing its purposes" not only with assessment, but also with the use of assessment results to resemble the Institutional Effectiveness Paradigm originated by the primary author of this document in 1987 and shown in Figure 1.

What then are the common components of institutional effectiveness or outcomes assessment?

Although regional and professional accreditation requirements differ in terms of semantics, most now call for those components identified by COPA (1986):

1. A sharpened statement of institutional mission and objectives;
2. Identification of intended departmental/programmatic outcomes or results; and
3. Establishment of effective means of assessing the accomplishment outcomes and results.

Added to this, implicitly, is the use of the assessment results to improve the function of the institution or program and enhanced student learning. These components also underlie the work being accomplished by NPB to define institutional effectiveness for the future.

The Institutional Effectiveness Paradigm

How then should an institution go about integrating these institutional effectiveness components into its ongoing academic and administrative operations so that they become a part of its fabric? What assistance does the literature and practice in the field of higher education administration offer? What current practices can be adapted to incorporate these components? One answer to these questions is graphically portrayed in Figure 1, the Institutional Effectiveness Paradigm, and is described in the following explanation.

This paradigm depicts activities that have been proposed, fostered, and occasionally practiced by many authors and institutions for a number of years. It is an important adaptation of the rational planning model that has existed and been discussed in the literature during the past. Skeptics will quickly ask, Why this rational model when we know that campuses are essentially political entities and often act irrationally? The answer is that its elements precisely fit those components required by most accreditation processes. Others will then ask, How is **this** version of rational planning different from those earlier that have been proposed and implemented, only to fail? The primary differences in implementation of this paradigm are its focus on assessment of results (as opposed to processes and resource requirements) and the fact that our peers from other institutions (representing the public directly or indirectly) are to visit our campus periodically to see if the components of institutional effectiveness are indeed being practiced as well as they are professed to be.

The critical elements of the Institutional Effectiveness Paradigm displayed in Figure 1, whose implementation is the subject of this *Handbook*, are as follows:

1. Establishment of an Expanded Statement of Institutional Purpose;
2. Identification of Intended Educational (Instructional), Research, and Service Outcomes/Administrative Objectives;

Figure 1

THE INSTITUTIONAL EFFECTIVENESS PARADIGM

Expanded Statement of Purpose

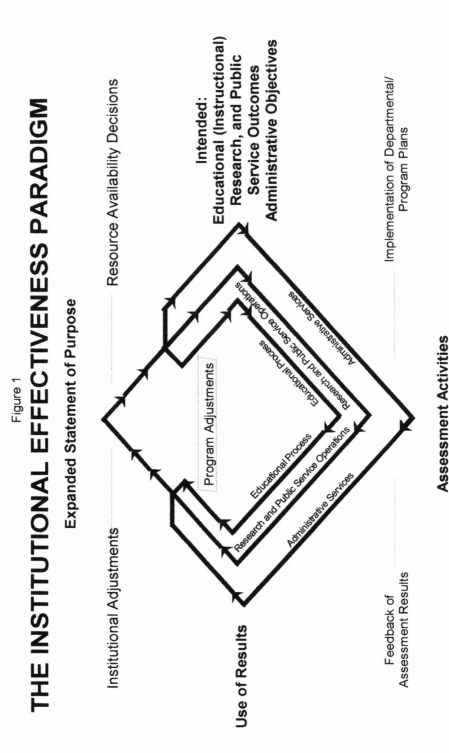

Resource Availability Decisions

Intended:
Educational (Instructional)
Research, and Public
Service Outcomes
Administrative Objectives

Implementation of Departmental/
Program Plans

Institutional Adjustments

Program Adjustments

Educational Process

Research and Public Service Operations

Administrative Services

Educational Process

Research and Public Service Operations

Administrative Services

Use of Results

Assessment Activities

Feedback of
Assessment Results

3. Assessment of the Extent to Which the Intended Outcomes and Objectives Are Being Accomplished; and
4. Adjustment of the Institution's Purpose, Intended Outcomes/Objectives, or Activities Based on Assessment Findings.

In recent years, regional accreditation has focused on accomplishment of the institution's "statement of purpose" or mission. Yet, today, the purpose or mission statements of any institutions are virtually interchangeable. Why is this the case? There are many reasons, but two are most apparent. First, up until the recent past, accreditation procedures have been primarily episodic. Every ten years, the institution's mission or statement of purpose has been studied by a faculty committee, reworded (usually retaining the same lack of substance), presented to the visiting committee, and afterward promptly filed and forgotten for another 10 years. Second, such disregard for the influence of the statement of purpose was possible because of the assumption (some would call it a "leap of faith") that if the institution could demonstrate adequate educational and administrative processes and financial resources, then surely it must be accomplishing its purpose. The result has been the singular lack of meaning or importance to actual institutional functioning that characterizes many existing statements of institutional purpose.

Institutional effectiveness (and outcomes assessment) is changing the role of the statement of purpose. Instead of "assuming" their accomplishment, institutions are being challenged to demonstrate their overall effectiveness through assessment of departmental/program outcomes and objectives linked closely to and supporting the institution's statement of purpose. This requirement changes the mission or statement of purpose from a shelf-document with little practical use to the basis for institutional action that it was intended to be. In order to provide a useful basis for the assessment of institutional effectiveness, most existing statements of purpose must be substantially expanded and refocused to reflect institutional intentions. Further, a working relationship between the revised statement of purpose and the intended outcomes and objectives at departmental and program levels must be established.

Expansion and refinement of the institutional statement of purpose are described in more detail in Chapter 3 as an essential early element of implementing institutional effectiveness. A separate resource section within that chapter offers further guidance concerning means for establishment of such an "Expanded Statement of Institutional Purpose." In addition, Appendix A contains an example of a statement for a four-year college, Appendix B for a two-year institution, and Appendix C for a major research university.

Many aspects of an institution's expanded statement of purpose will require no additional funding, only adjustment of institutional policies. In the case of those components of the expanded statement of purpose that do require increased funding, the institution will be required to set its priorities among what will assuredly be more components and proposals than funds available to support them.

Actual implementation of the institution's expanded statement of purpose will, in most instances, take place at the departmental and program levels through the identification of intended outcomes and objectives linked closely to the expanded statement of purpose and focusing on the institution's intended impact on its constituents or external environment. This intent will primarily consist of institutional assertions concerning its role regarding instruction, research, and public service. These institutional statements of intentions will principally be implemented by the institution's academic units through identification of their own intended educational (instructional), research, and public service outcomes.

The institution's administrative departments also have a vital, if less direct or obvious, role to play in institutional effectiveness. Some expanded institutional statements of purpose will undoubtedly contain specific references to necessary administrative and educational support services (computer, library, counseling, etc.) as being essential to the support of the institution's educational, research, and public service outcomes. In such cases, the institution's administrative departments will play a direct role and set objectives clearly related to the expanded statement of purpose. At other institutions, administrative units will not be as directly linked to the expanded statement of purpose, but should establish objectives that they believe provide an administrative or physical environment conducive to accomplishment of the institution's expanded statement of purpose.

The formulation of statements of intended outcomes and objectives and assessment of their accomplishments are described in Chapter 4 and its resource sections, entitled "Designing Assessment at the Departmental Level," "Setting and Evaluating Intended Educational (Instructional) Outcomes," and "Setting and Evaluating Objectives in Non-academic Units." A number of specific institutional examples of statements of intended outcomes and objectives are included in Appendix B of *Assessment Case Studies*. Once the expanded institutional statement of purpose and departmental statements of intended outcomes and administrative objectives are in place, the institution (primarily through its departments) will implement activities to accomplish these ends. Without much question, the single aspect of institutional effectiveness that has gained the highest level of public and institutional visibility is assessment. It is important to note that assessment, within the paradigm described, (a) occurs after establishment of the expanded statement of purpose and its supporting departmental or program statements of intended outcomes or administrative objectives, (b) is focused on ascertaining the extent of accomplishment of those outcomes and objectives identified, and (c) does not attempt to assess every aspect of an institution's operations. Originally among the most unnoticed—yet in the opinion of some, most important—elements of institutional effectiveness operations are the feedback or reporting of assessment findings and the use of such findings in adjusting institutional and departmental actions. This use includes adjustment of the expanded institutional statement of purpose, modification to departmental/program statements of intended outcomes and administrative objectives, and changes in departmental operations designed to accomplish the purposes intended.

The paradigm described and illustrated in Figure 1 is neither complex nor unfamiliar. The primary difference from earlier paradigms of this type lies in its focus on results rather than processes or resources. Thus, implementation of this paradigm and institutional effectiveness is *ends*, rather than *means*, oriented.

Implementation of the Institutional Effectiveness Paradigm

Although the Institutional Effectiveness Paradigm shown in Figure 1 relates the common institutional effectiveness or assessment requirements contained in accreditation criteria or standards to the literature and practice in higher education, it is apparent that implementation of the entire paradigm in a short period of time is not feasible on most campuses. This is true for the following reasons:

1. There is a clear sequential relationship between a number of the components (first, purpose; then, intended results, etc.);
2. Implementation in a short period (if possible) would leave little time for the institution's ongoing educational, research, and public service functions;
3. The nature of college and university governance requires participation and input by various constituents whose actions are relatively resistant to hasty action; and,
4. The fiscal implications of implementation of the paradigm in a short period could well be prohibitive.

How then does one go about implementing the Institutional Effectiveness Paradigm? The answer lies with the considerable thought, organization, and participation outlined in the next chapter and explained in the balance of this *Handbook*.

Scores of practitioners in various fields have observed as they have attempted to translate theory into practice, "Nobody ever said this was going to be either easy or quick." Implementation of institutional effectiveness is no exception. Unlike Shakespeare's Macbeth, who approached his mission by musing, "If it were done when 'tis done, then 'twere well / It were done quickly," those who implement institutional effectiveness should do so carefully and thoroughly or someone's corpse (career-wise) could be the result. The following suggested sequence of events is designed to accomplish substantive implementation of institutional effectiveness while offering a good chance for the survival of that individual or group therewith charged.

References: Cited and Recommended

Banta, T. W. and associates. (1993). *Making a Difference: Outcomes of a Decade of Assessment in Higher Education*. San Francisco: Jossey-Bass.

Bennett, W. (1983). *A Nation at Risk: The Imperative for Educational Reform*. Washington, DC: Government Printing Office.

Bennett, W. (1984). *To Reclaim a Legacy: A Report on the Humanities in Higher Education*. Washington, DC: Government Printing Office.

Boyer, C., Ewell, P., Finney, J. E., & Mingle, J. R. (1987). Assessment and Outcomes Measurement: A View from the States. *AAHE Bulletin, 39*(7), 8-12.

Cavazos presents higher educational goals. (1990, January 29). *Higher Education and National Affairs, 39*(2), 1.

Council on Postsecondary Accreditation (COPA). (1982). *Policy Statement on the Role and Value of Accreditation*. Washington, DC: Author.

Council on Postsecondary Accreditation (COPA). (1986). *Educational Quality and Accreditation: A Call for Diversity, Continuity, and Innovation*. Washington, DC: Author.

Criteria for Accreditation: Commission on Colleges. (1985). Atlanta, GA: Southern Association of Colleges and Schools.

Education Commission of the States. (June 1994). *Quality Assurance and Undergraduate Education: What the Public Expects.* Denver: Author.

Ewell, P., Finney J., & Lenth, C. (1990). Filling in the Mosaic: The Emerging Pattern of State-Based Assessment. *AAHE Bulletin, 42*(8), 3-5.

Farnsworth, S., & Thrash, P. (1990, February 1). *Letter to Chief Executive Officers of Commission Institutions Regarding Assessment from NorthCentral Association of Colleges and Schools.*

Federal Register, Department of Education (1987, September 8). *52 CFR Part 602 and 602.17, Secretary's Procedures and Criteria for Recognition of Accrediting Agencies: Focus on Educational Effectiveness.* Washington, DC: Government Printing Office.

Folger, J., & Harris, J. (1989). *Assessment in Accreditation.* Atlanta, GA: Southern Association of Colleges and Schools.

National Commission on Higher Education Issues. (1982). *To Strengthen Quality in Higher Education: Summary Recommendations of the National Commission on Higher Education Issues.* Washington, DC: Government Printing Office.

National Governors' Association, Task Force on College Quality. (1986). *Time for Results: The Governors' 1991 Report on Education.* Washington, DC: Author.

National Institute of Education (NIE) Study Group on Excellence in American Higher Education. (1984). *Involvement in Learning: Realizing the Potential of American Higher Education.* Washington, DC: Government Printing Office.

NPB. (1994). *Independence, Accreditation and the Public Interest: Special Report on Accreditation.* Washington, DC: Author.

Wingspread (1993). *An American Imperative: Higher Expectations for Higher Education.* Milwaukee: Johnson Foundation.

Resource Manual on Institutional Effectiveness. (1989). Atlanta, GA: Southern Association of Colleges and Schools. South Carolina Commission on Higher Education. (1989).

CHAPTER TWO

Overview of the Institutional Effectiveness Implementation Model: Its Assumptions, Basis, and Execution

Assumptions and Management Decisions Supporting Model Implementation

The **how** of institutional effectiveness and outcomes assessment is clearly the heart of this *Handbook*. However, it is important to understand the assumptions and basic management decisions that undergird the conduct of the implementation model described later in this chapter. The implementation model presented assumes the following:

1. **Institutional support for genuine implementation**—Nothing in this document provides a means through which to emphasize form rather than substance in institutional effectiveness implementation;
2. **Sensitivity of subject**—The most "sacred" activity in higher education is that which takes place behind the classroom door, and no effort should be made by the administration to dictate instructional process or content; and,
3. **Limited additional funding for institutional effectiveness implementation**— Implementation will cost time and money; however, the expenditure of both should be limited as much as possible.

Probably the most important initial plan management decision or realization in implementation of institutional effectiveness is the need to appoint a single individual to coordinate the process. Why is this the case? First, implementation of institutional effectiveness will be a considerable effort ultimately impacting most aspects of the institution, and the nature of the work required will call for coordination and logistical support across departments and between management levels. Second, implementation of institutional effectiveness is one project that, unlike class scheduling, registration of students, and the payroll, can be postponed unless there is an individual designated to continue moving (pushing) implementation toward culmination. A survey (Nichols & Wolff, 1990c) indicates that this appointment of a single individual to coordinate implementation is among the most often cited factors facilitating successful implementation.

Who should be appointed to coordinate institutional effectiveness implementation? There is no best answer that applies to all institutions to this question. Three general sources for such leadership are common on campuses:

1. **Academician**—Some institutions find that the credibility gained by appointment of an "interested" member of the faculty to head implementation is worthwhile, given the sensitivity of the subject;
2. **Institutional researcher**—Given the primarily quantitative nature of the assessment activity and the existence of an office with such expertise, a number of institutions have chosen to designate their institutional research officer to coordinate the implementation effort; and,
3. **Institutional planner**—Clearly the heart of institutional effectiveness is its relationship to campus planning efforts, and a number of institutions are choosing to emphasize the connection between institutional effectiveness and planning through appointment of a planning officer to coordinate the implementation effort.

Any of the type individuals described can be successful in the coordinator's role, as long as there is recognition that it is this individual's responsibility to see that implementation across the institution is being accomplished and, if not, to ensure that the institution's leadership knows why not.

Although the coordinator selected will have central responsibility for implementation, exercise of that role will necessarily be through a team appointed for that purpose, and actual implementation will be the responsibility of the individuals in the institution's administrative and academic departments. These roles often appear as part of the institutional effectiveness implementation team: the institutional planner, the departmental facilitator, and the assessment support person (Figure 2).

The Institutional Effectiveness Paradigm begins and ends with planning and assessment of the extent of success in achieving these plans. A key role emerging is that of coordinating and supporting the planning processes of an institution from the highest level through the academic and administrative departments on the campus. Most authorities in the field of college and university planning stress the importance of linking the ideas expressed in campus plans with the actions taken through fund allocation, and this link between planning and budgeting must be visibly maintained. However, on many campuses this linkage has grown to the point that planning has become little more than a useful form of budgeting. The planning required by institutional effectiveness, although related to budget planning as a means, is distinctly more ends-oriented and calls for an additional outcomes or results focus at the institution.

Academic and administrative departments will undoubtedly require further explanation of the concept and assistance in implementation of institutional effectiveness. The role of departmental implementation facilitator requires an individual with patience, credibility, and knowledge of institutional effectiveness to work with individual departments. Although such an individual cannot be expected to direct implementation within each department, he or she should explain the concept personally to each department (as it relates to their discipline or function), suggest a general course of action that the individual department might take toward implementation, and outline assessment options that are open to the department and are centrally supported.

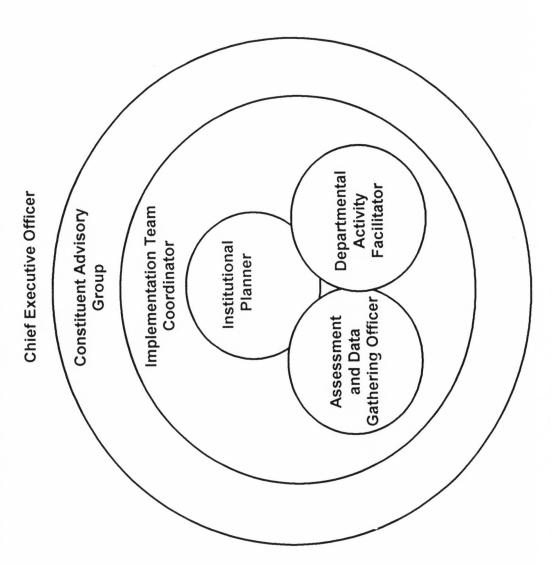

Figure 2

The Institutional Effectiveness Implementation Team

Chief Executive Officer

Constituent Advisory Group

Implementation Team Coordinator

Institutional Planner

Departmental Activity Facilitator

Assessment and Data Gathering Officer

Although the establishment of intended outcomes and objectives and (to a lesser degree) the conduct of assessment to determine if these intended ends have been accomplished are departmental responsibilities, a clear need exists for a centralized assessment support entity. This functionary (on many campuses the Office of Institutional Research) can provide (a) the assessment expertise needed to assist departments, (b) the logistical means for most efficiently conducting standardized testing and distributing/processing attitudinal instruments, and (c) a centralized point or clearinghouse for assessment results. The organizational implications of such an assignment of responsibility to the institutional research component are reviewed in articles in *New Directions for Institutional Research* (Nichols & Wolff, 1990a) and *AIR Professional File* (Nichols & Wolff, 1990b).

Probably the second most asked set of questions concerning institutional effectiveness (after how) relates to the cost and source of funding. Several basic points related to this subject need to be made:

1. There are clearly increased costs involved, both direct (out-of-pocket expenditures) and indirect (time).
2. The amount of additional direct cost incurred on each campus will depend on the institution's current activities (its existing level of expenditures for planning, institutional research, etc.), the nature of the assessment plan adopted, the size of the institution, and the extent to which the costs incurred are passed on to students through fees for testing. Hence, a cost estimate will be difficult until a number of policy issues are settled and an inventory of existing assessment assets conducted.
3. Many current institutional examples of successful outcomes assessment operations are the result of external grants for this purpose or of state funding mechanisms (formulas) that have been altered to encourage and reward such activity. Regrettably, these sources will not be available to most institutions as they go about institutional effectiveness implementation.
4. Initial funding for implementation should be relatively open-ended, although thoroughly justified and carefully monitored.

Given the preceding comments, institutions are best advised to acknowledge two important points: First, implementation of institutional effectiveness will require additional expenditures, for which they probably will not receive increased funding. Second, they should begin implementation activities by funding these activities from contingency or discretionary funds available at the highest levels of the institution until a number of policy-level decisions are made and historical cost data are available at the institution.

Overcoming campus inertia and encouraging institutional effectiveness implementation will take decisive action on the part of the institution's CEO and the establishment of incentives for departmental cooperation. The CEO must not only support implementation but also openly evidence that support. Most CEOs will make the expected verbal endorsement of institutional effectiveness implementation; however, it is their actions that will (or will not) convince those on the campus of their sincerity.

Among the actions that a CEO may take to demonstrate visibly his or her support for implementation are:

1. Taking an active (though not dominant) role in preparation of the Expanded Statement of Institutional Purpose;
2. Establishing his or her office's administrative objectives supporting the expanded statement of purpose;
3. Contributing to the formulation of his or her discipline's statements of intended educational, research, or public service outcomes; and,
4. Referencing assessment results in public statements.

At the departmental level there also must be incentives toward implementation. Probably the best incentive is the intrinsic value inherent in the concept of institutional effectiveness and the improvement of student learning. However, other more extrinsic (and some would say material) means such as the following may be necessary:

1. Incorporation of institutional effectiveness implementation into the reward system (rank, tenure, etc.) for faculty;
2. Provision of funding preferences within the institution to departments implementing institutional effectiveness; and,
3. Increase of institutional visibility for those departments actively and effectively pursuing implementation.

The Model for Implementation of Institutional Effectiveness and Assessment Activities

Figure 3 contains a model or sequence of activities for implementation of institutional effectiveness over a four-year period based on the assumptions and plan management decisions reviewed earlier in this chapter. Following the "Decision to Implement Institutional Effectiveness and Assessment Activities," events in the model are portrayed as developing simultaneously down separate, but closely related, activities tracks concerning planning and assessment.

Building the Necessary Institutional Foundation

During the first year of implementation, most activity of a planning/operational nature will be focused on "Establishment of an Expanded Institutional Statement of Purpose" as a foundation for further activities. The "Implementation of Attitudinal Surveys" and the "Conduct of an Inventory of Assessment Procedures" (as currently being employed at the institution or available to the institution) highlight the assessment/evaluation activities during the first year or period of implementation, and can be described as **Building the Necessary Institutional Foundation**. This first year of implementation activities is discussed in detail in Chapter 3, and six resource sections (including the new resource section on Assessment Planning) are provided to expand on the most important concepts contained in that chapter.

Figure 3
A Generic Model for Implementation of Institutional Effectiveness and Assessment Activities in Higher Education

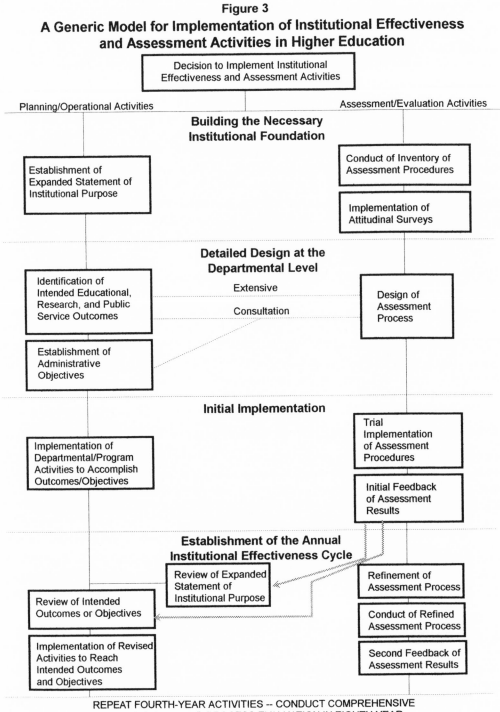

Detailed Design at the Departmental Level

The second year of implementation is characterized as **Detailed Design at the Departmental Level,** during which time the work accomplished the previous year at the institutional level will be extended to the departmental level. Planning/operational activities during the second year or period include the "Identification of Intended Educational, Research, and Public Services Outcomes" and the "Establishment of Administrative Objectives," both of which are closely linked with, and support accomplishment of, the expanded statement of purpose developed during the first year of implementation. These important statements of intended outcomes and objectives are closely coordinated with the "Design of the Assessment Process," through which accomplishment of these intentions will be evaluated. Second-year activities are described in Chapter 4, which features five resource sections (including new resource sections concerning Assessment in General Education and Continuous Quality Improvement) further explaining departmental outcomes/objectives and the design of an assessment process.

Initial Implementation

During the third year or period of implementation activities, the **Initial Implementation** of institutional effectiveness operations takes place. Based on their work during the previous year, the institution's components will be involved in "Implementation of Departmental/Program Activities to Accomplish Intended Outcomes/Objectives." The primary events during this third year or period will be the "Trial Implementation of Assessment Procedures," as designed during the previous year, and the "Initial Feedback of Assessment Results," as described in Chapter 5.

Establishment of the Annual Institutional Effectiveness Cycle

Establishment of the Annual Institutional Effectiveness Cycle (AIEC) is brought about in the fourth year of implementation activities and is described in Chapter 6. In that year, and each succeeding year, planning and operational activities will include a "Review of the Institutional Statement of Purpose," "Revision of Intended Outcomes or Objectives," and/or "Implementation of Revised Activities to Reach Original Intended Outcomes and Objectives." Likewise, during each year in the annual cycle, a "Refinement of the Assessment Process," "Conduct of Refined Assessment Procedures," and "Feedback of Assessment Results" will take place. It is within this AIEC that institutions will readily be able to demonstrate use of assessment results to improve programming and "Closing the Loop."

Why can't institutional effectiveness be implemented faster?

Some institutions, based on their existing planning and institutional research activities, may be able to shorten the institutional effectiveness implementation plan by a year or more. However, because most existing planning and institutional research functions are designed to support process-type decisions (budgeting, class scheduling, etc.) rather than assessment, the majority of institutions will require the full amount of time to complete implementation. The primary reasons for the lengthy period of time required for implementation are related to the assumptions regarding implementation enumerated earlier in this chapter.

Genuine implementation of institutional effectiveness will change the way many institutions operate. A change of this magnitude cannot be brought about in a short period without creating massive resistance to not only the substance of the change, but also the rapidity of the process of change.

In the academic area, institutional effectiveness deals with the most sensitive prerogatives of the faculty—those related to control of the curriculum and the classroom. Although there is absolutely no intention for institutional effectiveness to infringe on these prerogatives, an attempt to rush or force implementation may very well be viewed as such by many faculty. Faculty participation in curriculum design and assessment of the accomplishment of intended educational outcomes is essential to successful implementation of institutional effectiveness. One immutable law of college and university administration is that you can't rush the faculty without meeting more resistance than it's worth.

Acceleration of the process of implementing institutional effectiveness would require more personnel commitment (although over a shorter period) and higher out-of-pocket costs than most institutions can tolerate. Most institutions of higher learning do not have extra personnel who can readily be diverted to developmental tasks such as implementation of institutional effectiveness. Implementation will require a considerable amount of time on the part of various committees and most certainly within the academic and administrative departments as they identify intended outcomes and objectives as well as the means for their assessment. Frankly, there is only a limited amount of "extra service" in addition to teaching, research, and public service that faculty can be asked to assume over a short period. However, extended over the longer period of the proposed model, this amount of involvement is distinctly feasible.

Likewise, rapid escalation of direct out-of-pocket expenditures to support institutional effectiveness will not be feasible at most institutions. Rather, gradual escalation of funding to meet documented needs for activities will be found both more feasible and more acceptable to others on the campus over the longer period of time suggested.

If genuine institutional effectiveness implementation were either easy or quick, more successful examples would have been available earlier. On the other hand, careful, well-planned implementation stands a far greater chance for substantive success and continuation over a period of years.

What will be the greatest problems encountered in executing the proposed institutional effectiveness implementation model?

The problems will, of course, vary from campus to campus, but three of the most likely are (a) gaining the genuine commitment of the institution's administrators, (b) dealing with faculty resistance, and (c) maintaining momentum during the extended period of implementation.

Although verbal commitment (i.e., lip service) to institutional effectiveness implementation will come relatively easily from most administrators, follow-through into sustained support demonstrated by their actions may be another matter. For those not truly committed to the intrinsic value of institutional effectiveness, the key to their sustained support may lie in the extent to which they each become personally identified with the implementation effort and cannot afford to have it fail without reflection upon themselves.

Faculty resistance will arise during the implementation process. Indeed, the survey by Nichols and Wolff (1990c) indicates that "indifference or resistance on the part of faculty" is the most often cited factor impeding institutional effectiveness implementation. Such resistance will take forms varying from open resistance from faculty stating that nothing they intend to accomplish is subject to "measurement," to more serious passive resistance which may be found in departments that refuse to implement. In both cases, patience is the key to successful implementation. When gently pressed, even the most vocal faculty member must admit that *some* of the things his or her discipline intends to accomplish are ascertainable or observable over time. From that admission, the reluctant faculty member will often gradually accept institutional effectiveness implementation rather than risk a loss of credibility with his or her colleagues as a reasonable member of the community of scholars.

The department that passively resists implementation is a more serious problem, yet one that also is subject to being overcome with patience. Short of a change in leadership, which ultimately may be necessary, probably the best course of action is the structuring of the individual and departmental reward systems to make it abundantly clear that cooperation in implementation is in the best interest of those involved.

Probably the single greatest problem likely to be experienced with the implementation plan proposed is the maintenance of campus commitment and momentum over the four-year period. On those campuses motivated toward implementation of institutional effectiveness to satisfy accreditation requirements, the leverage provided by this activity will help to sustain momentum. On other campuses it will be necessary to arrange events, activities, announcements, and so forth that emphasize how important institutional effectiveness implementation remains, what has been accomplished to date, what the current activities are, and where those support final implementation.

For a more detailed treatment of issues likely to be encountered in implementation of institutional effectiveness or assessment on your campus, see *Assessment Case Studies* (1995), a companion work to this *Handbook*, to learn how 11 institutions ranging from community colleges to major research universities handled common problems in implementation. Learn what worked for them and what approaches were decidedly less than effective.

Summary

In this chapter, the essential components and the sequence of events for the proposed model for implementation of institutional effectiveness have been very briefly outlined, as well as the assumptions upon which that model is based and the management decisions that will need to be made. Finally, some of the problems that the practitioner is likely to encounter during implementation have been introduced. In the next several chapters, more detailed explanations of activities proposed during each year of institutional effectiveness implementation are presented.

References: Cited and Recommended

Nichols, J. O., & Wolff, L. A. (1990a). Organizing for Assessment. In J. B. Presley (Ed.) Organizing for Effective Institutional Research (pp. 81-92). *New Directions for Institutional Research, XVII*(2). San Francisco: Jossey-Bass.

Nichols, J. O., & Wolff, L. A. (1990b). The Role of Institutional Research in Implementing Institutional Effectiveness or Outcomes Assessment. *AIR Professional File*, no. 37.

Nichols, J. O., & Wolff, L. A. (1990c, October 11). *The Status of Institutional Effectiveness at* Institutions of Higher Education within the Southern Association of Colleges and Schools (SACS): Findings of Visitation Teams, Extent of Implementation, and Factors *Facilitating/Impeding Implementation*. Contributed paper at the 1990 meeting of the Southern Association for Institutional Research, Ft. Lauderdale, FL.

CHAPTER THREE

Building the Necessary Institutional-Level Foundation for Institutional Effectiveness: The First Year

Following the institution's initial "Decision to Implement Institutional Effectiveness and Assessment Activities," the first year of implementation activities will be focused on accomplishing the necessary homework to support the balance of the effort during the following three years. The first year's work, as shown in Figure 4, is based on the assumptions that:

1. There has been a visible and genuine campus commitment to institutional effectiveness implementation;
2. Adequate, though not unlimited, resources have been made available to begin implementation;
3. An individual has been named to assume leadership for coordination of overall institutional effectiveness implementation;
4. Team members with responsibility for institutional planning, departmental activity facilitation, and assessment (data gathering) have also been identified, along with an appropriate advisory group composed of representatives of a cross section of campus constituencies (see Figure 2, p. 15); and,
5. Basic institutional process-oriented data (enrollment, teaching loads, average salary, etc.) designed to support ongoing decision making at the institution are available.

Within the first year, and in each of the succeeding years, implementation activities will be conducted along the separate, but related, planning/operational and assessment/evaluation activities tracks as illustrated in Figures 3 and 4.

Planning/Operational Activities

Planning/operational activities undertaken during the first year of implementation include adaptation of the generic implementation model provided in this *Handbook* to the specific institution and the formulation of an expanded institutional mission statement.

Figure 3, "A Generic Model for Implementation of Institutional Effectiveness and Assessment Activities in Higher Education'' (see page 18) contains a depiction of the generalized or generic approach to implementation that forms the basis of this *Handbook*.

However, it is important to realize that this approach will need to be adapted to specific institutional circumstances. Based on their current situation, some institutions may be able to compress somewhat the process of implementation because of the prior existence of certain components (e.g., an enhanced or expanded mission statement) on their campus. Other institutions will find it necessary to extend the process or commit additional resources to offset initial deficiencies (e.g., lack of basic process-oriented institutional data). The implementation model depicted in Figure 3 should be modified to incorporate institution-specific terms, adjustments in estimated times, and specific dates by which activities should be completed on each campus. If implementation is in response to accreditation requirements, the institution will also want to ensure that the specific jargon (outcomes, expected educational results, intended student academic achievement, etc.) utilized by the accrediting association is also included in the adaptation.

The primary task along the planning/operational activities track during the first year of implementation is "Establishment of an Expanded Statement of Institutional Purpose." This is one of the single most important actions in implementation of institutional effectiveness operations. As stated in Chapter 1, the key difference between outcomes assessment for its own sake and institutional effectiveness is the purposeful manner in which assessment is focused on intended departmental/program outcomes or objectives linked to the Expanded Statement of Institutional Purpose in institutional effectiveness. This linkage is illustrated in Figure 5, and an understanding of it is essential to the concept of institutional effectiveness.

The Expanded Statement of Institutional Purpose is, then, the beginning and the end of the Institutional Effectiveness Paradigm shown in Figure 1. It provides the sense of direction or institutional intention that is supported by the statements of "Intended Educational, Research, and Public Service Outcomes" and "Administrative Objectives" identified by the academic and administrative departments. Ultimately, it is the extent to which these intended departmental/program outcomes or objectives have been reached that is reflective of accomplishment of the Expanded Statement of Institutional Purpose.

The term **Expanded Statement of Institutional Purpose** has been chosen for two reasons. First, implementation of institutional effectiveness and outcomes assessment operations greatly expands and enhances the traditional role of these document(s) as a guide to institutional priorities and operations. Second, the actual composition of the statement of purpose currently in existence at most institutions will need to be reviewed and substantially expanded. Many terms can be utilized to identify and structure such a statement (**mission, role and scope, purpose, goals, philosophy, etc.**), but the important concept to grasp is that the document(s) serving as the campus's Expanded Statement of Institutional Purpose should provide a clear and unequivocal statement of institutional-level intentions for the future so that departmental/program statements of intentions may be directly linked to support such institutional-level intentions.

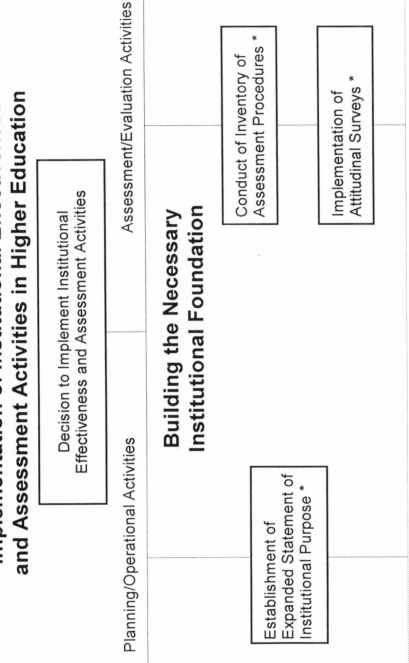

Figure 4

The First Year of a Generic Model for Implementation of Institutional Effectiveness and Assessment Activities in Higher Education

Assessment/Evaluation Activities

Planning/Operational Activities

Decision to Implement Institutional Effectiveness and Assessment Activities

Building the Necessary Institutional Foundation

Conduct of Inventory of Assessment Procedures *

Implementation of Attitudinal Surveys *

Establishment of Expanded Statement of Institutional Purpose *

* Resource section(s) included in chapter to support

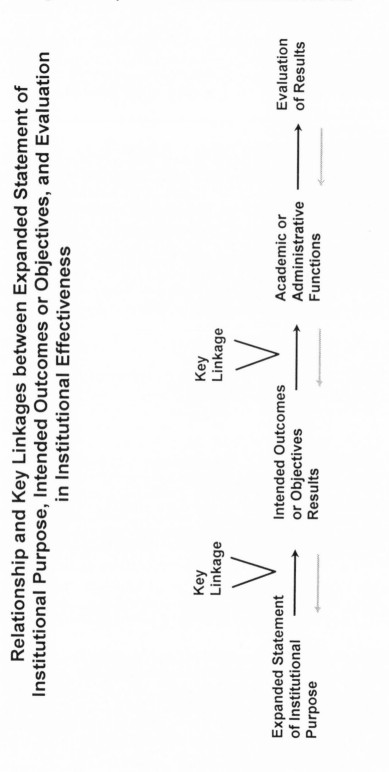

Figure 5

Relationship and Key Linkages between Expanded Statement of Institutional Purpose, Intended Outcomes or Objectives, and Evaluation in Institutional Effectiveness

Given the importance of the Expanded Statement of Institutional Purpose, how does an institution go about establishment or expansion of its statement of purpose? The answers are clearly as numerous as the institutions that must accomplish this delicate task. However, in the resource section entitled "Developing the Expanded Statement of Institutional Purpose," beginning on page 30, the author reviews the past and future roles of such statements, indicates desirable characteristics of such statements, and discusses the possible role of strategic planning in this effort. Finally, Appendixes A, B, and C contain examples of an Expanded Statement of Institutional Purpose for a four-year institution, a two-year college, and a major research university. All examples offer sufficient substance for use as a basis for institutional effectiveness operations on either type campus. Appendix D offers a sequence of events that (subject to institutional adaptation) can lead to establishment of the Expanded Statement of Institutional Purpose within 12 months.

Assessment/Evaluation Activities

Two major activities regarding assessment/evaluation should take place during the initial period of implementation: (a) the conduct of an inventory of existing and available assessment procedures and (b) the implementation of attitudinal surveys.

The "Conduct of an Inventory of Assessment Procedures" is clearly the place to begin along this track and will undoubtedly produce surprising results on most campuses. Among these surprising results will be the realization of how much assessment activity is already taking place in many of the institution's academic departments. Although the quality of the assessment-related activities found to be taking place will vary widely, there will probably be instances of truly excellent assessment activities already in place that can be utilized as examples to the rest of the institution's academic departments.

What are some of the types of assessment/evaluation activities that may already exist on your campus? You may find activities such as the following:

1. **Entrance examinations**—Although such examinations are not designed specifically to measure achievement at your institution, they are useful in establishing the level of academic competency of your entering students, from which your own accomplishments can be judged or as a measure of the achievement of remedial programming.

2. **Standardized and locally prepared tests of graduating students**—Although your institution may not require such testing of student knowledge (cognitive learning), some academic departments continue to administer or require such examinations. At least one national testing firm (the Educational Testing Service) provides summary data regarding test scores to the institutions from which those students who took the examination reported receiving their degrees. In a separate resource section entitled "Cognitive Assessment Instruments: Availability and Utilization," beginning on page 60, the advantages, disadvantages, and costs of both locally designed and standardized cognitive examinations are reviewed.

3. **Licensure examinations**—Among the best end-of-program assessment procedures, already widely implemented in various disciplines, are licensure-type examinations such as those in accountancy, nursing, and law.

4. **Performance examinations of graduating students**—Many academic departments will be found to have a rich history of performance examinations regarding acquired motor skills, such as painting and music, in which students are required to demonstrate their proficiency prior to graduation. Assessments of skills as well as of more long term changes in students are discussed in the resource section entitled "Assessment of Behavioral Change and Performance" in this chapter.

5. **Departmental alumni follow-ups**—Many departments attempt to stay in touch with their graduates and have received comments regarding their programs from that source.

6. **Existing institutional data systems**—Among the most frequently overlooked sources of assessment information is the institution's automated data system. Although most such data systems are likely to be designed for support of transactional (registration, fee payment, payroll, etc.) activities or, at best, process-type decision support (teaching loads, average salaries, space utilization, etc.), their potential for support of assessment is considerable. A resource section concerning this subject and entitled "Assessment-Related Information from Institutional Data Systems" is provided in this chapter and begins on page 107.

The process of conducting this initial inventory of existing and available assessment mechanisms should result in a comprehensive directory of existing assessment procedures and results. It should also result in a similar listing and analysis by discipline of those nationally available procedures (primarily standardized tests) that are not currently utilized on the campus.

The other major assessment/evaluation activity undertaken during the first year of implementation should be "Implementation of Attitudinal Surveys." The attitudes of an institution's constituents, including current and former students, employers, and the general public, are one important barometer of the extent to which an institution's purpose is being communicated and how accomplishment of that purpose is perceived. Some institutions and individual departments may already be utilizing separate survey instruments. However, it is unlikely that such instruments are focused on soliciting responses directly related to the accomplishment of the Expanded Statement of Institutional Purpose or linked to departmental/program intended outcomes or objectives. This first year is an ideal time to initiate implementation of a family of attitudinal surveys to be focused specifically on these subjects.

A resource section entitled "Attitudinal Surveys in Institutional Effectiveness" is provided for further exploration of this subject. It begins on page 43 and includes a discussion of (a) the types of attitudinal surveys, (b) various commercial instruments available for this purpose, (c) the local design or adaptation of attitudinal surveys, and (d) the benefits gained through centralizing the processing of such surveys while decentralizing the design process and emphasizing effective feedback of the results to the departmental/program level.

Complete implementation of attitudinal surveys will not be feasible until an Expanded Statement of Institutional Purpose and departmental/program statements of intended outcomes and objectives are finalized by the end of the first and second period of the implementation model, respectively. However, most survey and feedback design work can be completed parallel to these actions. By the end of the first year, pilot testing of the instruments can be accomplished, and their phased implementation can be initiated.

A separate resource section entitled "Assessment Planning" is provided for further guidance concerning this subject. It begins on page 123.

Summary

By the close of the first period of implementation activities, the foundation should have been laid and the tools gathered for constructing institutional effectiveness operations on the campus. The document(s) serving as the Expanded Statement of Institutional Purpose should be in place to guide planning/operational activities throughout the future. The completed campus "Conduct of Inventory of Assessment Procedures" and initial "Implementation of Attitudinal Surveys" serve to initiate identification and use of the means for assessment. Each of these actions at the institutional level supports a change in the focus of implementation activities to the department/program level in the second period of implementation of institutional effectiveness on the campus.

Developing the Expanded Statement of Institutional Purpose

Michael Yost

In the preceding chapter, the Expanded Statement of Institutional Purpose (ESIP) has been described as one of the most important parts of assessing institutional effectiveness. This document or collection of documents is developed in sequential steps in much the same way as an architect develops the blueprint for a new building; and as the blueprint gives direction to those who construct the building, the ESIP gives direction to those who develop the institutional effectiveness and assessment plans at a college or university.

In the pages that follow, we describe the content of the ESIP, give examples of the content, describe how to construct the ESIP, and explain the linkages between the content of the ESIP and the operation of the institution.

The ESIP should be thought of as being made up of two separate but related parts (Figure 6): the institutional mission and the institutional goals. The institutional mission statement is sometimes also referred to as the statement of purpose for an institution. Typically, this document is printed in the front of an institution's catalog or bulletin. Institutional goals, supporting or developed from the institutional mission, constitute the action plan for the institution. Collectively, these two documents give direction to the overall operation of the institution and clearly identify its intentions. Each of the regional accrediting agencies in the United States requires that institutions have a valid, up-to-date mission or purpose statement. As an initial part of the process of developing an institutional effectiveness program for an institution, this document must be evaluated, updated, and in most cases expanded.

The process of assessing institutional effectiveness is based on the degree of accomplishment of the institution's stated purpose as reflected in its mission or purpose statement. Because the institution is encouraged to formulate departmental/program statements of intentions consistent with the institution's purpose, great clarity and specificity are needed in the statements of institutional intentions contained in the ESIP. Although an institutional mission statement should not reach an operational level of detail, it should include substance sufficient to provide a clear framework for subsequent statements of institutional goals, which, in turn, would provide a clear sense of direction for the institution's departmental statements. The ultimate determination of effectiveness is the relationship of the statement of purpose and the accomplishment of institutional goals.

Figure 6

Components of the Expanded Statement of Institutional Purpose

Mission - Broad Statement of Institutional Philosophy,
Role, Scope, Etc.

Institutional Goals - Institutional-Level Action Statements
that Implement, Support,
and Are Derived from the Mission

a . . . .
b . . . .

Let us begin this process by examining the parts of an institutional mission statement. To facilitate in this presentation, an example ESIP and an institutional mission or purpose statement have been developed for an institution referred to as "Our University." These documents are located in Appendix A, and portions will be cited as needed in the text of this resource section.

First, let's look at the length and inclusiveness of the statement. As stated earlier, the institutional mission statement is usually included as the first major topic in the catalog or bulletin of an institution. As a part of the research in preparing to write this chapter, statements of purpose or institutional intentions from many institutions were reviewed. Typically, those documents were found to be between one and three single-spaced, typed pages in length. The institutional mission statement usually begins with a statement such as the following:

> Our University is an independent, nonsectarian, coeducational institution, in the tradition of the liberal arts and sciences. Seeking to be faithful to the ideals of its heritage, Our University is committed, in all of its policies and practices, to the unrestricted and rigorous pursuit of truth, to the certainty of values in human life, and to a respect for differing points of view.

This opening statement provides a brief history and philosophy of the institution, and states whether it is privately or publicly supported, whether it is coeducational or single sex, and what the institution represents. This portion of the mission statement for Our University is somewhat shorter than it is for most institutions.

Another part of the institutional mission statement describes the type of students that the institution enrolls and the geographic area (service area of the institution) from which they come.

...to provide an outstanding education for a relatively small number of talented and highly motivated students from a diversity of geographic, ethnic, and socioeconomic backgrounds.

The first part of this statement describes the clientele (highly motivated, talented, with diverse ethnic and socioeconomic backgrounds), the size of the institution (relatively small), and the geographic area that the institution seeks to serve (diverse geographic backgrounds). This statement would have been written very differently if Our University had been an institution supported by city, county, or state funds with restricted geographic service boundaries.

The next section of the mission statement deals with the faculty.

To achieve this end, we recruit and retain outstanding faculty members who are dedicated to the art of teaching and advising; to the search for and dissemination of truth through scholarship, research and creative endeavor; and to service to the University and the larger community.

This statement describes all of the major activities engaged in by faculty members. These include teaching, advising, research (or creative activities), dissemination of information, and service. Although this statement does not place more emphasis on one of these areas than another, this is not always true at all institutions.

The academic environment is described in the next statement.

We also seek to provide a supportive and challenging environment in which students can realize the full potential of their abilities and come to understand their responsibility of service in the human community.

This type of academic environment is appropriate for an institution that emphasizes the liberal arts and sciences. However, if Our University had contained an engineering school or had been an occupationally oriented institution, this statement would have been written very differently, as illustrated in Appendix B and C.

Because the major business of colleges and universities is to educate students, the description of the curriculum is one of the key elements of the institutional mission.

The principal focus of Our University's curricular programs is undergraduate education in the liberal arts and sciences, combined with a number of pre-professional fields. Relations between the liberal arts and the pre-professional fields are carefully nurtured to provide mutually reinforcing intellectual experiences for students and faculty. Our University also offers master's and doctoral degree programs in selected professional areas that will prepare individuals for positions of leadership in their chosen careers.

For a relatively small institution with a tightly focused curriculum, this statement can be very concise and relatively short. As the curriculum becomes more diverse, the amount of explanation required in the mission statement is greatly expanded. Two points in the example are noteworthy. First, the statement clearly defines the "principal focus" of the curriculum and, second, it states the relationship between the programs. These are both important ingredients of the institutional mission statement.

All public institutions and the majority of private institutions have a sense of responsibility for providing some level of service to the community in which they are located.

This service can take the form of faculty/staff participation in community events or non-university-sponsored events that take place on the university campus. In any event, if an institution does assume a public service role, it should be described in the institutional mission statement.

> In addition, recognizing its responsibility to the larger community, Our University provides a variety of carefully selected programs of continuing education and cultural enrichment.

Although some of the faculty at almost all institutions engage in research or other creative academic endeavors, not all institutions assume the responsibility of developing and maintaining a research program. Typically, small institutions do not have research programs and large institutions do. Much of the decision as to whether or not to have such a program is a function of faculty, staff, equipment, space, and funding. In the event that an institution assumes a research function, it also should appear as a part of the institutional mission statement.

> Our University recognizes its responsibility in maintaining a position of excellence and leadership in research.

It is difficult to believe that the administration and staff of an institution would exclude any individual from enrollment or employment because of sex, race, religion, or national origin. Along with the moral issues associated with discrimination are the many state and federal laws forbidding it. Because many individuals (students and employees) read the institutional mission statement, it is wise to include the institution's nondiscrimination statement in the mission statement:

> In its recruitment and retention of members of the university community, Our University, consistent with its academic and institutional heritage, maintains an openness to all qualified persons.

This sample nondiscrimination statement is a shortened form of the legal version published by the federal government.

Because the institutional mission or purpose statement defines the most fundamental criteria for assessing institutional effectiveness, it serves several important functions. It (a) provides guidance for administrative decisions regarding the overall direction of the institution through the Statement of Institutional Goals; (b) provides direction to each of the colleges, divisions, and departments of the institution, creating an umbrella under which those units may plan, operate, and evaluate their programs; and (c) establishes a general blueprint for the development of a process for assessing and improving institutional effectiveness. For these reasons, it is impossible to overstate the value and usefulness of mission statements as statements of purpose that articulate the institution's commitment to important outcomes for students.

Developing the Institutional Mission Statement

Given the importance attached to the institutional mission statement, a significant task for each institution is to conduct the research needed to formulate that critical document.

The potential approaches are, of course, as numerous as the institutions that must undertake the task. Assuming a broad perspective, much of the current literature in the field of higher education describes the general process of deriving the institutional mission statement as an outcome of "strategic planning." Numerous writers (Cope, 1981; Keller, 1983; Shirley, 1982, 1983) have provided descriptions of the process, and although procedures suggested vary widely, these authorities appear to agree on a number of important concepts. Strategic planning is an ends-oriented approach to planning that seeks to answer the questions, What is the business of the institution? and How does the institution fit into an educational picture of the city, region, state, or country? It focuses on assessment of the institution's internal strengths and weaknesses and the institution's fit with or niche in the external educational environment. Although various techniques may be used, the result of this assessment is identification of environmental opportunities that are a good match for the strengths of the institution. An assessment of the institution's internal strengths and weaknesses is a major component of strategic planning. Whether this assessment is informal or formal, oral or written, focused more on strengths or more on weaknesses, the findings are critical in planning for the future.

The result of strategic planning is a clear sense of institutional direction resulting from conscious decisions about the role of the institution. The ongoing objective is the creation of a match among environmental opportunities, institutional values, and strengths, coupled with resources available to support action in high-priority areas.

Now, let's consider an example of the application of strategic planning to Our University. Suppose that Our University had survived for nearly 100 years as a relatively small, private institution that had not undergone a great deal of change or reform. Suppose, further, that the institution was well endowed, and that it had a local and regional reputation of being a "good" institution, but one that did not appear to have any outstanding academic programs. The physical plant was in good condition, the budget was balanced, and enrollment was stable and at an acceptable level. The members of the board of trustees, after hiring a new president, decided that the mission of the institution should be reviewed and evaluated and, if necessary, changed.

At this point in time, the data required to support the evaluation of the existing mission (and possibly to support the development of a new mission) were gathered. Historic data indicated that the existing mission statement had not been evaluated since the last regional self-study, and at that time there was only a cursory review of the mission statement. Also, since the last review of the mission statement, there had been several changes in the administrative structure of the institution and several academic programs had been implemented that did not appear to fit within the existing mission statement and the curriculum as a whole. In the previous 10 years the institution had become a disjointed collection of academic units. The new president suggested that a study be conducted to determine whether it would be feasible for the "principal focus of Our University's curricular programs to be undergraduate education in the liberal arts and sciences, combined with a number of pre-professional fields."

With this potential mission in mind, studies of internal strengths and weaknesses and external market constraints were undertaken. An examination of the external market constraints indicated that the nearest institution with this type of curricular offering was almost 500 miles away; high school students in the city and region were traveling outside of the region to attend schools with this type of curricular offering; on a national basis, there was an increase in the enrollment in this type of institution; and noted experts in education were recommending that students acquire a liberal arts education. The assessment of internal strengths indicated that the new mission could be pursued in light of sufficient liberal arts curricular offerings in basic academic areas; talent and diversity in the faculty; and classroom, laboratory, and residence hall space; financial reserves; library resources; and faculty/staff support. The assessment of internal weaknesses indicated that selected graduate and undergraduate academic programs would need to be strengthened, and others phased out; selected classrooms and laboratories would need to be modified; selected academic programs would need to be initiated; faculty would need to be given opportunities for retraining; and university funds would have to be reallocated. When all of the positive and negative internal and external factors were assessed collectively, this portion of the new institutional mission statement was enthusiastically accepted by the governing board, the faculty, and the staff. At this point, the meaning of the mission had to be more clearly defined in terms of institutional goals; and following this, the operational plan for achieving the mission had to be developed and implemented in the individual departments and programs of the institution.

This example is but a brief sketch of the assessment and strategic planning needed to develop a small portion of a mission statement for an institution. A large amount of other data would have to be gathered and a tremendous number of judgments would have to be made in order to develop a new mission statement.

Staffing and timing are both critical components in conducting the research needed to support the strategic planning and the development of an institutional mission statement. The rule of thumb for staffing and participation is to have broad-based involvement and representation of both faculty and administrators. If a subcommittee working structure is used, then both faculty and administrators should be on each subcommittee. Also, faculty and administrators should both be used to chair subcommittees. Some institutions may also choose to involve students and staff in this process. Broad-based involvement and representation help ensure that the end product (the mission statement) will represent individuals at all levels within the institution and that these individuals (and hopefully those whom they represent) will assume ownership and identification with the mission statement.

Although a mission statement is seldom more than one to three pages long, a great deal of time is required for its development. Initially, decisions have to be made regarding what data and information need to be gathered. Once gathered, they must be reviewed and analyzed by the committee before a draft of the mission statement can be developed. It also takes a great deal of discussion and writing to develop what the committee considers to be the appropriate wording of the mission statement. Finally, getting approval of the document by the governing body of the institution, faculty, and administration will usually require the development of several revisions of the mission statement before it is acceptable to the members in each of these groups. At least six months are required to develop, write, and gain an acceptance of an institutional mission statement. Many institutions spend an entire academic year in the development of this document. One of the greatest challenges faced during the period of public review is retaining sufficient substance to provide a clear sense of institutional direction, rather than appeasing all aspects of the institution with a mission statement that is acceptable to all because it lacks any substance.

Obviously, there are many approaches that can be used to develop a new mission statement. Whatever an institution's approach, it is important to remember that the institutional mission statement forms the blueprint for identification of institutional goals and intended departmental and program statements of outcomes and objectives. This document, the institutional mission statement, also provides the ultimate basis for the evaluation of institutional effectiveness.

Developing Institutional Goals

The institutional mission statement should be worded so that persons reading it have no doubt as to the overall direction and orientation of the institution. However, this document does not articulate the mission of the institution at a level of detail that will support the development of a set of departmental/program priorities for action or intended outcomes.

If we return to the blueprint analogy, the mission statement is analogous to the initial plot-plan an architect develops for a new university. An initial plot-plan lays out which buildings and roads will be in which location without describing in great detail the internal structure of each of the buildings. Just as an architect develops more elaborate plans that accompany the plot-plan and describe each building in detail, the faculty and administration must add more specificity to the mission statement. As the architect develops detailed plans that a builder uses as to construct the buildings, the faculty and administration must add detail to their mission statement so that operational plans in the institution's departments/programs can be developed.

The development of institutional goals to accompany a mission statement is analogous to the development of the overall plan for the building from an initial plot-plan. Initially, an architect develops an overall plan for a building, and later he or she develops the many detailed drawings needed by the craftsmen who will build it. Institutional goals remain relatively general in nature, but they articulate the direction given to key concepts within the institution that identify what is to be accomplished. As a chief architect would give an initial or rough plan for a building to one of his or her colleagues who is going to develop the final plan, institutional goals should be developed and published within an institution to give direction to the development of operational plans and intended outcomes or objectives at all levels within the institution.

Who should develop the institutional goals? The personnel mix required to develop these goals is identical to that needed to develop the institutional mission. Broad-based involvement of faculty and administrators (and possibly students and staff) is a requirement. It is critical that each of these groups agrees to the validity of the goals, believes these goals represent both its own best interests and those of the institution as a whole, and accepts the need to work toward accomplishment of the goals. Without broad-based involvement and acceptance of the institutional mission and goals, the results of strategic planning will go unused, the institution will not grow and develop, and there will be no way to assess institutional effectiveness.

A great deal of data are gathered and used in the process of developing the mission statement. Along with the analysis of the data, there will be debate as to the relevance and meaning of the data to the institution. Because the goals form a document that is one level of specificity greater than the mission statement, all of the information gathered in the earlier endeavor will apply to the development of the goals.

In the development of the mission statement, some of the questions asked are as follows:

- Should we do ____?
- Can we move in "that" direction?
- Are we capable of doing ____?
- What will be the consequences of ____?
- What implications does this have for ____?
- Can we add ____?
- What will be the effect of ____?

The questions asked in developing the institution's goals are very different from these. Because the decision to move the institution in a particular direction(s) has already been made during development of the mission statement, the questions change from Should we? to How much? Some of the questions asked are the following:

- How much should we increase by ____ [date]?
- What administrative or academic organization will best accomplish ____?
- What level of funding will be required to reach ____ by ____ [date]?
- What level of enrollment (or staffing) must we reach in order to ____?
- What changes in the physical plant must be made by ____ [date] in order to ____?

The answers to these and other similar questions will result in the development of a valid set of goals for an institution.

There are several parameters that must be understood—and set—before an institution can begin to develop its institutional goals. The questions to be asked are:

- What structure will be used in organizing and sequencing the goals?
- What time frame(s) and level of specificity will be used in the writing of the goals?
- What level of the operation of the institution will warrant development of goals?

Each of these questions should be answered in detail before goals are written.

Although goals are typically written one at a time, the writers must have thought their way through some organizational structure before they begin. Without an organizational structure, it is easy to overlook important concepts and difficult to arrange the goals for presentation once they have been developed. The sample goals in Appendix A follow a modification of the overall administrative organization of Our University. In this document, there are goals established and approved at the **institutional level** for each of the major administrative subdivisions of the institution. For the most part, the goals for each administrative subdivision are ones that can be pursued more or less independently by the staff in that subdivision. Those goals that seem to cut across or require the joint effort of two or more administrative subdivisions appear in the first section of this statement. Because all of the subdivisions work to support the academic, research, and service missions of the institution, goals are developed for all of the administrative subdivisions. This implies that all of these subdivisions should participate in institutional effectiveness assessment. A different, more programmatic structure for the Expanded Statement of Institutional Purpose is illustrated in Appendix B, while still another approach is provided in Appendix C.

Whenever mission or goals statements are developed at an institution, they are built on assumptions that are relevant at the time those goals statements are developed. Because the purpose of this entire endeavor is to assess institutional effectiveness, it is essential that the assumptions upon which those goals have been developed be included. It is amazing how quickly institutions forget (or selectively modify) their original assumptions. If the assumptions are not recorded, it will be impossible to assess institutional effectiveness validly in the future.

Well-written institutional goals contain two major ingredients. First, they include a description of some well-defined end result. Examples of these types of statements include the following:

- Enrollment will reach ____.
- Admissions will achieve an acceptance rate of ____.
- Five new academic programs will ____.
- The business office will implement systems that will ____.
- The development office will reach an alumni giving rate of ____.
- Student services will have programs that will ____.
- The library will have holdings of ____.
- Financial aid will reach a support rate of ____.

Some of the goals specify or state that a specific number, percentage, or rate be reached, whereas others state that something of an operational nature will be accomplished. Both are equally important and valid goals. Also, note that the concepts stated in these goals are very broad and inclusive.

If these statements are written very specifically or narrowly, then they become departmental or program objectives or outcomes, not goals. Keep in mind that the purpose of developing the mission and goals statements is to develop documents that, when distributed on campus, can give others direction and assistance as they develop the outcomes and objectives they will operationalize. If the goals become too specific, they infringe on the work and professional responsibility of others. Also, if goals statements are written too specifically, then an inordinately large number of them must be developed. From an assessment point of view, an excessive number of goals create personnel, time, and cost problems.

The second ingredient of a goals statement is the time frame. In the examples of goals given earlier, the end result was stated, but the reader was never told when it would occur. There was no way of telling whether it would occur next semester, next year, or in five years. It is important that the time required to achieve the intended action be stated as a part of most goals. Just as some changes within an institution are easier to make than others, it takes more time to achieve one goal than another. Changes in academic programs sometimes take as much as four years, major changes in budget allocations can usually be made in two years, changes in admissions ratios can be made in one year, and changes in institutional investment strategies can be made in several months. Obviously, the time frame used in a goals statement must fit the aspect of the institution to which it applies. It is even possible to use longitudinal time frames in developing goals. For example, a reasonable goal of this type might be as follows: The student retention/graduation rate will increase by 1% in each of the next five years and reach 70% by 1998. There are many options open to the creative persons or groups who develop mission and goals statements.

What aspects or subdivisions of an institution warrant the development of institutional goals? The answer is that since no one major aspect or subdivision of the institution is independent of the others, they all warrant the development of goals. However, when an institution chooses to evaluate and change its mission, some aspects tend to become more critical than others. If, for example, an institution chooses to pursue academic excellence, then the quality of entering students, the quality of the faculty, the curriculum, and finances needed to support the endeavor would become key concepts of the plan for change. If these are the key concepts, then admissions, faculty recruiting, faculty development, curriculum council, financial aid, the development office, budget allocations, and so forth would become the key institutional operations within the plan for change. Assuming that this logic is valid and that the list of key concepts and institutional operations is complete, then the Mission and Goals Committee should pay special attention to developing the institutional goals to accompany what they consider to be the key to the plan for change. This approach will focus the attention of the institution on the key concepts and help avoid the development of an excessive number of goals. It is critical that all of the key concepts in the planned change be covered by a goal, but it is just as important that an institution not write so many goals that it is overburdened with their sheer number. Balance and inclusiveness are critical when it comes to developing the proper types and number of institutional goals.

The length of and time required to develop the ESIP vary significantly from institution to institution. Most mission statements do not exceed one page in length and the accompanying goal statements seldom exceed 20 in number depending upon the complexity of the institution. Most institutions take at least 12 months to substantially revise or expand their existing statement of purpose. Appendix D suggests a Sequence of Events leading to the establishment of the Expanded Statement of Institutional Purpose within this period of time. Revisions accomplished in less than a 12-month period should be questioned regarding the degree of comprehensiveness and broad-based participativeness. At some institutions, it takes less time to develop the institutional goals statement than it does to gather data, do the strategic planning, and develop the mission

Figure 7

Organization of Institutional Goals and Departmental/Program Outcomes or Objectives and Assessment

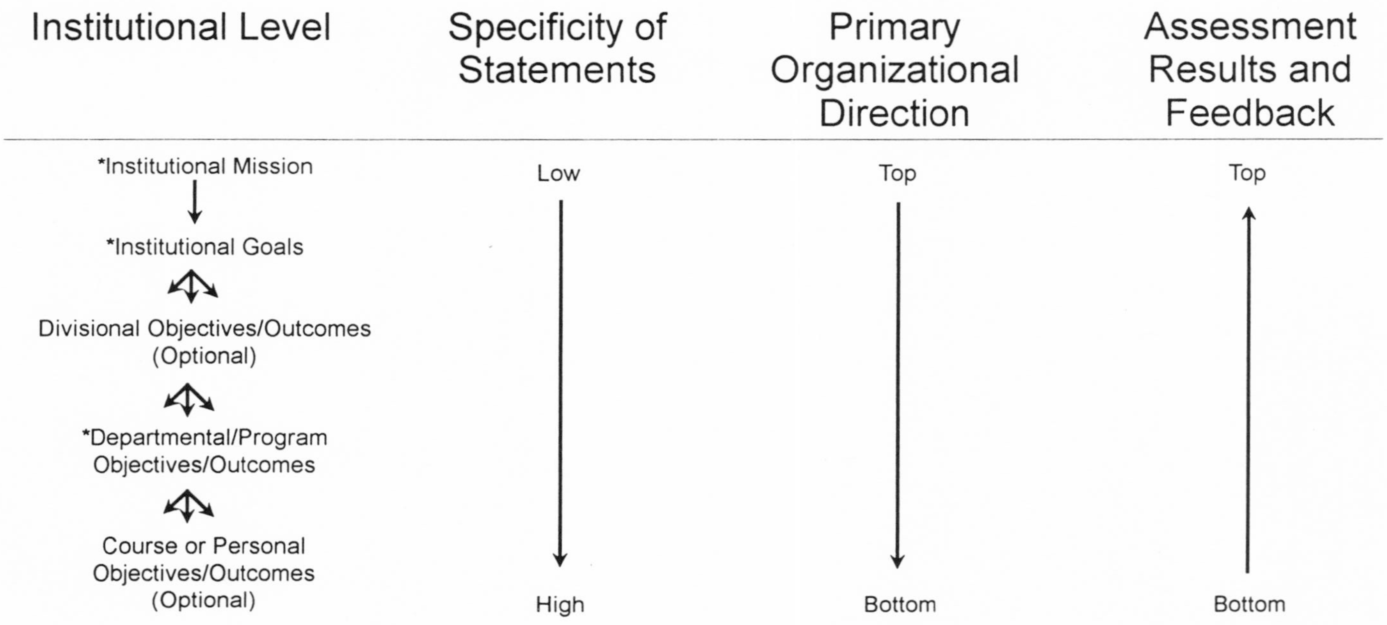

Institutional Level	Specificity of Statements	Primary Organizational Direction	Assessment Results and Feedback
*Institutional Mission	Low →→→→→ High	Top →→→→→ Bottom	Top ←←←←← Bottom
*Institutional Goals			
Divisional Objectives/Outcomes (Optional)			
*Departmental/Program Objectives/Outcomes			
Course or Personal Objectives/Outcomes (Optional)			

* Minimum Necessary

statement. It is conceivable that the goals statement can be developed in as little as three months. As with the mission statement, approval for the institutional goals statement should be obtained from the governing board of the institution, the faculty, and the administration.

Summary

When the institutional mission and goals statements are completed, they will provide direction for operational planning within all levels of the institution and, in turn, will give direction to the majority of the activities and efforts within the institution. These two documents comprise the Expanded Statement of Institutional Purpose, which, in conjunction with the more operational plans of the departments/programs, acts as the evaluation blueprint in assessing institutional effectiveness.

Figure 7 is a graphic summary of the text discussion. Institutions are administratively organized from the top down; as a result, goals, objectives, and assessments are also frequently organized in the same way. Some obvious exceptions to this approach exist within almost all institutions (particularly at larger ones), but it is not necessary to discuss them at this point. The goals, objectives, and assessments are hierarchically organized from top-to-bottom within an organization, with the activities near the top of the organization being very broad, general, and inclusive and the activities near the bottom being very task or activity specific. It is important that the reader see the necessity of maintaining key linkages between organizational levels within such a structure. Whereas the organizational structure has a top-to-bottom organization, the feedback of information is organized on a bottom-to-top basis. Think of the assessment process as one of **merging** the more specific assessments at the lower academic/administrative levels into assessments at successively higher levels within the organization. Assessment at any level within an institution becomes a summary of the assessment of the areas within and immediately below that level.

With all of this rhetoric, the reader needs to keep one major concept in mind: Assessment is not done solely for its own sake. Institutions assess to improve their operation or effectiveness. Assessment should be tied to operations so that the information obtained from the assessment can be used for improvement.

References: Cited and Recommended

Caruthers, J. K., & Lott, G. B. (1981). *Mission Review: Foundation for Strategic Planning*. Boulder, CO: National Center for Higher Education Management Systems.

Chaffee, E. E. (1985). The Concept of Strategy: From Business to Higher Education. In J. Smart (ed.), *Higher Education: Handbook of Theory and Research*, Vol. 1 (pp. 133-172). New York: Agathon Press.

Cope, R. (1981). *Strategic Planning, Management and Decision Making*. Washington, DC: American Association for Higher Education.

Dutton, J. L., Fahey, L., & Narayanan, V. K. (1983). Toward Understanding Strategic Issue Diagnosis. *Strategic Management Journal, 4,* 307-323.

Ewell, P. T. (ed.). (1985). Assessing Educational Outcomes. *New Directions for Institutional Research, 47.* San Francisco: Jossey-Bass.

Keller, G. (1983). *Academic Strategy: The Management Revolution in American Higher Education.* Baltimore, MD: Johns Hopkins University Press.

Kotler, P., & Murphy, P. E. (1981). Strategic Planning for Higher Education. *Journal of Higher Education, 52,* 470-489.

Shirley, R. C. (1982). Limiting the Scope of Strategy: A Decision Based Approach. *Academy of Management Review, 7(*2), 37-46.

Shirley, R. C. (1983). Identifying the Levels of Strategy for a College or University. *Long Range Planning, 16(*3), 92-98.

Attitudinal Surveys in Institutional Effectiveness

Gale Bridger and Lori Wolff

Gloria Raines, *Editor*

> O wad some Pow'r the giftie gie us
> To see oursels as ithers see us!
> It wad frae mony a blunder free us,
> And foolish notion.
> —**Robert Burns**, "To a Louse"

Surveys designed to measure the attitudes of an institution's various constituents provide important insights into the way others perceive the institution's purpose, programs, and performance. Attitudinal surveys take many forms, address a range of publics, and generate a wealth of information to be incorporated into the planning/evaluative process. As institutions receive increasing demands for accountability, surveys can be a valuable tool in assessing institutional effectiveness; however, if surveys are not carefully selected, administered, and utilized, they may simply generate reams of paper which are stored in the institutional research office. To assist those who wish to begin a survey program, this resource section includes:

- A review of commercial survey instruments;
- A consideration of contracted survey services;
- An examination of locally developed instruments;
- Identification of the types of information which can be acquired most effectively with survey techniques;
- Recommendations concerning the constituent groups who may best provide the information sought;
- A discussion of the campus groups which may benefit from the information generated; and,
- Practical steps for conducting surveys and disseminating information.

Commercially Available Surveys

The following agencies offer a full range of survey services which have been subjected to careful, long-term testing to provide valid and reliable attitudinal data from several population groups:

- The American College Testing Program (ACT);
- The National Center for Higher Education Management Systems (NCHEMS);
- The Educational Testing Service (ETS); and,
- The Cooperative Institutional Research Program (CIRP) of the University of California, Los Angeles, and the American Council on Education.

(a) American College Testing Program

The American College Testing Program Evaluation/Survey Service (ACT/ESS) offers 14 survey instruments for use by two-year and four-year postsecondary education institutions. Each is an optical-scan instrument containing two or four pages of questions designed to permit a general evaluation of an institution's programs and services. The institution has the option of designing up to 30 additional questions for inclusion in each survey. ACT also offers a catalog of additional items which institutions may use rather than writing their own questions. In addition, each instrument provides space for the participant to write comments or suggestions. Since 1979, several million ESS instruments have been administered at more than 950 institutions. This extensive use of the ACT materials has generated normative data for comparative studies as well as an opportunity for longitudinal studies within institutions. A brief description of each instrument follows:

1. **The College Student Needs Assessment Survey** is used to ascertain the educational and personal needs of enrolled college students and determine their career and life goals. This four-page questionnaire contains:
   - Background information including basic demographic data and information for subgroup selection for analysis of student responses;
   - Career and life goals with information on college major, occupational choice, and relative importance of various career and personal goals;
   - Educational and personal needs which asks the student to indicate assistance needed in the areas of career development, educational planning, intellectual skills development, and life skills development; and,
   - Additional questions, comments, and suggestions.

2. **The Adult Learner Needs Assessment Survey** can be used to examine the educational needs of adult learners and, in its four pages, includes the following items:
   - Background as related to previous educational experience, family, and employment;
   - Educational plans and preferences with emphasis on the special needs of the adults such as scheduling, location, and format of classes;

- Personal and educational needs including life skills development, educational planning, and association with others; and,
- Additional questions, comments, and suggestions.

3. **The Alumni Survey** is designed to measure the impact of an institution on its graduates. The survey solicits information concerning the continuing education and employment history of alumni; therefore, it is most useful to Alumni offices and fund raising efforts. Four-page surveys are available for two-year and four-year institutions and provide information in the following sections:
    - Background information tailored to the two-year or four-year graduate;
    - Continuing education which provides extensive information on formal education since graduation/departure;
    - Educational college experiences giving the alumni's perception of the value and impact of his or her education in areas such as quality of life, skills development, and independent living;
    - Employment history, which provides information for alumni and placement offices as well as for various academic program planners; and,
    - Additional questions, mailing addresses, comments, and suggestions.

4. **The Alumni Outcomes Survey** assesses alumni's perceived outcomes related to the institution's programs and services. This survey is focused on the institution and its effect on the lives of alumni. Survey results would be relevant to academic schools and departments which are attempting to measure graduates' reactions to their educational experiences. This survey covers the following areas:
    - Background including highest current and former lifetime educational goal;
    - Employment history and experience with an emphasis on how well educational experiences prepared them for their current positions;
    - Educational outcomes listing a variety of abilities and skills with an evaluation of their importance for success in today's world and the impact of students' educational experiences on the attainment of these abilities;
    - Educational experiences evaluation;
    - Activities and organizations in which the alumni participated while in school; and,
    - Mailing addresses, additional questions, comments, and suggestions.

5. **The College Outcomes Survey** is designed to obtain student feedback on the institution's impact on students' affective and cognitive development in order to improve student development and document outcomes for accreditation and other external requirements. The major sections of the instrument are:
    - Background information including a section on goals and a section to determine how the student spent time while in college (work, studying, care of family, etc.);
    - College outcomes which solicits feedback on the importance and progress made in a variety of academic outcomes; student evaluation of the general education program; institutional impact on meeting student goals; the extent of personal growth; and the institution's contribution to that growth in a variety of affective areas;

- Satisfaction with selected aspects of the institution;
- Summary of the institution's contribution to the student's growth and preparation; and,
- Local questions, comments, and suggestions.

6. **The Entering Student Survey**, a four-page form, is used to obtain information on the entering student's personal history, interests, and perception of the institution. The instrument contains:
   - Background information;
   - Educational plans and preferences. Unlike the ACT Profile, responses are gathered from entering college freshmen only;
   - College impressions which asks the student to rate the importance of various items in his or her decision to attend the institution. The student also is asked to indicate agreement or disagreement with various descriptors to provide a perception of the institution; and,
   - Additional questions, comments, and suggestions.

7. **The Student Opinion Survey**, with two-year and four-year forms, is used to examine the perception held by enrolled, continuing students of the institution's services and environment. The two-year form also includes items designed to explore the student's reasons for selecting the institution and his or her overall impression of the school. The following survey sections are included:
   - Background information;
   - Use of and level of satisfaction with various campus services and programs;
   - Level of satisfaction with the environment in the following areas: academic program, admissions, rules and regulations, facilities, registration, and general; and,
   - Additional questions, comments, and suggestions.

8. **The Survey of Academic Advising** is used to obtain information regarding student impressions of academic advising services. The four-page form includes the following:
   - Background information;
   - Advising information including frequency of advisor and advisee contacts and the period of time the student has been assigned to the current advisor;
   - Academic advising needs in which the student identifies topics discussed with the advisor and expresses his or her level of satisfaction with the advisor's assistance; and,
   - Additional questions, comments, and suggestions.

9. **The Survey of Current Activities and Plans** is designed for applicants to the institution who chose *not* to enroll. The survey requests the following:
   - Background information;
   - Impressions of the institution;
   - Educational plans and activities;

- Employment plans; and,
- Additional questions, comments, and suggestions.

10. **The Survey of Postsecondary Plans** is used with high school students to identify their occupational and educational plans after high school graduation. This survey also asks for the students' impressions of the particular institution conducting the survey and offers space for additional questions, comments, and suggestions. Information from the first part of this survey is not unlike that contained in the ACT Profile.

11. **The Withdrawing/Nonreturning Student Survey** is produced in two-page and four-page formats. In both, the student who chooses to leave the institution before completing a degree is asked to provide background information and to indicate reasons for leaving. These reasons are grouped in the following categories:
    - Personal (health, moving, marriage, social, etc.);
    - Academic (suspension, instructional quality, lack of challenge, etc.);
    - Institutional (scheduling problems, inadequate advising, programs or facilities, etc.);
    - Financial (availability of work or financial aid); and,
    - Employment (conflict between work and school, etc.).

    Both forms provide space for comments and suggestions. The four-page form also asks the student to rate his or her satisfaction with various institutional services and characteristics.

ACT offers a variety of flexible services; and, institutions may choose to purchase one or more of the survey instruments with or without ACT scoring and reporting services. Institutions can contract for mailing and scoring only or contract for a full range of mailing, scoring, and reporting services. ACT is developing new services to link various surveys together or with other data to provide multiple sources for answering key questions.

(b) National Center for Higher Education Management Systems

The National Center for Higher Education Management Systems (NCHEMS) has three major assessment programs. They are:

1. **Student Outcomes Information Service (SOIS)** is designed to obtain information on students' needs and reactions to their educational experiences. The six questionnaires are developed for the following student populations:
   - Entering students;
   - Continuing students;
   - Former students;
   - Graduating students;
   - Recent alumni; and,
   - Long-term (3-5 year) alumni.

   The questionnaires, available in both two-year and four-year institution versions, have a common set of questions which include information about student background, personal goals and career aspirations, factors influencing choice of college, satisfaction with college experience, activities while in college, educational plans and accomplishments, and career choices and career successes. Perhaps the most significant difference between the SOIS and ACT surveys is the coordinated, research-oriented approach of the SOIS which is supported by a carefully written handbook, *Student Outcomes Questionnaires: An Implementation Handbook* (2nd edition, 1983), by Peter T. Ewell. Ewell takes the novice practitioner through the process step by step and carefully points out tricks and essential steps to help guarantee successful, usable survey results. As with ACT, data processing and questionnaire analyses are available. Annual summaries of information from participating institutions are also made available.

2. **Comprehensive Alumni Assessment Survey (CAAS)**, in both two-year and four-year versions, is designed to solicit information concerning the effectiveness of an institution while allowing alumni to evaluate their personal development and career preparation. The survey contains the following areas:
   - Employment and continuing education includes information concerning first and current job titles, salaries, and relation to major;
   - Undergraduate experience provides information on academic advising, faculty contact, course availability and academic support services;
   - Development of intellect solicits alumni reaction to the importance of outcomes such as analytical and logical thinking and allows alumni to rate how the institution affected those abilities;
   - Achievement of community goals seeks alumni opinion on items such as engaging in a life of service to society;
   - Personal development and enrichment allows alumni to rate how well institutional experiences enhanced their abilities in areas important to personal development;
   - Community participation solicits the value of community activities to graduates; and,
   - Demographic/background information provides characteristics of alumni.

3. **Institutional Performance Survey (IPS)** is a comprehensive, one-hundred item instrument available in both two-year and four-year versions, which measures eight dimensions relating to institutional performance. The major areas are described below:
   - Institutional effectiveness measures performance and opportunities for educational experience and career development;
   - Leadership and decision styles assesses perceptions of how decisions are made and allows members of the institutional community to evaluate how decisions are made and implemented;
   - Institutional culture evaluates how well the institution's leadership and operation match its culture; and,
   - Institutional environment asks how outside factors affect policy decisions.

(c) Educational Testing Service

The Higher Education Assessment area of Educational Testing Service (ETS) offers a broad array of survey instruments focusing on program planning and evaluation. The following survey instruments are available from ETS Higher Education Assessment (i.e., Outcomes Assessment):

1. **The Goals Inventories** (IGI, CCGI, and SCGI) differ in content and focus in addressing the concerns of the three different types of institutions (i.e., university or large college, community college, and small college); however, they use the same format. Each has 90 statements of possible institutional goals, and participants are asked to indicate their opinions of the importance of each statement in terms of what exists and what they would like to see exist. The inventory is appropriate for use by students, faculty, and administrators; therefore, the institution gains varied perceptions of its goals and purpose. A Canadian IGI in both French and English, a Spanish/English IGI, and a Canadian CCGI in English only are available.

2. **The Program Self-Assessment Service (PSAS)** consists of a set of questionnaires which address areas such as curriculum, program purposes, departmental procedures, faculty activity, student accomplishment, and the general environment for work and learning. The PSAS assumes that the perceptions and assessment of those most directly involved with any department or program can contribute to improved quality and functioning of the area surveyed; therefore, the service offers assessment questionnaires for faculty, students who major in the department or program, and recent graduates of the program. Responses provide a profile of the targeted program or department and can assist in the program review process by identifying areas of strength as well as areas which require attention.

3. **The Graduate Program Self-Assessment Service (GPSAS)** is the parent of the previously described PSAS. GPSA is co-sponsored by the Graduate Record Examination Board and the Council of Graduate Schools in the United States. Instruments have been developed for both master's and doctoral level programs and address the parallel constituent groups identified in the PSAS discussion, students enrolled in the program, faculty, and recent graduates. Survey questions provide information on 16 areas of program characteristics including environment for learning, scholarly excellence, teaching quality, faculty concern for students, curriculum, departmental procedures, resources such as library and laboratories, faculty work environment, student accomplishments, and others.

4. **The Student Instructional Report (SIR)** is a brief, objective questionnaire which enables instructors to gain information concerning the students' reactions to their courses. The questionnaire offers students the opportunity to comment anonymously on their courses and instruction. Six factors are covered:
   • Course organization and planning;
   • Faculty and student interaction;

- Communication;
- Course difficulty and work load;
- Textbooks and readings; and,
- Tests and/or examinations.

The SIR is not intended to replace regular student and faculty communication; however, it does provide an additional means by which instructors may examine their teaching performance. Extensive comparative data are available through ETS based on SIR administrations in the United States and Canada. The questionnaire is available in Spanish and in a Canadian version in both French and English. All of the ETS instruments offer space for optional local items, and like ACT and NCHEMS, the services of basic data processing and reporting are available. Special services and professional assistance may be negotiated as well.

(d) Cooperative Institutional Research Program

The oldest and perhaps the most widely known survey targets one population only, college freshmen, and is included here; although, it is not in the truest sense commercial. The Student Information Form (SIF) used in the Cooperative Institutional Research Program (CIRP) contains standard biographic and demographic data-gathering items which have been included for each entering freshman class since the annual survey began in 1966. The instrument also contains research-oriented attitudinal questions which are modified from time to time. The SIF includes a wide-ranging set of questions, including items dealing with students' personal habits, reasons for attending college, political views, and others. The annual report, generated by the optical-scanned responses and provided to participating institutions, gives responses in percentages for each institution and comparative data for all institutions in the participant institution's category. Through a series of follow-up questionnaires CIRP also maintains longitudinal data on American higher education.

Contracted Services

Most management consultant services and marketing consultants are capable of developing and conducting surveys of the public to determine perceptions concerning a given institution's reputation, purposes, and programs. A number of agencies market themselves primarily to the higher education community. Because these organizations operate in a highly competitive market, individual groups will not be identified here; however, there are *several* advantages to contracting for survey services:

- The contract is usually for a turnkey process which includes designing the survey to meet the specific needs of the client; gathering and processing the data; and presenting and interpreting the results to appropriate groups. The contractual process may be regarded more favorably by those surveyed because it is individualized and carries the identity of the contracting institution. The contractor may provide on-site consultants who may lend added credibility to the process and the findings through discussion with constituents.

Some disadvantages of contracted services should be noted:

• An institution may expect the contract cost to run as high as $30,000 or $40,000.
• The resultant data will not have the benefit of comparability to normative data or summary data from other institutions of the same level or type.
• The time required for the full development of such services may be counterproductive. Institutions may be interested in gaining reputational kinds of information or community needs assessment data through telephone sampling or similar marketing techniques. Such services contracted with local sampling and marketing agencies may be quite successful and fairly inexpensive. This approach should be selected if available commercial instruments do not meet the institution's identified need; the expertise is not available in-house; or, the contracted arrangement can provide the data required in a cost-effective and timely manner.

Locally Developed Surveys

Locally developed or "in-house" surveys require time and expertise to design. On most campuses, the responsibility for designing such instruments is assigned to the staff of the institutional research office or to faculty members from disciplines which emphasize research design and statistical analysis. One of the primary reasons for using locally developed surveys is cost-effectiveness; however, regardless of the potential cost savings, one should heed the caution from H. R. Kells in *Self-Study Processes* (1980) that "a poorly designed instrument, used at the wrong moment with an unreceptive audience, will yield little or no useful information and it may damage the sense of community and morale at the institution involved" (p. 69). Designing and utilizing locally developed survey instruments can be an effective way for the institution to gain a sense of ownership and personalize the entire assessment and evaluation process.

When evaluating the use of locally developed instruments for an individual institution, one valuable resource is Peter Ewell's (1987b) presentation of a general set of pros and cons regarding the use of either standardized or locally developed instruments. This set, although it refers specifically to tests, is applicable to assessment or survey instruments. The complete outline of the pros and cons is provided in the resource section entitled "Cognitive Assessment Instruments: Availability and Utilization," beginning on page 60; therefore, it will not be repeated in this section. However, the list should be consulted when deciding whether or not to use locally developed instruments. Perhaps the most important advantage of using locally developed instruments is that they can be designed to reflect the specific curriculum or program which is being evaluated. A locally designed survey instrument "improves the fit between the questionnaire content and the institution's concerns" (Stevenson, 1985, p. 5). Kells in *Self-Study Processes* (1980) also emphasizes that if an institution uses locally developed surveys, the instrument must be matched to the special circumstances of the institution if the goals of the assessment process are to be achieved. Rhode Island College administered its own entering student questionnaire to obtain data to be used in developing individualized learning plans for its students. Such in-house surveys allow the institution to collect and analyze information "that people [at the institution] care about so as to answer unique questions about a program" (Dennison & Bunda, 1989, p. 51). Designing and using locally developed instruments encourages the university to work as a community. Although the need for an assessment instrument may be conceived in the office serving the institutional research or planning function, numerous campus departments or offices can benefit from the survey process and should play an essential role in the development of the survey instrument (Fisher, 1988).

Peter Ewell in *Student Outcomes Questionnaires: An Implementation Handbook* (1983) emphasizes the need for campus involvement (even though his publication deals primarily with a standardized set of questionnaires) by noting that such involvement "will help ensure better response rates and will ultimately facilitate effective use of the questionnaire results" (p. 17). As with virtually any process, involving more people can cause frustration, but it also can bring in different perspectives that may lead to new insights about the institution (Ewell, 1985). A secondary benefit from the use of an instrument designed on campus is the institutional personalization which can be accomplished. Northeast Missouri State University, which has one of the foremost models for institutional effectiveness, exemplifies this personalization. Their set of instruments has included the prominent use of the institution's name on the survey form. The use of an institutional symbol or logo gives the instrument a professional look and becomes a recognizable symbol which can be associated with the survey and its results (Fisher, 1988). This personalization may create a feeling of ownership of the assessment process for those who develop the survey and also may encourage respondents to take the time and effort to answer the questionnaire. If the decision is made to use a locally developed survey instrument, adherence to a general outline of procedures in designing the instrument may expedite the process. The steps in the development of a localized instrument do not vary substantially from those an institution would pursue when using a standardized instrument and are presented in the following list:

1. Conduct a meeting with those initiating or requesting the instrument and those responsible for design of the instrument;
2. Make firm decisions concerning who will cover the cost, handle the mailing and receiving, data entry, and statistical analysis, and oversee the publication of and access to the results;
3. Conduct a meeting with those responsible for the survey design and those who might benefit from the survey results. All persons involved should be asked to provide suggestions for questionnaire items;
4. Throughout the process, focus on developing an institutional logo which will appear on the instrument and in any other publication concerning the survey or its results;
5. Contact several off-campus vendors and obtain standardized instruments dealing with the topic of interest;
6. Contact other institutions or a clearinghouse to obtain locally developed instruments in the area to be surveyed;
7. Ask those personnel responsible for the design and those who might benefit from

the survey and its results to review the different standardized and localized instruments;

8. Design a draft instrument;
9. Revise drafts as needed based on the suggestions from the faculty, staff, and administrators who play a role in the overall process;
10. Conduct a trial administration using volunteer students, staff, and/or faculty to test the instrument in draft form;
11. Approve the final instrument design;
12. Arrange to have the survey printed at the institution's printing operation or an off-campus vendor; and,
13. Follow through with plans the institution has made regarding distribution, data entry, analysis, and publication of results.

In terms of the actual structure of the survey instrument, reviewing several commercial standardized instruments allows the faculty, staff, and administrators to identify the general areas which would be appropriate to include in the assessment process. Another approach might be to seek out locally developed instruments created at other institutions. These actions may allow the institution to make a smooth transition from a standardized instrument to one which is designed locally to meet the specific institution's needs, goals, and circumstances. A panel at the 1990 American Association for Higher Education (AAHE) Assessment Forum (Amiran et al., 1990) focused on the issue of "borrowing" locally developed instruments from other institutions. The panel and audience identified a need for a clearinghouse to facilitate collaboration among institutions. Designing a survey instrument utilizing on-campus personnel, although less expensive in terms of out-of-pocket cost, will not be as cost effective in terms of time. Undertaking an assessment process which involves the use of a locally developed instrument requires strong commitment from those who are responsible for the design. An institution should weigh Ewell's pros and cons carefully and choose the type of instrument, whether standardized or locally developed, which is best for the circumstances of a given institution.

Characteristics of Survey Information

Survey information falls into two categories: factual/demographic and opinions/perceptions. A caution about each category is in order here. Some demographic data are verifiable by checking other sources of student information; however, that process is time-consuming and is not generally needed. The caution is that responses to survey items may not be absolutely accurate. A participant may subtract or add years to his or her age; an alumni may exaggerate income; however, most respondents tend to answer honestly and accurately and, for the purposes of the survey, the information has value. A more significant caution regards the second category, opinions or perceptions. The institution's leadership must recognize that these results are perceptions and are not necessarily reality or fact. Survey results may tell us a great deal about how we are viewed by others or by ourselves; but, these perceptions must be considered with other quantitative, measurable data to form a complete picture of the institution, its strengths and its shortcomings.

Survey Populations

By referring to the various surveys developed by the testing agencies and reviewed in the first pages of this section, we may identify some of the survey populations whose opinions and perceptions we value. These include students, faculty, administrators, non-teaching staff, alumni, and subgroups of those such as entering students, nonreturning students, recent alumni, and tenured faculty. The general population in the institution's service area is an appropriate population for reputational-type surveys. Any group using the institution's services or having contact with and knowledge of the institution is an appropriate survey population, depending on the kind of information sought. Employers of the institution's graduates are another valuable survey group. This was one of the findings of a recent dissertation which dealt with the various components of educational quality (Martin, 1989). Employer satisfaction with graduates as a component of quality generated a consensus among the four groups surveyed: members of the board of trustees, members of the state legislature, university administrators and faculty, and alumni. This component was ranked first to fifth in overall importance by 25 of the 28 subgroups and was listed as a top ten component of quality in the remaining subgroups. "What do we want to know?" is the first question an institution should ask when considering attitudinal surveys. The second question is, "Who can tell us best?" Once the populations are chosen, good research practices must be followed in sampling the populations. Wherever possible, surveying the total group is helpful. For example, faculty, administrators, or nonreturning students may be surveyed as a total group.

Information Users

With surveys selected and information gathered from defined populations, the results should not be relegated to a shelf. Who will use the information? Each campus will have its own individualized list, but these suggested users may assist in planning meetings for dissemination of information.

Information/Perceptions	**Users**
Student Services	*Admissions Personnel Registrar*
	Student Affairs Officers
	Counselors
	Student Activities Staff
	Student Government Association
	Financial Aid Officers
	Career Planning & Placement Staff
	Housing Staff
Academic Programs	*Academic Vice President*
	Academic Deans
	Department Chairs
	Curriculum Commitees
	Faculty

Facilities	*Central Administrators*
	Physical Plant Director
	Building Managers
	Librarians
	Athletics/Intramural Sports Staff
Administration	*President*
	Administrative Staff
	Vice Presidents

To ensure the most efficient use of results, a comparison of a group's intended attitudinal outcomes or objectives with related data generated through survey processes will bring these relationships into focus. Groups then may proceed with action plans to test the effectiveness of their programs and services or to revise those offerings. A carefully prepared presentation related specifically to the user group using that group's language and frame of reference is essential.

Design for Survey Implementation and Dissemination of Results

The implementation of an attitudinal survey program should be undertaken systematically with clear results in mind. Representatives from each of the potential user groups should be involved in the process and participate in the identification of survey populations and the kinds of information desired. The following sequence of activities should occur. The subpoints are given as examples and should trigger additional items specific to the institution's needs.

1. Identify intended results for the survey activity:
   - Personal and demographic information about various student, alumni, and other population groups;
   - Information for program improvement;
   - Perceptions of institutional quality; and,
   - Inform external publics of the institution.

2. Select appropriate instruments considering:
   - Available financial resources;
   - In-house expertise and data processing support;
   - Content of commercially available instruments; and,
   - Feasibility of longitudinal use.

3. Establish a time schedule for administration:
   - Entering students (each orientation period);
   - Continuing students (every third year or alternate years);
   - Exiting/noncontinuing students (as a part of the exiting process);
   - Graduating seniors (as a part of the diploma application, graduation checkout, or similar activity);
   - Recent alumni (every year within 6 months of graduation);

- Alumni follow-up (each year for graduates 5 years out or, every other year or every third year for classes 3 to 5 years out);
- Program-related questionnaire (at the time of program review or every 5 years); and,
- External publics (at 5-year to 10-year intervals, particularly during mission review or as needed to identify new constituencies or new programs).

4. Collect and interpret data: Contractual arrangements for mailing, processing, tabulating, and summarizing data;
   - Assignment of personnel and allocation of release time for these activities; and,
   - Establishment of types of reporting desired (means, percentages, comparisons, simple frequencies, by subgroups or aggregated only).

5. Disseminate information:
   - Identification of key user groups;
   - Partitioning of data into manageable segments; and,
   - Scheduling of small-group sessions for presentation and interpretation of data.

6. Conduct follow-up sessions to review:
   - Usefulness of information as catalyst for change or in reaffirmation of status quo, or for initiation of new programs and services;
   - Need for additional data;
   - Need for instrument redesign or continued use; and,
   - Longitudinal implementation of survey cycle.

As one examines the preceding, a number of additional questions, items for inclusion, or cautions will come to mind. The cross-fertilization of ideas and needs which surfaces in discussions with key user representatives may be valuable to the health of the institution and to the resultant survey data. Some key elements which ensure the effectiveness of the program follow:

1. **Avoid overcontact with survey populations**. The same community leaders, alumni, or continuing students should not be asked at too frequent (one year or less) intervals to participate in survey activities. The key to avoiding overcontact is to establish a central office which, at the least, serves as a clearinghouse for all such activity and, at the most, conducts the gathering and dissemination of all such data. Oversurveying populations is not cost-effective, provides fragmented information, and may alienate the survey participant, thus yielding less dependable data and creating public relations problems for the institution. Alumni are an example of a population which is often oversurveyed. The Placement Office conducts a career satisfaction survey; the Development Office asks many of the same questions in a survey designed to identify potential donors; and the graduate's academic department asks similar questions to determine achievement of programmatic goals. One survey which is centrally coordinated with all users involved in survey development

and planning for dissemination of results will create much more positive relation-ships between the institution and its alumni.

2. **Establish a plan for multiple contacts for mail surveys to increase response rate**. A letter from the university president, chief academic officer or the student's dean explaining the need for the information and appealing to the person's loyalties as a member of the institutional community, will convey the importance of the sur-vey and improve the response rate. Inclusion of a postage-paid return envelope is advisable as is the mailing of surveys at forwarding-address-requested level of post-age rather than at a lower rate. A follow-up postcard reminder is helpful. A personal phone call which may be linked to calls for other purposes such as recruitment calls to applicants, calls encouraging continuing students to preregister, or fund drive calls to alumni and community members can be very effective. Some institutions have included a dime, a pencil or pen with the school's name stamped on it, a small note pad or some other small token. These items are not expensive and may be an additional incentive to the person being surveyed. Other institutions have increased survey response rates by announcing that a prize will be awarded to a winner drawn randomly from those completing the survey. The prize can be a cash award, book-store gift certificate, football tickets, etc. Conducting a drawing does not affect the confidentiality of the response if a separate card is included for the respondent to use to write his or her name and address.

3. **If work is being done in-house, be certain that the time, personnel, and facilities are adequate to complete the task**. If support is inadequate, the project is very likely to fail. Appropriate follow-up cannot occur if data are not processed in a timely fashion. Any positive effect of the earlier activities is lost if user groups can-not see the results of their earlier efforts and if the public surveyed sees no evidence that results are being used. It may be more cost-effective and profitable to forgo some individualized information needs to take advantage of the efficiency of basic services offered by the various testing services.

4. **Select segmented elements of data for presentation over a continuing period of time, and be certain to follow up on their use**. Peter Ewell, in *Assessment, Ac-countability, and Improvement: Managing the Contradiction* (1987a, p. 19), made this point emphatically: "Don't show everything at once." Ewell's point is to guar-antee that the institution will continue to have new information to report and to dem-onstrate ongoing commitment. Accountability to our external constituencies may require this kind of juggling of information. Internal accountability, however, re-quires this segmentation of information for a different purpose. A user may focus on narrower areas for improvement and change, and that concentration of effort is more likely to result in a stronger institution than are attempts to address all areas simulta-neously.

Summary

Patricia Hutchings, in *Six Stories: Implementing Successful Assessment* (1987), says, "In some ways the important point may be less what one does than the need to do something. Yes, everything will be imperfect, it's better on paper" (p. 13). Certainly, a plan for attitudinal surveys is a way to "do something" and offer constructive, useful results in the early stages of an assessment process. The institution which takes the steps necessary to implement attitudinal surveys will indeed see itself as others see it, and it will, if the information is carefully used, free itself from many a "blunder" and "foolish notion."

References: Cited and Recommended

The ACT Evaluation/Survey Service, *Specimen Set* [Instruments]. (1994). Iowa City, IA: American College Testing Program.

Amiran, M. R., Golden, A., & Wright, B. D. (1990, June 29). *Why Reinvent the Wheel? The Gentle Art of "Borrowing" Instruments.* Panel discussion at the fifth annual American Association for Higher Education Assessment Forum, Washington, DC.

Assessment Resource Center Bibliography. (1987). Knoxville, TN: Assessment Resource Center, University of Tennessee.

Cavanagh, D., & Soellner, P. (1987). *The FIPSE Value Added Grant for Rhode Island College.* Paper presented to the second National Conference on Assessment in Higher Education, Denver, CO.

Cooperative Institutional Research Institute. (1986). *The American Freshman: National Norms for Fall 1986.* Los Angeles, CA: University of California.

Dennison, G. M., & Bunda, M. A. (1989). Assessment and Academic Judgements in Higher Education. In P. J. Gray (ed.), Achieving Assessment Goals Using Evaluation Techniques. *New Directions for Higher Education*, *XVI*(3). San Francisco: Jossey-Bass.

ESS in Action. (1987). Iowa City, IA: American College Testing Program.

ETS College and University Programs. (n.d.). [Brochure]. Princeton, NJ: Educational Testing Service.

Ewell, P. T. (1983). *Student Outcomes Questionnaires: An Implementation Handbook* (2nd ed.). Boulder, CO: National Center for Higher Education Management Systems.

Ewell, P. T. (1984). *The Self-Regarding Institution: Information for Excellence.* Boulder, CO: National Center for Higher Education Management Systems.

Ewell, P. T. (1985). Some Implications for Practice. In P. T. Ewell (ed.), Assessing Educational Outcomes. *New Directions for Institutional Research*, *XII*(3). San Francisco: Jossey-Bass.

Ewell, P. T. (1987a). *Assessment, Accountability, and Improvement: Managing the Contradiction.* Washington, DC: American Association for Higher Education Assessment Forum.

Ewell, P. T. (1987b). Establishing a Campus-Based Assessment Program. In D. F. Halpern (ed.), Student Outcomes Assessment: What Institutions Stand to Gain. *New Directions for Higher Education*, *XV*(3). San Francisco: Jossey-Bass.

Fisher, M. B. (1988). Surveying Your Alumni. In G. S. Melchiori (ed.), Alumni Research: Methods and Applications. *New Directions for Institutional Research*, *XV*(4). San Francisco: Jossey-Bass.

Hutchings, P. (1987). *Six Stories: Implementing Successful Assessment.* Washington, DC: American Association for Higher Education Assessment Forum.

Institutional Performance Survey [Instrument]. Boulder, CO: National Center for Higher Education Management Systems.

Kells, H. R. (1980). *Self-Study Processes: A Guide for Postsecondary Institutions.* Washington, DC: American Council on Education.

Lenning, O. T., Beal, P., & Sauer, K. (1980). *Retention and Attrition: Evidence for Action and Research.* Boulder, CO: National Center for Higher Education Management Systems.

Martin, L. (1989, December). *Perceptions of the Importance of Various Components of Educational Quality in Mississippi Public Universities*. Unpublished doctoral dissertation, University of Mississippi. (University Microfilms no. 319591, catalog no. 9019274.)

McClain, C. J. (1987, Winter). Assessment Produces Degrees with Integrity. *Educational Record*, *68*(1), 47-52.

Resource Manual on Institutional Effectiveness. (1987). Atlanta, GA: Commission on Colleges of the Southern Association of Colleges and Schools.

Section III. (1989). *Criteria for Accreditation: Commission on Colleges*. Atlanta, GA: Southern Association of Colleges and Schools.

Stevenson, M. R., Walleri, R. D., & Japely, S. M. (1985). Designing Follow-Up Studies of Graduates and Former Students. In P. T. Ewell (ed.), Assessing Educational Outcomes. *New Directions for Institutional Research*, *XII*(3). San Francisco: Jossey-Bass.

Student-Outcomes Questionnaires [Instruments]. Boulder, CO: National Center for Higher Education Management Systems.

Cognitive Assessment Instruments: Availability and Utilization

Marsha V. Krotseng and Gary R. Pike

The increased calls for accountability which have resounded over the past decade have led to a heightened focus on student assessment in higher education. In the eyes of many, assessment is synonymous with testing. After all, paper-and-pencil tests remain the most common and widely understood means of determining a student's progress. However, number 2 pencils and optically scanned forms comprise just one (albeit highly visible) element of the process—the act of cognitive assessment. While the disputations characteristic of medieval universities and their offspring, the American colonial college, are no longer the order of the day, creative assessment options such as portfolios have gained more widespread use. Based on the systematic scheme represented by the Institutional Effectiveness Paradigm in Figure 1 (see page 8), individual institutions have adopted unique strategies for cognitive assessment in the realization that the only truly effective assessment will be tailored to their own culture and clientele.

Appropriate Assessment: Which One of the Above?

This resource section advances a wide array of cognitive assessment alternatives: standardized tests of both general knowledge and learning in the major field, locally developed instruments for assessing general and specialized knowledge, tests of critical thinking, and portfolios. The discussion extends beyond the design of such instruments to incorporate their appropriate application, capabilities, flexibility, advantages, and pitfalls.

Of the six goals that former U.S. Secretary of Education Lauro F. Cavazos placed before the higher education community in early 1990, three directly address cognitive assessment:

- All associates and bachelor's degree recipients should be able to demonstrate proficiency in college-level math and science;
- All graduating students should be able to write coherent, grammatically correct papers and display a basic knowledge of world history, geography and culture appropriate to their degree level; and,
- All students leaving colleges and universities should possess higher order critical thinking and problem-solving skills needed to contribute productively to the economic and political life of the nation. ("Cavazos presents," 1990, p. 1).

At the state level, members of the State Higher Education Executive Officers association have reported the growing use of student and institutional outcomes measures in evaluating educational effectiveness (SHEEO, 1990).

No longer is the critical question whether to saddle this assessment steed, but, rather, how to harness its full potential without being thrown. As the seasoned rider analyzes a thoroughbred's nature before leaving the gate, colleges and universities can similarly avoid a false start at cognitive assessment by scrutinizing the ever-expanding universe of available methods detailed in the following pages.

Two primary queries posed by Halpern (1987a) necessarily precede the selection of an appropriate instrument: "What do you want to know?" and "Why do you want to know it?" (p. 109). "Clear and succinct answers to these questions will [then] provide direction to the secondary questions, 'What should you measure?' and 'How should you measure it?'" (p. 109). In the present context, the reason for assessment is readily apparent—to analyze an institution's intended (and actual) educational outcomes. Comprising this path to institutional effectiveness or program improvement are such discrete stepping-stones as the determination of students' academic progress and the use of examinations as "gateways" to upper-division course work or as benchmarks for budget decisions and accountability (Halpern, 1987b). Once an institution has set forth its Expanded Statement of Institutional Purpose and the supporting departmental/program statements of intended outcomes/objectives, the identification of proper instruments can proceed logically and smoothly. As Harris (1985) concluded, "You can compare your students to [others] nationally on standardized tests without having definite educational goals.... But without such goals, you can't be sure the tests reflect your curriculum" (p. 13).

Resnick and Goulden (1987) cited 13 basic methods of assessment of learning originally reported in an American Council on Education (ACE) survey of 450 college and university presidents and academic vice presidents:

- College-level skills or minimum competency tests;
- Tests of general knowledge in the humanities and sciences;
- Comprehensive tests in a student's major;
- Tests of critical thinking;
- Tests of quantitative problem solving;
- Tests of oral communication;
- Tests of writing;
- Value-added measures of student gains while in college;
- Mathematics placement tests for entering students;
- English placement tests for entering students;
- Reading placement tests for entering students;
- Placement tests in other skills for entering students; and,
- Pretest and posttests for remedial courses.

By 1991, basic skills testing was in place at 72% of all higher education institutions. Almost all (90%) public two-year institutions had programs to assess basic skills

(El-Khawas, 1991).[1] Beyond the basics, El-Khawas reports that more than half of all colleges and universities assess higher-order skills (e.g., writing) as an expected outcome of college study. By 1993, El-Khawas stated that only 43% of all higher education institutions had extensive activity in planning and improvement of student outcomes assessment. This figure was anticipated to increase as State Postsecondary Review Entities (SPREs) became more prevalent in the legislative processes of educational assessment. (For additional information see the Resource Section "Assessment in General Education," starting on page 172.) Among the most widely evaluated and recommended means for assessing college's cognitive outcomes are the specific instruments highlighted in the following sections.

Assessment of General Knowledge

Emphasizing breadth across the curriculum rather than in-depth study, tests of general knowledge reveal the students' grasp of basic concepts and skills in the liberal arts (Hartle, 1985). Communication, computation, and critical thinking join elements from the social and natural sciences on both standardized and local instruments intended for this purpose. The variety of tests available for the assessment of general knowledge is evident in the catalogs developed by the Clearinghouse for Higher Education Assessment Instruments (Smith, Bradley, & Draper, 1994a; 1994b).

Standardized Tests of General Knowledge

Since 1987, state mandates, accrediting associations, and revised campus policies have spurred tremendous growth in the number of institutions interested in assessing general education outcomes. Paralleling this development is the increased availability of instruments for measuring general learning. Prior to 1987, five tests were available for general education assessment: the ACT Assessment Program examinations, the College-Level Examination Program (CLEP) General Examinations, the College Outcome Measures Program (COMP) examination, the Graduate Record Examination (GRE) General Test, and the Scholastic Aptitude Test (SAT). Four new tests have been introduced since 1987: the Academic Profile, the College Basic Academic Subjects Examination (College BASE), the Collegiate Assessment of Academic Proficiency (CAAP), and the Education Assessment series.

All but one of the tests available prior to 1987 were initially designed for other purposes (e.g., undergraduate or graduate admissions considerations), not for evaluating general education programs. Although tests such as the ACT and SAT (which have, themselves, been revised in recent years) have been shown to predict initial undergraduate or graduate success, their relationship to course work and experiences during the last two years of college is much less clear.

---

1. For more explanation of Basic Skills, see Addison Greenwood (author), *National Assessment of College Student Learning: Getting Started.* National Center for Educational Statistics, 1993.

(a) ACT Assessment

The ACT Assessment Program was designed as a battery of college entrance and placement examinations. The original ACT Assessment includes four tests requiring 30 to 50 minutes each: (1) English usage, (2) mathematics usage, (3) reading in the natural sciences, and (4) reading in social studies. A composite (total) score also is provided. Depending on the coefficients used, reliability estimates for the individual tests have ranged from 0.73 to 0.91. Alpha reliability for the composite score is reported to be 0.85. Research has found that the ACT Assessment is capable of predicting subsequent performance in college, including cumulative grade point average and performance in specific classes (Munday, 1968; Richards, Holland, & Lutz, 1967). However, studies at Tennessee Technological University have failed to demonstrate a relationship between gains on the ACT Assessment exams and students' experiences in college (Dumont & Troelstrup, 1981).

Several years ago, the American College Testing Program also introduced the Enhanced ACT Assessment exams. ACT provides concordance tables that translate composite, English, and mathematics scores on the original ACT Assessment exams into Enhanced ACT scores. Scores for social studies reading and natural sciences reading are not available for the Enhanced ACT Assessment because they have been replaced by the Reading and Science Reasoning tests. Data on the reliability and validity of Enhanced ACT scores for outcomes assessment are not available.

Note. The ACT and Enhanced ACT Assessment examinations are published by the American College Testing Program, P.O. Box 168, Iowa City, IA 52243.

(b) College Outcome Measures Program

Of the five tests developed prior to 1987, only the American College Testing Program's COMP exam was designed specifically to measure general education outcomes of a post-secondary nature. The purpose of the COMP exam is to assess the knowledge and skills necessary for effective functioning in adult society (Forrest, 1982). Available as a two and one-half-hour Objective Test of 60 multiple-choice items or a longer (4½-hour) Composite Examination, the COMP exam provides a total score, three content subscores, and three process subscores (Forrest & Steele, 1982). The Composite Examination also contains measures of writing and speaking ability (Steele, 1979).

In the technical manual for the COMP exam, ACT staff report that the alpha reliability (internal consistency) of the total score is 0.84 for individuals (Forrest & Steele, 1982). Reliability estimates for the six subscores range from 0.63 to 0.68. Steele (1989) reports that the group means generalizability coefficient for total score is 0.96, assuming a sample size of 300 students. Generalizability coefficients for the six subscores range from 0.87 to 0.94 for samples of 300 students. Using Steele's data, Pike (1990) reports that the 95% confidence interval about universe score for total score is slightly more than +6 points for groups of 300 students.

The technical report for the COMP exam also contains several studies intended to provide evidence of the convergent and discriminant validity of the Objective Test. These studies generally reveal that scores on the COMP exam are related to patterns of course work and other outcomes measures but generally unrelated to students' demographic characteristics (Forrest & Steele, 1982). Somewhat troubling, from the perspective of discriminant validity, is the fact that the best predictor of performance on the COMP exam is entering academic ability as measured by the ACT Assessment examination (Forrest & Steele, 1982).

Studies at several institutions have indicated that the COMP exam is highly sensitive to students' precollege characteristics and relatively insensitive to instructional effects (Davis & Murrell, 1989; Pike, 1989, 1990). In a study of college sophomores at 6 four-year and 8 two-year institutions in Washington State, the Council of Presidents and State Board for Community College Education (1989) reported that students' background characteristics are significantly related to total score and subscores on the Objective Test. The authors concluded that the COMP exam is basically a measure of aptitude or ability, and the test is relatively insensitive to educational effects.

Note. Further information on the College Outcome Measures Program is available from the publisher, American College Testing Program, P.O. Box 168, Iowa City, IA 52243.

(c) Collegiate Assessment of Academic Proficiency

The CAAP exam is intended to measure skills typically attained during the first two years of college. This test consists of five 40-minute modules that can be administered individually or in combination: (1) writing (either multiple-choice questions or a writing sample), (2) mathematics, (3) reading, (4) science reasoning, and (5) critical thinking (ACT, 1989). The first four modules parallel the tests in the Enhanced ACT Assessment.

KR-20 reliability (internal consistency) estimates for scores on four of the modules range from 0.76 to 0.93 (ACT, 1989). Reliability estimates are not available for the Science Reasoning test. Studies of students at two-year and four-year colleges found low to moderate correlations between CAAP scores and end-of-sophomore year grades (0.34 to 0.38) and also discovered that CAAP scores have moderate predictive validity for grades during the junior year. In addition, research indicates that average CAAP scores increase from the freshman to the end of the sophomore year (Bailey, 1994). Of particular interest to institutions using the ACT assessment series as an input measure to their institution will be the statistical relationship developed between those measures and CAAP scores two years later. Using this procedure ACT can estimate CAAP scores (based upon national normative data) of groups of entering students taking ACT input measures such as ACT, and ASSET.

Note. The publisher of the CAAP is the American College Testing Program, P.O. Box 168, Iowa City, IA 52243.

(d) Scholastic Aptitude Test

Like the ACT Assessment exams, the Scholastic Aptitude Test was designed for use as a college entrance and placement examination. The SAT is composed of two tests, verbal and quantitative, with a combined score also available. Research findings show that both the verbal and quantitative scores on the SAT are related to performance during the first two years of college (CEEB & ETS, 1988). Although the publishers of the SAT describe the exams as measures of problem-solving ability, studies have failed to demonstrate that the tests are sensitive to the effects of college course work. Research by Ratcliff (1988) incorporates the SAT as a pretest in order to control for the effects of entering ability on posttest scores.

Note. The Scholastic Aptitude Test is published by the Educational Testing Service, Princeton, NJ 08541.

(e) College-Level Examination Program

The College-Level Examination Program (CLEP) General Examinations originally were designed to provide college credit for noncollege learning (CEEB, 1984). The General Examinations consist of five tests requiring 90 minutes each: (1) English composition, (2) humanities, (3) mathematics, (4) natural science, and (5) social science and history. Reliability estimates for the five tests range from 0.91 to 0.94 (CEEB, 1984).

Using experts in each content field, the CLEP development process has achieved high levels of content validity. In addition, research has linked performance on the CLEP exams to performance in introductory college courses (CEEB, 1986). Studies have not been conducted to evaluate the validity of the CLEP exams as program evaluation instruments.

Note. Further details on these CLEP exams can be obtained from the College Entrance Examination Board, 45 Columbus Avenue, New York, NY 10023-6917.

(f) Education Assessment Series

The Education Assessment Series (EAS) tests are modifications of the CLEP exams and are designed to provide information about student outcomes for program evaluation. The EAS consists of two tests intended to provide comprehensive nationally normed data in a relatively short administration time (45 minutes per module) and at a low cost. Because multiple forms of the tests will be available, institutions may administer the tests twice and examine changes in students' scores over the course of their college careers. The EAS was first pilot-tested in 1988, so data on the reliability and validity of the tests are still not available.

Note. Additional information may be obtained by contacting the College Entrance Examination Board, 45 Columbus Avenue, New York, NY 10023-6917.

(g) Graduate Record Examinations

A test usually given at the end of a student's undergraduate career, the Graduate Record Examinations (GRE) General Test has also been used to evaluate the effects of college curricula on student learning at several institutions (Ratcliff, 1988). The GRE General Test actually comprises three nationally normed tests designed to assess learned abilities that are not related to any particular field of study but that are related to skills necessary for successful graduate study (Adelman, 1985).

Three scores are provided: verbal (antonyms, analogies, sentence completions, reading passages), quantitative (quantitative comparisons, mathematics, data interpretation), and analytical (analytical reasoning, logical reasoning) (Graduate Records Examinations

Board, 1987). The full test is administered during a three and one-half hour period. Research on the General Test has revealed high levels of reliability for the three tests, ranging from 0.89 to 0.92 (Conrad, Trismen, & Miller, 1977).

In addition to scores on the three tests, it is possible to obtain nine item-type scores on the exam: (1) antonyms, (2) analogies, (3) sentence completions, (4) reading passages, (5) quantitative comparisons, (6) mathematics, (7) data interpretation, (8) analytical reasoning, and (9) logical reasoning (Wilson, 1985). Ratcliff (1988) has shown that clusters of undergraduate course work can be formed that discriminate among performance on the nine item types. In addition, Wilson (1985) has reported that item-type scores are related to undergraduate performance and success in graduate school.

Note. The publisher of the GRE is the Graduate Record Examinations Board, Educational Testing Service, CN 6000, Princeton, NJ 08541- 6000.

(h) Academic Profile

Of the four tests marketed since 1987, the Academic Profile is the oldest. Developed by the Educational Testing Service and the College Entrance Examinations Board to assess the effectiveness of general education programs, the Academic Profile is available in two forms: a short (1-hour) form designed to provide group data and a long (3-hour) form designed to provide data about individuals (ETS College & University Programs, 1987).

A norm-referenced total score and seven subscores (also norm-referenced) are provided. Subscores include three content areas (humanities, natural science, and social science) and four skill areas (reading, writing, mathematics, and critical thinking). The newest form of the Academic Profile also provides proficiency scores in the areas of writing, mathematics, and reading/critical thinking (ETS, 1990). Research demonstrates that these proficiency scores can be used to evaluate student change over the course of a college career. Reliability estimates for the norm-referenced subject and skill scores range from 0.74 for critical thinking to 0.85 for reading. The KR-20 reliability estimate for the total score is 0.94, and the average reliability for the total score across the four short forms is 0.80 (Leininger, 1994).

The content validity of the Academic Profile was insured during instrument development by working with faculty to address concerns expressed in the Association of American Colleges 1985 report *Integrity in the College Curriculum*. Detailed information on the convergent and discriminant validity of the Academic Profile is available in the *Academic Profile User's Guide: Part I* (Educational Testing Service, 1991).

Note. Additional information concerning the Academic Profile can be obtained from Higher Education Assessment, ETS College and University Programs, Princeton, NJ 08541-0001.

(i) College BASE

The College Basic Academic Subjects Examination is a criterion-referenced achievement test that can be used to evaluate individuals or programs. (National norms also are provided for comparative purposes.) One- and three-hour versions of the test are available.

College BASE provides a composite score, four subject scores (English, mathematics, natural science, social studies), and three reasoning scores (interpretive, strategic, and adaptive reasoning) (Riverside Publishing Company, 1989). Subject scores are further subdivided into cluster scores and skill scores. For example, the mathematics score is composed of three cluster scores: (1) general mathematics, (2) algebra, and (3) geometry. The general mathematics cluster score contains skill scores for practical applications, properties and notations, and using statistics (Riverside Publishing Company, 1990).

The subjects, clusters, and skills assessed by *College BASE* are based on the work of the College Board's Educational Equality Project (Osterlind & Merz, 1990). Initial specifications for the test were drawn from the Educational Equality Project's report *Academic Preparation for College: What Examinees Need to Know and Be Able to Do* (College Entrance Examination Board, 1983). More than 100 persons representing 50 colleges and universities revised the competencies and skills identified by the Educational Equality Project, modifying them to reflect the general education knowledge and skills expected of college graduates (Osterlind & Merz, 1990). Evidence of the reliability and validity of *College BASE* can be found in research by Pike (1992a; 1992b).

Currently, the exam is being used in Missouri for admission to teacher education programs, and it has been used by more than 25 institutions to evaluate their general education programs.

Note. The College BASE examination is published by Riverside Publishing Company, 8420 Bryn Mawr Avenue, Chicago, IL 60631-3476.

Localized General Knowledge Alternatives

With increasing numbers of states and state higher education system offices mandating student outcomes assessment, these entities inevitably have fashioned their own substitutes for the familiar standardized route in search of instruments more closely paralleling a particular curriculum. According to ACE, fully 55% of all colleges and universities reported developing their own instruments for student assessment by 1989, a 10% rise from the previous year. Although many of these state-, system-, and institution-devised alternatives are not strictly local in the sense of being confined to a single place, they are more limited in scope and application and, hence, are referred to in this publication as "local instruments." Obviously, such general knowledge examinations can be better tailored to local circumstances and needs.

By Florida state statute, every community college and state university student must successfully complete all four tests of that state's College Level Academic Skills Project (CLASP). This examination is required for all community college associate degrees as well as for admission to upper-division status in all public universities. Developed by faculty from the Florida community colleges and state universities, CLASP is used to assess skills in both communication (reading, listening, writing, and speaking) and mathematics (algorithms, concepts, generalizations, and problem solving). Although this measure was specifically constructed for Florida institutions of higher learning, the Florida State Department of Education honors legitimate requests from individuals and institutions interested in the CLASP Technical Report and Test Administration Plan (Harris, 1985).

The New Jersey College Basic Skills Placement Test (NJCBSPT) is a series of five tests designed to meet the requirements of the assessment and evaluation program developed by the New Jersey Board of Higher Education. In addition to the five individual test scores (writing, reading comprehension, sentence sense, math computation, and elementary algebra), two composite scores can be derived from the language assessment parts of the test—one for Total English and the other for composition. This 168-item test is administered over a three-hour period. Reliability estimates for the seven subscales range from 0.83 to 0.92. The content validity of the NJCBSPT was achieved by providing for constant review during test construction by a panel of experts from the New Jersey Basic Skills Council. Studies on the construct validity and predictive validity of the NJCBSPT have found that instructors are satisfied with it as a placement test. The same studies have found moderate positive correlations between NJCBSPT scores and course grades (Cerreto & Colijn, 1994). As of this publication, the continuation of the NJCBSPT is unlikely due to changes in the structure of higher education in New Jersey.

A well-known system-level requirement, the Regents' Testing Program of the University System of Georgia, is administered to all rising juniors in the state's community colleges, four-year colleges, and universities. A prerequisite to graduation, the Regents' Program evaluates both reading comprehension and essay construction. The reading portion, a one-hour test of 60 items, "consists of ten…passages, with five to eight questions on each, that test comprehension in terms of vocabulary, literal comprehension, inferential comprehension, and analysis" (Harris, 1985, p. 20). Review of the essay section involves multiple faculty evaluators (who have not taught the students) trained to use a consistent scoring procedure (Harris, 1985).

On the West Coast, the California State University System's Graduation Writing Assessment Requirement (GWAR) demands writing proficiency of all upper-division and graduate students. However, each of the 19 CSU campuses has implemented its own version of this requirement; whereas some campuses designate certain upper-division and graduate-level courses that entail "a large amount of writing," others "allow students to demonstrate proficiency on an actual writing test" (Harris, 1985, p. 20). As in Georgia and New Jersey, multiple faculty evaluations and a consistent grading procedure have proved integral to the process.

Finally, a few hardy institutions like Olivet Nazarene, dissatisfied with the standardized status quo, have assumed the entire burden of developing more satisfactory tests of general education for their students.

Standardized or Local?

Confronted with this complex assortment of instruments, college faculty members and administrators are well advised to consider their intended educational outcomes together with the strengths and weaknesses of standardized and locally developed examinations before committing to any particular program. Standardized instruments such as the COMP, ACT, GRE, and SAT obviously have weathered a number of prior applications and are readily available. More important, Ewell (1987) has described them as:

1. Relatively easy to administer;
2. Acceptable in terms of faculty time invested, although costly if used in volume;
3. Generally less open to charges of subjectivity; and,
4. Nationally normed, allowing comparison across institutions.

On the other hand, standardized examinations suffer major disadvantages in that:

1. They may or may not reflect the content of a specific institution's curriculum;
2. The results often are reported as a single performance score (or, at best, four to six subscores), obscuring both the laudable and the less healthy aspects of the curriculum; and,
3. Normative comparison scores may be inappropriate for general curriculum evaluation (e.g., GRE norms, compiled from those taking the test, may not be suitable for comparison with scores from an entire graduating class [Ewell, 1987]).

As suggested earlier, the attributes of state- and system-wide examinations alleviate several of these concerns. Specifically, such faculty-developed instruments will be:

1. Tailored to the individual curriculum;
2. Available for more detailed analysis of results;
3. Amenable to a variety of formats including essays or task and problem-solving exercises; and,
4. Perceived as legitimate by faculty because at least key colleagues have played a role in the tests' design (Ewell, 1987).

But, neither are these examinations absent from certain drawbacks. According to Ewell (1987), they:

1. Reflect only the priorities of a particular institution or system and may, therefore, hold less external credibility;
2. Cannot be compared with results from other institutions or programs outside the system or state;
3. Can be costly to produce, especially in terms of that precious commodity—faculty time; and,
4. Will not necessarily be well constructed without special on-campus training or expertise.

Specialized Knowledge: Assessment in the Major Field

Historically, assessment of student learning in the major field has been an important topic in higher education (Banta & Schneider, 1988). "Comprehensive exams in the major fields or across fields, using essays and oral interrogation and modeled on English university practice, [were] common in American higher education through most of the nineteenth century" (Resnick & Goulden, 1987, p. 80). Indeed, descriptions of senior culminating experiences at Swarthmore and St. Johns have become almost legendary. For the majority of today's institutions, however, standardized examinations in the major field of study afford a practical alternative for assessing in-depth understanding of a specific subject, commonly referred to as specialized knowledge.

Standardized Instruments

According to Harris (1985):

> If a department is primarily interested in assessment for program evaluation, it may not need to administer outside tests. Rather, it may be able to use the test results its students and graduates ordinarily provide in their application for graduate or professional education, or for licensure or certification. A post-graduation examination [such as the CPA]… will have obvious leverage on the department's faculty. Departments often develop 'batting averages' out of such information. (p. 20)

If, instead, circumstances clearly call for outside measures, viable standardized alternatives are suggested in the following paragraphs. Given the tremendous number of tests that are currently available, this review covers only a limited number of measures in detail, focusing primarily on the disciplines of business, chemistry, and psychology. However, the same publishers produce similar tests for most other major fields as well.

(a) Major Field Achievement Tests (Business)

The Educational Testing Service provides 16 tests in specific academic disciplines. Of these, the most recently introduced test (April 1990) is in business. Subscores cover seven areas: (1) accounting, (2) economics, (3) finance, (4) legal and social issues, (5) marketing, (6) management, and (7) quantitative business analysis (ETS, 1990).

Unlike the other major field examinations, the Business Test is not based on the Graduate Record Examinations. (There is no GRE area test for business.) Instead, faculty from across the country participated in developing the Business Test, which is intended to measure material covered in a core curriculum (ETS, 1990). Institutions may add as many as 50 locally developed questions to the test to tailor it to their own core curriculum. Information on the reliability and validity of the Business Test is not currently available. However, a recent report by Wyse (1994) suggests that the test can be a viable placement tool.

(b) Major Field Achievement Test in Chemistry

The Major Field Achievement Test (MFAT) in Chemistry is a modification of the Graduate Record Examinations area test in chemistry. This test is much shorter than the GRE version and has a significantly lower level of item difficulty (ETS, 1990). Areas covered in the test include analytical, inorganic, organic, and physical chemistry (ETS, 1989). Only a total score is provided for this MFAT component. The reliability estimate for total score on the test is 0.91. National norms also are provided for the test.

(c) Major Field Achievement Test in Psychology

Like the test in chemistry, the MFAT in psychology is a modification of the GRE area test in psychology. However, unlike the MFAT for chemistry, the psychology test yields a total score and two subscores: one for experimental psychology and the second for social psychology. Reliability estimates are 0.91 for total score, 0.80 for experimental psychology, and 0.83 for social psychology (ETS, 1989).

This MFAT draws on material from cognition and perception, comparative psychology, sensation, developmental psychology, clinical and abnormal psychology, social psychology, and measurement and methodology. Dizinno (1994) provides a description of the use of this test at St. Mary's University in *Reviews and Descriptions of Assessment Instruments: Major Field Assessments*, edited by Smith, Draper, and Bradley.

Information regarding these or any of the other Major Field Achievement Tests is available from the publisher, Higher Education Assessment (18-U), ETS College and University Programs, Princeton, NJ 08541-0001. As of this writing ETS was in the process of discontinuing its MFATs in the fields of Engineering and Geology.

(d) CLEP Subject Tests (General Chemistry)

The College Entrance Examination Board has developed approximately 30 subject area tests, including a test in general chemistry. These tests are designed to provide college credit for noncollege learning.

Research on the General Chemistry exam indicates that the test exhibits adequate levels of reliability (approximately 0.89), and expert review by a test development committee has established its content validity (matched to introductory chemistry courses). In addition, studies have found that test scores are moderately correlated with grades in general chemistry courses.

Note. The College Entrance Examination Board, 45 Columbus Avenue, New York, NY 10023-6917, publishes this and other CLEP subject examinations.

(e) Graduate Record Examinations (General Chemistry)

The Graduate Record Examinations Program (GRE) offers subject tests in 17 disciplines, including chemistry. Each of these tests yields a total score, and eight tests provide subscores (Conrad, Trisman, & Miller, 1977). Research indicates that all of the tests evidence acceptable levels of reliability (0.82 to 0.96) (DeVore & McPeek, 1985). Reliability (internal consistency) is 0.86 for the chemistry examination.

Because the GRE subject tests are designed to predict performance in graduate school, norms are not available for college seniors, and subscores are not matched to patterns of undergraduate course work. The Educational Testing Service is attempting to overcome these limitations by providing shorter versions of the subject tests, removing the most difficult items, providing norms for college seniors, and developing a flexible report format.

Note. The GRE subject instruments are published by the Graduate Record Examinations Board, CN 6000, Educational Testing Service, Princeton, NJ 08541-6000.

(f) Graduate Record Examination (Psychology)

The Graduate Record Examinations Board also provides a subject-area test in psychology. Unlike the test in chemistry, the psychology test yields two subscores: experimental and social psychology (Conrad, Trisman, & Miller, 1977). Reliability estimates are 0.93 for total score, 0.87 for experimental psychology, and 0.85 for social psychology. Further description of this examination is available from the Graduate Record Examinations Board, CN 6000, Educational Testing Service, Princeton, NJ 08541-6000.

(g) AACSB Business Management Test

The American Assembly of Collegiate Schools of Business (AACSB) has commissioned the development of outcomes measures for evaluating the quality and effectiveness of business management programs. These measures include a paper-and-pencil test of knowledge in business and a series of assessment center exercises designed to test students' abilities in applying their knowledge.

The AACSB Business Management Test covers content in seven areas: (1) accounting, (2) business strategy, (3) finance, (4) organization theory, (5) marketing, (6) management information systems, and (7) quantitative analysis and operations research (AACSB, 1987). The AACSB (1987) reports that reliability estimates for the paper-and-pencil measures range from 0.79 to 0.86. Interrater reliability estimates for the assessment center exercises are not available.

Because the Business Management Test has been under development, extensive information on its validity is not available. Thus far, the only indication of the instrument's validity is based on the use of content experts in test development. Additional research on the validity of the test is progressing.

The publisher of this subject-specific instrument is the America Assembly of Collegiate Schools of Business, 605 Old Ballas Road, Suite 220, St. Louis, MO 63141. Because of concerns about an accrediting association marketing an outcomes assessment instrument, the AACSB has adopted the practice of selling its item bank to interested institutions.

(h) AICPA Achievement Test for Accounting Graduates (ATAG)

The AICPA Accounting Testing Program has been developed by the American Institute of Certified Public Accountants (AICPA) to provide information for accounting educators and the accounting profession. Four tests are available through this program: (1) the Accounting Orientation Test; (2) the Accounting Aptitude Test; (3) the Achievement Test, Level I (for college sophomores); and (4) the Achievement Test for Accounting Graduates, originally named the Level II Achievement Test (AICPA, 1987). Of these four tests, the Achievement Test for Accounting Graduates is most appropriate for assessment in the major at four-year institutions. The ATAG is available in either 50-minute or two-hour versions and covers five content areas: (1) financial accounting, (2) cost and managerial accounting, (3) auditing, (4) taxation, and (5) information systems.

Although the brochure from the publisher does not provide information concerning the reliability and validity of these exams, research at the University of Tennessee, Knoxville indicates that KR-21 reliability estimates are fairly high. These studies also document the validity of using the ATAG as an assessment instrument (Herring & Izard, 1992).

Norms, in the form of percentile ranks, are available for all four AICPA tests. These norms are based on number of years spent studying accounting and are updated regularly (AICPA, 1987). Test fees are based on the number of answer sheets ordered.

Note. These instruments may be obtained from the American Institute of Certified Public Accountants Project, The Psychological Corporation, 555 Academic Court, San Antonio, TX 78204.

(i) ACS Test in General Chemistry

The General Chemistry examination developed by the American Chemical Society (ACS) is a confidential, norm-referenced test of the outcomes of instruction in general chemistry. According to the ACS (1985), research has shown the reliability (internal consistency) of the test to be 0.86. The ACS also reports that the content of the test has been drawn from information presented in introductory chemistry courses. Scores on the General Chemistry exam are moderately correlated with grades in introductory college chemistry courses.

Note. Additional information may be secured by contacting the Examinations Committee, American Chemical Society, University of South Florida, Chemistry Room 112, Tampa, FL 33620.

(j) National Teacher Examinations

State and local mandates for teacher education reform frequently have resulted in use of the National Teacher Examination (NTE) as a rite of professional passage into the elementary or secondary classroom. The NTE program offers three Core Battery Tests and 30 Specialty Area (subject-area) Tests, all of which are designed to provide measures of achievement for students in teacher education programs (NTE Policy Council, 1985). Reliability estimates are in the high 0.80s to low 0.90s for the Core Battery Tests as well as the Specialty Area Tests, and research has linked the content of the tests to the curricula of colleges and universities (NTE Policy Council, 1984). However, NTE score reports are not designed for program evaluation purposes, and modifications of the report format have not been undertaken.

Note. The National Teacher Examination is published by the Educational Testing Service, CN 6051, Princeton, NJ 08541-6051.

As suggested earlier, a number of professional licensing and certification examinations routinely taken by students afford readily available outcomes measures. Prospective attorneys agonize until receiving official results of their state's bar examination; likewise, accounting majors anxiously approach the rigorous certified public accountants (CPA) examination. Physicians, nurses, psychologists, and other health care professionals also are subject to national and state licensing board requirements, such as the examination by the National League of Nursing. Departments and institutions keep close track of their graduates' performance on such measures, often vying with one another for the highest percentage of successful completions. Moreover, graduate schools of business, law, and medicine have access to students' entry scores on the GMAT, LSAT, and MCAT, respectively.

(k) Student Occupational Competency Achievement Testing series

The National Occupational Competency Testing Institute offers a variety of services to schools, community/technical colleges, and the business community through its Student Occupational Competency Achievement Testing (SOCAT) series (Wells, personal communication). As of 1992, 65 instruments were available in the SOCAT series, covering fields such as Accounting/Bookkeeping, Electronics, Mechanical Drafting, and Welding. Results provided by the National Occupational Competency Testing Institute include individual (percent correct) reports, norm-based comparisons for individuals and groups, and performance-criterion listings for individuals (Wells, personal communication).

Locally Developed Alternatives

Locally constructed instruments aimed at program improvement through assessing the accomplishment of intended educational outcomes have arisen out of necessity—"in the absence of available standardized alternatives" (Ewell, 1987, p. 18). For instance, the University of Tennessee at Knoxville (UTK) combines some 45 faculty-developed instruments with the GRE's standardized tests to measure the competencies of various departmental majors. A number of publications by UTK's Center for Assessment Research and Development extensively discuss this nationally recognized assessment program, together with the process of test evolution.

Other locally designed examinations have emerged from "dissatisfaction with the match in content and coverage between available standardized tests and the curriculum" (Ewell, 1987, p. 18). Among the prime examples are an experimental sophomore-junior project at King's College (Pennsylvania) and pilot activities at Berea, Carson-Newman, and Mars Hill colleges testing institutionally prepared written and oral examinations for senior English, religion/philosophy, and political science majors (Weiner, 1987).

At Indiana University of Pennsylvania, an innovative program known as the Pre-Teacher Assessment Project employs trained teacher-evaluators to assess sophomore education majors on each of 13 skill dimensions: planning and organizing, monitoring, leadership, sensitivity, problem analysis, strategic decision making, tactical decision making, oral communication, oral presentation, written communication, innovativeness, tolerance for stress, and initiative. Among the vehicles for this evaluation are videotaped scenarios, teaching simulations, and organization of an educational fair (Orr, 1987).

Recently, the Clearinghouse for Higher Education Assessment Instruments completed reviews of these, and other, locally developed instruments (Pike, in press). Additional information can be obtained by contacting Dr. Michael K. Smith, 212 Claxton Education Building, College of Education, University of Tennessee, Knoxville, TN 37996-3400, (615) 974-5894.

Thus, the prevailing assessment mode has brought higher education full circle. As Ewell (1987) has pointed out, recent "pressures for enhanced assessment have stimulated colleges and universities to reexamine the senior comprehensive—in general education or, more commonly, in the major field—as an alternative to standardized testing" (p. 18).

An integral component of the curriculum and, more significantly, the gateway to graduation, the traditional senior comprehensive examination "entailed objective demonstration of a student's mastery of core concepts and material...[and] application of these concepts to an extensive critical essay or problem-solving exercise" (p. 18). However, in contrast to the institutional effectiveness paradigm advanced in this *Handbook*, the "primary intent...was to determine what students knew and not to identify the strengths and weaknesses of the curriculum" (p. 18).

To Buy or Not to Buy?

Arguments favoring the use of standardized versus locally developed major subject tests echo those presented on page 69. Nationally normed and less susceptible to charges of subjectivity, standardized examinations also may prove to be poor measures for a particular department's curriculum and, thus, its intended educational outcomes. Although local examinations can easily be customized, they, in turn, consume faculty time and yield no external norms. Ultimately, the best advice is to carefully compare intended educational outcomes for the department or program with the material examined on each standardized test prior to reaching this crucial decision. And, there is no single "correct" solution. Whether the choice is to buy or to build a test, the appropriate answer can vary from field to field within an institution.

Assessment of Cognitive Development

Although most institutions tend to focus on the assessment of basic skills, general education, and learning in the major, many colleges and universities are becoming increasingly concerned with the assessment of higher-order thinking skills. As Mentkowski and Chickering (1987) have noted, "Many faculty are now working to teach and assess competence in critical thinking (e.g., problem-finding, problem-framing, and problem analysis with the marshalling of supportive evidence and argumentation) as a more enduring outcome of undergraduate education" (p. 153). By 1989, ACE found 14% of all higher education institutions already assessing critical thinking skills, with nearly half planning to introduce assessment of these skills. As with the assessment of other types of learning, a variety of instruments are available (see Smith, Bradley, & Draper, 1994a; 1994b). Yet, assessment of cognitive development and critical thinking differs from other types of outcomes assessment in that production measures become much more prominent.

One difficulty with instruments currently available for assessing cognitive development is their high correlation with measures of general intelligence (Baird, 1988). As a consequence, many of the efforts to assess effectiveness of programs designed to enhance critical thinking have not produced any significant results (McMillan, 1987).

(a) Analysis of Argument

The Analysis of Argument is a production measure designed to assess clarity and flexibility of students' thinking skills. After reading a passage representing a particular position on a controversial issue, students are asked to write a response disagreeing with the position taken in the passage. After five minutes they are told to write a second short essay supporting the original position (Stewart & Winter, 1977). The two essays are then scored using a 10-category scheme.[2]

Because interrater agreement is a function of training, the authors do not provide estimates of reliability. However, Stewart and Winter (1977) report that studies have shown scores on the Analysis of Argument test to be significantly related to other measures of cognitive development and to students' educational experiences.

(b) Erwin Scale of Intellectual Development

The Erwin Scale of Intellectual Development (SID) is an untimed instrument designed to measure intellectual development based on the Perry (1970) scheme. Three of Erwin's four subscales (dualism, relativism, and commitment) parallel Perry's categories of intellectual development (Erwin, 1983). The fourth subscale is empathy.[3]

Research by Erwin (1983) indicates that all four subscales have acceptable levels of reliability (from 0.70 to 0.81). This research also shows that scores on the SID are significantly related to other measures of development, including measures of identity and involvement.

(c) Measure of Epistemological Reflection

The Measure of Epistemological Reflection (MER) provides a bridge between recognition and production measures. Six stimuli corresponding to Perry's levels of development are presented to subjects, who are asked to justify the reasoning contained in each stimulus. Standardized scoring procedures provide a quantified measure of intellectual development (Baxter-Magolda & Porterfield, 1985).[4]

Alpha reliability (internal consistency) estimates across stimuli may be as high as 0.76, and interrater reliability has ranged from 0.67 to 0.80, depending on the amount of training provided to the raters. Research also reveals support for the theory underlying the MER, indicating significant score differences for different education levels (1985). A review of this instrument is available in a review by Hanson (1994a).

(d) Reflective Judgment Interview

Like the Measure of Epistemological Reflection, the Reflective Judgment Interview (RJI) provides a bridge between recognition and production measures. Requiring approximately 40 minutes to administer, the RJI consists of four dilemmas that are pre-

---

2. The author of this instrument is David G. Winter of the Department of Psychology, Wesleyan College, Middletown, CT.
3. This 86-item intellectual development scale is named for its author, T. Dary Erwin of the Office of Student Assessment, James Madison University, Harrisonburg, VA.
4. This untimed measure was developed by Mareia Baxter-Magolda of the Department of Educational Leadership, Miami University, Miami, OH.

sented to students individually. Each dilemma is followed by a series of questions designed to identify the stage in Perry's scheme being used to deal with the dilemma (King & Kitchener, 1985). A subject's score is the average rating across the four dilemmas and across raters.[5]

Based on research results, the Reflective Judgment Interview evidences acceptable levels of reliability (ranging from 0.73 to 0.78). In addition, the RJI has been found to be significantly correlated with other measures of critical thinking and to level of education (Kitchener & King, 1981). Additional information about this instrument is available in Hanson's (1994b) recent review.

(e) Test of Thematic Analysis

The Test of Thematic Analysis assesses students' critical-thinking skills using a compare-and-contrast format. Students are given two sets of data and asked to describe (in writing) how these sets differ. This process requires approximately 30 minutes. The content of the essays is scored on a nine-point scale (Winter, 1977), yielding a total score; in addition, measures derived from human information processing research (differentiation, discrimination, and integration) can be used to evaluate the structure of the written responses (Schroder, Driver, & Streufert, 1967).[6]

Studies have revealed high levels of interrater agreement for the Test of Thematic Analysis (Winter & McClelland, 1978), and scores have been found to be significantly correlated with both academic ability and course work (Winter, McClelland, & Stewart, 1981). In addition, measures of the structural characteristics of students' essays have been found to be significantly related to other measures of critical thinking, as well as to educational experience (Winter & McClelland, 1978).

(f) Watson-Glaser Critical Thinking Appraisal

The Watson-Glaser Critical Thinking Appraisal (CTA) is a 100-item multiple-choice measure designed to assess students' critical-thinking abilities. In addition to a total score, five subscores are provided: (1) inference, (2) recognition of assumptions, (3) deduction, (4) interpretation, and (5) evaluation of arguments (Crites, 1965; Helmstadter, 1965).[7]

Research indicates that the CTA is a reliable instrument. Total-score reliability estimates range from 0.85 to 0.87 (Crites, 1965; Helmstadter, 1965). Moreover, scores on the CTA are significantly related to students' college experiences and are predictive of performance in courses emphasizing critical thinking (Westbrook & Sellers, 1967; Wilson

---

5. The coauthors of this instrument are K. S. Kitchener, School of Education, University of Denver, Denver, CO, and P. M. King, Department of College Student Personnel, Bowling Green State University, Bowling Green, OH.
6. David G. Winter of the Department of Psychology, Wesleyan University, Middletown, CT, authored this test of critical thinking.
7. The publisher of this 50-minute critical-thinking measure is Harcourt, Brace, and Jovanovich Publishers, 6277 Sea Harbor Drive, Orlando, FL.

& Wagner, 1981). Hoops (1994) and Annis (1994) have provided descriptions of the use of this test at both the department and institutional levels at Ball State University.

The Educational Testing Service (ETS) has developed an instrument entitled *Tasks in Critical Thinking* to provide performance-based assessment of the critical thinking skills of analysis, inquiry, and communication through the use of an "extended task" format.[8] Students are each given one 90-minute task, which consists of a problem and the guiding of students through various steps necessary to solve it. Each task consists of eight to ten short-answer questions followed by an essay or report, which is related to issues introduced by the task (i.e., no multiple choice formats). Each task relates to one academic area (e.g., humanities, social sciences, or natural sciences), but is not course-specific (i.e., independence of courses and dependence on general field). The tasks are constructed in such a manner as the content increases in difficulty as the students progress through each task.

Portfolio Assessment

Clearly, cognitive assessment comprises much more than standardized and locally developed test instruments. Student portfolios have gained increasing acceptance and use over the past several years as a viable means of evaluating both general knowledge and learning in the major (see Smith, Bradley, and Draper, 1994c). Once confined primarily to the fine arts, today's portfolios appear in a variety of departments and can encompass a wide array of indicators, including writing samples, summaries of accomplishments, students' reflections on their college experience, videotapes, and speeches. Former AAHE Assessment Forum Director Pat Hutchings (1990) characterizes portfolio assessment as "a collection of student work done over time. Beyond that, the rule is variety—and appropriately so" (p. 6). According to Hutchings, new instances of portfolio use arise almost weekly—from the music department at Kean College to Spanish at the University of Virginia and entry-level placement at Miami University of Ohio (p. 6).

The following brief illustrations drawn from Hutchings's (1990) work reflect the range of institutions—public and private, four-year and two-year—that have turned to some form of portfolio assessment alternative. The diversity of applications and materials incorporated in these portfolios is indeed striking.

(a) Alverno College

Recognized as a pioneer in outcomes assessment, Alverno College has applied portfolio evaluation in the context of general education as well as in specific majors. Several approaches used in general education include an Academic Career and Resource Journal, a Communication Portfolio, and a General Performance Portfolio. Providing students with an introduction to portfolio assessment, the Academic Career and Resource Journal is used throughout each student's orientation course and includes assessment findings in beginning course work and test results from learning and lifestyle invento-

---

8.   For further information consult the Educational Testing Service, Princeton, NJ.

ries. The Communication Portfolio includes separate speaking and writing sections. Videotaped speeches and written feedback from general education and major courses, as well as from the Integrated Competence Seminar (described in a moment), are among materials maintained in the speaking portfolio. Samples of work from introductory writing classes and written self-assessments have become part of the writing portfolio; systematic collection of more advanced work may be undertaken in the future. The General Performance Portfolio focuses on social interaction skills and on the specific individual and collaborative skills that all students must demonstrate through grappling with crucial social issues in the Integrated Competence Seminar. The departments of English, natural sciences, and psychology also have employed portfolio assessment to enhance development among their respective majors.

(b) Butler University (Indiana)

The College of Business at Butler University employs portfolios to assess problem solving, communication styles and abilities, and metacognitive processing. Among the various indicators maintained are scores, student work samples, and student self-evaluations. Future portfolios may expand to include materials relevant to ethical, global, and interpersonal and intrapersonal development.

(c) College of William and Mary

Faced with Virginia's statewide mandate requiring assessment of student learning, the College of William and Mary's foremost concern was to design useful measures for a student population that already scored well on standardized tests. Thus far, portfolios have proven quite successful for assessment in major fields such as philosophy and music. The college also has pilot-tested portfolio assessment of general educational objectives.

(d) Dundalk Community College (Maryland)

Dundalk Community College, a two-year institution, is pursuing portfolio use in assessing not only student writing but also development of an aesthetic sense and critical-thinking skills.

(e) Kenyon College (Ohio)

Each student in Kenyon College's history department must complete a portfolio containing two course-assigned papers, one revised and expanded research paper, and an autobiographical essay regarding his or her work as a historian. Two history department faculty evaluate this portfolio and conduct an oral interview with the student.

(f) SUNY at Fredonia

Portfolios form part of a larger assessment of the SUNY General College Program at Fredonia. Students compile materials from entrance through the senior year, including a final self-evaluation. The pedagogical intent is to heighten students' awareness of their own learning processes, encourage reflective thinking, and involve them in their own learning.

(g) San Diego State University

Among the many programs employing portfolios at San Diego State University are classics, social work, and recreation. For 1,700 students in the teacher education program, portfolios track students' individual growth as learners, multicultural sensitivity, and insights from field experience. This information provides a basis for exit interviews conducted through core courses.

Pros and Cons of Portfolios

As Hutchings (1990) cautions, one "sure route to nowhere is to have assessment come forward as an ''add-on' activity unrelated to the regular work of faculty and students" (p. 6). Portfolio assessment allays this concern because it builds on papers, projects, and other assignments that students have completed for courses. Portfolios also provide deeper insight into students' progress, revealing not only the final outcomes—or ends—of four, five, or more "critical years" but also the means by which students have arrived at those outcomes. Thus, portfolio assessment can prove effective either as a stand-alone measure or as a supplement to the other cognitive measures just discussed. Further advantages associated with this form of assessment include its value in sparking conversation between faculty advisor and student, its practical utility for the faculty member asked to compose a letter of recommendation, and its circumvention of the misuses of and possible biases inherent in standardized tests. In providing a natural opportunity for students to make connections among their diverse subjects, portfolios can serve as a potent learning device.

On the other hand, this relatively new assessment technique is still being "debugged"—even by institutions that have employed it extensively. Portfolios are "difficult to make neat sense of" and, thus, do not always satisfy requirements of external audiences such as employers and graduate schools (Hutchings, 1990, p. 8). Some of their unwieldiness, however, can be surmounted with the incorporation of more traditional outcomes indicators (e.g., standardized test results). Portfolio review and evaluation can prove time-consuming as well; not only because each set of materials is unique, but because individual student conferences generally are involved. Among their other disadvantages, portfolios present storage problems over time, may lead to duplication of materials when used to assess both general education and learning in the major field, and entail an initial period of development and acclimation for new faculty. Finally, it can be expensive to initiate and sustain portfolio assessment. Alverno College has addressed this last issue by having the unit that houses the materials pay directly for them; hence, the institution supplies materials maintained in the Assessment Center and departments, and students are responsible for their own copies as well as for their Academic and Resource Career Journals.

Toward Assessment of Learning with Proper Perspective

Gregory R. Anrig, president of the venerable Educational Testing Service, ironically has cautioned that although individual institutions may find ETS (and similar standardized) examinations "helpful," externally imposed tests actually may prove detrimental. He continues, "There is not a consensus about what the core of learning should be, making it difficult to develop **a quality test** [emphasis added] to be used for institutions in an entire state" (Anrig quoted in Jaschik, 1985, p. 16). Thus, experts would wager that institutions will not be fully satisfied with only one of the many assessment measures outlined in this *Handbook*. Alverno College, Northeast Missouri State University, and the University of Tennessee at Knoxville are just several of the institutions currently incorporating multiple methods—and doing so successfully. Within a particular field, combining multiple cognitive measures such as standardized and locally written examinations, oral examinations, portfolio analyses, and demonstrations yields a more thorough picture of effectiveness than using any single instrument.

Whatever the method(s) of assessment, Marchese (1987) reminds us that the process invariably entails judgment by external parties—faculty members reviewing achievement across courses, outside examiners, or even the producers of standardized instruments. "Somebody beyond the agent of instruction [often an accrediting team] is asking the questions, What does it add up to? What was learned? Is that good enough?" (p. 7). Institutions, however, must move beyond these queries toward answers that enhance instruction and educational outcomes, and, ultimately, their effectiveness. As Marchese (1987) has noted, "Assessment per se guarantees nothing by way of improvement, no more than a thermometer cures a fever" (p. 8). Faculty and administrators who respond to the assessment siren with "a data-gathering effort only" have missed the whole point and set themselves up for the proverbial fall (Marchese, 1987). Yes, cognitive assessment does involve testing. But, evidence of an institution's true commitment to assessment does not emerge from an impressive slate of examinations alone; the real proof lies in its reply to the question, Where do we go from here? In the oft-imitated song, Sam Cooke claims, "I don't know much about history...biology...a science book...or the French I took." Colleges and universities can easily verify such statements through testing. However, what they subsequently do with that information will determine their actual effectiveness. The first three letters in **cognitive** represent an important point about the assessment of learning: it is just one component of a much larger process; the other pieces of the paradigm ensure that the results will be analyzed and judiciously applied.

References: Cited and Recommended

Adleman, C. (1985). *The Standardized Test Scores of College Graduates, 1964-1982*. Washington, DC: Study Group on the Conditions of Excellence in American Higher Education.

American Assembly of Collegiate Schools of Business (AACSB). (1987). *Outcomes Measurement Project: Phase III Report*. St. Louis, MO: Author.

American Chemical Society (ACS). (1985). *Norms for the ACS Test in General Chemistry*. Unpublished manuscript. Tampa, FL: Author.

American College Testing Program (ACT). (1989). *Report on the Technical Characteristics of CAAP*. Iowa

City, IA: Author.

American Institute of Certified Public Accountants (AICPA). (1987). *AICPA Accounting Testing Program.* San Antonio, TX: Psychological Corporation.

American Psychological Association. (1985). *Standards for Educational and Psychological Testing.* Washington, DC: Author.

Annis, D. B. (1994). Watson-Glaser Critical Thinking Appraisal. In M. Smith, J. Bradley, & G.Draper (eds.), *Reviews and Descriptions of Assessment Instruments: Basic Skills, General Education, and Critical Thinking* (pp. 125-126). Knoxville, TN: Clearinghouse for Higher Education Assessment Instruments.

Bailey, B. E. (1994). Collegiate Assessment of Academic Proficiency. In M. Smith, J. Bradley,& G. Draper (eds.), *Reviews and Descriptions of Assessment Instruments: Basic Skills, General Education, and Critical Thinking* (pp. 43-46). Knoxville, TN: Clearinghouse for Higher Education Assessment Instruments.

Baird, L. L. (1988). Diverse and Subtle Arts: Assessing the Generic Outcomes of Higher Education. In C. Adelman (ed.), *Performance and Judgment: Essays on Principles and Practice in the Assessment of College Student Learning* (pp. 39-62). Washington, DC: Government Printing Office.

Banta, T. W., & Schneider, J. A. (1988). Using Faculty-Developed Exit Examinations to Evaluate Academic Programs. *Journal of Higher Education, 59*, 69-83.

Baxter-Magolda, M., & Porterfield, W. D. (1985). A New Approach to Assess Intellectual Development on the Perry Scheme. *Journal of College Student Personnel, 26*, 343-351.

Borg, W. R., & Gall, M. D. (1983). *Educational Research.* New York: Longman.

Cavazos Presents Higher Education Goals. (1990). *Higher Education and National Affairs,39*(2), 1, 4.

Cerreto, F., & Colijn, G. J. (1994). New Jersey College Basic Skills Placement Test. In M.Smith, J. Bradley, & G. Draper (eds.), *Review and Descriptions of Assessment Instruments* (pp. 71-74). Knoxville, TN: Clearinghouse for Higher Education Assessment Instruments.

College Entrance Examination Board (CEEB). (1984). *Technical Manual Overview.* Princeton, NJ: Educational Testing Service.

College Entrance Examination Board (CEEB). (1986). *Outcomes Assessment in Higher Education.* Princeton, NJ: Educational Testing Service.

College Entrance Examination Board and Educational Testing Service (CEEB & ETS). (1988). *Guide to the Scholastic Aptitude Test.* Princeton, NJ: Educational Testing Service.

Conrad, L., Trismen, D., and Miller, R. (1977). *Graduate Record Examinations Technical Manual.* Princeton, NJ: Educational Testing Service.

Council of Presidents and State Board for Community College Education. (1989). *The Validity and Usefulness of Three National Standardized Tests for Measuring the Communication,Computation, and Critical Thinking Skills of Washington State College Sophomores: General Report.* Bellingham, WA: Western Washington University Office of Publications.

Crites, J. O. (1965). Test Review. *Journal of Counseling Psychology, 12*, 328-330.

Curry, W., & Hager, E. (1987). Assessing General Education: Trenton State College. In D. F. Halpern (ed.), *Student Outcomes Assessment: What Institutions Stand to Gain* (pp. 57-65). San Francisco: Jossey-Bass.

Davis, T. M., & Murrell, P. H. (1989). *Joint Factor Analysis of the College Student Experiences Questionnaire and the ACT COMP Objective Exam.* Unpublished manuscript, Memphis State University, Center for the Study of Higher Education, Memphis, TN.

DeVore, R., & McPeek, M. (1985). *Report of a Study of the Content of Three Advanced Tests.* GRE Research Report no. 78-4R. Princeton, NJ: Educational Testing Service.

Dizinno, J. B. (1994). Major Field Test: Psychology. In M. Smith, G. Draper, & J. Bradley (eds.), *Review and Descriptions of Assessment Instruments: Major Field Assessments* (pp. 281-283). Knoxville, TN: Clearinghouse for Higher Education Assessment Instruments.

Dumont, R. G., & Troelstrup, R. L. (1981). Measures and Predictors of Educational Growth with Four Years of College. *Research in Higher Education, 14*, 31-47.

Educational Testing Service (ETS). (1989). *Major Field Achievement Tests: Comparative Data Guide.* Princeton, NJ: Author.

Educational Testing Service (ETS). (1990). *Higher Education Assessment Newsletter*. Princeton, NJ: Author.

Educational Testing Service (ETS) College and University Programs. (1987). *The Academic Profile*. Princeton, NJ: ETS.

Educational Testing Service (ETS) College and University Programs. (1991). *Academic Profile User's Guide Part I*. Princeton, NJ: ETS.

El-Khawas, E. (1991). *Campus Trends, 1991*. Washington, DC: American Council on Education.

Erwin, T. D. (1983). The Scale of Intellectual Development: Measuring Perry's Scheme. *Journal of College Student Personnel*, *24*, 6-12.

Ewell, P. T. (1987). Establishing a Campus-Based Assessment Program. In D. F. Halpern (ed.), *Student Outcomes Assessment: What Institutions Stand to Gain* (pp. 9-24). San Francisco: Jossey-Bass.

Forrest, A. (1982). *Increasing Student Competence and Persistence: The Best Case for General Education*. Iowa City, IA: ACT National Center for the Advancement of Educational Practice.

Forrest, A., & Steele, J. M. (1982). *Defining and Measuring General Education Knowledge and Skills*. Iowa City, IA: American College Testing Program.

Graduate Record Examinations (GRE) Board. (1987). *GRE Guide to the Use of the Graduate Record Examinations Program*. Princeton, NJ: Educational Testing Service.

Halpern, D. F. (1987a). Recommendations and Caveats. In D. F. Halpern (ed.), *Student Outcomes Assessment: What Institutions Stand to Gain* (pp. 109-111). San Francisco: Jossey-Bass.

Halpern, D. F. (1987b). Student Outcomes Assessment: Introduction and Overview. In D. F.Halpern (ed.), *Student Outcomes Assessment: What Institutions Stand to Gain* (pp. 5-8). San Francisco: Jossey-Bass.

Hanson, G. R. (1994a). Measure of Epistemological Reflection. In M. Smith, J. Bradley, & G.Draper (eds.), *Reviews and Descriptions of Assessment Instruments: Basic Skills, General Education, and Critical Thinking* (pp.93-94). Knoxville, TN: Clearinghouse for Higher Education Assessment Instruments.

Hanson, G. R. (1994b). Reflective Judgment Interview. In M. Smith, J. Bradley, & G. Draper (eds.), *Reviews and Descriptions of Assessment Instruments: Basic Skills, General Education, and Critical Thinking* (pp.115-118). Knoxville, TN: Clearinghouse for Higher Education Assessment Instruments.

Harris, J. (1985). Assessing Outcomes in Higher Education. In C. Adelman (ed.), *Assessment in American Education: Issues and Contexts* (pp. 13-31). Washington, DC: Office of Educational Research and Improvement.

Hartle, T. W. (1985). The Growing Interest in Measuring the Educational Achievement of College Students. In C. Adelman (ed.), *Assessment in American Education: Issues and Contexts* (pp. 1-11). Washington, DC: Office of Educational Research and Improvement.

Helmstadter, G. C. (1965). Watson-Glaser Critical Thinking Appraisal. *Journal of Educational Measurement*, *2*, 254-256.

Herring, H., & Izard, C. (1992, Spring). Outcomes Assessment of Accounting Majors. *Issues in Accounting Education*, 1-17.

Hoops, R. A. (1994). The Watson-Glaser Critical Thinking Appraisal. In M. Smith, J. Bradley,& G. Draper (eds.), *Reviews and Descriptions of Assessment Instruments: Basic Skills, General Education, and Critical Thinking* (pp. 121-123). Knoxville, TN: Clearinghouse for Higher Education Assessment Instruments.

Hutchings, P. (1990). Learning over Time: Portfolio Assessment. *AAHE Bulletin*, *42*(8), 6-8.

Jaschik, S. (1985, September 18). Public Universities Trying Tests and Surveys to Measure What Students Learn. *Chronicle of Higher Education*, pp. 1, 16.

King, P. M., & Kitchener, K. S. (1985). *Reflective Judgment Theory and Research: Insights into the Process of Knowing in the College Years*. Paper presented at the annual meeting of the American Educational Research Association, Boston.

Kitchener, K. S., & King, P. M. (1981). Reflective Judgment: Concepts of Justification and their Relationship to Age and Education. *Journal of Applied Development Psychology*, *2*,89-116.

Leininger, E. (1994). Academic Profile. In M. Smith, J. Bradley, & G. Draper (eds.), *Reviews* and Descriptions of Assessment Instruments: Basic Skills, General Education, and Critical *Thinking* (pp. 19-23). Knoxville, TN: Clearinghouse for Higher Education Assessment Instruments.

Marchese, T. J. (1987). Third Down, Ten Years to Go. *AAHE Bulletin*, *40*(4), 3-8.

McMillan, J. H. (1987). Enhancing College Students' Critical Thinking: A Review of Studies. *Research in Higher Education*, *26*, 3-30.

Mentkowski, M., & Chickering, A. W. (1987). Linking Educators and Researchers in Setting a Research Agenda for Undergraduate Education. *Review of Higher Education*, *11*(2),137-160.

Munday, L. A. (1968). Correlations Between ACT and Other Predictors of Academic Success in College. *College and University*, *44*, 67-76.

National Teacher Examination (NTE) Policy Council. (1984). *A Guide to the NTE Core Battery Tests*. Princeton, NJ: Educational Testing Service.

National Teacher Examination (NTE) Policy Council. (1985). *Guidelines for Proper Use of NTE Tests*. Princeton, NJ: Educational Testing Service.

Orr, J. (1987, September 29). Pre-Teacher Assessment: Plan to Upgrade Teaching Quality. *Indiana (PA) Gazette*, p. 13.

Osterlind, S. J., & Merz, W. R. (1990). *College BASE Technical Manual*. Columbia, MO: Center for Educational Assessment.

Perry, W. G., Jr. (1970). *Forms of Intellectual and Ethical Development in the College Years*. New York: Holt, Rinehart & Winston.

Pike, G. R. (1989). Background, College Experiences, and the ACT COMP Exam: Using Construct Validity to Evaluate Assessment Instruments. *Review of Higher Education*, *13*,91-117.

Pike, G. R. (1990). *Alternative Scoring Schemes for the ACT COMP Exam: A Research Note*. Paper presented at the annual meeting of the American Educational Research Association, Boston.

Pike, G. R. (1992a). *A Generalizability Analysis of the College Basic Academic Subjects Examination*. Unpublished research report, Center for Assessment Research and Development, Knoxville, TN.

Pike, G. R. (1992b). The Components of Construct Validity: A Comparison of Two Measures of General Education Outcomes. *Journal of General Education*, *41*, 130-159.

Pike, G. R. (in press). Assessment Measures: The Clearinghouse for Higher Education Assessment Instruments. *Assessment Update*.

Ratcliff, J. L. (1988). *Development of a Cluster-Analytic Model for Identifying Coursework Patterns Associated with General Learned Abilities of College Students*. Paper presented at the annual meeting of the American Educational Research Association, New Orleans.

Resnick, D. P., & Goulden, M. (1987). Assessment, Curriculum, and Expansion: An Historical Perspective In D. F. Halpern (ed.), *Student Outcomes Assessment: What Institutions Stand to Gain* (pp. 77-88). San Francisco: Jossey-Bass.

Richards, J. M., Jr., Holland, J. L., & Lutz, S. W. (1967). Prediction of Student Accomplishment in College *Journal of Educational Psychology*, *58*, 343-355.

Riverside Publishing Company. (1989). *College BASE: Guide to Test Content*. Chicago: Author.

Riverside Publishing Company. (1990). *Preliminary Summary of the College BASE Technical Manual*. Chicago: Riverside.

Schroder, H. M., Driver, M. J., & Streufert, S. (1967). *Human Information Processing*. New York: Holt, Rinehart & Winston.

Smith, M. K., Bradley, J. L., & Draper, G. F. (1994a). *Annotated Reference Catalog of Assessment Instruments in Basic Skills, General Education, and Critical Thinking*. Knoxville, TN: Clearinghouse for Higher Education Assessment Instruments.

Smith, M. K., Bradley, J. L., & Draper, G. F. (1994b). *Reviews and Descriptions of Assessment Instruments: Basic Skills, General Education, and Critical Thinking*. Knoxville, TN: Clearinghouse for Higher Education Assessment Instruments. Smith, M. K., Bradley, J. L., & Draper, G. F. (1994c). *Reviews and Descriptions of Assessment Instruments: Portfolios*. Knoxville, TN: Clearinghouse for Higher Education Assessment Instruments.

Smith, M. K., Draper, G. F., & Bradley, J. L. (1994). *Reviews and Descriptions of Assessment Instruments: Major Field Assessments*. Knoxville, TN: Clearinghouse for Higher Education Assessment Instruments.

State Higher Education Executive Officers (SHEEO). (1990). *State Priorities in Higher Education: 1990.* Denver, CO: Author.

Steele, J. M. (1979). *Assessing Speaking and Writing Proficiency Via Samples of Behavior.* Paper presented at the annual meeting of the Central States Speech Association, St. Louis, MO.

Steele, J. M. (1989). *College Outcome Measures Program (COMP): A Generalizability Analysis of the COMP Objective Test (Form 9).* Unpublished manuscript, American College Testing Program, Iowa City, IA.

Stewart, A. J., & Winter, D. G. (1977). *Analysis of Argument: An Empirically Derived Measure of Intellectual Flexibility.* Boston: McBer.

Weiner, J. R. (1987). *National Directory: Assessment Programs and Projects.* Washington, DC: American Association of Higher Education Assessment Forum.

Westbrook, B. W., & Sellers, J. R. (1967). Critical Thinking, Intelligence, and Vocabulary. *Educational and Psychological Measurement, 27,* 443-446.

Wilson, D. G., & Wagner, E. E. (1981). The Watson-Glaser Critical Thinking Appraisal as a Predictor of Performance in a Critical Thinking Course. *Educational and Psychological Measurement, 41,* 1319-1322.

Wilson, K. M. (1985). *The Relationship of GRE General Test Item-Type Part Scores to Undergraduate Grades.* GRE Research Report 81. Princeton, NJ: Educational Testing Service.

Winter, D. G. (1977). *Thematic Analysis: An Empirically Derived Measure of Critical Thinking.* Boston: McBer.

Winter, D. G., & McClelland, D. C. (1978). Thematic Analysis: An Empirically Derived Measure of the Effect of Liberal Arts Education. *Journal of Educational Psychology, 70,*8-16.

Winter, D. G., McClelland, D. C., & Stewart, A. J. (1981). *A New Case for the Liberal Arts.* San Francisco: Jossey-Bass.

Wyse, R. E. (1994). Major Field Test in Business. In M. Smith, G. Draper, & J. Bradley (eds.), *Reviews and Descriptions of Assessment Instruments: Major Field Assessments* (pp. 69-71). Knoxville, TN: Clearinghouse for Higher Education Assessment Instruments.

Assessment of Behavioral Change and Performance

Mary K. Kinnick and R. Dan Walleri

What can you do or do better as a result of an educational experience? How much better or in what different ways can you perform a particular task or demonstrate a skill, be it cognitive (e.g., ethical analysis, study skills, test-taking skills), affective (e.g., empathizing, valuing), psychomotor (e.g., keyboarding, dancing with flexibility), or some combination? What do you do—how do you behave—as a result of your educational experience in ways that distinguish you from your noncollege cohorts, from those who experienced a different educational program, or from other subgroups of students? During your educational experience, how do you make use of your environment, and what do your experiences infer about outcomes?

Although admittedly oversimplified, these questions help frame the assessment arena of this resource section—using assessments of behavior and performance as indicators of institutional effectiveness. Other resource sections in this volume provide information about cognitive assessment instruments and attitudinal surveys, primarily focusing on assessing general and specialized knowledge and self-reported attitudes, beliefs, and values. This section focuses exclusively on methods and approaches designed to collect information directly and indirectly on behavior and on performance from sources other than paper-and-pencil cognitive and attitudinal instruments.

Increasingly, many of these kinds of assessments are being referred to as "authentic," those that reflect behaviors and performances in the "real world." In addition, many are becoming part of "portfolios." Portfolios are a special kind of notebook or file where evidence of various kinds and from various sources (e.g., writing samples, results from standardized tests, evaluations from internship supervisors, self-assessments, etc.) are kept that document student learning over time.

Illustrations, rather than an exhaustive listing and description of this kind of assessment, are provided in this resource section. The section is designed to steer the reader toward written resource material, to identify red flags associated with this kind of assessment, and to promote creativity in identifying and implementing these kinds of assessment approaches and measures.

The national education reform effort will likely increase the prominence of behavioral and performance assessment approaches. Chartered with the 1989 establishment of six

National Education Goals, work continues on setting national performance measures and standards covering kindergarten through higher education (Commission on the Skills of the American Workforce, 1990; Secretary's Commission on Achieving Necessary Skills, 1991; Goal 5 Work Group, 1993). The most influential of these is referred to as the SCANS competencies (Secretary's Commission, 1991). Many of the states have initiated their own reform efforts fashioned after or incorporating similar sets of performance standards. For example, the *Oregon Education Act for the 21ST Century* (1991) resulted in a sweeping restructuring of education in that state with the SCANS competencies a key part of the assessment framework (Oregon Department of Education, 1993).

Stripped of the jargon and rhetoric, the education reform effort is designed to "push up" standards from the lower grades through higher education for **all** students. The emphasis is on what students "can do" rather than "seat time," grades, or even standardized test results. Perhaps a bellwether of the future, the Oregon State System of Higher Education recently adopted a new proficiency-based admissions system, known as PASS, that should be fully implemented by 1999 (Conley, 1994). For admissions consideration, students will present a composite of scores derived from a variety of assessments that attest to their proficiency in a number of specific learning outcome areas.

Most likely in the future, approaches such as portfolio assessment will be favored, approaches that can capture multiple assessments and multiple outcomes (Black, 1993). As education reform continues, both the amount and variety of assessment will expand, especially behavioral and performance assessment.

The authors accepted the challenge of this resource section for several reasons. First, some behaviors that institutions intend to—and most likely can and do—affect are neglected in our assessment practices. For instance, faculty at Portland Community College were asked to identify the kinds of student success they perceived as most important for their students (Gerber, 1994). Then they were asked to identify the kinds of information about student success they perceived as potentially most useful to them in planning their classes, curricula, programs, and services to students. In the set of top ten "student success outcomes," four suggest the assessment of behavior or performance: (1) developing positive behaviors (e.g., initiative, honesty, self-discipline); (2) setting educational and career goals for themselves; (3) identifying educational or career goals relevant to their talents and abilities (i.e., self-assessment); and (4) achieving self-identified goals. Although these student success outcomes reflect the values of faculty at only one particular community college, they call attention to the need for approaches beyond paper-and-pencil cognitive tests and attitude surveys.

Second, the area of psychomotor skills is almost totally neglected in the literature and, to a large extent, in actual assessment practice. Student development in this area appears to be an implicit, rather than an explicit, goal of higher education. The explicit goal of developing psychomotor skills appears more in the elementary and secondary sectors of education. These observable skills, however, relate to success in many vocational, technical, and professional education programs and careers, and are a part of numerous college offerings (Lenning, 1977).

Third, behavioral and performance assessment approaches may allow us to document some of the more potent and far-reaching effects of college on students. Howard Bowen's classic text *Investment in Learning* (1977) is a rich source of information on these potential effects and how they have been measured. Some of these outcomes include motivation to continue learning, citizenship, consumer behavior, employability, and job performance.

Social skills and interpersonal skills and behaviors such as intercultural communication, collaboration, conflict resolution, and team building are receiving more attention as valued outcomes of higher education. Behavioral and performance assessment approaches offer promise in documenting changes in these outcomes areas.

Getting Started: Critical Issues

The first step is to adopt a working definition of **behavior** and **performance**. The following definitions are used in this resource section (adapted from Carroll & Schneier, 1982, pp. 2-3):

> Behavior: refers to anything a person does…writing reports, solving mathematical problems on a computer, repairing machines, voting, getting a job, using the library, talking with faculty outside of class, etc.

Information on behavior may be collected in three distinct ways: by (1) direct observation, (2) self-report, and (3) unobtrusive measures such as physical traces, archives or records, simple observation, and contrived or hidden observation using videotapes or audiotapes (Webb, Campbell, Schwartz, & Sechrest, 1966).

> Performance: refers to how well a person does something…how well reports are written, how well math problems are solved, how quickly and properly the machine is repaired, how good the painting is, etc.

Performance may refer to a process as well as a product. Level of performance may be judged using relative standards (i.e., comparisons of one's performance to that of others, of the performance of those in a control group versus those in an experimental group, or of one's own performance over time), or absolute standards (i.e., arbitrary or intuitive and value-based ones) (Clarkson, Neuburger, & Koroloff, 1977).

Assessing behavioral changes in students and using observation and judgment to assess performance raise a host of conceptual and methodological issues, especially when the identified behavioral and performance changes involve values and motivational factors. The problems associated with such assessment efforts include analysis of outcomes unrelated to an institution's mission, inadvertent measurement of one outcome when the intent was to measure something different, and drawing of unwarranted causal inferences.

A key point of departure in ensuring reliability and validity is the design stage. Here are eight important questions that should be answered before initiating an assessment program:

1. What are the valued outcomes, and which ones lend themselves to assessment using either behavioral data or direct appraisal of performance?
2. What criteria should be used to judge performance?

3. What, if any, are behavioral manifestations of the valued affective, cognitive, or psychomotor outcomes sought?
4. Where can we make reasonable inferences from behavior to changes in cognition and affect?
5. What is the unit of analysis? the institution? a specific program or discipline? a particular class? all students? particular subgroups of students?
6. What will be the time frame? Assess while in college? after leaving college (and how long out—one, five, or more years)? or both?
7. What approach and data sources will be used—qualitative, quantitative, or both? Rely on self-report, observation, or both? Who will judge performance?
8. Does the institution have the resources, expertise, and time to adopt a behavioral and/or a performance appraisal approach?

Somewhat unique to this area of assessment is the dichotomy of outcomes subsumed under "behavioral changes" and "performance." On the one hand, there are psychomotor skills, such as keyboarding, where the behavior is concrete and relatively simple to observe and measure; that is, the outcomes are fairly clear and quantifiable. On the other hand, there are behavioral changes purportedly influenced by the college experience that can serve as indicators of civic and moral development, referred to hereafter as "constructs."

Valued Outcomes and Performance

The first and foremost question to answer is, What behaviors fall within the domain of a particular college's Expanded Statement of Institutional Purpose (ESIP), program outcomes, or administrative objectives? In the case of psychomotor skills, few college catalogs list behaviors associated with these skills as explicit expectations of the college experience, even in the case of community colleges that offer a wide array of vocational programs. Psychomotor skills are certainly implicit in many academic and professional programs (e.g., speech, art, dentistry, nursing, dance), and assessment of student performance is directly or indirectly related to such skills.

Many colleges explicitly incorporate behavioral constructs, such as citizenship and leadership, as part of their ESIP, especially private colleges and colleges with a religious affiliation (Grandy, 1988). For many other colleges, such behaviors are undoubtedly implicit within their educational or co-curricular program.

Of particular concern in assessing construct behaviors is the consistency between institutional and student values. If the students do not share institutional values and act on this difference, a valid assessment program will demonstrate this incongruity and suggest that the college is failing in its efforts to produce desired outcomes.

Construct behaviors apply to all students but are not necessarily a consequence of a specific class, discipline, or other college experience. Assessment requires institutional consensus, which may be difficult to achieve, as in the determination of general education requirements. Even if consensus can be achieved on desired outcomes, the underlying values may be in conflict. These value conflicts can produce just the opposite from desired behaviors. As Grandy notes (1988, p. 156):

What can happen is "reverse maturation." Students may question the values learned in childhood, and actually "grow" in the opposite direction from that intended by the college. It is generally a goal of college to teach students to question authority and think for themselves. Indeed, they will probably do that even if it is not an institutional goal. Thus, it should not come as a surprise that some students enter college being religious and respecting authority and leave with negative feelings towards religion and authority.

Assuming that the fostering of certain behaviors lies within the ESIP or statements of intentions at the department or program level, what constitutes demonstration of the behavior in measurable terms? What criteria will be used? Examples for psychomotor skills might include typing speed for a student in office occupations, or time to task completion (e.g., changing a transmission) for a student in automotive technology. Behavioral constructs, however, pose a whole range of measurement problems, as Grandy (1988, p. 141) has noted:

> Often we use words like "citizenship," "responsibility," "moral," and "ethical" without thinking much about what we mean. For purposes of assessment, and for program development as well, it can be useful to move away from those words and find more specific words that communicate more clearly. If a person develops "citizenship," does that mean that he always votes in national elections? Does that mean he is gainfully employed? Or does he simply have to stay out of jail?

Once a set of valued outcomes has been identified, a hard look should be taken at whether or not change in behavior or performance can reasonably be expected, given the extent to which students are able or encouraged to practice these behaviors and performances during the course, program, or institution-wide experience. To illustrate, consider the college that wants its students to produce written communications at the end of the college experience that meet a series of technical and artistic or creative standards. Let us suppose these criteria are not shared with the students, and few experiences are provided during the college years for them to produce papers and receive feedback. Why, then, should the college expect students to improve performance as a consequence of the college experience?

Once specific behaviors and performance areas have been identified, the challenge is to develop strategies by which the behaviors and performance skills can be systematically assessed and, more importantly, inferred as a consequence of the college experience. To what extent can the behaviors and skills be taught? How does one control for preexisting aptitude, behavior traits, maturation, and other effects independent of the college experience? Those planning the assessment should have some reasonable set of evidence that the behaviors and skills of interest can be affected by the college experience. This means becoming familiar with the available research literature on the effects of the college experience or aspects of it on specific behaviors or behavioral constructs of interest (e.g., leadership or service to community). Two texts we recommend highly are *How Colleges Affect Students* by Pascarella and Terenzini (1991) and *What Matters in College?* by Astin (1993).

One final issue should be considered: When "behavior" is assessed, the main interest is in assessing "typical" or usual behavior, not behavior unique to the situation and moment (Harris, 1985). To what extent do observed behaviors in simulated experiences in the classroom generalize to behaviors that occur in other settings, in "real life"? Further-more, even if change in behavior while attending college is observed, is it reasonable to assume that the behavior will generalize to noncollege settings and persist after college? Consideration of these questions should accompany discussions of the situations or circumstances under which behavioral data will be collected.

Unit of Analysis

Just as the type of indicators will vary with the behaviors under study, so will the unit of analysis. Many psychomotor skills are discipline or program specific. In this case, the assessment strategy is similar to that for any other competency, with the exception that demonstration of the competencies extends beyond paper-and-pencil operations. With the advent of computer technology, some psychomotor skills, such as keyboarding, may be more generalizable across the curriculum.

Construct behaviors are less concrete and relate to the whole of the college experience or general education program (Baird, 1988; Grandy, 1988). Thus, the unit of analysis shifts from program or discipline to the individual student or groups of students in the assessment of construct behaviors. Regardless of the unit of analysis chosen, it is unlikely that all students attending a particular institution will be involved in an assessment of behavioral change and performance. In some cases, students will be excluded by design, as when the assessment is based on a sample of students. In other cases, students may be excluded by the scope of the design, as when an institution's continuing education program is not included in the assessment effort.

In assessing behavioral change and performance, individual students or groups of students would normally be the unit of analysis. Program, discipline, and institutional effectiveness is assessed indirectly through inferences drawn from the assessment of students.

Time Frame

The time frame for assessment can be critical. Both psychomotor and construct behaviors can be measured during the college experience. However, desired outcomes should be validated through after-college experiences whenever possible. A student may demonstrate all the necessary task skills associated with an occupation or profession; but if he or she cannot retain a job due to poor social skills or a poor work attitude, the college's desired outcome has not been realized. Likewise, indicators of ethical behavior during college may not provide a test commensurate with subsequent life experiences.

Also, some behaviors and performances cannot be assessed adequately until the student has moved beyond the educational experience. Examples include career mobility, motivation to continue learning, and citizenship.

Approach and Data Sources

Both quantitative and qualitative approaches may be used in the assessment of behavioral changes. Prominent among them is the use of direct observations by assessors of a product, a work sample, or a performance. Assessing behavioral change is likely to involve a higher degree of subjective evaluation than assessing the cognitive domain through the use of standardized or locally developed tests. This, in turn, places even greater demands on ensuring reliable and valid measures, particularly ones with high interrater and intrarater reliability. Another major source of data will be students' self-reports of behavior and "running records" of student progress through the institution and behaviors after college (e.g., attendance patterns, employment status, transfer status).

Resources, Expertise, and Time

Adopting an assessment strategy, such as ethnography and case study, that involves direct and indirect (unobtrusive) observation of behavior has resource implications. The applicable approaches require special training and expertise, and data collection may be very time-consuming (with the exception of collecting self-reports of behavior by means of a survey). When first considering these approaches, institution or program staff and faculty must evaluate the resource implications and feasibility of such approaches. The existence of local graduate programs with opportunities for projects by graduate students and faculty may increase the feasibility of some of these approaches.

Assessment Strategies: Examples

This section reviews a variety of assessment strategies and the strengths and limitations of each. References to further information and resources available are provided.

(a) Using What Is Available

As a first step, review by discipline or program area, especially for vocational, technical, and professional programs, external certification examinations or other external assessment exercises taken by graduates for entry into a specific occupation or profession. Do these examinations include the use of behavioral measures and/or observations of skill performance? For instance, a performance component of the National Teachers Examination might already be used to examine students before they enter a teacher education program and could be repeated upon their completion of the program.

A review should also be made of faculty members' means of assessing students' progress in courses and programs. To what extent and in what areas are practices such as the following being used: case analysis, simulation exercises, competency-based curricula, or portfolio development and assessment? Although these approaches may be used primarily to assess the progress and performance of individual students, over time they might become the source of information for assessing the performance of groups of students.

The use of externally normed assessment instruments offers savings of time and dollars as well as an increased awareness by faculty of what graduates are being expected to perform and at what levels of proficiency. One limitation is that for many areas, use of such instruments as pretests will not make sense because students will have had little or no experience performing an expected task (e.g., replacing a transmission, filling a tooth). Here, the institution may elect to compare its students with those in other programs and/or to compare the behavior and performance of new groups of graduates with those of previous ones.

Other limitations are that such examinations will not exist for many specific programs or will be primarily paper-and-pencil ones, will fail to cover specific kinds of performances and behaviors valued by the local faculty, or will not cover many valued outcomes of general education (either for the first 2 years of college or for the experience as a whole). For further references, see Conoley and Kramer, *The 10th Mental Measurements Yearbook* (1989), especially the section on the National Occupational Competency Testing Institute; also, check with state and national licensing boards for information on examination content and processes used for specific vocational/technical fields and the professions.

(b) Student Flow and Tracking Systems

Inferring institutional effectiveness from observing the results of student attendance/enrollment tracking systems or student flow, is more complicated than in the past. Assessment of performance in terms of student flow has traditionally focused on retention as measured through student tracking systems (or "running records" in the language of unobtrusive measurement). However, tracking has taken on greater importance (i.e., Can the institution retain students until they complete a degree or certificate?), the characteristics and enrollment behaviors of students have undergone fundamental change, making interpretation of student tracking results problematic at best.

Increasingly, a majority of postsecondary students are following nonlinear paths in the pursuit of educational and career goals. Creating a student tracking system on the basis of assumptions about students' intention to earn a degree or about the time to degree completion will produce assessment results that are incorrect or misleading in terms of student and institutional achievement. Inaccurate inferences will be drawn from data that track enrollment behavior. To limit such misinterpretation, students' self-reported motivation and goals should be incorporated within an institution's tracking system.

Updating existing student tracking systems or creating new ones that take into consideration motivation and goals can be accomplished by soliciting and monitoring students' declared intentions. By combining such data with other student characteristics (e.g., gender, ethnicity, socioeconomic class, high school performance, attitudes, values), researchers are beginning to employ student "typologies" in efforts to assess patterns of student flow (Richardson, 1990). The distribution of student types at an institution has significant implications for the delivery of student services and the instructional environment needed to ensure student success. Over time, the success of various subgroups of students in achieving their own original or updated goals could be assessed. For further information, see Ewell (1987), Richardson (1990), Terenzini (1987), Walleri, Seybert and Cosgrove (1992), and the resource section beginning on page 107.

The potential problems associated with the shift in focus to student defined goals and satisfaction in outcomes assessment go beyond a more complex research design. As Palmer (1993, p. 4) notes:

> ...an over-reliance on outcomes indicators that reflect relative rather than absolute measures has its drawbacks. One lies in the potential alienation of the public. Accountability to

our external publics increasingly requires a calculation of the return on investment demonstrated through retention and graduation rates, student proficiency in specified skills, employment and income generation. This accountability concern must be balanced against the desire to describe accurately outcomes that reflect students' life-long learning goals.

(c) Psychomotor Skill Assessment

The first challenge faced in assessing psychomotor skills is the paucity of specific research in this area. Lenning noted this in his 1977 review, and the problem remains. Nevertheless, psychomotor skills have been and still are an integral part of numerous college offerings (Lenning, 1977, pp. 61-62):

> It is certainly true that college courses in physical education, science (laboratory courses), music, drama, art, speech, and so forth, require primary emphasis on motor activity and coordination. Professional programs such as medicine, engineering, and architecture also emphasize this area. Furthermore, if an outcomes taxonomy is to cover all of postsecondary education, the vocational programs that enroll millions of students must also be considered. Most of these programs emphasize psychomotor skills such as perception, dexterity, and coordination.

The scarcity of formal assessment models, despite the importance of psychomotor skills across numerous disciplines and programs, derives, first, from assumptions within curriculum objectives. As discussed earlier, few institutions explicitly address these skills in their ESIP. Instead, psychomotor skills are treated either as unstated prerequisites or as inherent limitations that are only marginally affected by drill and practice. When explicitly addressed, such skills are more often considered in terms of accommodation, as in the admission of handicapped students to a program in compliance with Office of Civil Rights guidelines.

A second reason for the lack of "pure" assessment of psychomotor skills is that they are interrelated with cognitive and affective factors, which are the usual focus of assessment. The advent of computer technology is likely to accelerate this integration rather than differentiation. For example, one of the projects being funded through the National Center for Research in Vocational Education (1990, p. 10) addresses the question of how machinists learn to use computer numerical control (CNC) technology. This technology was selected because it represents a prototype of changes in work which require an integration of traditional machining knowledge with the symbolic knowledge and logical skills involved in the new "informatics" that are affecting not just machining but many industrial occupations.

The research on cognitive and affective factors has tended to rely on standardized testing programs. Such an approach fails to address direct observation and performance assessment by faculty both within the context of assessment in general and psychomotor skills in particular. This situation has led Stiggins and Bridgeford (1986, p. 470) to conclude:

> If measurement researchers continue to emphasize only those tests that serve large-scale assessment purposes, we may fail to serve teachers' primary measurement needs. Mea-

surement training that relies on traditional objective tests does not meet the day-to-day assessment needs of teachers. It disregards the full range of measurement options available to teachers and, more important, it fails to help teachers obtain the types of data needed to address the day-to-day decisions they face.

One promising path out of this dilemma is found in the growing interest in "classroom research," a subject to which we shall return later in this resource section. Given the state of the art in assessment of psychomotor skills, then, the key issue is whether and to what extent an institution or program desires to address this domain. If the answer is a definite yes, then the first step is to develop a structure for the psychomotor domain.

Lenning (1977) offers a review of nine previously developed classifications. The Harrow taxonomy (p. 74), for one example, includes the following: reflex movements; basic/fundamental movements (locomotor, nonlocomotor, manipulative); perceptual abilities (kinesthetic discrimination, visual discrimination, auditory discrimination, tactile discrimination, and coordinated abilities); physical abilities (endurance, strength, flexibility, agility); skilled movements (simple adaptive, compound adaptive, and complex adaptive ones); and nondiscursive communication (expressive movement and interpretive movement). Berk (1986) offers both a discussion of the methodological issues and practical applications in the area of performance assessment, which is directly related to psychomotor skills (see chapters by Cascio and by Stiggins and Bridgeford). Key guidelines include explicit performance standards and direct observation as the basis of evaluation. The chief pitfall to avoid is allowing personal characteristics of students and other unrelated factors to influence the assessment.

(d) Experimental Design

The classic research model for studying human behavior has been the experimental design. When applied to education, the intent is usually to test for effects of subject content, teaching technique or some other instructional or programmatic intervention (Byrnes & Kiger, 1988; Cottrell & St. Pierre, 1983; Serdahely, 1980; Yarber & Anno, 1981). This approach can best be used at classroom-specific and program-specific levels of assessment, where educationally and ethically students can be randomly assigned to different "treatments" or treatment levels (or educational experiences) designed to promote particular valued behavioral or performance outcomes. The usefulness of the resulting information can be increased by the accumulation of longitudinal data from "experiments" used with specific classroom or program treatments. Areas of emerging concern to colleges and universities hold promise for the use of experimental design: drug education, sexual behavior, health/wellness, sensitivity to racial differences, and knowledge about and use of the campus resources and environment (often a focus of new-student orientation programs).

(e) Student Follow-up and Employer Satisfaction

Many outcomes require data after students leave the institution and are related to further educational performance, job performance, and behavioral manifestations of general education outcomes judged as important (e.g., leadership, moral development, citizenship). Student self-reporting as part of alumni surveys has been a primary means for documenting the outcomes of postsecondary education. Pace (1979) offered an extensive review of the history of efforts in this area. Bowen (1977) provided one of the most comprehensive reviews of evidence of the effects of higher education on students using data from government surveys of the general population (i.e., the census) and national surveys by polling agencies. The effects of the college experience on students are organized into the following categories (see chapters 5 and 6 of Bowen):

> *General traits of value in practical affairs:*
> * *Need for achievement*
> * *Future orientation (planning ahead, saving, deferring gratification, prudently taking risks)*
> * *Adaptability (being receptive to change)*
> * *Leadership*
> * *Citizenship*
> * *Attitudes*
> * *Interest/involvement in political affairs*
> * *Information on public affairs*
> * *Party affiliation*
> * *Voting*
> * *Community participation*
> * *Crime*
> * *Economic Productivity*
> * *Quantity of product*
> * *Quality of product*
> * *Kinds of products (high/low value)*
> * *Labor force participation*
> * *Versatility-mobility*
> * *Job satisfaction*
>
> *The Family*
> * *Sex roles*
> * *Marriage*
> * *Divorce*
> * *Family planning*
> * *Rearing of children*
>
> *Consumer Behavior*
> * *Allocation of consumer expenditures*
> * *Savings and investment*
> * *Ability to cope (dealing with red tape, asserting oneself)*
>
> *Leisure*
> * *How time is spent and amount of time for leisure*

Health
  * *Use of health services*
  * *Lifestyle related to health*
  * *Health status*

A major concern with the alumni or former-student survey approach in terms of assessment is the response rate, which determines to a great extent the perceived credibility of such studies by both internal and external constituencies. Since such studies deal with the total population, the concern is not with sampling or other methodological issues but with the response rate broken down by program or discipline and with the unknowns created by the nonrespondent population. The relevancy to faculty and policy makers will be determined primarily by their perception of an acceptable response rate, and thus, the only meaningful guideline for researchers is to strive for the highest response rate that can be obtained with the time and resources available.

One approach to the response-rate problem that is gaining favor across the nation and is specific to community colleges is cooperative interinstitutional projects involving data exchange. In Florida, Oregon, and other states, community colleges can match student records with employment security records maintained by the state (Walleri, 1990). This approach has produced match rates as high as 90% and provides information on the industry of employment and wages. A crosswalk between Classification of Instructional Programs (CIP) codes and the Standard Industrial Classification (SIC) system can be used to determine the rate at which students are employed within the field of their training. Cooperative efforts between community colleges and four-year institutions have focused on transfer rates and success in terms of community college students pursuing a bachelor's degree (Washington State Board for Community College Education, 1989).

Employer surveys offer yet another means of determining institutional effectiveness. Many institutions work regularly with business and industry with regard to training needs, cooperative work experiences, and placement. In terms of assessment, however, the issue is documentation. There are basically two approaches in surveying employers about their satisfaction with students' training or education and job performance. When the survey is tied to a specific student, as with employer surveys built from alumni survey results, care must be exercised to protect the student's confidentiality. In this case, student permission, gained through the alumni survey, for example, would be necessary. The drawback to this approach is that the employer population and response rate will be a function of the student response rate. The alternative is to survey the general population of employers known to employ graduates from the particular institution.

Change in behavior or performance using these approaches is noted across time, from one alumni or former-student group to the next. The change, however, may not be due to the college or program experience but rather to changes across time in characteristics of entering student populations. Thus, great caution must be taken in drawing causal inferences.

Other sources of information include the Student Right-to-Know and Campus Security Act of 1990, Carl D. Perkins Vocational and Applied Technology Education Act Amendments of 1990, and the Higher Education Act (HEA) amendments of 1992. These laws portend continued federal interest in having colleges and universities compile and publish student outcomes information. In the case of the Student Right-to-Know Act, the focus is on graduation rates. The vocational program review requirements of the Perkins Act are specifically tied to assessing student performance using "measurable objective criteria" (Public Law 101-392, Section 116), with the states required to develop evaluation plans designed to measure occupation-specific competencies. The HEA amendments of 1992 require the establishment of State Postsecondary Review Entities (SPRE) which will review Title IV eligible institutions under specified statutory provisions. It is anticipated that the SPREs will incorporate the assessment of student outcomes in their review standards.

(f) Data on the Use of the College Environment

Depending on how the student uses the college environment (including course taking patterns, influences or contributes to desired student outcomes), information about such use can complement the direct assessment of outcomes. In addition, use of the environment, such as the library, may be the desired student outcome that is used as an indicator of institutional effectiveness. An instrument designed to assess student use of the college environment is the College Student Experiences Questionnaire (CSQ), designed by C. Robert Pace (1986, 1989, 1990). A community college version of the questionnaire is also available (Friedlander, Murrell and MacDougall, 1993). The questionnaire asks students to report the frequency with which they have done different kinds of things while in attendance at the institution. Categories include use of classrooms, the library, facilities related to the arts, and the student union; experiences with faculty; experiences in writing; and topics of conversation. The ten resulting scales include items that indicate "difficulty," from low to high, also called "quality of effort."

Institutional effectiveness, then, can be assessed across time by observing students' behavior as they use the college environment. To the extent that their quality of effort promotes desired student outcomes, direct assessment of their use of the social, psychological, and physical environment can provide useful information about institutional effectiveness.

Another source of data on the use of the college environment is course taking patterns. Some recent research has demonstrated an association between groups of courses taken by students and improvements in student learning. The "coursework cluster analysis model" has been developed and used to analyze student transcripts for relationships between general areas of student learning and course taking patterns (Ratliff, 1992). When these relationships can be established locally, information on course taking patterns alone can become indicators of improved student learning and also of institutional effectiveness.

(g) Product and Observable Performance Assessment

Direct assessment of products and performance, or what is increasingly being called "authentic" assessment, typically involves one or more raters or judges describing the qualities of either a product (e.g., an essay, an architectural plan, a play, a movie) or a performance (e.g., a dance, a character portrayal in a play, a role play in a class, the process of replacing a transmission, the development of a participatory decision-making process in a small group). This approach to assessment can apply at the course, program, or institutional level. The special case of the Assessment Center is described in the following section.

Three important stages are involved in using the direct observation approach to assessing products and performances. First, the criteria to be used by the raters or judges must be identified and clearly specified. The development of the criteria might involve faculty as well as practitioners from the field who employ and supervise graduates of the program or institution. For instance, in rating a play, what qualities should be included? Specifically, what technical qualities should be reviewed? What artistic or creative qualities? Which are the qualities this particular program attempts to develop? For particular technical and professional fields, standards of performance may already exist and may be used as part of certification and licensing processes. For instance, international quality standards are beginning to have an impact on U.S. institutions as a consequence of requirements for conducting business with the European Community after 1992 (Johnson, 1990). The quality management standards of the International Standards Organization are similar to the student performance and employer satisfaction measures discussed here.

Examples will most likely be needed to clarify further what the specified criteria mean. For instance, in the case of an essay, if "persuasive" is a valued quality, what are some of the specific devices a student might use (that could be identified by a reviewer) to argue a particular position persuasively? In playing a character in a play, how might the rater or judge note the extent to which the performance was "convincing" or "well paced"?

Second, the raters or judges must be selected and provided the opportunity in advance to practice using the criteria to rate or judge a product or performance using rating scales, behavioral observation scales, checklists, the critical-incidence technique, and so on. Third, the level of inter-rater reliability should be determined and every effort made to increase such reliability. For a readable discussion of these issues, see Carroll and Schneier (1982), regarding performance appraisal techniques designed for on-the-job situations; chapters 7 and 8 in Worthen and Sanders (1987), for a discussion of performance standards and consumer- and expertise-oriented evaluation approaches; and Berk (1986), for a description of a wide variety of performance assessment methods and applications.

An alternative to the direct observation and rating of a product or performance is the use of paper-and-pencil instruments or interview schedules that ask the respondent questions designed to assess performance indirectly. For instance, in the field of educational administration many instruments of this kind are available (Arter, 1988). Critical issues here are the reliability and validity of the instrument or interview process. Evidence on each should be reviewed before adoption.

(h) The Assessment Center

An assessment center is a support service that is separate from or external to the ongoing instructional process. The assessment center approach used by Alverno College (1979) is a special case of an institution's commitment to the use of multiple assessment techniques designed to document as well as promote the desired and valued learning. Many of the assessments are not paper-and-pencil tests and would fall in the category of behavioral, product-and-performance assessment strategies. The Alverno curriculum seeks to promote growth of the following eight general abilities: effective communication, analysis, problem solving, valuing in a decision-making context, effective social interaction, effectiveness in individual-environment relationships, responsible involvement in the contemporary world, and aesthetic responsiveness. Each student must demonstrate competence at six levels in each of these abilities.

The assessment center approach has earlier origins in business and industry (Thornton & Byham, 1982). Commonly used assessment techniques include the following (Moses, 1979, p. 4): "group exercises, business games, in-basket exercises, pencil-and-paper tests, and interviews. They may also include specially designed role-playing problems, phone calls, or simulated interviews."

Another example of this approach is the Assessment Center program of the National Association of Secondary School Principals. The program involves a two-day assessment of performance, involving six to eight exercises (e.g., leadership group exercises, in-basket exercises involving simulations of decision-making situations, fact-finding exercises, structured interviews). Assessors are trained over a four-day period. Currently, 47 centers are operating in 35 states. Prospective principals are the primary audience for the center experience. According to Moses (1977), successful centers, compared with less successful ones, involve assessors who are quite familiar with the job or duties they are assessing; use simulation exercises more than paper-and-pencil tests; and make predictions about "specific outcomes rather than ...personality traits or individual characteristics."

For a concise, thoughtful discussion of assessment in professional education that describes and advocates the use of performance approaches (e.g., simulations, role plays, case study analyses, videotaped exercises, and auditing and feedback) of a master's level curriculum of the American Management Association, see Elman and Lynton (1985). Another useful treatment of the approach, with a focus on teacher education, is provided by Millward (1993).

(i) Naturalistic and Qualitative Approaches

Naturalistic (i.e., observing behavior in field or "natural" settings) and qualitative (i.e., nonnumerical treatment of data) approaches to assessing behavioral change and performance are especially appropriate if a goal is to understand or illuminate what is taking place or has taken place and the meaning those involved in the experience give to it. Included in these categories of approaches are ethnographic field studies, case studies, participant observation, the use of critical incidence logs, the keeping of journals or diaries, and the use of open-ended questions in interviews and surveys.

The use of full-blown ethnographic field studies and case studies as primary assessment strategies will most likely be limited due to time and personnel resource constraints. They can, however, provide rich information about student development and the role of the institution or program in such development. Classic studies such as the following provide illustrations of these approaches: Heath (1965), *The Reasonable Adventurer: The Development of Thirty-Six Undergraduates at Princeton*; Becker et al. (1961), *Boys in White: Student Culture in a Medical School*; and Clark (1960), "The Cooling-Out Function in Higher Education," a study conducted at a community college.

The use of the other less elaborate approaches, however, is more likely. One important goal of these approaches is to prepare descriptive accounts or portrayals of the behaviors occurring in a natural setting or settings. The goal is to do more than simply document behavior; it is to increase our understanding about the how and why of such behaviors and what meaning they have to the individuals exhibiting them.

Fundamental to these methods is the assumption that as individuals we see the world differently and ascribe to experiences our own socially constructed reality. We make our own meanings. In simpler language, this means that what I do and what you do may look the same and be coded the same by an outside researcher or evaluator. Each of us, however, may ascribe to the behavior a very different meaning. Take the example of two individuals who have a consistent record of not voting in national elections. If we use voting record as one indicator of strength of citizenship, then both are measured low. Interviews might suggest a different conclusion. Imagine that one says she just doesn't have time to be involved in politics and really doesn't keep up on the issues. The other says she believes there really is no choice offered, that her decision not to vote is a political statement, and that she works instead with special interest groups to bring about change in the society. Wh… …ates greater "citizenship"? The point being made … …m ethnographic and case studies, can ill… …having, the actor, helps the observer int…

…development and use of these approa… …ve are being underutilized. Not all of th… …resources (e.g., the use of diaries, critic… …of open-ended survey data). Good resou… …Guba and Lincoln (1981), *Effective E*… …*aphy and Qualitative Design in Educa*… …et al. (1966), *Unobtrusive Measures*; … …ardson (1965), *Interviewing: Its Form a*…

(j) Class…

K. Patrici… …h National Conference (held in Berkele… …one of the authors), referred to the "thre… …de accountability (what the public has … …the institution contributes) and classroo… …w an individual classroom makes a dif… …ment must be more than classroom assessment, but that institutional assessment without classroom assessment will be too sterile and involve too few faculty. The assumption is that without significant faculty involvement, efforts to improve student learning in desired directions will likely be ineffective.

Much of the literature currently available about classroom assessment focuses on assessing specific cognitive skills and performance, and so is included in this resource section. Cross and Angelo (1988, p. 1) define classroom research as follows:

> We believe that classroom teachers can, through close observation, collection of feedback on student learning, and design of experiments, learn more about how students learn, and more specifically, how students respond to particular teaching approaches. We call this process of involving teachers in the formal study of teaching and learning *classroom research*.

We would add that, unlike some forms of assessment (for instance, that which is conducted to certify performance), classroom research is not punitive. The sole purpose is to help students to learn better and teachers to teach better.

In their search for and selection of classroom assessment techniques, Cross and Angelo (1988, p. 4) used the following questions as a guide:

1. Will the assessment technique provide information about what students are learning in individual classrooms?
2. Does the technique focus on "alterable variables"—aspects of teacher or learner behavior that can be changed to promote better learning?
3. Will it give teachers and students information they can use to make mid-course changes and corrections?
4. Is the assessment technique relatively simple to prepare and use?
5. Are the results from the use of the technique relatively quick and easy to analyze?

Their expanded second edition (Angelo and Cross, 1993) includes descriptions of 50 different techniques for assessing academic skills and knowledge, assessing students' self-awareness and self-assessment of learning skills, and assessing student reactions to teaching and courses, and more. The techniques reflect current thinking about cognition, ways to obtain feedback on what is happening to students cognitively (e.g., critical thinking, skill in analysis, creative thinking, and skill with synthesis), and adults as learners.

We believe that attention to practices in classroom assessment will continue to increase in pursuit of the goal of improving institutional effectiveness. For examples of classroom assessment activities taking place at a variety of colleges and universities, see *Classroom Research Project, Conference Proceedings* (1990).

A Perspective on the Future

Before closing this section, the authors are compelled to share their perspective on the future of outcomes assessment and institutional effectiveness. This perspective calls for equal attention by the assessment movement to behavioral and performance measures of outcomes **and** of institutional processes that limit or promote the desired outcomes. Dewey (1944, p. 19) said:

> We never educate directly, but indirectly by means of the environment. Whether we permit chance environments to do the work, or whether we design environments for the purpose makes a great difference. And any environment is a chance environment so far as its educative influence is concerned unless it has been deliberately regulated with reference to its educative effect.

As a result of this perspective, we offer three recommendations:

First, to promote student growth and development in our institutions, we must look beyond measures of behavior and performance of students to include measures of behavior and performance of aspects of the institutional environment that may promote or hinder student learning and development. We might assess directly aspects of the environment such as faculty roles and behaviors, the clarity of expectations for student performance, and the opportunity structure as it functions to promote student leadership or peer and student-faculty interaction.

Second, we should seek not only to document and report change in behavior and performance but to promote it. The assessment processes used should themselves promote or facilitate learning while at the same time providing documentation that learning has occurred and/or that the college experience has had an effect. Experiencing or participating in the assessment process should add something positive to a student's education. When this is not the case, most likely the student will not be motivated to perform at his or her best. And, we question the ethics of asking students to do something for which there may be little or no individual educational benefit.

Third, we are convinced that constructs such as "motivation" and "involvement" in the educational experience are important variables that help to account for the kinds and direction of learning that is taking place among our students. These constructs should be assessed directly as indicators of institutional effectiveness in their own right.

This resource section has described a variety of strategies for assessing student behavior and performance as indicators of institutional effectiveness. Many behavioral and performance outcomes are ones that are highly valued, are subject to influence by institutions, and offer the opportunity for documenting some of the more far reaching effects of college on students. In addition, a focus on these kinds of measures highlights the need for more attention to psychomotor skills.

Those considering use of these strategies are advised to address a series of questions before diving in. Included are questions about the extent to which either behavioral data or direct appraisals of performance are relevant to assessing the valued outcomes; the specific behavioral manifestations of the valued cognitive, affective, or psychomotor outcomes sought; the unit of analysis; the time frame; criteria to be used in judging performance; and the time, resources, and expertise needed and available to adopt these approaches.

The specific assessment strategies reviewed included inventories and use of what is already available, student flow and tracking systems, psychomotor skill assessment, experimental design, student follow-up and employer satisfaction, use of the college environment, assessment of products and observable performance, the assessment center, naturalistic and qualitative approaches, and classroom assessment. Three recommendations are offered: (1) measure the behavior and performance of the institutional environment as well as the students, (2) promote change in behavior and performance through the students' experiences with assessment rather than conduct assessments solely to document behavior and performance, and (3) directly assess student motivation and involvement—key variables that are related to the kind and quality of student outcomes.

In conclusion, we challenge all those interested in improving our assessment practices, as they serve to improve institutional effectiveness, to develop instruments that help in assessing the extent to which higher education environments are designed and function to promote development. Also, we challenge our colleagues to develop and use simultaneously behavioral and performance measures of both environment and student.

References: Cited and Recommended

Arter, J. A. (1988). *Assessing Leadership and Managerial Behavior*. Portland, OR: Northwest Regional Educational Laboratory.

Alverno College Faculty (1979). *Assessment at Alverno College*. Milwaukee: Alverno College.

Astin, A. (1993). *What Matters in College?* San Francisco: Jossey-Bass, Inc.

Baird, L. (1988). Diverse and Subtle Arts: Assessing the Generic Outcomes of Higher Education. In C. Adelman (ed.), *Performance and Judgment: Essays on Principles and Practice in the Assessment of College Student Learning* (pp. 39-62). Washington, DC: U.S. Department of Education.

Becker, H. S., Geer, B., Hughes, E. C., and Strauss, A. L. (1961). *Boys in White: Student Culture in Medical School*. Chicago: University of Chicago Press.

Berk, R. A. (ed.). (1986). *Performance Assessment: Methods and Applications*. Baltimore, MD: Johns Hopkins University Press.

Black, L. C. (1993). Portfolio Assessment. In T. W. Banta and Associates, *Making a Difference: Outcomes of a Decade of Assessment in Higher Education* (pp. 139-150). San Francisco: Jossey-Bass.

Bowen, H. R. (1977). *Investment in Learning: The Individual and Social Value of Higher Education*. San Francisco: Jossey-Bass.

Byham, W. (1988). Using the Assessment Center Method to Measure Life Competencies. In C. Adelman (ed.), *Performance and Judgement: Essays on Principles and Practice in the Assessment of College Student Learning* (pp. 39-62). Washington, DC: U.S. Department of Education.

Byrnes, D., & Kiger, G. (1988, October 7). *Ethical and Pedagogical Issues in the Use of* Simulation Activities in the Classroom: Evaluating the "Blue Eyes-Brown Eyes" Prejudice *Simulation*. Paper presented at the annual meeting of the Northern Rocky Mountain Educational Research Association, Jackson, WY.

Carroll, S. J., & Schneier, C. E. (1982). *Performance Appraisal and Review Systems: The Identification, Measurement, and Development of Performance in Organizations*. Glenview, IL: Scott, Foresman.

Cascio, W. F. (1986). Technical and Mechanical Job Performance Appraisal. In R. A. Berk (ed.), *Performance Assessment: Methods and Applications* (pp. 361-375). Baltimore, MD: Johns Hopkins University Press.

Clark, B. (1960). The Cooling-Out Function in Higher Education. *American Journal of Sociology, 65*, 569-576.

Clarkson, Q., Neuburger, & Koroloff, N. (1977). A System for Establishing Evaluation Standards. *CEDR Quarterly*, Spring, pp. 17-19.

Classroom Research Project. (1990). Conference proceedings, university extension, University of California, Berkeley, 2223 Fulton St., Berkeley, CA 94720.

Commission on the Skills of the American Workforce. (1990). *America's Choice: High Skills or Low Wages!* Rochester, NY: National Center on Education and the Economy.

Conley, D. T. (1994). *Proficiency-Based Admission Standards Study* (PASS). Eugene, Oregon: Office of Academic Affairs, Oregon State System of Higher Education, P. O. Box 3175, Eugene, OR 97403.

Cottrell, R., & St. Pierre, R. (1983). Behavioral Outcomes Associated with HRA Use in a College Level Health Education Course Utilizing a Lifestyle Theme. *Health Education, 14*(7), pp. 29-33.

Cross, K. P. (1990, June 16). Collaborative Classroom Assessment. In *Proceedings of the First National Conference on Classroom Research.* Berkeley, CA: University of California-Berkeley Classroom Research Project and University of California Extension.

Cross, K. P., & Angelo, T. A. (1988). *Classroom Assessment Techniques: A Handbook for Faculty.* Ann Arbor, MI: National Center for Research to Improve Postsecondary Teaching and Learning.

Dewey, J. (1944). *Democracy and Education: An Introduction to the Philosophy of Education.* New York: Free Press. (Original work published 1916)

Elman, S. E., & Lynton, E. A. (1985, October 13-15). *Assessment in Professional Education.* Washington, DC: American Association of Higher Education. Paper prepared for AAHE under contract to the National Institute of Education for the National Conference on Assessment in Higher Education, Columbia, SC.

Ewell, P. (1987). Principles of Longitudinal Enrollment Analysis: Conducting Retention and Student Flow Studies. In J. Muffo & G. W. McLaughlin (eds.), *A Primer on Institutional Research* (pp. 1-19). Tallahassee, FL: Association for Institutional Research.

Friedlander, J., Murrell, P. H., and MacDougall, P. R. (1993). The Community College Student Experiences Questionnaire. In Banta, T. (ed.), *Making a Difference: Outcomes of a Decade of Assessment in Higher Education* (pp.196-210). San Francisco: Jossey- Bass, Inc.

Gerber, L. (1994). *A Study of Community College Instructional Stakeholder Attitudes Toward Student Outcome Goals.* Unpublished doctoral dissertation. Portland State University, Portland, Oregon.

Goetz, J. P., & LeCompte, M. D. (1984). *Ethnography and Qualitative Design in Educational Research.* Orlando, FL: Academic Press.

Goal 5 Work Group (1993). *Reaching the Goals: Goal 5.* Washington, DC: Office of Educational Research and Improvement, U.S. Department of Education.

Grandy, J. (1988). Assessing Changes in Student Values. In C. Adelman (ed.), *Performance and Judgment: Essays on Principles and Practice in the Assessment of College Student Learning* (pp. 139-162). Washington, DC: U.S. Department of Education.

Guba, E. G., & Lincoln, Y. S. (1981). *Effective Evaluation.* San Francisco: Jossey-Bass.

Harris, J. (1985). *Assessing Outcomes in Higher Education: Practical Suggestions for Getting Started.* Washington, DC: American Association of Higher Education. Paper prepared for AAHE under contract to the National Institute of Education for the National Conference on Assessment in Higher Education, October 13-15.

Heath, R. (1964). *The Reasonable Adventurer: A Study of the Development of Thirty-Six Undergraduates at Princeton.* Pittsburgh, PA: University of Pittsburgh Press.

Johnson, F. (1990, May 13-16). *Quality Measurements for Postsecondary Technical and Vocational Education.* Paper presented at the annual forum for the Association for Institutional Research, Louisville, KY.

Lenning, O. (1977). *Previous Attempts to Structure Educational Outcomes and Outcome-Related Concepts: A Compilation and Review of the Literature.* Boulder, CO: National Center for Higher Education Management Systems.

Lenning, O. (1988). Use of Noncognitive Measures in Assessment. In T. Banta (ed.), Implementing Outcomes Assessment: Promise and Perils (pp. 41-52). *New Directions for Institutional Research, 59*(3). San Francisco: Jossey-Bass.

McCracken, G. D. (1988). *The Long Interview.* Newberry Park, CA: Sage.

Millward, R. F. (1993). Assessment Centers. In T. Banta (ed.), *Making a Difference: Outcomes of a Decade of Assessment in Higher Education,* (pp.231-243). San Francisco: Jossey-Bass, Inc.

Moses, J. L. (1977). The Assessment Center Method. In J. L. Moses & W. C. Byham (eds.) *Applying the Assessment Center Method.* New York: Pergamon.

National Center for Research in Vocational Education. (1990). *The 1990 Agenda for the National Center for Research in Vocational Education*. Berkeley, CA: University of California-Berkeley.

Oregon Department of Education (1993). *Restructuring Professional Technical Education in Oregon: The Perkins Perspective*. Salem, OR: Office of Professional Technical Education.

Pace, C. R. (1979). *Measuring Outcomes of College*. San Francisco: Jossey-Bass.

Pace, C. R. (1986). *Measuring the Quality of College Student Experiences*. Los Angeles: Higher Education Research Institute, Graduate School of Education, University of California-Los Angeles.

Pace, C. R. (1989). *The Undergraduates: A Report of their Activities and Programs in College in the 1990s*. Los Angeles: Center for the Study of Education, University of California, Los Angeles.

Pace, C. R. (1990). *College Student Experiences Questionnaire*. Los Angeles: Higher Education Research Institute, Graduate School of Education, University of California-Los Angeles.

Palmer, J. C. (1993). *Student Outcomes Data at the Community College*. Washington, DC: National Center for Academic Achievement and Transfer, Working Papers 4(1).

Pascarella, E. T., and Terenzini, P. T. (1991). *How College Affects Students*. San Francisco: Jossey-Bass, Inc.

Ratliff, J. (1992). Assessment and Curriculum Reform. *New Directions in Higher Education*, *80*. San Francisco: Jossey-Bass, Inc.

Richardson, R., Jr. (1990). Strategies for Serving Underprepared Students. *Leadership Abstracts*, *3*(8).

Richardson, S. A., Dohrenwend, B. S., & Klein, D. (1965). *Interviewing: Its Function and Form*. New York: Basic Books.

Secretary's Commission on Achieving Necessary Skills (1991). *Skills, What Work Requires of Schools: A SCANS Report for America 2000*. Washington, DC: U.S. Department of Labor.

Serdahely, W. (1980). A Factual Approach to Drug Education and its Effects on Drug Consumption. *Journal of Alcohol and Drug Education*, *26*(1), 63-68.

Stiggins, R. J., & Bridgeford, N. J. (1986). Student Evaluation. In R. A. Berk (ed.), *Performance Assessment: Methods and Applications*. Baltimore, MD: Johns Hopkins University Press.

Terenzini, P. T. (1987). Studying Student Attrition and Retention. In J. Muffo & G. W. McLaughlin (eds.), *A Primer on Institutional Research* (pp. 20-35). Tallahassee, FL: Association for Institutional Research.

Thornton III, G. C., & Byham, W. C. (1982). *Assessment Centers and Managerial Performance*. New York: Academic Press.

Washington State Board for Community College Education. (1989). *A Study of the Role of Community Colleges in the Achievement of the Bachelor's Degree in Washington State*. Olympia, WA: Author.

Webb, E. J., Campbell, D. T., Schwartz, R. D., & Sechrest, L. (1966). *Unobtrusive Measures: Nonreactive Research in the Social Sciences*. Chicago: Rand McNally.

Worthen, B. R., & Sanders, J. R. (1987). *Educational Evaluation*. New York: Longman.

Yarber, W., & Anno, T. (1981). Changes in Sex Guilt, Premarital Sexual Intimacy Attitudes and Sexual Behavior During a Human Sexuality Course. *Health Education*, *12*(5), 71-81.

Yin, R. (1984). *Case Study Research*. Beverly Hills, CA: Sage.

Assessment Related Information from Institutional Data Systems

Bobby Sharp and Sheri Blessing

> Whenever possible, methods of assessment should be based on existing information. …Such attention to existing data will be both educationally and economically efficient (*NASULGC Statement of Principles*, 1988).

Institutions of higher learning routinely maintain and report vast amounts of information about themselves. This occurs if for no other reason than to comply with reporting requirements of governmental and accrediting agencies. Yet this source of assessment information may be overlooked as institutions focus attention on innovative ways to demonstrate their effectiveness. As ascertained during the "Initial Inventory and Evaluation of Assessment Procedures" phase mentioned earlier, useful indicators of institutional effectiveness already may be available from institutions' existing information systems. Such institutional data can serve as critical evidence offered by institutions regarding their effectiveness.

This resource section is predicated on a basic assumption that is emphasized throughout this publication and depicted graphically in Figures 3 and 5 (pp. 18 and 26):

> For existing institutional systems to contribute meaningfully to outcomes assessment, their products must be fundamentally linked to appropriate statements of purpose by the institution and its various units.

Taken alone, institutional data are of little, if any, value as evidence of institutional effectiveness. The meaningfulness of existing institutional data derives directly from focusing them as information on specific statements of intentions that have been composed within the whole system of institutionaleffectiveness and assessment activities. The mere ability to generate impressive reports is of secondary importance to their appropriateness in helping an institution tell whether it is accomplishing its stated goals. Institutional data generated to support institutional effectiveness must relate to intended educational, research, and service outcomes and administrative objectives established by the institution.

Purpose of the Resource Section

The purposes of this resource section are:

1. To review currently maintained institutional data that may be used as indicators of institutional effectiveness;
2. To critique limitations of typical institutions' information systems when called on to support outcomes assessment; and,
3. To suggest ways for increasing the value of information systems to assessment activities.

The components of this resource section are represented graphically in Figure 8. Institutional information systems exist in some form at all institutions of higher learning. Statements of purpose serve as screens through which these data are filtered to produce information for use in assessment efforts. In this way relevant parts of the considerable amount of institutional data will become focused and useful in assessing institutional effectiveness.

Throughout this resource section it is assumed that no two institutional data or reporting systems are alike, even when the same commercially available database and report-writing software are used. Unique institutional policies and procedures have resulted in quite diverse data-maintenance and data-reporting systems.

Keeping this variety of institutional data systems in mind, an additional objective of this resource section is to stimulate individuals involved in assessing institutional effectiveness to (1) recognize the potential usefulness of existing data and reports, and (2) evaluate the capabilities of their own institutions' information systems to contribute to the assessment process. In some cases, modifications to the systems may be needed to address inadequacies and make them more useful to institutional assessment efforts.

Institutional Information Systems

For the purposes of this discussion, information systems refers to the collection of databases, formatted reports, and interactive inquiry tools available within an institution. How these are administered varies widely with institutions, from highly centralized to decentralized. Most reflect the primary types of activities or processes they were designed to support. Some common systems are described here.

(a) Operational Support Systems

Routine but complicated institutional activities such as registering students, collecting and recording student fee payments, maintaining accurate student records, and meeting faculty and staff payrolls have been quite suited to automation with the use of computers. These data systems obviously provide valuable support to institutions in carrying out essential operations. However, the initial implementation of these data systems was largely to support the many transactions that routinely occur within institutions rather than to provide easily accessed, aggregated information to high-level policymakers. They were developed with the processing of student, staff, and financial records in mind.

For that reason, their usefulness to institutional effectiveness and outcomes assessment may be limited to those stated purposes or objectives that pertain to operating procedures

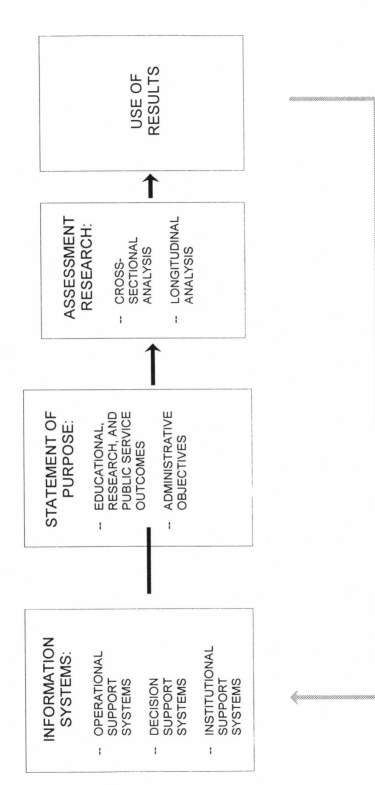

Figure 8

ASSESSMENT USING INSTITUTIONAL INFORMATION SYSTEMS

and practices by selected offices or departments. Examples of how transactional data systems can be focused on administrative goal statements are as follows:

1. Financial and budgetary units may use revenue and expenditure data to focus on administrative objectives related to effective budget control, accounting practices, and financial reporting.
2. A Registrar's Office may use course registration data to focus on objectives related to the mechanics of the registration process, the prompt production of class rolls, or the timely release of student grades.
3. An Office of Financial Aid may use financial aid data to focus on objectives related to the timeliness and fairness of financial aid awards.

(b) Decision Support Systems

Traditional data systems also offer information that is used in administrative decisions and policy setting. On many campuses, data elements are added to operational support systems in order to provide information used by top-level administrators. With the availability of sophisticated "executive information systems" (EIS), "executive support systems" (ESS), and "decision support systems" (DSS), attention is being drawn to the development of information systems specifically to provide readily accessible information on multiple levels of aggregation. One recent edition of *New Directions for Institutional Research* was devoted to developing such systems (Glover & Krotseng, 1993).

Decision support data systems have most often been developed in such policy areas as:

1. Admissions and institutional marketing dynamics;
2. Student graduation and attrition;
3. Faculty hiring practices;
4. Faculty workload and productivity measures;
5. Faculty salary summaries;
6. Space utilization rates;
7. Course and program offerings;
8. Academic and support services (e.g., library holdings); and,
9. Sponsored research values.

The importance of such data to administrators in setting policy cannot be overemphasized. This has been confirmed by El-Khawas's (1986, 1987, 1988, 1989, 1990, 1991, 1992) annual *Campus Trends*. The vast majority of those administrators responding to the American Council on Education surveys on practices in higher education included many of those data as appropriate measures of institutional effectiveness.

For decision support data to be of value as indicators of institutional effectiveness, however, they must be focused on articulated statements of objectives or expected outcomes. For example, graduation rates after four years, an indicator of institutional effectiveness frequently used by senior institutions, have meaning only when assessing intended educational outcomes that pertain to students completing degree requirements. When appropriately applied, decision support data may provide key information about the extent to which various policies (e.g., intervention efforts with high-risk students) implemented throughout the campus are successful.

(c) Institutional Reporting Systems—Federal

Data to support the assessment of many institutional objectives may be available in the various reports routinely submitted to federal agencies. Once part of the Higher Education General Information Surveys (HEGIS) system of reports, one set of reports is collected under the aegis of the Integrated Postsecondary Education Data System (IPEDS). The purpose of IPEDS reporting has been to obtain information about institutions— who attends them and who completes degree programs at them, what degree programs are offered, and what human and financial resources are used in providing higher education services. In addition to IPEDS reports, other reports have been routinely submitted to various federal agencies such as the Office of Civil Rights (OCR), the Office of Vocational and Adult Education (OVAE), the Office of Postsecondary Education (OPE), and the Equal Employment Opportunity Commission (EEOC).

On many campuses several offices have shared responsibilities for submitting the IPEDS and other federal reports. Thus, one of the first tasks may be to assemble copies of these reports into a complete set for use in the assessment effort. These reports contain a considerable amount of information on students, faculty, and finances, and taken together, represent a rich historical data source for use in an institutional effectiveness program. In addition, these reports represent a concerted effort to adhere, over time, to consistent and standard data definitions. This effort adds credibility to the information contained in these reports.

The specificity of these reports necessitates carefully applying the data contained within them. In reporting degrees awarded, for instance, the levels of disaggregation reach to the six-digit Classification of Instructional Programs (CIP) level by gender of the degree recipient. Enrollment is typically disaggregated by CIP, by level of the program, by racial/ethnic status, and by gender. Faculty salaries are usually reported by rank, by gender, and by tenure status. Library loan transactions are reported by type of collection. Clearly, such detail has meaning only to the extent that it is focused on intended educational, research, or service outcomes. When particular institutional objectives are articulated in ways that allow for direct linkages between the objectives and the information reported to the federal agencies, these reports are ready-made sources of evidence of institutional effectiveness.

(d) Institutional Reporting Systems—State and Multi-Institution

To supplement the reports submitted to federal agencies, state and system agencies often require their own data reports. These reports should also be assembled and reviewed for their usefulness to the assessment program. These reports, like those submitted to IPEDS, typically have been developed through thought and deliberation, lending credibility to their contents.

• An increasing number of states are mandating state-level assessment reporting.
  Ewell, Finney, and Lenth (1990) indicated that 27 of the 48 states that responded to

a survey "report having in place an identifiable 'assessment initiative' consisting of legislation or board policy" (p. 4), and another six states provide incentives for assessment efforts.

Indicators included in state-mandated assessment reports vary widely and include such standard reporting elements as academic preparation of enrolling students, enrollment in academic programs, demographic diversity, retention rates, graduation rates, faculty credentials, public service, and other similar measures. In addition, other measures of student achievement include reporting licensing and certification exam performance, job placement data, alumni follow-up studies, and external program evaluation results. Institutions located in states that require various assessment-related data obviously may incorporate the state-mandated reports into the overall institutional assessment program. The design and implementation of the institutional assessment effort can allow for both meeting the state mandate and utilizing the data within the institution's own planning process.

(e) Institutional Reporting Systems—Internal

Another source for decision support information that may be useful to a program of institutional assessment includes the myriad of both routine and ad hoc studies and reports produced within every institution. These studies range widely and include such subjects as admissions practices (e.g., rates of applications, acceptances, and matriculation), graduation rates, affirmative action practices (e.g., hiring, promoting, and terminating practices), faculty flows, and faculty salaries. As expected of internal studies, the level of sophistication and the usefulness of these reports vary. Nevertheless, part of the inventory of assessment procedures phase should involve compiling an inventory of the federal, state, and any additional reports and internal studies available. A detailed look at the different definitions or procedures of these reports and studies is necessary to apply these data to the assessment process. In some instances, reconciling incongruous figures may be required.

Orientation of Information Systems

(a) Cross-Sectional Orientation

Despite the vast amount of data maintained and reported by institutions, many data systems have an inherent weakness when called on to support outcomes assessment. That weakness is the cross-sectional orientation of data elements and report formats within those data systems.

Institutional "census files," from which many of the reports mentioned thus far are generated, typically represent snapshots of institutional databases. Because these databases constantly change as fields of data are overwritten with "updates," the snapshots show the contents of the files at an instant in time. For most institutions, these snapshots become the historical record for each reporting period and represent the institutional condition at a given point in time.

Since outcomes assessment examines change over time, cross-sectional studies alone will be inadequate. The practice of inferring change from cross-sectional studies is, of course, common among researchers. For example, in a given semester the distribution of freshmen across an institution's programs of study may differ significantly from the distribution shown by seniors. Institutional effectiveness goals related to institutional and program retention may be addressed in part by comparing these distributions. Further research questions may be suggested from such an examination. However, this analysis is limited in scope due to other possible explanations for observed differences between or among the subgroups.

(b) Longitudinal Orientation

One way to overcome the limitations of cross-sectional analyses is to use census files to study changes over time by comparing measures across multiple time periods. Like cross-sectional analyses, the composition of the subpopulations change from point-to-point measures, but unlike cross-sectional analyses, trend studies or time-series studies look at changes across successive time periods. A common example is the comparison made in admissions acceptance and yield rates over consecutive years. Another example is a multiyear comparison of average salaries for various subpopulations of faculty. In both examples, relative differences and trends are identifiable through comparing cross-sectional snapshots across time. Quite useful indicators of institutional effectiveness may be readily available through this method.

Such analyses, however, are based on comparisons of different populations or subpopulations at different points in time. They do not track individuals' experiences or responses over time. Outcomes assessment requires at least some analyses that allow for that type of study. These analyses, commonly referred to as panel studies, follow a group of individuals (i.e., the panel) across multiple reporting periods.

Panel analysis is particularly suited to student data. Progress of individuals through their educational programs can best be shown when various measures of their performance are collected and maintained across successive time periods. Built-in referents for measuring progress or change then exist. Traditional data systems thus may require modification or supplementation in order to provide the longitudinal orientation crucial to outcomes assessment.

Along with developing the capability of data systems to support longitudinal orientations, analysts must develop proficiency in handling these data and in applying appropriate research methods to them. For example, thoroughly understanding experimental design may be necessary. Or, interpreting panel attrition's effect on the generalizability of the findings, a typical problem for researchers using panel data, may require new research skills. Procedures used to analyze panel data, such as repeated-measures analysis, are not as well known to researchers as are other research techniques. This will mean that the development of unfamiliar, specialized research skills may be necessary at many institutions.

(c) Data Elements Supportive of Outcomes Assessment

The particular data elements used to support outcomes assessment necessarily will depend on an institution's assessment program. However, for most institutions there are at a minimum two types of data elements that can be maintained and will be required for either cross-sectional or longitudinal studies:

1. **Demographic data elements**—These typically will come from admissions data files and may not change throughout the tracking period. Included here are such variables as the following:
    a. Student identifier;
    b. Birth date;
    c. Race;
    d. Sex;
    e. Entrance test scores;
    f. High school grades;
    g. High school rank;
    h. Household socioeconomic status;
    i. Prior institution(s) attended;
    j. Prior degree(s) earned;
    k. Proposed major and degree; and,
    l. Predicted college success measures (e.g., predicted grade point average).

These data elements both broaden the scope of outcomes analysis and offer referents against which progress may be measured.

2. **Academic progress data elements**—"Term" files usually provide most of these data elements. That is, these data elements are term specific, varying from one term to the next. Examples of these data elements include the following:
    a. Declared major each semester;
    b. Financial aid and tuition status each semester;
    c. Current semester course-taking data (e.g., number, name, section, credit hours, grade);
    d. Semester and cumulative grade point average (GPA) or quality points; and,
    e. Graduation data (e.g., date, major, degree), when available.

These data elements allow the tracking of academic performance by term or by year, if preferred. Among questions answered by this collection of data elements are those related to the history of program demand as well as the calculation of retention/attrition and graduation rates. Data are then available to assess the progress of an entire cohort, a subgroup, or even an individual student.

Most institutional data systems are fairly well equipped to provide the demographic and academic process data elements just identified. The primary task is to extract them and assemble them into a longitudinally designed file. Various hardware and software tools are now available to facilitate that process.

A file developed with typically available institutional data, however, still will require supplemental measures important to demonstrating institutional effectiveness. Increasingly, institutions are collecting a considerable amount of data from attitudinal surveys and cognitive tests. Other sections of this chapter address the development and use of these instruments within outcomes assessment. The results of these surveys and tests may be used to demonstrate institutional effectiveness and should be incorporated and used along with those progress-type data elements previously listed. For example, responses to items in an entering freshmen survey can be compared to responses to items in other surveys administered both during students' enrollment and after they graduate from or otherwise leave an institution. These survey responses also can be related to current major, current GPA, or other measures captured in the file. Test performances at various times during students' enrollment also can be compared as measures of academic progress. To make such analyses possible, however, institutional data systems must contain these types of measures.

Using Institutional Data Systems in Assessment

How institutional data systems are used in outcomes assessment depends on several factors:

1. The extent to which data systems are automated will either limit or expand the opportunities for their use. During systematic outcomes assessment over time, a considerable amount of data will be collected for analysis. Sufficient and accessible automated storage will be essential. The capability of extracting data from institutional data systems is assumed. Powerful, easily used data analysis tools (e.g., statistical packages) will be necessities. Already limited computing facilities simply may be overburdened by extensive longitudinal data files, thereby constraining users of longitudinal data. As has been demonstrated by Ewell (1983; 1987a) and others, however, modest but quite effective longitudinal tracking files can be built using microcomputers with sufficient hard disk storage. Usually, though, mainframe computing support will be required.

2. As indicated in Chapter 1, the way assessment data will be used depends on the commitment of institutional leaders to the entire institutional effectiveness and outcomes assessment program. The best possible outcomes data will be of little use to an institution when appropriate outcomes questions have not been composed. To get the most use out of assessment data, institutions must have thoughtfully articulated why they are collecting it in the first place.

3. Potential users of assessment data must be taught how those data can be used. Thinking in terms of longitudinal data collection and analysis is still a relatively novel approach and is unfamiliar to many researchers. As a new way of measuring the effectiveness of all aspects of institutions, outcomes assessment data require the development of users. However, once involved in applying sound assessment practices, users will see benefits of this approach and explore new uses for the collected data.

Possible uses of institutional data systems in assessment are numerous. Many have been suggested and alluded to already in this resource section. Thus, those offered in the following section are but a few among many.

(a) Calculating Retention and Graduation Rates

In El-Khawas's (1986) report, 88% of those higher education administrators surveyed indicated that retention and graduation rates were appropriate measures of institutional effectiveness. Their appropriateness, as emphasized throughout this publication, depends on statements of institutional and departmental intentions that have been formulated. For most institutions, however, facilitating the successful progress of students through academic programs to graduation represents a fundamental purpose for their existence. Measuring the extent to which students persist to graduation thus may offer indications of how effectively institutions have accomplished one of their fundamental purposes.

Thorough analysis of retention and graduation rates can best be conducted by using a longitudinal-oriented data system. Then cohorts of students entering the enrollment "pipeline" can be followed as long as information on them is deemed important to the assessment program.

Questions about retention and graduation rates usually require disaggregation into subgroups. That is, it is one thing to know that a certain percentage of entering full-time freshmen will persist to graduation, but it is quite another to know retention and graduation rates of student subgroups and to be able to identify those that are relatively high risk and in need of special intervention programs. These disaggregated retention and graduation rates provide institutions with considerably more useful information in answering pertinent questions, such as:

1. For an entering freshmen cohort, how do retention and graduation rates differ among ethnic groups? among entry-level skill groupings?
2. How do retention and graduation rates differ among majors?
3. How do retention and graduation rates differ among ethnic groups within majors?
4. If there are differences that cause concern, how will the outcomes of strategies adopted to deal with the issue be measured?

The answers given to questions such as these may determine the success or failure of institutional effectiveness and assessment programs.

The questions posed in the preceding paragraph reemphasize the importance of having a carefully designed longitudinal data system. Systems that permit answering only the first or second question (i.e., regarding rates for ethnic groups, for certain entry-level skill groupings, or for majors), but not the third (i.e., rates for ethnic groups within majors), may be of limited help in identifying those individuals most in need of remediation and developmental programs. The extent of the disaggregation should be considered in conjunction with the levels of cross analysis anticipated.

(b) Comparing Successive Test Scores and Inventory Results

Some institutions have begun employing batteries of cognitive tests as part of their outcomes assessment. Institutions promoting a "value-added" concept of higher education, for example, must develop means to demonstrate that students perform better academically as a result of their educational experiences. One way to do this has been to require standardized test scores for students at different points in their educational experience. Thus, entering freshmen, rising juniors, and graduating seniors may be required to take standardized tests and have their scores maintained in longitudinal data systems.

Taken individually at one test point, these test scores offer little evidence of "value" having been "added." Compared over time, however, the results of the exams may indeed serve as measures of educational progress and may stimulate changes in such areas as curricula and course offerings. Studies comparing successive test scores may employ such statistical procedures as repeated-measures analysis to examine the data.

Along with cognitive tests, opinion and attitudinal surveys may be administered over successive time periods and may serve as useful indicators of educational progress. Differences in responses between the point of entry as freshmen and the point of exit as graduates can tell institutions how students perceive their own progress as related to the academic and support programs offered to them. The capacity to compare successive inventory results, though, presupposes some kind of longitudinal data system.

In comparing both cognitive test scores and inventory results over time, institutions should remember that the focus customarily is on **institutional effectiveness**, not individual student performance. The purpose of various tests and inventories administered to students is to assess the effectiveness of institutions and their subunits. Students do not pass or fail these instruments. Rather, their performances on these tests and inventories should be used by institutions as but one means among many for evaluating policies intended to enhance institutional effectiveness.

(c) Determining Course-Taking Patterns

A longitudinal data system that retains students' course enrollment histories also can provide useful information about educational progress. When considered along with other assessment indicators such as retention and graduation rates as well as cognitive test scores, the results obtained can be especially useful in several ways. For instance, information learned from relating graduating students' cognitive test scores to their course-taking patterns may help improve:

1. Curricular requirements/offerings;
2. Student advising programs;
3. Course offerings;
4. Faculty teaching assignments; and,
5. Space allocation.

Results of such an analysis thus range from happier, more successful students to improved use of institutional resources.

(d) Providing Inter-institutional Follow-up Information on Students

Among the data elements within longitudinal data systems that support outcomes assessment are those pertaining to activities of students following graduation. Over 80% of the administrators responding to El-Khawas's (1986) survey indicated that "honors and other achievements of recent graduates," "job placement rates of graduates, by field," and "graduates' performance on the job" each were appropriate measures of institutional effectiveness. Paulson (1990) found alumni follow-up studies to be a common assessment initiative within the states responding to the Education Commission of the States' survey. Mechanics of conducting alumni surveys can be found in various publications as well as in workshops offered by professional organizations. The subject is also treated in another resource section in this volume.

Along with follow-up studies of graduates, surveys of students who elect not to return to school can also reveal useful information. Institutions may find these students' evaluations of educational and associated programs to be one helpful means of assessing the effectiveness of those programs.

Equally important indicators of institutional effectiveness are an institution's graduates who successfully continue their education at other institutions; for example:

1. Two-year institutions whose missions include preparing students to complete their baccalaureate degrees at four-year institutions need to know how their graduates perform at the senior institutions;
2. Four-year institutions need to know how their baccalaureate graduates perform when they enroll in graduate programs; and,
3. Master's degree programs need to know how their graduates perform in doctoral degree programs.

To support outcomes assessment, institutions at all levels should prepare for providing "feeder" institutions and programs with follow-up information on their former students. Longitudinal data systems containing data elements for prior institutions attended and prior degrees obtained, along with current status and performance measures, will facilitate the interinstitutional cooperation required. Regular reports provided to feeder institutions can then become part of the longitudinal data systems supportive of those institutions' assessment programs.

The provision of such data to feeder institutions is authorized under USCS 1232g, Family Educational and Privacy Act. In that legislation, information other than "directory information," as defined in the act, may be released to "(F) Organizations conducting studies for, or on behalf of, educational agencies or institutions for the purpose of developing, validating, or administering predictive tests, administering student aid programs, and improving instruction, if such studies are conducted in such a manner as will not permit the personal identification of students and their parents by persons other than representatives of such organizations; and, such information will be destroyed when no longer needed for the purpose for which it is conducted; (G) Accrediting organizations in order to carry out their accrediting functions."

The release of student data to feeder institutions assumes the data will be used for "improving instruction," a component within the overall institutional effectiveness initiative. Further, the stipulations regarding use of the data and protecting the individual student's anonymity must be strictly enforced.

Responding to Federally Mandated Reporting

Two particular legislative actions by Congress place new demands on institutions to report certain types of information. This unprecedented accountability demanded by federal agencies requires that institutions develop appropriate databases and reporting systems.

First, in 1990 Congress passed the "Student Right-to-Know and Campus Security Act" (Public Law 101-542) amending the Higher Education Act of 1965. Title I of this legislation requires institutions of higher education receiving Federal financial assistance to provide information on graduation rates of both regular students and student athletes. Title II requires institutions to disclose campus security policies and statistics on a variety of reported crimes. Information under Title I first was made available beginning July 1, 1993, and under Title II beginning September 1, 1992, with both extending each year thereafter.

Title I of the Act calls for detailed reporting of graduation rates related to "potential institutional outcomes," and "with respect to athletically related student aid." This detail includes graduation rates broken down by programs of study and by academic divisions, licensure and certification pass rates, employment-in-field rates, and "other institutional outcomes that may be appropriate." It also requires information specifically about student athletes: numbers of students receiving athletically related student aid broken down by selected sports, average graduation rates also broken down by selected sports, by race, and by sex, and graduation rates for both non-student athletes and student athletes for the four most recent graduating classes. In an effort to collect and publish information that is "substantially comparable" to that required by the Act, the National Collegiate Athletic Association modified its reporting form, completed annually by member institutions, in order to collect appropriate information.

Second, in 1992 Congress reauthorized the Higher Education Act of 1965 with far ranging legislation entitled the "Higher Education Amendments of 1992" (Public Law 102-325). Part H, entitled "Program Integrity," amended Title IV of the Act of 1965 with specific and potentially onerous reporting requirements for institutions.

One provision under Part H requires that each state establish a State Postsecondary Review Entity (SPRE) to be responsible for the conduct and coordination of review criteria and standards specified in the legislation. Reviews of institutions may be triggered by excessive student loan default rates, by transfer of ownership, or by consumer complaints from students, faculty, and others. "Relevant" information specified by the Act in Section 494C that must be made available by institutions include: "the success of the program at the institution," including:

1. The rates of the institution's students' program completion and graduation, taking

into account the length of the program at the institution and the selectivity of the institution's admissions practices;

2. The withdrawal rates of the institution's students;
3. With respect to vocational and professional programs, the rates of placement of the institution graduates in occupations related to their course of study;
4. Where appropriate, the rate at which the institution's graduates pass licensure examinations; and
5. The variety of student completion goals, including transfer to another institution of higher education, full-time employment in the field of study, and military service."

Another provision under Part H defines the nature and role of accrediting agencies. Among the criteria for determining valid accrediting agencies is a list of twelve areas in which such agencies must establish standards of quality. These include an institution's "success with respect to student achievement in relation to its mission, including, as appropriate, consideration of course completion, State licensing examination, and job placement rates."

Proposed regulations implementing the Act specify and extend its provisions. The result is a substantial increase in federal activism with respect to institutional accountability and effectiveness. Whether or not an institution is susceptible to a SPRE review, which as of this writing is unfunded, the provisions of the legislation that pertain to accrediting agencies assures additional record keeping and reporting by institutions.

Summary

Successful efforts to assess institutional effectiveness must be supported by appropriate data systems. For most higher education institutions, a considerable amount of useful data already exists and requires cataloging and formatting into useful information. Examples of these data are the many federal, state, system, and internal reports regularly produced over many years. These existing reports may be a quite efficient and relatively inexpensive means of demonstrating institutional progress toward stated goals.

Many institutions, however, will find that their data systems lack a sufficiently longitudinal orientation to fully support their efforts to measure institutional effectiveness. Inherent in measuring institutional effectiveness is the capability for following the progress of individual students over time. Data systems must be configured to support longitudinal analyses relating academic programs to demographics, academic performance, personal development, and job placement. Information systems must guarantee that questions, raised as both internally prerogatives and externally mandates, related to institutional effectiveness can be answered with confidence.

The commitment of resources to adapt, supplement, or otherwise modify institutional information systems to support institutional effectiveness should be considered early in the institutional effectiveness initiative and reviewed periodically as new initiatives appear. It is very important that institutional information systems link directly to the institution's and departments' statements of intentions. This tie-in with the statements of outcomes gives institutional information systems their utility. When these systems are focused correctly on intended educational, research, and service outcomes and administrative objectives, expenditures to more fully utilize existing data may be among the most cost-effective actions that institutions can take.

References: Cited and Recommended

Banta, T. W. (ed.). (1988). Implementing Outcomes Assessment: Promise and Perils. *New Directions for Institutional Research, 59*(3). San Francisco: Jossey-Bass.

Berk, R. A. (ed.). (1986). *Performance Assessment: Methods and Applications*. Baltimore: Johns Hopkins University Press.

Criteria for Accreditation: Commission on Colleges. (1989-1990). Atlanta, GA: Southern Association of Colleges and Schools.

El-Khawas, E. (1986). *Campus Trends, 1986* (Higher Education Panel Report No. 73). Washington, DC: American Council on Education.

El-Khawas, E. (1987). *Campus Trends, 1987* (Higher Education Panel Report No. 75). Washington, DC: American Council on Education.

El-Khawas, E. (1988). *Campus Trends, 1988* (Higher Education Panel Report No. 77). Washington, DC: American Council on Education.

El-Khawas, E. (1989). *Campus Trends, 1989* (Higher Education Panel Report No. 78). Washington, DC: American Council on Education.

El-Khawas, E. (1990). *Campus Trends, 1990* (Higher Education Panel Report No. 80). Washington, DC: American Council on Education.

El-Khawas, E. (1991). *Campus Trends, 1991* (Higher Education Panel Report No. 81). Washington, DC: American Council on Education.

El-Khawas, E. (1992). *Campus Trends, 1992* (Higher Education Panel Report No. 82). Washington, DC: American Council on Education.

Ewell, P. T. (1983). *Information on Student Outcomes: How to Get It and How to Use It.* Boulder: National Center for Education Management Systems.

Ewell, P. T. (ed.). (1985). Assessing Educational Outcomes. *New Directions for Institutional Research, 47.* San Francisco: Jossey-Bass.

Ewell, P. T. (1987a). Establishing a Campus-Based Assessment Program. In D. F. Halpern (ed.), *Student Outcomes Assessment: What Institutions Stand to Gain* (pp. 9-24). New Directions in Higher Education, *59*(3). San Francisco: Jossey-Bass.

Ewell, P. T. (1987b). Principles of Longitudinal Enrollment Analysis: Conducting Retention and Student Flow Studies. In J. Muffo & G. W. McLaughlin (eds.), *A Primer on Institutional Research* (pp. 1-19). Tallahassee, FL: Association for Institutional Research.

Ewell, P. T. & Lisensky, R. P. (1988). *Assessing Institutional Effectiveness*. Washington: Consortium for the Advancement of Private Higher Education.

Ewell, P. T., Parker, R., & Jones, D. P. (1988). *Establishing a Longitudinal Student Tracking System: An Implementation Handbook*. Boulder: National Center for Education Management Systems.

Ewell, P. T., Finney, J., & Lenth, C. (1990). Filling in the Mosaic: The Emerging Pattern of State-Based Assessment. *AAHE Bulletin, XLII*(8), pp. 3-5.

Fendley, Jr., W. R. & Seeloff, L. (eds.). (1993). *Reference Sources: An Annotated Bibliography for Institutional Research*. Tallahassee, FL: Association for Institutional Research.

Frank, R. F. & Lesher, R. S. (1991). Planning for Executive Information Systems in Higher Education. *Cause/Effect, XIV*(3), pp. 31-39.

Glover, R. H. & Krotseng, M. V. (1993). Developing Executive Information Systems for Higher Education. *New Directions for Institutional Research, 77*(1). San Francisco: Jossey-Bass.

Gray, P. J. (ed.). (1989). Achieving Assessment Goals Using Evaluation Techniques. *New Directions in Higher Education*, *67*(3). San Francisco: Jossey-Bass.

Halpern, D. F. (ed.). (1987). Student Outcomes Assessment: What Institutions Stand to Gain. *New Directions in Higher Education*, *59*(3). San Francisco: Jossey-Bass.

Handbook of Accreditation, 1990-92. (1990). Chicago: North Central Association of Colleges and Schools; Commission on Institutions of Higher Education.

Harris, J. (1985). *Assessing Outcomes in Higher Education: Practical Suggestions for Getting Started.* Unpublished manuscript, David Lipscomb College, Nashville, TN.

Howard, R. D., Nichols, J. O., & Gracie, L. W. (1987). Institutional Research Support of the Self-Study. In J. Muffo & G. W. McLaughlin (eds.), *A Primer on Institutional Research* (pp. 79-88). Tallahassee, FL: Association for Institutional Research.

Kauffman, J. F. (1984). Assessing the Quality of Student Services. In R. A. Scott (ed.), Determining the Effectiveness of Campus Services (pp. 23-36). *New Directions in Institutional Research*, *41*(1). San Francisco: Jossey-Bass.

Keller, G. (1983). *Academic Strategy* (see especially pp. 131-133). Baltimore: Johns Hopkins University Press.

Klepper, W. M., Nelson, J. E., & Miller, T. E. (1987). The Role of Institutional Research in Retention. In M. M. Stodt & W. M. Klepper (eds.), Increasing Retention: Academic and Student Affairs Administration in Partnership (pp. 27-37). *New Directions in Higher Education*, *60*(4). San Francisco: Jossey-Bass.

Melchiori, G. S. (ed.). (1988). Alumni Research: Methods and Applications. *New Directions for Institutional Research*, *60*(4). San Francisco: Jossey-Bass.

Miller, R. I. (1981). Appraising Institutional Performance. In P. Jedamus, M. W. Peterson, & Associates (eds.), *Improving Academic Management* (pp.406-431). San Francisco: Jossey-Bass.

Mingle, J. R. (1985). *Measuring the Educational Achievement of Undergraduates: State and National Developments*. Unpublished manuscript, State Higher Educational Executive Officers, Denver.

Paulson, C. P. (1990). *State Initiatives in Assessment and Outcome Measurement: Tools for Teaching and Learning in the 1990s.* Denver: Education Commission of the States.

Resource Manual on Institutional Effectiveness. (1989). Atlanta, GA: Southern Association of Colleges and Schools.

Seldin, P. (1988). *Evaluating and Developing Administrative Performance*. San Francisco: Jossey-Bass.

Statement of Principles on Student Outcomes Assessment. (1988). Washington, DC: National Association of State Universities and Land Grant Colleges.

Terenzini, P. T. (1987). Studying Student Attrition and Retention. In J. Muffo & G. W. McLaughlin (eds.), *A Primer on Institutional Research* (pp. 79-88). Tallahassee, FL: Association for Institutional Research.

Assessment Planning

James O. Nichols

There are both extrinsic and intrinsic reasons for an institution to carefully plan its assessment program. As states or regions begin the assessment process, an institution may find itself required to submit an assessment plan to an external agency such as the legislature, state governing board, or regional accrediting agency within a relatively short time frame. Often the institution is given little guidance and few suggestions about specific format. Unfortunately, such guidance may be provided later when the reviewing agency explains why the institution's assessment plan has been found to be unacceptable.

The other primary reason for comprehensive campus assessment planning is the need to coordinate various assessment activities that would otherwise be carried on independently. It is in service of this latter purpose (coordination of campus activities) that the balance of this resource section is intended. Most of the following comments are structured around the four different periods or years described in the generic model for implementation shown in Figure 3 on page 18.

Three general concepts underlie assessment planning as described in this resource section. They are that the assessment plan:

- Focuses upon intended educational outcomes or administrative objectives;
- Is dynamic in nature; and,
- Only secondarily involves the preparation of a document which might bear the title "Assessment Plan."

The event immediately preceding evaluation of achievement or assessment in the Institutional Effectiveness Paradigm shown in Figure 1 (page 8) is the identification of "Intended Educational, Public Service, and Research Outcomes and Administrative Objectives," which are linked to and support the statement of purpose for the institution. Therefore the focus and target of assessment planning activities at the institution is the determination of the extent to which the outcomes and objectives identified have been achieved. Any other assessment planning or action at the institution not directly attributable or connected with ascertaining the accomplishment of identified intended outcomes or objectives is superfluous and wasteful of institutional resources. Among the institutions taking part in *Assessment Case Studies*, it was estimated that somewhat less than half the effort expended on assessment activities was not as clearly focused on intended outcomes or objectives as would have been desirable, and in many cases was wasted.

One of the great misconceptions about documents bearing the title "Assessment Plan" is that once conceived, and if necessary approved by whatever external agency, they are "written in stone." In fact, assessment planning is exceedingly dynamic in nature and must respond rapidly to changes in intended outcomes or objectives as well as experiences with means of assessment.

Too often, the focus of assessment planning becomes the creation of the written document entitled "Assessment Plan." When the focus of attention is the written document, the emphasis frequently shifts to the acceptability of the "Assessment Plan" to off-campus authorities rather than coordination of on-campus operations. When this happens, the plan tends to be seen on campus as less important in terms of feasibility or workability. It is not uncommon for an "Assessment Plan" to be submitted to and found to be entirely acceptable by off-campus authorities, and then prove to be totally unworkable on campus.

The following sections are organized around the key components of the generic model for implementation of institutional effectiveness found on page 18.

Planning for the Institutional Level Foundation of Assessment

As has been alluded to earlier, there are a series of organizational and policy level issues which initially need to be addressed in planning for assessment implementation on the campus. Philosophically, among the first issues to be addressed in implementation planning is the degree of centralized or decentralized assessment coordination and support to be practiced on the campus.

There are many advantages to a highly centralized approach to assessment activities on a campus. These include the ability to focus the best expertise available on assessment issues within departments; relative efficiency as resident "experts" replace novices and as economies of scale reduce the per unit cost of assessment activities, such as questionnaires, etc.; and, the ability to control the process, thus insuring uniform and comprehensive implementation throughout all disciplines in the institution. On the other hand, the primary limitations of this approach are its very considerable and apparent additional cost resulting from the significant growth in budgets associated with centralized implementation and the probable lack of faculty interest, involvement, or responsibility in the assessment process.

The completely decentralized approach to assessment implementation (otherwise known as the "dump it on the faculty" approach), practiced at too many institutions in this author's opinion, has a number of apparent liabilities and benefits as well. From the administration's standpoint, there will be apparently little centralized cost escalation involved with such an effort and faculty involvement will be guaranteed since the responsibility is exclusively their own. On the other hand, such a totally decentralized approach provides no assurance that individual academic departments will implement the desired assessment activities; is extremely inefficient as few economies of scale can be realized and each lesson learned must be repeated in every department; and, distracts from instructional operations as departments are required to commit their already limited resources to support assessment activities.

On most campuses, a compromise between a totally centralized and totally decentralized approach to assessment implementation is put into effect. A judgment is necessarily made regarding which aspects of implementation can best be handled at the institutional level. These activities frequently include overall coordination, the conduct of survey research, and administration of standardized testing instruments. Responsibility for locally developed cognitive testing, performance testing, and other matters is often decentralized to the departmental level.

The role of the faculty in planning for assessment implementation on the campus is essential. Research clearly indicates that among the most important factors in the success or failure of implementation efforts is the degree to which faculty participate in and accept (if not support) assessment activities (Nichols & Wolff, 1990). Normally, faculty oversight or "control" of the process is brought about through the establishment of a faculty oversight committee known in some regions as "The Assessment Committee" (NCA Briefing, 1992). This committee can play a number of roles in assessment planning. By its very existence, it conveys a sense of academic legitimacy. It can be utilized readily as a means of communication to the components of the institution. Among the other roles which the Assessment Committee can play is dealing with the policy issues (use of assessment data, clearinghouse function, student motivation, etc.) associated with implementation. The committee can also be utilized for monitoring implementation activities within the components of the institution. Finally, as a last resort, the committee constitutes a set of willing hands potentially necessary for logistical support of assessment activities.

Speaking of logistical support, plans need to be made early in the process for both the technical and logistical support necessary for implementation throughout the institution. There will be a need for technical support regarding the conduct of survey research, expertise in test and measurement, knowledge of standardized assessment means available, and (to a limited extent) data processing skills. Many institutional research offices do not have the necessary personnel to provide portions of this technical support within their current means, and will need to augment their staff to provide the technical support necessary for implementation. On other campuses, this type of technical support will spring from the academic community in the form of contributed services by faculty interested in becoming involved with assessment activities. No small amount of thought and planning should be given to the logistical support needed for assessment activities to take place. At the institutional level, examples of this type of logistical support are the distribution and processing of graduating student, alumni, and employer surveys, as well as the administration of standardized test. At the departmental level, logistical support will need to be provided to support comprehensive locally developed test development and administration as well as performance type test conducted by the department faculty.

The person power necessary to provide both logistical and technical support for implementation of assessment activities is a key ingredient. For many years institutions have hired temporary clerical support for assessment implementation to stuff envelopes, distribute questionnaires, make follow-up phone calls, etc. However, during the last year, this author in working with the case study institutions has become acutely aware of the need to provide some (even if limited) faculty release time within academic departments, if not to administer and score, at least to develop locally constructed means of cognitive and performance assessment. On several of the case study campuses, a lack of release time was indicated as the primary reason limiting or precluding the use of such locally developed means of assessment which are often the most appropriate form. While the funding implications of faculty release time for this purpose are not insignificant, the appearance of institutional willingness to support the process by providing even very limited release time, is probably well worth the cost to motivate the faculty and ensure their feeling of institutional commitment to the process.

Few events concerning the implementation of institutional effectiveness or assessment of educational outcomes can be described as "sure things." However, the relative surprise on the part of most institutions when discovering how much assessment is already taking place on their campus is among those events which can be described with these words. Because the academic enterprise tends to be separated into colleges, schools, departments, and even down to the course level, communication from one department to another about activities which are taking place only is at best limited. Figure 9 on the following page provides a format for identifying existing assessment data and activities on a campus. In the author's opinion, usually between 30% and 35% of the assessment data ultimately needed by an institution is already available on the campus and can be identified through the early conduct of an inventory of assessment activities currently underway on the campus. Once this inventory is complete, it is important that its results be published for those on the campus to see examples of where assessment activities are already in place in many aspects of the institution.

Among those disciplines likely to report assessment activities already in place are the allied health areas—nursing, inhalation therapy, etc., and other areas with professional accreditation requirements, such as the National Council for the Accreditation of Teacher Education (NCATE) and the American Association of Collegiate Schools of Business (AACSB). In addition to these areas, it is likely that assessment activity will also be taking place in disciplines within which there are professional licensure requirements. In both of these instances, professionals practicing in the field have taken the initiative to assure the overall quality of their graduates and in so doing, often established an assessment program both to improve the performance of their programs and to ensure the public of at least minimal levels of competence by the practitioners in the field.

In addition to inventorying that which is available on the campus, a review and dissemination of the commercially available means of assessment is appropriate at this time. As individual academic departments plan for assessment activities in their fields, it is important that they understand what colleagues on the campus are doing in regards to assessment as well as knowing what is available in the field from commercial sources and colleagues in their field at other institutions.[1]

---

1. An excellent reference in this regard is the Clearinghouse for Higher Education Assessment Instruments publication available by writing to 212 Claxton Education Building, College of Education, University of Tennessee, Knoxville, TN 37996-3400 (Tel. 615-974-5894 or 615-974-3748).

FIGURE 9

FORMAT FOR IDENTIFYING EXISTING ASSESSMENT DATA

For each study or data set, identify the following:

What is it (brief description)?	Who has it (office/person)?	What population does it cover (e.g., freshmen, remedial students, etc.)?	When was it done (i.e., term, year, etc.)?	Special features or limitations

Source: Peter T. Ewell and Robert P. Lisensky, ASSESSING INSTITUTIONAL EFFECTIVENESS. (Washington: Consortium for the Advancement of Private Higher Education, 1988, p. 55).

As institutions complete their initial institutional level planning for implementation, consideration should be given to the use of existing institutional data (see resource section beginning on page 107 as well as how the attitudinal instruments discussed in the resource section beginning on page 43) will be utilized. Careful consideration needs to be given to the procedures for distributing and collecting each of the questionnaires described in the resource section referenced as well as to the choice of commercial surveys, contracted service, or locally developed instruments for survey research purposes. Should the institution choose to utilize standardized attitudinal surveys such as those described earlier, it can be assured of: the ready availability of the instruments for immediate distribution; flexibility to add institutional items to the survey forms; provision of both paper and data tape processed reports; as well as comparative data from other institutions. Regretfully this approach is more costly than some others and provides limited institutional identity for the purpose of publicizing the institution while gathering the data desired.

Should the institution choose to employ one of a number of consulting agencies, such as the National Center for Higher Education Management Systems (NCHEMS), to conduct their survey research, it can expect an instrumentthat is more tailored to the institution's needs and that will have added credibility for the participants as well as the institution itself. However, this choice is usually the most costly alternative, can be relatively time consuming, and in some cases, also results in a lack of data when compared with other institutions.

Many institutions, particularly those with larger institutional research staffs, will choose to design their own family of attitudinal surveys. The advantages of this approach include the customization of the survey to specific institutional needs and service identities, (such as the names of particular libraries, etc.), which in combination with color schemes, signatures, etc., can provide a very high level of institutional identity. Once these surveys are designed, their per unit cost to implement and continue is the lowest of the three alternatives in most cases. Unfortunately, the disadvantages of locally developed attitudinal surveys include the relatively extended design process duration (estimated at six months to a year from inception to survey results) and the high developmental cost within the institutional research staff for such endeavors. The development of a single instrument, such as a graduating student survey, alumni survey, etc., can be expected to consume roughly half-time of a single professional staff member for a year from inception through working with individual departments to design the survey and its data processing input and report formats. Additionally, little comparative data, other than that available from related items appearing on commercially available surveys, will be available for use on the campus.

Assessment planning for the first year should have included, as a minimum:

- Determination of organizational and support responsibilities;
- An inventory of existing and available means of assessment;
- Identification of existing institutional data; and,
- Completion of attitudinal survey design or selection.

Detailed Planning of the Assessment Process at the Department Level

As shown in the generic implementation model on page 18, detailed design or planning of the assessment processes at the institution will need to take place in collaboration or consultation with identification of intended educational outcomes and administrative objectives. **There is a clear order to this process. First, educational outcomes and administrative objectives are formulated by respective academic and administrative or educational support departments. Then, means of assessment are identified.**

The natural tendency of many institutions at this point in the implementation process is to focus upon the means of assessment first rather than upon the outcomes or objectives the achievement of which they are intended to measure. This was done at several of the case study institutions and is the author's experience on campus after campus (Nichols, 1995). Why shift planning from the obvious identification of intended educational outcomes to the means of assessment at this point? Several reasons emerge from the case study reports and the author's experience. First, the means of assessment themselves are **tangible** (tests, surveys, performance exams, etc.), which can be observed by the participants; and on which much of the national attention has been focused. Second, by moving immediately (and incorrectly) to the means of assessment, necessary substantive discussions concerning the nature of the discipline and individual differences of opinion can be avoided or at least postponed. In planning for assessment implementation, it is absolutely essential that planning for the means of assessment follow or flow from the identification of intended educational outcomes and administrative objectives. If this is not the case, two events tend to transpire on campuses. First, much effort is wasted as institutions "do assessment," and then try to ascertain what they had intended to measure. Second, the degree of use of assessment results, not focused upon the intended educational outcome originally identified by the faculty, is greatly diminished.

The single greatest mechanism for saving money in the cost of assessment activities is to limit the amount of assessment accomplished to barely enough to verify accomplishment of intended educational outcomes and administrative objectives. The best assessment techniques in the world, not focused upon intended educational outcomes or administrative objectives, are in essence wasted and should be eliminated in the planning stage before ever taking place on the campus.

The relationship in assessment planning between selection of intended educational outcomes and identification of the means of assessment is a sensitive one. Frequently, faculty will initially identify intended educational outcomes which can only be described as "ideal." Whereas on the other side of the table (literally in some cases), those charged with assisting in the design or planning of the institutional assessment process are more likely to be concerned with more "pragmatic" issues regarding feasibility. In the long run, what most often takes place is the selection of important intended educational outcomes which have been refined or focused into "operational terminology" more subject to identification of accomplishable means of assessment. In this process, neither faculty "idealist" nor assessment "pragmatist" are victorious, but a working compromise between the two extreme points of view is often established.

FIGURE 10

ASSESSMENT PLANNING CONCEPTUAL MATRIX

Undergraduate English Program	Means of Assessment				
	Cognitive Measures			Attitudinal Measures	
Intended Outcomes	Local	MFAT	Licensure	Graduating Student	Alumni
1. Students completing the Baccalaureate program in English will compare very favorably in their knowledge of literature with those students completing a similar program nationally.		√		√	

Figure 11

ASSESSMENT PLANNING
DETAILED DOCUMENTATION

Program/Department: Undergraduate English Program

Intended Outcome/Objective: Students completing the Baccalaureate program in English will compare very favorably in their knowledge of literature with those students completing a similar program nationally.

Means of Assessment	What	When	Responsible	Type of Feedback	Use of Results
1a. The average scores of the graduates of the Baccalaureate program in English on the "Literature in English" MFAT subject test (which they will be required to take shortly before graduation) will be at or near the 50th percentile compared to national results.					
1b. Ninety percent of the graduates of the English Baccalaureate program will "agree" or "strongly agree" with the statement "In the field of literature I feel as well prepared as the majority of individuals nation wide who have completed a similar degree during the past year."					

While the emphasis in assessment planning for use to guide campus implementation is on "planning rather than the paperwork associated therewith," the patterns of thought reflected in Figure 10, Assessment Planning Conceptual Matrix, and Figure 11, Assessment Planning Detailed Documentation on the preceding pages, may be useful. The Conceptual Matrix shown in Figure 10 relates a specific intended educational outcome to the types of assessment activities to be utilized to ascertain the accomplishment of that outcome. It is important to keep this "one on one" relationship between intended educational outcomes and means of assessment clear to all parties. Otherwise, means of assessment tend to take on a life of their own, cease to be a means, and become an end in themselves.

Figure 11, Assessment Planning Detailed Documentation, takes the logic outlined above one step farther and for each means of conduct and assessment identified in the conceptual matrix, poses a series of questions concerning its utilization. Carried to their extreme across a large and complex institution, either of these figures would create a mountain of assessment planning paper, which is unnecessary on most campuses. However, the organizational constructs upon which these figures are premised should be considered by those planning and designing the assessment process on any campus.

Planning for the use of various types of assessment, standardized cognitive tests, locally developed cognitive tests, performance types of assessment, and behavioral types of assessment share some similarities, but each type represents some distinct challenges within itself.

Planning for the use of standardized cognitive test regarding the major or general education begins with a review of the instruments available. All of the major testing companies will provide a copy of the instrument or its technical description to a central campus location for review of its content by the faculty. It is suggested that one office be established for ordering such specimen tests and that as a minimum, on four-year college campuses all appropriate ETS Major Field Assessment Tests and, on two-year campuses, all appropriate Student Occupational Competency Achievement Tests (SOCAT) be forwarded to that office for review by the faculty in the various departments. At the very least, review of specimen examinations will provide the departmental faculty with a feeling for what a national panel of experts in their field believes constitutes the body of knowledge for which a graduate should be responsible.

Who should administer standardized tests on the campus? In the author's opinion, administration of standardized tests is best left to the professionals in the institutional testing service, counseling center, etc. On most campuses there exists one office or another that is widely identified as the entity administering standardized tests for the institution. With experience in proctoring and processing standardized test, the clerical and professional staff in this area are much better equipped to deal with the sometimes formidable test administration bureaucracies established by the testing services than are departmental faculty.

The feedback and use of results of standardized test results by departmental faculty are of particular concern in assessment planning. Where possible, test results should be analyzed centrally, graphically portraying such results, compared with the normative population.

One planning issue common to all of the forms of assessment discussed in this re-source section is that of documentation of the use of results. Because the ultimate end of the assessment process is the use of its results to improve academic and administrative programming, documentation of how these results are utilized becomes increasingly important as the implementation process matures. The individual responsibility for documentation should be identified on each campus as part of the assessment planning process. The author's recommendation is that this responsibility be lodged at the department chair level. The documentation of use of results need only be quite informal in nature. However, this documentation should be scheduled and reviewed by a senior academic or administrative officer on a periodic basis to ensure that the documentation is, indeed, being kept.

Locally developed cognitive measures require a considerably different approach than that utilized concerning standardized instruments. The primary issue regarding locally developed cognitive tests is the expenditure of considerable amounts of time over an extended period of time to design, administer, score, and refine such instruments by the faculty. At virtually no institutions across the country is release time provided for this arduous task. Regretfully, the case study institutions reported this lack of provision of release time as resulting in a relatively small number of departments utilizing locally developed instruments. This was true to the extent that one case study institution's correspondent identified the need for better incentives for the construction of locally developed tests as the most important single item to be passed on to those starting the assessment implementation process. It is the author's suggestion that some, even if very limited, release time be provided in recognition of the amount of work required.

Once the results of locally developed cognitive, performance, or behavioral type assessments are completed by the department, the issue of forwarding these results to an institutional "clearinghouse" for assessment results can be anticipated. The advantages of having such a clearinghouse are: its coordination of a number of similar means of assessment at the departmental level into a more efficient overall institutional pattern; the provision of technical support in test and measurement services; and the offering of logistical support in production and administration of locally developed means of assessment. Faculty on some campuses feel quite safe and secure in forwarding potentially damaging information concerning their programs to such a central clearinghouse that has the respect of all engaged in implementation on the campus. On other campuses, the level of such trust does not allow the "airing of dirty laundry" beyond the department level for fear of retribution. If politically feasible given the environment on the campus, the provision of assessment results to a central point or clearinghouse should be planned in the design of the assessment process.

Preparing for program level performance assessment requires the most comprehensive assessment planning discussed to this point. While responsibility for this type of assessment is normally lodged at the departmental level, support by institutional level assets is not uncommon. The logistical implementation of performance assessment can sometimes be a formidable challenge. Arranging just the right circumstance within which to ask the students to perform as they will when they go into society requires careful planning regarding equipment, facilities, and timing.

A considerable less arduous form of performance assessment involves the utilization of individuals off the campus who supervise the performance of students taking part in operations within society. This is typified by student teaching, internships, cooperative education programs, practicum, clinical experiences, etc., in which the students actually go into the community to perform on a trial basis those skills which they have developed during their matriculation through the degree program.

The training of evaluators or supervisors for either on campus performance assessment or off campus internship/practicum assessment requires careful planning. In most cases, both on- and off-campus evaluators are provided with something resembling a checklist which identifies the skills which the student is asked to demonstrate while taking part in the performance assessment. In some cases, video tapes of the student's performance are made and forwarded to the campus for evaluation by independent panels utilizing the "checklist" concept. The consistency or reliability of evaluations will be enhanced if either on campus or video tape facilitated training/exercises are provided so that trial evaluations using the "checklist" may be accomplished by each evaluator and then compared to the evaluation "standard," thus creating a better norm for all evaluations.

The primary issue regarding behavioral type of assessment planning is the identification of the sources of information concerning the students' "behavior." On the campus this information may come from the placement service, the students/graduates themselves on Graduating Student Surveys, as well as other sources, such as point of contact surveys. Sources of information from off the campus include the opinions of employers as well as records provided to the institutions from "follow-on institutions" that the student has attended. Such follow-on institutions include the four-year colleges and universities to which two-year college graduates transfer to complete their baccalaureate programs as well as graduate schools for four-year institutions' baccalaureate recipients. In both cases, careful articulation with many agencies is necessary in order to provide the breadth of information necessary to support the overall assessment process.

Planning for Initial Implementation of Assessment Activities

Following the necessary organization/institutional activities and detailed design at the important departmental level, careful planning needs to take place regarding initial implementation of assessment activities in roughly the third period of implementation.

The timing of assessment activities on most campuses tends to be "spring loaded" as most institutions, even community colleges, tend to graduate the majority of their students at the close of the second semester in approximately May of each year. Because so much assessment activity is geared around end of program measures, this particular time of year is one of very heavy assessment effort.

Every attempt should be made through careful planning to spread those assessment activities that can be moved out of the late second term into other parts of the academic year. As an example, Alumni and Employer Surveys can be conducted in the fall term without doing damage to response rates, etc. Wherever possible, the assessment work-load should be spread as evenly as possible throughout the academic year.

The sheer logistics or "person power" necessary to accomplish most institutions' assessment activities is staggering. Volunteer assistance from members of the faculty as well as professional and clerical staff will provide some of the hands necessary to conduct assessment activities while the student government can be expected to provide a modest level of assistance on some campuses. However, it may well be necessary to employ on a temporary basis additional personnel to stuff envelopes, administer examinations, etc., during the late spring semester or potentially the early summer. It is unfortunate that the highest demand for assessment activities occurs just as much of the voluntary assistance (faculty) is leaving for the summer.

Planning for initial implementation at institutions with the foresight to begin this process well in advance provides the luxury of being able to phase in implementation over a several year period. This phase-in can take the form of one or more components initially beginning the implementation process while others begin the next year. This approach has the advantage of learning lessons from the pilot components of the institution which can be put into use in the other units of the institution beginning implementation the following year. On the author's own campus, implementation was commenced over a two-year period with one-half of the academic programs (spread across all colleges or departments) beginning assessment activities during academic year 1992-93 and the balance of the university during 1993-94. This approach allows the luxury of easing in to the assessment burden sure to follow initial department implementation.

There is little way to plan for the level of anxiety that will probably accompany initial implementation of assessment activities on campus. Speaking at the 1994 meeting of the Association for Institutional Research, Dr. Frank Newman, Chairperson of the Education Commission of the States, stated that there are three cardinal rules of evaluation or assessment: "Nobody wants to be evaluated, nobody wants to be evaluated, and finally, nobody wants to be evaluated." In order to allay as much apprehension as possible, institutions need to plan to ensure that (a) the process is thoroughly explained on the campus, (b) it is clearly separated from appraisal of individual faculty members or staff, and (c) that the faculty, in particular, feel that they have relative control over the process and the use to which assessment data will be put on the campus.

Planning for the initial feedback of assessment information to individual academic and administrative programs will be a key to successful implementation on many campuses. The guiding principle regarding feedback of this information is that it should focus on the educational outcomes or administrative objectives identified by the institution's academic and educational support of administrative programs. As data are collected from a number of sources, they should be drawn to intended educational outcomes and administrative objectives as a magnet draws iron filings. If some iron filings (i.e., assessment results) don't seem to find a home (intended educational outcomes or administrative objectives), then there was no reason for that assessment to begin with and the institution has squandered a portion of its valuable assessment effort and funding.

In order to make more efficient the initial feedback of assessment information, the institution should initially plan for relatively simple tabular and graphic presentation techniques. Some institutions may wish to consider personal verbal and written communication of assessment results back to academic departments in order to guarantee that the "message is delivered," and to explain in some detail the initial assessment findings.

Assessment Within the Annual Institutional Effectiveness Cycle

Assuming that the annual institutional effectiveness cycle has been initiated by the feedback of assessment results concluding the previous implementation phase as shown in Figure 3 on page 18, most of the assessment activity within the institutional effectiveness cycle can be described as refinement and readministration.

After the initial iteration of assessment activities on the campus, any assessment plan which had originally been considered even remotely complete will be acknowledged to have been greatly inadequate. Gaps and shortcomings in the assessment activities just concluded will be more than apparent. Also new means of assessment and techniques for their use will be available. In general, this can be described as a period of time usually taking place during the fall term in which institutions identify "what worked" and the means to improve shortcomings noted in their previous iterations of assessment procedures.

The refined assessment procedures each year can be expected to be somewhat smoother with fewer obvious administrative and logistical problems associated therewith. In addition, these activities may be conducted more efficiently; in many cases resulting in no greater expenditure of funds for assessment activities while the scope of these activities are both broadened and improved in depth. However, practitioners should also be aware that with each iteration, new assessment problems may emerge from previously successful procedures. Means of assessment, that were initially planned and carefully articulated with a department's intended educational outcomes, may function smoothly during the first several years of implementation; however, flounder when the department changes its intended educational outcomes without adjusting the means of assessment.

As iterations in the annual institutional effectiveness cycle are conducted, the feedback and the use of information can be expected to improve. In general, a greater variety in the format of assessment information feedback is experienced at institutions more mature in assessment activities as they become sensitized to the best means of communication with their various constituents. In addition, the focus tends to shift toward the documentation of the use of assessment information to improve program planning as iterations of the annual institutional effectiveness cycle are experienced.

Concluding Remarks

Assessment planning is essential to successful implementation; however, it should be acknowledged that it is impossible to cover all eventualities in any assessment planning. Therefore, the refinements to assessment planning, made annually, constitute a never ending dynamic adjustment to institutional assessment practices. It was clear from the experiences of the case study institutions (Nichols, 1995) that those institutions which had made the effort to establish a clear plan for assessment activities were among those likely to have been able to ultimately demonstrate the use of results for the improvement of academic programming and there is no reason to doubt that this will not be the case at the majority of institutions nationwide.

References: Cited

NCA Briefing. (December 1992). *Assessment: Comments from the APR Process, 10*(3), 8.

Nichols, J. O. (1995). *Assessment Case Studies: Common Issues in Implementation with Various Campus Approaches to Resolution.* New York: Agathon Press.

Nichols, J. O., & Wolff, L. A. (1990). Organizing for Assessment. In J. B. Presley (ed.), *New Directions for Institutional Research, 66*(2), 81-92.

Nichols, J. O., & Wolff, L. A. (1990, October 11). *The Status of Institutional Effectiveness at Institutions of Higher Education within the Southern Association of Colleges and Schools (SACS): Findings of Visitation Teams, Extent of Implementation, and Factors Facilitating/Impeding Implementation.* Contributed paper at the 1990 meeting of Southern Association of Institutional Research, Ft. Lauderdale, FL.

CHAPTER FOUR

Detailed Design at the Departmental Level

The activities accomplished at the institutional level during the first year or period of the process are preparatory to the majority of the campus's efforts toward implementation of institutional effectiveness or educational outcomes assessment that will take place within the academic and administrative departments beginning in the second period of implementation (see Figure 12). As in so many other instances, ultimate success in institutional effectiveness implementation is dependent on the service provided to the institution's constituents (students, alumni, etc.) by its operating elements (departments/programs).

Among the more difficult tasks that must be accomplished in implementation during this second period is gaining the confidence and active support of academic and administrative department chairs and/or heads. What are the obstacles to be overcome in gaining this confidence and support?

Probably the first obstacle is the inertia of academic and administrative practices, which have for years focused almost exclusively on the processes that take place in a department rather than the end "results" or outcomes to which those departmental processes contribute. In the academic sector, these processes relate to class scheduling, grade reporting, and so forth. Within administrative departments, process-oriented activities such as conducting registration, acquiring books, cutting the grass, and preparing the payroll all seem more familiar and urgent than outcomes assessment. Second, implementation of institutional effectiveness will be an additional task rather than a replacement for any of the process-oriented tasks required in continuation of day-to-day operations. This will be a particularly difficult obstacle to overcome at relatively smaller institutions or in smaller departments within larger institutions, where the departmental-level administrative personnel may already be overburdened with process-oriented requirements for which little release time or support is provided.

A third major obstacle to departmental leadership support will, in all likelihood, be a large measure of skepticism regarding implementation of institutional effectiveness as just another fad or redirection of effort and doubt about the institution's commitment to following through with implementation. Many departmental administrators have witnessed the great fanfare surrounding announcements of significant institutional initiatives in the past, which proved to be only lip service.

Figure 12

The Second Year of a Generic Model for Implementation of Institutional Effectiveness and Assessment Activities in Higher Education

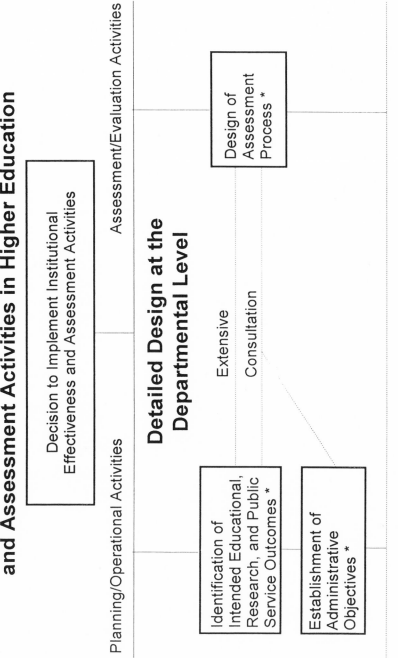

Planning/Operational Activities

Assessment/Evaluation Activities

Decision to Implement Institutional Effectiveness and Assessment Activities

Detailed Design at the Departmental Level

Extensive Consultation

Design of Assessment Process *

Identification of Intended Educational, Research, and Public Service Outcomes *

Establishment of Administrative Objectives *

* Resource section(s) included in chapter to support

Given these obstacles, winning the confidence and active support of departmental administrators for implementation will take a concerted effort. However, this confidence can be stimulated by the following:

1. Visible commitment in word and deed by the institution's Chief Executive Officer (CEO) and Chief Academic Officer (CAO);
2. Complete and professionally executed staff work at the institutional level during the first year of implementation;
3. Implementation plans that identify each department as one component of an ongoing project involving other departments and extending into the future; and,
4. Presence of an external stimulus, such as an accrediting or state governmental agency, requiring implementation.

.Gaining the active support of departmental administrators will require allowing them to choose institutional effectiveness implementation over, or at least along with, their process-oriented responsibilities. Such a choice will doubtlessly require the extension of various incentives for implementation. However, it is also important that the institution avoid apparent punishment of those units in which implementation is not being aggressively pursued.

Although activities on the planning/operational and assessment/evaluation tracks remained relatively separate during the first period of implementation, extensive coordination between such activities is required in the second period. As the various academic and administrative departments go about establishing their intended outcomes and administrative objectives, it is important that the departments identify (in general) the means through which assessment of their actual results will take place. At the same time, those parties designing the institution's assessment/evaluation process need to be well informed regarding the objectives on which that process will focus. Neither the interests of the planning/operational track nor those of the assessment/evaluation track should be paramount in this relationship. Rather, a give-and-take process should occur between the two, yielding the most appropriate intended departmental/program outcomes or objectives that can be supported by a feasible assessment plan.

For a further discussion of issues and solutions in departmental implementation see *The Departmental Guide* and *Assessment Case Studies* (1995).

Planning/Operational Activities

During this second period of implementation, planning/operational activities are extended to the departmental/program level through establishment of "Intended Educational (Instructional), Research, and Service Outcomes or Administrative Objectives."

All of these results-oriented statements should be carefully linked to support of the institution's expanded statement of purpose (see Figure 13). On some campuses, the Expanded Statement of Institutional Purpose will be utilized as the starting point, and results-oriented statements will flow "down" from this statement to the individual departments. At other institutions, departmental/program statements of intentions will be

Figure 13

Undergraduate English Program

Example of Linkage between Expanded Statement of Institutional Purpose and Departmental/Program Intended Outcomes/Objectives at Our University

Expanded Statement of Institutional Purpose

Mission Statement:

The principal focus of Our University's curricular program is undergraduate education in the liberal arts and sciences combined with a number of directly career related and preprofessional fields.

Goal Statements:

Each graduate of Our University will be treated as an individual, and all graduates of baccalaureate-level programs at the University will have developed a depth of understanding in their major field and been afforded the opportunity to prepare for a career or profession following graduation.

Departmental/Program Intended Outcomes/Objectives

1. Students completing the baccalaureate program in English will compare very favorably in their knowledge of literature with those students completing a similar program nationally.

2. Graduates will be able to critique a brief draft essay, pointing out the grammatical, spelling, and punctuation errors and offering appropriate suggestions for correction of the deficiencies.

3. Students completing the baccalaureate program will be capable of writing an acceptable journal article and having it published.

directed "up" to support the Expanded Statement of Institutional Purpose. Whether these results-oriented statements are voluntarily originated by the institution's departments or are directed from a central level, it is imperative that a clear and identifiable linkage be established between the expanded statement of purpose and such departmental results-oriented statements of intentions.

In the instructional area, results-oriented statements of intentions will primarily take the form of "Intended Educational Outcomes" by degree program offered and for general education. In acknowledgment of the difficulty of general education assessment, a separate resource section regarding this subject, beginning page 172, has been added to this 3rd edition of the *Handbook*. It may also be desirable to establish separate statements of intended outcomes regarding educational programs (such as, premedicine or certificate programs) not resulting in a specific degree.

The example depicted in Figure 13 is that of the Undergraduate English Program at Our University. It depicts the linkage of the Intended Educational Outcomes identified for that program by the faculty in the English Department back to support the Institutional Goal of offering students the ability to develop a depth of understanding in their major field, which in turn supports a portion of the Our University Mission Statement. It is this type of linkage, connection, and support from the program level to the institutional level which ties assessment of student academic achievement with the rest of the institution into a program of overall institutional effectiveness.

Additionally, intended outcomes should be identified for the other two traditional areas included in statements of purpose (research and public service). These statements of "Intended Research and Public Service Outcomes" should also be linked to the Expanded Statement of Institutional Purpose.

Finally, the institution's administrative and educational support units should play a major role in accomplishment of institutional effectiveness through establishment of "Administrative Objectives" supporting the Expanded Statement of Institutional Purpose. Direct linkage with portions of the expanded institutional statement of purpose by some units (payroll, auditing, physical plant, etc.) may be difficult to achieve. In this case, the objectives established by these units should focus on creation of an academic and administrative environment conducive to more direct support of the Expanded Statement of Institutional Purpose by other departments/programs. Nonetheless, such statements of objectives or intentions should be established in all organizational units.

In the resource sections entitled "Setting and Evaluating Intended Educational (Instructional) Outcomes" and "Setting and Evaluating Objectives and Outcomes in Nonacademic Units," these concepts are discussed further (see pages 157-171 and 186-204). Appendix B of *Assessment Case Studies* contains over 50 examples of statements of intended educational outcomes and administrative objectives developed at colleges nationwide.

Among the trends or movements in higher education which parallel or support assessment/institutional effectiveness implementation on campus is that set of activities commonly described in the business community as Total Quality Management or TQM. While these concepts, and certainly the title, are widely scorned by some academicians, the same structures and procedures under the pseudonym Continuous Quality Improvement are supportive of institutional effectiveness activities. The resource section beginning on page 205 outlines the nature of the relationship between the "quality" movement in higher education and assessment of intended educational outcomes and administrative objectives.

Assessment/Evaluation Activities

Based on the institutional-level activity in the previous period (initial design and implementation of attitudinal surveys, inventory of existing assessment procedures, adjustments of institutional data systems, identification of cognitive tests, etc.), assessment/ evaluation activities in this second period of implementation also shift to the departmental/program level.

By the beginning of the second period of implementation, those charged with implementing assessment procedures on the campus should be prepared to work closely with each department/program in identifying appropriate ways to assess accomplishment of the statements of intention being developed within the unit. These means of assessment include the following:

1. Attitudinal measures;
2. Measures of cognitive learning;
3. Behavioral change;
4. Performance measures;
5. Information drawn from the institution's automated files; and,
6. Other means.

Data from these sources are derived from both locally developed and standardized instruments, tests, and procedures.

In the educational (instructional) sector of the institution, a wide variety of assessment means probably will be brought to bear on departmental/program statements of "Intended Educational Outcomes," although it should be understood that not all accomplishments identified in such statements can be measured or ascertained. Attitudinal surveys and more direct measures (counts of patrons, external funding received, library circulation, etc.) will predominate as means of assessment in the institution's administrative departments.

The resource section entitled "Statements of Outcomes/Objectives and Assessment at the Departmental Level" contains not only a much more detailed review of these concepts, but also a discussion of the importance of multiple assessment procedures for each intended outcome or objective, the design of feedback mechanisms, and logistical support of the assessment process.

Figure 14 represents the continued development of the Undergraduate English Program Example begun earlier in this chapter. Added to what had been shown earlier in Figure 13, are the means of assessment and criteria for program success identified by the faculty. It is important that the linkage illustrated by the arrows be maintained, as pointed

Figure 14

Undergraduate English Program

Example of Linkage between Expanded Statement of Institutional
Purpose, Departmental/Program Intended Outcomes/Objectives,
and Assessment Criteria and Procedures at Our University

Expanded Statement of Institutional Purpose	Departmental/Program Intended Outcomes/Objectives	Assessment Criteria & Procedures

Mission Statement:

The principal focus of Our University's curricular program is undergraduate education in the liberal arts and sciences combined with a number of directly career related and preprofessional fields.

Goal Statements:

Each graduate of Our University will be treated as an individual, and all graduates of baccalaureate-level programs at the University will have developed a depth of understanding in their major field and been afforded the opportunity to prepare for a career or profession following graduation.

1. Students completing the baccalaureate program in English will compare very favorably in their knowledge of literature with those students completing a similar program nationally.

2. Graduates will be able to critique a brief draft essay, pointing out the grammatical, spelling, and punctuation errors and offering appropriate suggestions for correction of the deficiencies.

3. Students completing the baccalaureate program will be capable of writing an acceptable journal article and having it published.

1a. The average score of the graduates of the baccalaureate program in English on the "Literature in English" MFAT subject test (which they will be required to take shortly before graduation) will be at or near the 50th percentile compared to national results.

1b. Ninety percent of the English baccalaureate program will "agree" or "strongly agree" with the statement "In the field of literature I feel as well prepared as the majority of individuals nationwide who have completed a similar degree during the past year."

2a. As part of a "capstone course" during the students' final semester prior to graduation, they will critique a short draft essay; identify grammatical, spelling, and punctuation errors; and offer suggestions for correction of the deficiencies. Eighty percent of the program's graduates will identify and offer appropriate suggestions for remediation of 90% of the errors in the draft essay.

3a. All graduates of the baccalaureate level program in English will prepare a journal article for submission and forward it to the English department.

3b. Eighty percent of those journal articles submitted will be judged acceptable for publication by a jury of English department faculty from an institution comparable to Our University.

3c. Twenty percent of those articles submitted will be published in student or other publications.

out in the resource section Assessment Planning, so that the means of assessment themselves do not take on a life of their own, but remain subservient to the identification of that which we value in our instructional programs and want to insure is being accomplished.

Second, it is important to note that in the development of the Undergraduate English Program Example a clear identification of intended educational outcomes precedes, rather than follows, identification of the means of assessment. On most campuses, there is a strong tendency to identify means of assessment which are highly visible, tangible, and concrete, and then to develop the intended educational outcomes which they are designed to ascertain the accomplishment thereof. This natural tendency results in many cases in a substantial waste of resources, lack of willingness on the part of many faculty to use the results to improve programming, and the forfeiture by the faculty of their right to control the curriculum through identification of intended educational outcomes. **There is a logical progression from intended educational outcomes to means of assessment**. If it is followed, identification of the means of assessment will flow readily; otherwise, the assessment process may well bog down.

Finally, Figure 14 illustrates the setting of criteria for program success. The percentages, averages, etc., shown, represent how well the faculty believe that students **ought** to perform in their program based upon the nature of the students at the time they enter the program, the resources available, as well as the duration of the instructional process. The experience of the case study institutions in *Assessment Case Studies* clearly indicated that institutions and departments, who answered the "ought" question initially, were far more likely to use assessment results at a later time than those who failed to set such criteria judgmentally at the beginning of the process.

Together with the second period implementation activities illustrated in Figure 12 (page 139) these five resource sections can be used to guide the final preparations for implementing institutional effectiveness operations the following year.

Statements of Outcomes/Objectives and Assessment at the Departmental Level

Linda Pratt

In designing a campus-wide assessment process, it is important to assure that each administrative department's objectives and programs statements of intended educational outcomes are clearly linked to the institution's Expanded Statement of Purpose and that the specific assessment procedures are appropriate for evaluating the extent to which the institution as a whole is moving toward achievement of its goals. The focus in implementing institutional effectiveness is, by definition, at the institutional level. The President (CEO), the Vice President for Academic Affairs (CAO), and the Dean must all assume responsibility for implementing the assessment process. These roles will be relatively direct at the institution and college level; however, at the department level the roles of these senior administrative officers must be to offer encouragement, support and resources, but not to direct the process. The linkage of academic and administrative outcomes and objectives to an Expanded Statement of Institutional Purpose is necessary to assure that subunits support the institution-wide mission. In order to be effective, to become an integral part of the activities of the department, the process of developing objectives and implementing the assessment process must be designed by the faculty of the department with the support of the department chairperson. The faculty must be active in every step of the process—in planning, in developing or selecting measurement devices, in collecting data, in interpreting the results, and in using the results to improve the curriculum.

Linkage of Assessment Results Through Outcomes and Objectives to Statement of Purpose

There are a variety of formats for writing objectives and defining desired outcomes. The *Resource Manual on Institutional Effectiveness* (1989), published by the Commission on Colleges of the Southern Association of Colleges and Schools (SACS), suggests one format for development of outcomes/objectives at the unit level that ensures linkage between the institution's statement of purpose and the unit objectives by including an excerpt from the mission as a part of the objective. Assessment criteria and procedures, as well as ways assessment results will be used, are then described. This format, and any other which ensures that the assessment results are consistent with the intended outcomes/objectives and that the linkage with the institution's statement of purpose is assured, provides solid evidence concerning accomplishment of institutional-level intentions.

In order to ensure linkage of institutional and department/program statements of intention, SACS suggests the development of a series of matrices that relate planning and evaluation components to each of the traditional areas of institutional mission (e.g., teaching, research, and public service) as well as to an institution's major operational areas such as admissions, curriculum, instruction, faculty, library, physical resources, and so forth. Essential planning and evaluation components identified by SACS include:

1. The statement of institutional purpose;
2. The definition of expected results (outcomes or objectives);
3. The description of appropriate means of evaluation;
4. The assignment of responsibility for implementation; and,
5. The description of the use of evaluation results (SACS, 1989, pp. 11-13).

Sometimes difficulties arise in attempting to link the Expanded Statement of Institutional Purpose (mission statement and goals statements) and their related outcomes/objectives. As Fincher (1978) notes, "Goals may not be present at the beginning of an activity or function, but they are believed to be a future state, destination, or end product that will help guide and direct the progression of that activity or function" (p. 4). Not all outcomes are intended, encouraged, planned, or anticipated, and side effects may be as important as intended outcomes. In this case, Institutional Effectiveness may on occasion be as concerned with movement in "the right direction" as with the measurable achievement of narrowly defined outcomes/objectives. Thus, although institutions must attempt to state clearly their missions, goals, and outcomes/objectives, they must maintain sufficient flexibility to permit revisions as the process unfolds.

Linkage of the Expanded Statement of Institutional Purpose from the top down is probably preferable to linkage from the bottom up on many campuses. Certainly this type of linkage more nearly matches many familiar planning models. Such top-down linkage is more appropriate for institutions with a clearly articulated Expanded Statement of Institutional Purpose, for smaller institutions, and for selected colleges or universities where the existence of a unique ethos is all-pervasive. Charismatic presidential leadership or strong traditions of centralized leadership may also increase the likelihood of common acceptance of a well-defined mission statement that guides the development of institutional goals as well as departmental/program statements of intentions.

On the other hand, the bottom-up linkage of intended outcomes/objectives to an Expanded Statement of Institutional Purpose may be more effective for some institutions. In larger research institutions with diverse units, the tradition of decentralized funding patterns and governance structures may mean that institutional goals emerge from the broad statements of a loose confederation of largely autonomous schools and departments. In these instances, the Expanded Statement of Institutional Purpose springs from the activities of the institution's subunits.

Finally, in many institutions, a combination of bottom-up and top-down development may be preferable. For example, in large universities, each school or college may develop goals for top-down use by departments, while, at the same time, the amalgamation of the goals of the schools or colleges may drive the institution's Expanded Statement of Institutional Purpose in an essentially bottom-up process. Much of the preceding section is directed at institutions in the early stages of implementing an effectiveness and assessment process. As an institution matures in its implementation of the assessment process and in particular in the assessment of student outcomes, the curriculums of the departments and schools will be reviewed and revised. This is the point at which the most effective assessment processes can be developed. Measurement of student outcomes can be integrated directly into the design of the curriculum, not superimposed.

General Factors to Be Considered

In identifying and defining intended outcomes/objectives and the assessment procedures for measuring those outcomes/objectives within the various administrative units on campus, key factors to consider are the time and effort needed to develop the outcomes/objectives and to implement the assessment process. If the number of outcomes/objectives is too large or the assessment procedure is too cumbersome, the process is likely to be abandoned in midstream. As Miller (1980) indicated, "The process of collecting data should be established in such a way that it can continue beyond the first self-assessment as a routine function of the master planning and decision-making process" (p. 425). For this to occur, the number of such departmental statements of intentions should be reduced to those that can be effectively addressed in any single time period, and the outcomes/objectives and related assessment procedures should be simple and directly related to the most important goals of the institution and of the individual unit. When addressing the gains achieved by students enrolled in courses and degree programs, the most effective assessment procedures and those which are most likely to be used on a continuous basis are those which are developed as an integral part of the curriculum.

It is not necessary or even desirable for any unit of the institution to develop a comprehensive set of outcomes/objectives that describe every detail of the operations of that unit. Rather, each unit must identify the most important or key outcomes or objectives and concentrate on assessment of those outcomes. In practice, this may mean choosing outcomes/objectives related to an area identified as being troublesome, addressing only those related to new or revised initiatives, or selecting only those outcomes deemed absolutely essential to unit operations. As an example, a department with a faculty that has an excellent reputation in the teaching area might want to increase its emphasis on faculty research and publication. The department could identify the accomplishment and publication of significant research findings as an intended outcome but would not, at the same time, identify improvement in teaching as an area for increased emphasis. An alumni office that has had an efficient system for identifying and tracking graduates of the institution since 1960 might set as an objective the improvement of the database of pre-1960 alumni. Critical to the success of any such effort is the identification of outcomes/objectives judged important to the operation of the unit and linked as directly as possible to the Expanded Statement of Institutional Purpose.

Once a set of departmental/program outcomes/objectives has been identified, the next step is to further refine and complete these statements for use within institutional effectiveness assessment. The format for describing intended outcomes/objectives may vary according to the reference, but the questions to be answered remain consistent:

1. Is the outcome/objective consistent with the institution's Expanded Statement of Institutional Purpose?
2. Does the outcome/objective describe a reasonable or achievable outcome?
3. Is the outcome/objective clear and measurable?
4. Is the outcome/objective written at a reasonable level of specificity?
5. Does the outcome/objective specify the time frame in which it will be accomplished?

Within the context of these general questions, there are many formats for presenting objectives. The National Laboratory for Higher Education (1974) recommended that an objective (or intended outcome) take the form of a single statement with the following elements:

1. **Responsibility**—what person or unit is responsible for carrying out the objective;
2. **Outcome** (or result)—what is expected to occur;
3. **Time**—when the goal will be completed;
4. **Measurement** (or assessment)—what will be used to measure accomplishment of the objective;
5. **Performance standards**—what level of attainment is required; and,
6. **Conditions**—what conditions must be met before the objective can be accomplished.

An example of an objective written in this format is the following:

By fall of the 1992-93 academic year [**time**], the Admissions Office [**responsibility**]—assuming that there are tuition increases of no more than 7% [**condition**]—will enroll an entering class [**outcome or result**] of 1,200 [**performance standard**]; the number of full-time registrations will be used to verify achievement [**measurement**].

Translated into the format suggested by one regional accrediting association, the Commission on Colleges of the Southern Association of Colleges and Schools (SACS) (*Resource Manual*, 1989), this objective would read as follows:

1. **Statement of Purpose**—Our University will recruit students of high academic credentials.
2. **Expected Results** (outcome/objective)—By Fall of the 1992-93 academic year, Our University will admit 2,000 students from a pool of 3,200 applicants, yielding a fall semester entering class of 1,200 students.

3. **Assessment Procedures**—The number of full-time registrations for first-time freshmen in the fall semester, as indicated by the records in the Registrar's Office, plus the number of applicants and number of students accepted for admission during those periods, as indicated by the records in the Office of Admissions, will constitute the basic data for assessment of the extent of accomplishment.

4. **Administration of Assessment Procedures**—The Office of Institutional Research will report the number of applicants, the number of those accepted, and the number of entering freshmen as a part of the regular fall enrollment report. The Office of Admissions will verify the applicant and admission data, and the University Registrar will verify the number of first-time freshmen.

5. **Use of Assessment Findings**—The Office of Admissions will review the results on a yearly basis and, if the results are below expectation, either initiate procedures to increase the number and the quality of applicants, or raise the matter for consideration at the institutional level.

Note that the SACS format includes a description of the way the assessment results will be used. Addition of this, or a similar, section to each objective improves the probability that the assessment process will become more than an exercise. The format just described might be slightly altered so that the "Expected Results" and "Assessment Procedures" sections are completed early in the fiscal or academic year with additional sections describing the results of the assessment and the use of the assessment results completed at the end of the period as part of an annual update or an annual report.

A third format is very similar to the one recommended by SACS but substitutes a section called "Progress Toward Achieving Objective" for the "Administration of Assessment Procedures" section. The format just described might be implemented by requiring that the "Expected Results" and "Assessment Procedures" sections be completed early in the fiscal or academic year with additional sections describing the results of the assessment and the use of the assessment results completed at the end of the period as part of an annual update or an annual report. Since some administrators and faculty tend to confuse expected results with strategies for achieving objectives, it may be advantageous to include a "Strategies for Achieving Objectives" section along with the objective.

These are only two examples of formats for writing objectives. Each institution must identify a format that is compatible with its own planning and evaluation system. The format itself is not as important as the elements included, and many perfectly acceptable statements of departmental/program intentions will not explicitly contain all of the elements suggested. The sample outcome/objective just described, for example, could also have been presented in the form of a table or with separate paragraphs for each element, and the second could have been written as a single statement with all of the elements included.

Selection of Assessment Procedures

One of the most challenging aspects of writing objectives and of identifying outcomes for higher education, particularly for administrative units, is the problem of selecting the assessment procedures to determine whether expected outcomes have been achieved.

While in the process of developing new outcomes/objectives, the department or administrative unit can easily identify assessment procedures that will be so time- and resource-consuming that they will become an end in themselves and not a means of determining whether a specific outcome/objective has been achieved. If this occurs, the long-term result is likely to be abandonment of the process.

Pratt and Reichard (1983) recommend developing, wherever possible, assessment procedures using existing institutional records such as registration records, logs of student or public contact, monthly or weekly records of books checked out of the library, or any other records, particularly those that can be reduced to monthly, quarterly, or yearly reports. If such records are not available or if the existing records are not appropriate for assessing a particular outcome/objective, special reports must be developed. Even in this case, the more completely the assessment procedures can be incorporated into existing operations of a unit, the more likely the assessment is to be continued over the long term. In a few instances, the particular academic or administrative unit may wish to collect data through a special procedure such as a survey of students, faculty, alumni, or local business operators. If this form of assessment is undertaken, it should generally be regarded as a long-term, repetitive effort, with the initial survey data used to form a baseline for future studies as well as to answer immediate assessment needs. Institutions should seriously consider centralization of the logistical aspects of such surveys to avoid duplication of effort and excessive cost.

As the individual assessment plans are developed for each outcome/objective, the use of subjective measures should not be neglected. Although objective measures are generally easier to collect and less open to question, they are not appropriate in every case. As Miller (1980, pp. 425-426) indicated:

> ...institutional evaluation should use objective data where available and purposeful but make no apologies for using subjective data. Or, it is better to be generally right than precisely wrong. Objective data is important, yet considerable variation exists in the availability and quality of such evidence....The lack of "hard" data should not deter careful and systematic decision making about important institutional matters. Solid bases for decision making can be developed by using whatever hard data are available along with experience, judgment, and common sense. Important institutional process-type decisions often are made on much less.

Whatever the source of data, whatever the type of evidence available, the careful selection of educational, research, and service outcomes and administrative objectives is one of the most important activities in the process of assessment. If outcomes and objectives are important and meaningful to the department/program, if the assessment procedures are easily incorporated into ongoing operations, and if those procedures provide useful information that can be used to improve those operations, then the process is likely to be sustained over time.

Importance of Multiple Assessment Procedures for Each Outcome/Objective

In any area of research, the reliability of the results depends in part on the various procedures used to develop the situation and collect the data and in part on the appropriateness of the particular measure chosen. As in other research endeavors, reliability can be improved by the use of multiple measures. Although the term **multiple measures** is generally interpreted to mean two or more different measures of the same effect, it can also mean repeating the same measure at different intervals or, more rarely, having more than one observer measure the same effect at a single point in time.

Some outcomes are stated in such a way that a single measure will provide appropriate information for assessment of that objective. For example, Our University has a goal to "increase the level of organized or sponsored research expenditures by 5% per year for the next five years." An audit report indicating the increase in expenditures each year would be a single measure adequate to assess that goal. On the other hand, the goal to "study Our University's general education program to determine whether revisions are desirable" would probably require more than one outcome/objective measure for adequate assessment. Some type of test or examination measuring student achievement might be paired with portfolios including examples of student work in critical areas of the general education curriculum, measures of student success in subsequent upper-level courses, evaluation of course syllabi to determine whether course content is consistent with the goals of the program, and possibly a review of the program by an outside group or individual. A third goal, to "give increased emphasis to recruitment of minority students (Hispanic, African American, Asian, and Native American) and increase their representation in the overall student population" might best be assessed by establishing a base of the number and percentage of students in each racial category and monitoring changes in both number and percentage over a period of several years. In this case, repeated measures of the same data element provide the most appropriate method of assessment.

In summary, as in selecting the specific method of assessment, the determination of the number of different methods of assessment or the number of times each needs to be repeated to establish trend data is a decision that must be made based on the content of the goal or objective.

Progressive Revision of Standards

As the Expanded Statement of Institutional Purpose objectives and outcomes are reviewed on a continuous basis, the standards by which their achievement is measured also need to be reconsidered periodically. If, for example, the percentage of students successfully passing board exams in nursing increased at the rate of 2% per year over three years, it might be logical to consider adopting statements of intentions that would require progressively higher percentages of students to pass such exams. Judgment will play a crucial role in determining realistic performance standards.

Design of Feedback Mechanisms

Based on the assessment of outcomes and objectives, reports for presentation to academic and administrative departments should be prepared. Mechanisms for providing feedback from the evaluation should include written documents, probably in the form of a report addressing each of the stated outcomes/objectives as well as tabular data. Although narrative descriptions of the findings are suggested, graphic presentations are usually more effective. An objective of the assessment process might be to summarize the data for each outcome/objective on one page through either a table or graph, with a short explanatory paragraph highlighting the major findings. Faculty and staff committees may be involved in analyzing and reporting the information that is disseminated to the entire department for review. Time for faculty and staff to discuss the report and to offer their interpretation of the results is essential. Rather than discussing the results at a regular departmental meeting, the chairperson or director may identify a special meeting at the beginning of the academic year for the interpretation of the assessment findings. A retreat or workshop may be the best mechanism for communicating how well the department met its objectives. Combining oral presentations with supporting visual materials can effectively draw attention to the data.

Interpretation of the data requires comparison of the results to norms or expectations, depending on how the standards are established. When outcomes are presented as desired states, then comparisons of obtained results with desired outcomes may be effective in focusing on strengths and weaknesses. If standardized instruments are used, comparison of the department's performance with an appropriate normative sample aids in interpretation of the results. If an institution-wide survey is conducted, the department can be compared with the institution as a whole or some subgroup, such as a division, college, or school. At the very least, the same data should be collected over a period of time to show progress toward goals. Graphical presentations can clearly illustrate trends over time and progress toward goals. After the results have been interpreted, faculty and staff should focus on the implications for changes in courses, curriculum, instructional methods, faculty development, advising, and other areas. The assessment findings must be communicated to an institution's chief executive officer (CEO) or an institution-wide committee that has responsibility for the evaluation of institutional effectiveness. This will be facilitated by processing assessment results through a centralized clearinghouse for assessment results.

Peter Ewell (1984) cited three examples of "self-regarding institutions" that engage in a continuous assessment process and use assessment results for curriculum and institutional improvement. Alverno College, Northeast Missouri State University (NMSU), and the University of Tennessee at Knoxville (UTK) differ in their approaches to assessment as well as in their motivation for carrying out assessments. However, both NMSU and UTK link the results of assessment to budgeting processes, and NMSU uses the results in its budget requests to the state. UTK is responding to the Tennessee Higher Education Commission's "performance funding" program, which distributes additional state money based on measures of student outcomes and program evaluations.

Given Ewell's analysis of effective assessment programs of postsecondary institutions, I conclude that, to be effective in promoting institutional change, the review of departmental outcomes must be incorporated into the regular resource-allocation and budget-planning processes. The linkage of departmental evaluations to institutional-level assessment is most effectively accomplished through the planning and budgeting processes. Departmental requests for budgets could be presented to an institution-wide committee for review of progress toward last year's goals and objectives and determination of resource needs to support the proposed objectives.

If the departmental evaluations result in increases or decreases in budgets to support change and improvement, then faculty and staff will view the process as more than a mere exercise. The tangible ramifications of the evaluation process will lead to serious efforts to demonstrate departmental outcomes, although a tendency to set aspirations or intentions that are easily attained and/or to lower standards over time may be observed in some departments. Therefore, senior administrators or an institutional committee should carefully review the revised outcomes and objectives to ensure that criteria and standards are appropriate.

The institutional review will result in revisions of outcomes and objectives in light of institutional goals and resource availability. The senior administrator of the institutional committee and department heads can negotiate the outcomes and objectives for the next cycle to ensure compatibility with the Expanded Statement Institutional Purpose and feasibility within given resources.

At the departmental level, the reports of assessment findings are reviewed, discussed, and revised by members of the department. After discussions with senior administrators or the institutional committee, the director or department chairperson/head can agree to certain revisions in objectives. Finally, the director or department chairperson should communicate these changes to the faculty and staff. Resource allocations would be directly linked to the proposed objectives and to the departmental strengths and weaknesses identified in the evaluation reports.

The Logistical Support of Assessment

Assessment can be a costly process, in terms of both money and human resources. Throughout these resource sections the authors have encouraged the use of simple assessment procedures. Both academic and administrative units have repeatedly been encouraged to use existing data wherever possible, to minimize the use of special reports, and to use special instruments and surveys sparingly. However, even the most carefully designed process will require extra expenditures and added effort on the part of faculty, administrators, and staff.

Student outcomes assessment is one area where additional expense is almost unavoidable. Although attitude assessment instruments are relatively inexpensive, the total cost of administering a survey can be high. The costs of an initial mailing, return postage, and the mailing of one or more follow-up postcards must be considered as well. A simple alumni survey of a graduating class of 1,000 could cost well over $1,000, depending on the particular survey and the method of scoring and analysis. Academic assessment instruments are even more costly. Freshman placement testing can be less expensive, provided instruments are scored on campus, but even this is a major expenditure. A decision to purchase commercially available surveys or services rather than invest one's own staff resources ends up as a trade-off requiring judgment as to which resource is most limited.

Each campus should review the assessments planned—particularly those that require student testing or surveying of campus or outside groups—to determine whether the needs of several units can be met by a coordinated effort. In many cases, a single survey can meet the needs of not only several administrative units but also several academic departments or schools. Where this is possible, the time and effort to prepare, administer, and score the instrument as well as the actual costs of mailing and follow-up can be greatly reduced. As an added benefit, the return rate is likely to be higher if the same individuals do not receive multiple instruments from different units within the college or university.

As the assessment procedures are being developed and identified, campus planning groups should be identifying sources of funds to be used for assessment. The success of a student outcomes assessment process will depend, in large part, on whether assessment can become a regular budget item. If new sources of funds must be identified each year, the process will eventually die as other priorities intervene. It is also important for some person or group to be given responsibility for carrying out those parts of the assessment that are coordinated and for that individual (or group) to be given the time and resources to complete the tasks on an ongoing basis.

As the assessment process progresses, a large body of data concerning the students and the operations of the university will accumulate. At this point, two questions arise: (1) How will the information be stored or maintained? and (2) Who will have access to what data? Each campus will need to determine, for each type of information, who is to have access and who is to maintain that data. The campuses will then need to identify an office that will be responsible for maintaining a consolidated list of information sources, a library of reports, and documented computer files of survey and student academic assessment data. Following the campus determination of access, that office would serve as a clearinghouse for assessment data. Most information would be available in either raw data or report form. Some information, such as that included in detailed annual reports, might be available only in the offices generating the reports and the files of supervisors receiving the reports. However, even in those cases, the clearinghouse would maintain copies of unit outcomes and objectives reports indicating which assessments are appropriate and the current assessment results relating to each.

As indicated by this discussion, a major assessment program—even one carefully planned to decentralize and simplify the procedure—requires a major commitment by the institution. This commitment must take the form of providing resources as a part of the regular budget and of assigning responsibility for overall coordination to a single office or individual.

Summary

It would be a mistake to picture the design of the assessment process solely in terms of the blueprint analogy utilized by Yost in a preceding resource section concerning the development of the Expanded Statement of Institutional Purpose, because the assessment process must by its design be reactive in nature. Rather, those charged with responsibility for coordination of assessment activities must gather the best materials available, apply these assessment materials to the blueprint provided by intended outcomes/objectives, assist in development of new materials to fill the gaps in assessment coverage, seek to make the application of various assessment methodologies across the campus as efficient as possible, and feed back the information to the various levels of the institutions as effectively as possible.

Institutions can expect a considerable degree of variance in the technical merit of statements of departmental/program intended outcomes/objectives. Particularly at inception of institutional effectiveness operations, such differences are not only acceptable but desirable to the extent that they reflect active involvement by the institution's departments. However, this resource section and the examples contained in Appendix B suggest that outcomes/objectives should be linked to the Expanded Statement of Institutional Purpose, exhibit (explicitly or implicitly) many of the attributes described earlier, and in most cases be subject to ascertainment of accomplishment.

References: Cited and Recommended

Ewell, P. T. (1984). *The Self-Regulating Institution: Information for Excellence*. Boulder, CO: National Center for Higher Education Management Systems.

Fincher, C. (1978). Importance of Criteria for Institutional Goals. In R. H. Fenske (Ed.), Using Goals in Research and Planning (pp. 1-15). *New Directions for Institutional Research*, No. 19, Vol. 8. San Francisco: Jossey-Bass.

Miller, R. I. (1980). Appraising Institutional Performance. In P. Jedamus, M. W. Peterson, and Associates (eds.), *Improving Academic Management*. San Francisco: Jossey-Bass.

National Laboratory for Higher Education. (1974). *Developing Measurable Objectives*. Durham, NC: Author.

Pratt, L. K., and Reichard, D. J. (1983). Assessing Institutional Goals. In N. P. Uhl (Ed.), Using Research for Institutional Planning (pp. 53-66). *New Directions for Institutional Research*, no. 37. San Francisco: Jossey-Bass.

Resource Manual on Institutional Effectiveness. (1989). Atlanta, GA: Commission on Colleges of the Southern Association of Colleges and Schools.

Setting and Evaluating Intended Educational (Instructional) Outcomes

Brenda Rogers

At the level of the academic department, successful implementation depends on the involvement and commitment of faculty, who are the direct link to students and the educational process. Educational outcomes, defined as changes that result from instruction, must be focused on student learning and the improvement of teaching and learning. Institutions may refer to educational outcomes as expected results, intended outcomes, instructional outcomes, or intended student academic achievement. The focus should be not on the terminology, but on a common understanding of the purpose of statements of outcomes. Specifically, academic departments must state in relatively behavioral terms their expectations for student achievement. Because faculty have responsibility for developing the curriculum and courses, as well as for teaching and testing students, they should also be responsible for defining reasonable expectations for groups of students, and hence their program.

Setting Intended Educational (Instructional) Outcomes

In the normal cycle for curriculum planning and course development, educational outcomes originate from the faculty. The plan for implementing institutional effectiveness integrates course and curriculum planning with institutional planning processes. The degree to which institutional effectiveness is implemented at the academic department level depends largely on faculty perceiving that the activities are appropriate departmental planning and evaluation processes. Demonstrating to faculty that the institutional effectiveness process will enhance normal departmental planning and will link departmental planning with the institutional budgeting cycles is imperative.

That faculty must have primary responsibility and concomitantly ultimate authority for setting the educational outcomes within their respective academic departments. For any other group to do so would be usurping the power of the faculty over curriculum and course development. In fact, a major source of faculty resistance to the assessment movement in higher education is a perceived threat to their academic freedom in the selection of course content and instructional methods, the development of testing procedures that might not be educationally sound for the discipline, and the establishment of grading standards.

In general, faculty support is enhanced when the actions as well as the rhetoric of the administration demonstrate a commitment to assessment "as a tool for the improvement of teaching and learning" (Chandler, 1986, p. 5). Peter Ewell (1985), in a description of successful assessment programs, notes that model programs often have "an explicit focus on the assessment and improvement of an individual curricula" and that "many programs fail because assessment and improvement is only undertaken for the institution as a whole" (p. 22). Incentives for planning and evaluation activities, such as seed money to support a faculty planning retreat or to develop a set of assessment measures, are visible signs of that commitment. Departments that set challenging objectives and have creative ways of measuring their accomplishments should be recognized and rewarded whenever possible.

The Study Group on the Conditions of Excellence in American Higher Education (1984) emphasized assessment as a form of feedback to improve teaching and learning. This group specifically recommended faculty involvement in the design and implementation of assessment programs for the following reason:

> The best way to connect assessment to improvement of teaching and learning is to insure that faculty have a proprietary interest in the assessment process...such involvement will help faculty to specify—far more precisely than they do at present—the outcomes they expect from individual courses and academic programs. And the more precisely they can specify the outcomes, the more likely they are to match teaching approaches to those ends (p. 45).

The success of assessment efforts depends on more than focusing those efforts on academic departments, the curricula, and courses; it also depends on faculty consensus within the department as to the appropriate means for assessing outcomes. Faculty will be skeptical if they believe that assessment information lacks relevance for the improvement of teaching and learning processes. A standardized test measuring computational and writing skills, adopted by the institution to measure "general education," will probably not be meaningful to the art, drama, and music departments, although their courses may satisfy some of the general education requirements. The faculty may, however, accept measures of critical thinking applied specifically to their disciplines as appropriate outcomes.

Faculty must also agree on the proper use of the assessment results. Although faculty may agree that normative data will assist in evaluating their program, they may be rightfully concerned about the misuse of the data. Faculty need answers to the following questions: Who will have access to the departmental information, and how will this information be used? Will programs be eliminated based on student outcomes? Will results be used to promote and terminate faculty? To minimize these legitimate concerns about the misuse of the assessment results, faculty must engage in discussions at the planning stage, during which the ground rules for the dissemination and use of the information are established. Unless faculty are assured that they will maintain control over the information at the academic department level, they may not provide the essential support in setting meaningful educational outcomes for their programs.

Thus, as the administration develops policies and procedures for institutional assessment, it must consult faculty and respond to their concerns. Faculty representing a wide range of academic disciplines should serve on every committee and should have input about the implementation of assessment.

However careful the facilitators of the planning and evaluation processes are, faculty participation in planning and implementation will not ensure that all faculty fully support institutional efforts. Rarely do faculty reach total consensus on any issue. However, for the implementation of institutional effectiveness to have the desired impact on the overall quality of the institution, the majority of the faculty, particularly those who function as strong leaders, should support the planning and evaluation efforts, if not every activity. Clearly, the faculty, as the specialists in their academic disciplines and as the direct link to students in the classroom, must be responsible for defining and revising intended instructional outcomes. At the departmental level, outcomes must form a bridge between institutional goals for student learning/development and specific course and curriculum content. The educational outcomes must be broad enough to encompass the total curriculum yet concrete enough to have implications for changes in instructional methods and curriculum design. Therefore, faculty should limit the number of outcomes to be assessed to those that are meaningful at the departmental level and are related to institutional goals. Concentration on assessing a few critical outcomes is more productive than incomplete coverage of all departmental expectations.

As desired states of behavior, outcomes should focus on problem areas where improvements are needed and changes are expected. A continuation of the current conditions, although important, is not appropriate in an outcome statement. Thus, outcomes should be stated in terms of expected behaviors within a set time frame. Educational outcomes focus primarily on student behavior; however, faculty development can also be included since changes in faculty may have indirect effects on student learning.

How do departmental faculty begin the process of developing meaningful outcomes statements? A good resource is the manual *Developing Measurable Objectives* (National Laboratory for Higher Education, 1974), which contains a discussion of procedures for developing program goals and objectives. A beginning step is to complete a content analysis of current courses and curricula. A review of course syllabi and the study of the overall curriculum should be conducted, perhaps as a part of a regular program review. This curriculum review should not be limited to current local course offerings alone but should extend to other institutions that offer strong academic programs in the same field which may serve as models for the institution to emulate. Consultation with colleagues from other institutions is often helpful. In addition, faculty should consult reports from national commissions, standards of the professional accrediting agencies, and professional associations to identify outcomes. Then faculty can select those outcomes that are appropriate for their students as well as consistent with both the purpose of the institution and the overall orientation of the department.

To ensure that outcomes are aimed at appropriate levels of performance, faculty must know the achievement levels of the typical entering student in order to set the expected performance level of the typical exiting student. Outcomes frequently are statements of gains or changes that occur as a result of the college experience. Knowledge of high school preparation will assist in setting reasonable outcomes for first- and second-year college students. In some disciplines it is highly desirable to have placement test data not only to establish valid procedures for assigning students to remedial or advanced courses, but also to describe skills and knowledge of the typical entering student. For upper-level undergraduate programs, faculty need to be familiar with prerequisite courses taught not only at their institution, but at institutions from which students transfer. A more difficult question is the expected level of performance for the exiting student, which should be stated in the educational outcomes. For departments that primarily provide general education courses at the freshman and sophomore levels, outcomes may include the knowledge, skills, and attitudes judged necessary for success at upper-division levels. Some questions for departments to consider are the following: Do the expectations differ for those students who major in the discipline versus those who take only the introductory courses? Do the courses teach general skills that should continue to develop in other courses outside of the department? When is the appropriate time during the student's academic career to measure the attainment of these outcomes?

For departments offering degrees, diplomas, or certificates, faculty should determine the outcomes that are necessary for graduates to succeed in jobs or advanced academic programs. If the undergraduate degree provides the foundation for graduate or professional programs, faculty must be aware of the performance levels required by post-baccalaureate programs. If the degree, diploma, or certificate is primarily aimed at job preparation, then the outcomes must relate to entry-level skills required for employment. If a requirement for job entry is passing a licensing, certifying, or qualifying examination, then the knowledge and skills have already been defined, probably by a professional organization. In the absence of such examinations, faculty must work with other professionals to conduct job analyses of entry level positions. A job analysis specifies the skills, knowledge, and behaviors necessary for a recent graduate to perform the job adequately.

Institutional goals in the educational area are not limited to development of "a depth of understanding in the major field and preprofessional programs preparing the graduate for employment" (Appendix A, p. 262). In the Expanded Statement of Institutional Purpose of the hypothetical institution Our University, academic programs are to ensure an "academic foundation in liberal studies in order to enhance students' communication and analytic skills, to provide an understanding of their intellectual and cultural heritage, and to assist them in the development of self-awareness, responsible leadership, and the capacity to make reasoned moral judgments" (Appendix A, p. 259). Thus, departments must address areas of social and personal development as well as cognitive development, which is usually the primary focus of curriculum objectives. Faculty must consider how their academic disciplines contribute to social and personal development. For example, the study of foreign languages may contribute to students developing an interest in and tolerance of people from different cultures. The sociology, political science, and business management programs may focus on defining "responsible leadership" and having students judge the value of such leadership to our society.

Thus, outcomes should not be limited to the cognitive domain, but should adequately cover the affective and skill areas. The classification of outcomes into these three areas—cognitive (knowledge), affective (attitudes), and skills (performance)—is helpful to ensure broad coverage of student changes. Erwin (1991) classifies objectives as subject matter—knowledge obtained in specific disciplines; developmental—including cognitive and affective objectives that have a lasting impact and are more general than subject-specific objectives; and skills—defined as "the means by which knowledge is acquired and communicated" (Erwin, p. 44).

The cognitive domain, as described in Bloom's taxonomy of educational objectives (Bloom et al., 1956), includes knowledge, comprehension, application, analysis, synthesis, and evaluation. Faculty should specify the level of cognitive complexity required for students to demonstrate that learning has occurred. Is it sufficient for the student to pass an objective test that measures knowledge, or is the application of knowledge in simulation exercises a more appropriate measure?

The affective domain, described by Krathwohl, Bloom, and Masia (1964), includes attitudes, beliefs, values, goals, and expectations which predispose a person to behave in certain ways. Affect or attitude must be directed toward a person, object, place, or idea. For example, to say that a student has a positive attitude is meaningless, but to add "toward writing" allows us to make some predictions about the student's behavior. We might expect the student to write frequently, to write with observable pleasure, or to ask for help in writing.

Although such outcomes are generally not stated in course objectives, faculty frequently want to increase student interest in the subject matter—an affective outcome. Departments may be less inclined to state affective outcomes because of the problems associated with the measurement of attitudes. Henerson, Morris, and Fitz-Gibbon (1978, p. 13) described those problems. First, it is impossible to measure attitudes directly; we must infer attitudes from behavior. Second, there may be inconsistency between attitudes and behavior; thus, more than one observation of behavior is essential in order to infer the attitude. Third, it is difficult to develop instruments that meet the accepted standards for reliability; attitudes change, and stability in measuring them over time is often unattainable. Finally, since attitudes are constructs that cannot be directly observed, people disagree on the conceptual and operational definitions of specific attitudes.

Skills include, but are not limited to, psychomotor tasks that develop through imitation and practice. Physical education departments; the performing arts; professional programs like nursing, teaching, and dentistry; and technical, vocational, and trade programs all focus on skill development. Although knowledge of information may be a necessary condition to perform certain tasks, knowledge alone is not sufficient; practice is often the key to psychomotor performance. For example, the music department cannot adequately assess the aspiring musician through an objective test that measures recognition of musical notes, time, and rhythmic patterns. Actual performance of several pieces in which a student demonstrates the ability to read music and play musical instruments, using correct time and rhythms, is necessary to determine the student's level of proficiency.

In addition to psychomotor skills, general skills expected of all students are usually identified. The Expanded Statement of Institutional Purpose for Our University explicitly states five general skills that all students should master before exiting the institution. Our University's students are expected to:

1. Express themselves clearly, correctly, and succinctly in a written manner;
2. Make an effective verbal presentation of their ideas concerning a topic;
3. Read and offer an analysis of periodical literature concerning a topic of interest;
4. Complete accurately basic mathematical calculations; and,
5. Demonstrate a sufficient level of computer literacy.

These skills are usually addressed in the general education component of the curriculum, which crosses academic departments. Reading, writing, speaking, mathematical computation, and computer literacy may be directly related to specific courses; however, the skills should continue to develop across the entire curriculum. For example, students may be required to take a speech course that will provide them with fundamental skills in developing an idea and presenting it orally. In theory, students should practice these skills in many other courses, through class discussions if not formal oral presentations. Although the speech department should accept primary responsibility for this skill, all academic departments should provide students with both practice in and evaluation of oral presentations.

Who should be responsible for setting the educational outcomes for general education? This is a question that each institution must address, for it also implies responsibility for assessing these skills. Perhaps, as with our hypothetical institution, these should be institution-wide outcomes, set by a faculty committee that broadly represents the academic community. This approach supports the notion of shared responsibility for the development of general education skills. The task confronting each department is to define the expected outcomes for its own courses and programs in ways that can be assessed. The academic department then has responsibility for reviewing its courses and programs, examining the professional literature, and collaborating with colleagues from other institutions—including high schools, two-year colleges, four-year colleges, institutions with professional and graduate programs, and employers—to determine desirable outcomes for its students.

Each academic department must develop for its students meaningful educational outcomes that capture the overall objectives of the courses and curricula within the context of the institution's purpose. Although defining procedures for assessing outcomes is the next step, the process of setting educational outcomes should not be restricted by measurement considerations. Often the most meaningful objectives may be less amenable to direct observation or testing. If faculty are committed to the educational outcomes, they may find very creative and innovative ways to infer the accomplishment of these objectives. Creativity and innovation should be encouraged, not stifled by measurement considerations.

Evaluating Intended Educational (Instructional) Outcomes

As emphasized previously, it is important to allow educational outcomes to emerge without overemphasis on assessment procedures. Probably some separation in time between the development of the outcomes and the selection of assessment procedures is healthy. (However, once meaningful objectives are established, the next step is to define in operational terms how the educational outcomes will be evaluated.)

For faculty to agree on which outcomes are important for their students to attain is difficult enough, but then to agree on the operational definitions of those outcomes—how they will be observed and measured—may be a major stumbling block in the process. Multiple measures that use a variety of assessment methods (for example, interest inventories, interviews, and direct observation of behavior) may be essential for faculty to endorse the assessment process.

In evaluating student outcomes, faculty first should inventory existing data collection efforts and assessment procedures. The resource section beginning on page 123 contains a detailed discussion of this process. It may be that departments or the institution is currently conducting a follow-up survey of graduates that may be useful in the assessment of educational outcomes.

Most institutions maintain computerized files with historical data on students, faculty, and staff. A wealth of information about retention, enrollment and graduation trends, grades, and course-taking patterns is available from student information systems. Computerized files and report programs may have to be designed to answer important questions— for example, on the average, how long it takes an undergraduate to complete a baccalaureate degree in a particular discipline. However, the data are available without new collection efforts. Peter Ewell (1987) has described the basic principles in building cohort files and conducting retention studies from data maintained on college campuses, and this subject was explored in some detail in the resource section beginning on page 107.

To assist in the evaluation of departmental outcomes, computerized reports must present separate analyses for each department. Assuming that a fourth-generation language, like SAS (1985), is used to build the files and generate the reports, a programmer can modify slightly the standard program to produce departmental reports. Coordination with the institutional research office or administrative data processing is essential to ensure that reports, like retention studies, answer questions at the departmental level.

Routine reports required by the governing board, state agencies, the federal government, and professional accrediting agencies offer additional sources of information. The IPEDS (formerly HEGIS) reports required by the federal government are useful if the data are analyzed over several years to identify trends in enrollment and graduation. The institutional research office should be able to identify the standard reports that may help departments with assessment.

If, however, existing data do not provide information appropriate for assessing departmental outcomes, then other approaches will have to be considered. Faculty must reach agreement as to the approaches that will generate the most meaningful information about their students. Not only tests and surveys but also direct observations, interviews, student performances, journals and other written materials, portfolios of student work, oral presentations, and self-evaluations should be considered as sources of information about educational outcomes and student learning. The major consideration is whether the method provides useful, credible information about the accomplishment of the educational objectives.

Faculty may choose qualitative methods in order to explore student change and development. Qualitative approaches may utilize unobtrusive observations of students, unstructured interviews, content analysis of historical documents, analysis of autobiographies or journals, and holistic judgments of student performances or products, such as oral presentations or writing samples. Qualitative approaches do not yield scores; rather, faculty use the information to make overall judgments about the attainment of the stated outcomes. A good introduction to qualitative research methods is *Qualitative Data Analysis: An Expanded Sourcebook* (Miles, 1994).

It will be helpful for faculty to categorize the educational objectives as pertaining to cognitive, affective, and psychomotor outcomes. Educational testing will be most appropriate for cognitive outcomes. Surveys, interviews, and qualitative approaches may be more appropriate for affective, rather than cognitive, outcomes. Performance measures and direct observations are good techniques for measuring psychomotor skill attainment. A variety of approaches will be reviewed with emphasis on resource materials helpful to academic departments.

Assessment of Cognitive Outcomes

In the past few years the dominant approach toward the assessment of cognitive outcomes in general education and the academic major has been standardized tests. However, institutions have reported limited success in using the results effectively for improving teaching and learning. Often the standardized cognitive instruments do not provide adequate coverage of the content nor do they tap the more complex cognitive processes that college requires of students. We would do well to heed the remarks of Shulman, Smith, and Stewart (1987, p. 8): "There's some magical thinking going on in the assessment community. And that magical thinking is that if we can somehow lay a comprehensive 90-minute exam on top of an otherwise absolutely disintegrated curriculum, we're doing general education."

Testing that is not preceded by sound curriculum planning and development may be a useless activity. Furthermore, testing cognitive processes and content unrelated to the course and curriculum objectives is a waste of time if the aim is the improvement of teaching and learning at the departmental level. Western College of Miami University (Banta, 1993, pp. 78-80) found that the battery of tests had little impact on the curriculum. One reason given was that there was a lack of connection between the measures and the instructional objectives in their classes. Baird (1988) argues strongly that existing measures of "generic academic outcomes," such as those developed by testing companies, are not linked to the specific goals of the institution and the academic programs, and therefore scores from such measures are not effective measures of student learning and teaching strategies at the program and course levels. Rather than limiting assessment to the search for the "right test," faculty should select from a broad array of methods, using multiple measures to increase the reliability of the results.

While cognizant of the limitations of standardized measures of cognitive outcomes for departmental use, departmental faculty should conduct a critical review of existing instruments. New instruments are being marketed every day. The innovative Project for Area Concentration Achievement Testing at Austin Peay State University is developing surveys academic curricula by content area, has faculty write test items corresponding to the content, and constructs area achievement tests. Assessment efforts underway at colleges and universities will inevitably yield new instruments. The research literature and technical manuals accompanying the instruments should provide evidence for the validity of the instruments for specific purposes. Assessment instruments are available not only from testing companies, but also from individuals who have developed instruments for research purposes. A thorough review of existing instruments includes an evaluation of the following:

1. Content validity — The match between the test content and the departmental objectives;
2. Reliability — The consistency of scores over time and across alternate forms;
3. The appropriateness of the instrument for the target population; and,
4. The normative data to assist in interpreting the measures or scores.

Several resources will assist in the search for published tests. In *Tests in Print III: An Index to Tests, Test Reviews, and the Literature of Specific Tests*, Mitchell (1983) attempts to list all commercial tests printed in English. The *Mental Measurement Yearbook* series contains reviews of tests as well as factual information about the author, publisher, publication date, cost, administrative time, and grade levels for which appropriate. Research instruments developed by individual researchers may be obtained simply by requesting copies and permission to use them from the authors. Often these questionnaires and scales are available free of charge simply by contacting the researcher.

Banta and Schneider (1988) have reported on the use of faculty-developed exit examinations. The process undertaken by academic departments in the development of the examinations is briefly described in the article. An excellent discussion of "Assessment Through the Major" is provided by Mark I. Appelbaum (1988). A variety of approaches for evaluating the quality of education obtained by the student majoring in a discipline is presented. Issues surrounding the assessment of the major are explored in some depth.

The development of tests to measure cognitive gains is a time-consuming task requiring much expertise in the field of tests and measurement. Departments that choose to develop their own achievement tests will likely need assistance from testing experts. Testing companies will work with institutions in the development of instruments. As indicated in the resource section on cognitive instruments, some institutions committed to outcomes assessment have established their own assessment centers, staffed with experts to assist departments in the process of setting outcomes and selecting or developing appropriate measures. However, most institutions will be hard pressed to justify such an expenditure without specific external funding.

Although speaking primarily about elementary and secondary education, Morris and Fitz-Gibbon (1978) have described the general process for measuring achievement as one part of a program evaluation. To construct a departmental achievement test, faculty must carefully state the outcomes/objectives to be covered in the test. The objectives should include specification of both the content and the cognitive processes. Test items are then constructed to measure the outcomes/objectives with the item format carefully chosen to require the cognitive processes described by the objectives. Items and the reliability of the instrument should be analyzed. Finally, validity of the scores for the intended use should be examined. Although many excellent references describe the process of developing achievement tests, this is not a simple task. However, when no existing achievement test adequately covers the program outcomes/objectives, the only alternative may be the development of departmental examinations.

Another approach is the use of an external examiner, as proposed by Bobby Fong (1987) at the American Association for Higher Education Assessment Forum. He suggests that an outside expert in the academic field can be an "effective way to assess both student learning and curricular coherence in a major," which can lead to "valuable information and recommendations as to where curricular requirements need to be more specific and how course offerings need to be strengthened" (p. 17). The outside consultant could be asked to address the outcomes specified by the departments and to critique the curriculum. Separate resource sections at the end of Chapter 3 have expanded on specific instruments used to assess cognitive outcomes.

Assessment of Affective Outcomes

The resource section on attitudinal surveys to assess institutional effectiveness provides a thorough review of survey instruments (see page 43). The ETS instruments that are most appropriate for use at the academic department level are the Program Self-Assessment Service and the Graduate Program Self-Assessment Service. The perceptions of three constituencies—currently enrolled students, alumni, and faculty—concerning the strengths and weaknesses of the program can be compared. The ability to add up to 20 items to the printed questionnaire offers the opportunity to obtain information directly relevant to the affective objectives of the program.

Another attitudinal instrument is the College Student Experiences Questionnaire (CSEQ), developed by UCLA's Robert Pace (1990). This is a self-report instrument measuring student involvement in 16 college activities, 21 areas in which students estimate gains as a result of attending college, and 7 dimensions of the college environment. Comparative data are available for participating institutions. The CSEQ assesses student behaviors, such as the percentage of students using the library or various student services. Thus, it may be particularly helpful in establishing baseline measurements for a range of activities, which may be helpful in setting institutional or subunit goals. Although the research is promising, the primary application of research findings thus far has been at the institutional, rather than the departmental, level.

The research literature on college student development is a good resource for identifying measures of affective outcomes. The *Journal of College Student Personnel* should be reviewed regularly for new instruments and innovative approaches to assessment. If changes in values or level of motivation are the focus of departmental objectives, then Grandy (1988) and Graham (1988) provide a good review of existing instruments as well as a review of issues relating to the measurement of these affective outcomes.

In the absence of existing surveys that match the educational objectives, the department must develop its own surveys, if surveys of students, alumni, and/or faculty are judged as the best sources of information. Attitudinal surveys are generally easier to construct than achievement tests. The key is to develop items that elicit truthful responses and relate to the intended outcomes. Existing surveys should be examined for examples of the types of questions and response formats. After the questionnaire is constructed, experts should review it. A pretest with an analysis of the results should be conducted prior to implementation.

Faculty should explore methods other than surveys to assess affective outcomes. Attitudinal surveys may lack specificity or may be so reactive in nature that faculty will question the validity of the results. In such cases, faculty must select alternate assessment methods and possibly develop new approaches. Unobtrusive measures offer alternatives to paper-and-pencil measures (Grandy, 1988; Terenzini, 1986; Webb, Campbell, Schwartz, & Sechrest, 1981). Examples of unobtrusive measures are records of student use of facilities and services. For example, professors often place supplemental reading material on reserve in the library. Frequency of use is an indicator of students' interest in the subject. Physical education departments may be able to monitor student use of recreational and exercise facilities. Such "counts" may be good indicators of attitudes as well as actual behavior.

Interviewing students is another way to collect evaluation data on affective outcomes. Questions may be highly structured and standardized, or they may emerge as a skilled interviewer probes the responses for underlying meaning. In either case, interviewers should be trained and have a very clear understanding about the goal of the interviews. Either individual or group interviews may be used. Research on focus groups suggests that this method is useful for exploring attitudes and perceptions.

The interview method, if conducted properly, may yield a wealth of both quantitative and qualitative data regarding students' perceptions, expectations, and values. If faculty or advisors conduct the interviews, an unintended outcome may be an increase in meaningful dialogue between students and faculty/advisors. A study of changes in students over their four years at Stanford University, *Careerism and Intellectualism Among College Students* (Katchadourian & Boli, 1985), illustrates the use of the interview method to analyze change in undergraduates over the college years.

From observations of student behavior we may draw inferences about attitudes. Observations can be highly controlled with checklists for recording and quantifying discrete behaviors. On the other hand, faculty may observe during classroom settings, later recording and interpreting events. Students' responsiveness, from which interest in the subject matter is inferred, may be observed in the classroom. Faculty advisors may observe and record in advising notes the way students make educational and career decisions during their college years. From such notes, inferences may be made about students' career maturity, attitudes toward college and work, and academic motivation. The less obtrusive and the more naturalistic the observations, the more likely the behavior is reflective of student attitudes rather than a desire to please or exhibit socially desirable behavior.

Self-reports from students and faculty offer another alternative. The degree of structure in self-reports can vary from inventories and checklists to life histories, journals, and self-evaluations. As a part of course assignments or faculty advising, students may be asked to report their attitudes toward the course content, instructional methods, their own progress in attaining the goals of the course, or their growth and development as a result of taking a course or majoring in a subject. Faculty may report their own attitudes toward teaching, research, and departmental and institutional service. As with all measures of attitudes, self-reports can be faked; therefore, it is important that self-reports be used only in areas where there is clearly no "right" or desirable attitude. Also, student grades and faculty evaluations for promotion, tenure, or merit moneys should be clearly divorced from these self-reports.

Because attitudes are not directly observable but must be inferred from observations of behavior, it is essential to use multiple methods for measuring affective outcomes. Conclusions based on the convergence of results from multiple methods will stand up under close scrutiny; whereas, a single measurement, based on one observation, is probably a very unreliable indicator of attitudes.

The Assessment of Skills and the Psychomotor Domain

Having experts observe performance is the most appropriate way of ascertaining the attainment of psychomotor skills as well as other skills, such as writing, speaking, problem solving, managing, and leading. Physical education instructors observe students in sports and physical activities and rate the level of skill attainment. Similarly, faculty in the performing arts rate their students based on actual performances of music, dance, and drama. Products created in studio art and design classes are judged by faculty. Technical and vocational instructors observe their students performing tasks related to job skills and judge how adequately prepared they are for job entry.

Performance assessments are also appropriate for judging highly complex cognitive processes that require demonstration, such as writing and speaking (Dunbar, 1988). Performance measures, such as writing a paper, delivering a speech, or using a computer to solve a problem, are appropriate for many general education outcomes. In fact, performance measures may be more relevant to the instructional methods and intended outcomes than multiple-choice questions.

The degree to which the performance task is structured and planned, related to theory, systematically observed, and reduced to numerical ratings determines whether the method is quantitative or qualitative. Rating separate components of writing, such as grammar, paragraph structure, complexity of sentence structure, and diction, will yield a quantitative measure of writing. A holistic approach—in which an expert examines the entire piece of writing and makes an overall judgment as to how well the purpose is accomplished—is a qualitative assessment.

Some other examples of performance assessments appropriately adopted by academic departments are field experiments; interviews with students in a foreign language to determine their fluency and comprehension; diagnoses by medical students; clinical interviews by counseling, psychology, and social work students; and practice teaching and simulations of classroom teaching by education students. A more complete review of performance and behavioral assessment is contained in the resource section beginning on page 86.

Portfolio assessment, a method for determining student change and growth over time, is also discussed in the resource section beginning on page 86. A portfolio is a collection of student performance information over time, which may be judged in terms of growth or change in knowledge, skill, and values. The portfolio may contain written works, such as essays, journals, and autobiographies; self-evaluations; audio tapes and videos of speeches delivered or other performances; a collection of art work, drawings, designs, and so forth; or computer programs written or printouts demonstrating mastery of programming. The performances selected for the portfolio may be left up to the students' imaginations, or they may be assigned by the faculty. Typically, the portfolio follows the student throughout his or her college career and is assessed at different points in time. At Evergreen State College in Washington, the student's portfolio replaces the college transcript, and the portfolio contains written assessments of the student by faculty members.

Some outcomes of higher education may be shared by many departments but transcend the specific content of any single discipline. **Life competencies** is a term used to describe behaviors that are best observed, such as leadership, decision making, communication, planning and organizational skills, problem analysis, innovation, and social interaction (Byham, 1988). One approach to assessing life competencies, originally adopted by business and industry but feasible for institutions of higher education, is the assessment center. The assessment center is defined as "a comprehensive, standardized process in which techniques such as situational exercises and job simulations (e.g., discussion groups and presentations) are used to evaluate individuals" (p. 256). The assessment center requires a full-time director and many part-time assessors who are trained observers. Faculty might participate as observers, particularly for the evaluation of objectives directly related to their departmental student outcomes. In fact, the credibility of the results from assessment centers depend in large part on faculty defining the simulation exercises and judging the performances.

Summary

Educational outcomes describe changes in students in the cognitive, affective, and skill dimensions. Departments should limit the outcomes to those that are most important for their students and most significantly related to the institutional purpose. The process of identifying educational outcomes should be a natural, ongoing part of course and curriculum planning; however, the new dimension in the process is developing the linkages between institutional purpose and departmental activities.

A variety of approaches are available for assessing educational outcomes. Methods closely related to the teaching and learning processes are likely to be successful, whereas the administration of instruments—tests, surveys, and so on—with little connection to regular course activities may yield useless data. Methods appropriate for the type of educational outcome should be selected. Achievement tests, as well as written work and other products, are appropriate measures of cognitive outcomes. Surveys, interviews, observations, and portfolio analysis may be appropriate measures of affective outcomes. Skills, including psychomotor, interpersonal, life competencies, and complex cognitive skills, may best be evaluated through performance measures. The assessment procedures must match the objective and yield information that will be useful to faculty in changing teaching strategies, improving course content, and revising curricula.

References: Cited and Recommended

Appelbaum, M. I. (1988). Assessment Through the Major. In C. Adelman (ed.), *Performance and Judgment: Essays on Principles and Practices in the Assessment of College Student Learning* (pp. 117-137). Washington, DC: U.S. Department of Education, Office of Educational Research and Improvement.

Angelo, T. A., and Cross, K. P. (1993). *Classroom Assessment Techniques: A Handbook for College Teachers*. (2nd ed.) San Francisco: Jossey-Bass.

Baird, L. L. (1988). Diverse and Subtle Arts: Assessing the Generic Outcomes of Higher Education. In C. Adelman (ed.), *Performance and Judgment: Essays on Principles and Practices in the Assessment of College Student Learning* (pp. 39-62). Washington, DC: U.S. Department of Education, Office of Educational Research and Improvement.

Banta, T. W. and Associates. (1993). *Making a Difference: Outcomes of a Decade of Assessment in Higher Education*. San Francisco: Jossey-Bass.

Banta, T. W., & Schneider, J. A. (1988). Using Faculty-Developed Exit Examinations to Evaluate Academic Programs. *Journal of Higher Education, 59*, 69-83.

Bloom, B. S., Englhard, M., Funst, E., Hill, W., & Krathwohl, D. (eds.). (1956). *Taxonomy of Educational Objectives: The Classification of Educational Goals: Handbook I: Cognitive Domain*. New York: David McKay.

Byham, W. C. (1988). Using the Assessment Center Method to Measure Life Competencies. In C. Adelman (ed.), *Performance and Judgment: Essays on Principles and Practices in the Assessment of College Student Learning* (pp. 255-278). Washington, DC: U.S. Department of Education, Office of Educational Research and Improvement.

Chandler, J. W. (1986). *The College Perspective on Assessment*. ETS Invitational Conference on Assessing the Outcomes of Higher Education, New York, NY.

Dunbar, S. (1988). States of Art in the Science of Writing and other Performance Assessments. In C. Adelman (ed.), *Performance and Judgment: Essays on Principles and Practices in the Assessment of College Student Learning* (pp. 235-254). Washington, DC: U.S. Department of Education, Office of Educational Research and Improvement.

Ewell, P. T. (1985). *Levers for Change: The Role of State Government in Improving the Quality of Postsecondary Education*. ECS working paper. Denver, CO: Education Commission of the States.

Ewell, P. T. (1987). Principles of Longitudinal Enrollment Analysis: Conducting Retention and Student Flow Studies. In J. A. Muffo & G. W. McLaughlin (eds.), *A Primer on Institutional Research* (pp. 1-19). Tallahassee, FL: Association for Institutional Research.

Erwin, T. D. (1991). *Assessing Student Learning and Development: A Guide to the Principles, Goals, and Methods of Determining College Outcomes*. San Francisco: Jossey-Bass.

Fendley, W. R., Jr. and Seeloff, L. T., ed. (1993). *Reference Sources: An Annotated Bibliography for Institutional Research*. Tallahassee, FL: Association for Institutional Research.

Fong, B. (1987). *The External Examiner Approach to Assessment*. Paper commissioned by the American Association for Higher Education Assessment Forum for the Second National Conference on Assessment in Higher Education, Denver, CO.

Gardiner, L. F. (1989). *Planning for Assessment: Mission Statements, Goals, and Objectives*. Trenton, NJ: Office of Learning Assessment, New Jersey Department of Higher Education.

Goldman, B. A., & Mitchell, D. F. (1990). *Directory of Unpublished Experimental Mental Measures: Volume V*. Dubuque, IA: W. C. Brown.

Graham, S. (1988). Indicators of Motivation in College Students. In C. Adelman (ed.), *Performance and Judgment: Essays on Principles and Practices in the Assessment of College Student Learning* (pp. 163-186). Washington, DC: U.S. Department of Education, Office of Educational Research and Improvement.

Grandy, J. (1988). Assessing Changes in Student Values. In C. Adelman (ed.), *Performance and Judgment: Essays on Principles and Practices in the Assessment of College Student Learning* (pp. 139-161). Washington, DC: U.S. Department of Education, Office of Educational Research and Improvement.

Henerson, M. E., Morris, L. L., & Fitz-Gibbon, C. T. (1978). *How to Measure Attitudes.* Beverly Hills, CA: Sage.

Hutchings, P. (1990). "Learning over Time: Portfolio Assessment." *AAHE Bulletin, 42*(9), 6-8.

Katchadourian, H. A., & Boli, J. (1985). *Careerism and Intellectualism among College Students.* San Francisco: Jossey-Bass.

Krathwohl, D. R., Bloom, B. S., & Masia, B. B. (eds.). (1964). *Taxonomy of Educational Objectives: The Classification of Educational Goals: Handbook I: Affective Domain.* New York: David McKay.

Krueger, R. A. (1988). *Focus Groups: A Practical Guide for Applied Research.* Newbury Park, CA: Sage.

Light, R. (1990). *The Harvard Assessment Seminars: Explorations with Students and Faculty about Teaching, Learning, and Student Life.* Cambridge, MA: Harvard University Press.

Light, R. (1992). *The Harvard Assessment Seminars Second Report: Explorations with Students and Faculty about Teaching, Learning, and Student Life.* Cambridge, MA: Harvard University Press.

Miles, M. B., & Huberman, A. M. (1994). *Qualitative Data Analysis: An Expanded Sourcebook.* Beverly Hills, CA: Sage.

Mitchell, J. V. (ed.). (1983). *Tests in Print III: An Index to Tests, Test Reviews, and the Literature on Specific Tests.* Lincoln, NE: Buros Institute of Mental Measurements.

Mitchell, J. V. (ed.). (1989). *The Tenth Mental Measurements Yearbook.* Lincoln, NE: Buros Institute of Mental Measurements.

Morris, L. L., & Fitz-Gibbon, C. T. (1978). *How to Measure Achievement.* Beverly Hills, CA: Sage.

National Laboratory for Higher Education. (1974). *Developing Measurable Objectives.* Durham, NC: National Laboratory for Higher Education.

Pace, C. R. (1990). *The College Student Experiences Questionnaire.* Los Angeles: Higher Educational Research Institute, University of California.

SAS Users' Guide: Basics, Version 5 Edition (1985). Cary, NC:SAS Institute.

Shaw, M. E., & Wright, J. M. (1967). *Scales for the Measurement of Attitudes.* New York: McGraw-Hill.

Shulman, L. S., Smith, V. B., & Stewart, D. M. (1987). *Three Presentations: From the Second National Conference on Assessment in Higher Education.* Washington, DC: American Association for Higher Education.

Study Group on the Conditions of Excellence in American Higher Education. (1984, October 24). Text of New Report on Excellence in Undergraduate Education. *Chronicle of Higher Education*, pp. 35-49.

Terenzini, P. T. (1986). *The Case for Unobtrusive Measures.* ETS Invitational Conference on Assessing the Outcomes of Higher Education, New York, NY.

Webb, E. J., Campbell, D. T., Schwartz, R. D., & Sechrest, L. (1981). *Unobtrusive Measures* (2nd ed.). Chicago: Rand McNally.

Assessment in General Education

Heidi A. Tickle

This section summarizes the history of general education, the many components comprising general education, assessment instruments, and procedures that have been employed. In short, this is a "cookbook" for how to assess general education today.

General education (GE) is a term that has been employed since the 1930s to describe a movement in higher education toward a reform of educational curriculum, teaching effectiveness, and broad-based, long-term application of those skills learned in the academic setting (GE and Liberal Education are terms often mistakenly used interchangeably, but in this discourse the two are distinctly separate). Over the successive generations of the 1950s through the 1970s, societal demands also affected the progress of GE. Academicians were discontented with the trends they believed liberal education had been assimilating, such as the use of the acquisition of knowledge over the application of method and the employment of rational assumptions based on abstract universal truths passed down over generations, which had formed the basis of liberal education in an earlier time (Corbett and Wilson, 1991; Miller, 1988; e.g., Dressel and Lorimer, 1960; e.g., The Fund for Adult Education, 1957). Alternatively, GE is a collection of ideas, principles, and methods of employing the two (i.e., ideas and principles) with strong influence by intrinsic and societal forces in nature over time (Miller, 1988).

GE is a paradigm designed to be an outline (i.e., not a script) by which institutions may instill the ability for lifelong learning and application of skills to many areas of life with the additional ability to specialize learning in a specific area of interest. The particular characteristics of GE are: (a) a great focus placed on the needs of the students followed by the relationship of the students to their communities; (b) a comprehensive program of both a broad-based curriculum that extends beyond the limited courses preparing students only for a specialized area and a multifaceted milieu in which students learn; (c) constant testing and evaluation of the goals and procedures, insuring that the institution maintains its focus on the above-stated characteristics; and (d) primary emphasis not on the acquisition of knowledge but rather on the application of knowledge to pressing issues and future societal problems (Leavens, Young, Gordon, Vorkink, Easley, and Magruder, 1994; Miller, 1988). Ultimately, GE shapes not only the curriculum but also societal interactions between students and their instructors that apply in the classroom setting.

Where GE has fallen short of its original effective edge is that institutions seldom have common goals (agreement on the purposes of the GE program throughout all departments), which are needed to construct a solid program within the GE framework. Departments have loosely constructed their own goals and means of outcomes assessment, lacking a common thread uniting the curricula. Not only have departments lacked common goals in GE, but on a larger scale institutions across the nation lack a standard that specifies which divisions of academia should be included in a GE program. In many instances, components of GE vary with each institution. Nevertheless, a common outline for eliminating such disorder is available.

One must first recognize that GE intended educational outcomes and assessment procedures are inseparably associated. Foremost in the development of an effective GE program is a clear understanding of intended outcomes: (a) concentration on the individual and the individual's relationship to society, (b) focus on developing in students outlooks based on inquiry, (c) the development of problem-solving skills, and (d) the continuous growth of individuals over a lifetime with the evolution of the self within a democratic society (Leavens et al., 1994). With these fundamental truths at the forefront, a solid base upon which to build additional department facets can be formed.

GE programs, without focusing on specific departments and courses, concentrate their efforts on the nurturing of the following skills in their students: (a) philosophical awareness, (b) ethics and values, (c) communication, (d) mathematical, (e) aesthetic, (f) scientific, and (g) analytical and critical thinking (Leavens et al., 1994; General Education Review Steering Committee, 1991). A clearly defined set of outcomes accompanied by assessment measures that demonstrate program effectiveness and students outcomes are essential in the documentation of goal achievement.

ASSESSMENT

The process by which institutions implement assessment measures of GE have been subjective and largely inadequate thus far. No longer is blind approbation of program effectiveness acceptable. Leavens et al. (1994) contends that "the university must develop measures to demonstrate its program performance…provide patterns of evidence for performance on multiple objectives…[and] use the collected data in order to achieve improved quality" (pp. 184-185). The use of data to objectively view the strengths and weaknesses of the academic areas of an institution empowers the administration with numerical evidence for program accreditation, educational improvements, allocation of institutional funds, professorial expansion or reduction, and the like. Without the data gained through assessment, acting on any of the stated change venues is haphazard at best.

Assessment of GE is accomplished in many ways. As institutions vary according to available funds, population characteristics, the student body's numerical size and number of faculty, etc., the methods by which these institutions assess their program effectiveness and student outcomes contrast. It is then appropriate to introduce not only the tools available to institutions for assessing their programs and student outcomes but also the varying means by which these tools may be employed.

Approaches to General Education Assessment

There are two primary approaches to GE assessment—application of the process to the institution as a whole or in terms of its individual components or departments (math, English, etc.). Choosing between these two approaches is the institution's most basic as well as perhaps the most difficult judgment. Also, the institution must choose whether to use locally developed or nationally standardized measures for assessing GE.

As can be ascertained from the previous discussion, GE of a student is most desirably a holistic rather than a fragmented experience. Nevertheless, even on most campuses that have dealt with the difficult issue of identifying intended educational outcomes for GE, these statements tend to focus not on the development of the individual, but rather on the development of specific skills (e.g., reading, writing, mathematics). In many cases this inability to conceptualize the whole GE program as something other than the accumulation of specific knowledge and skills in particular disciplines results in the persuasion by assessors to assess the skills individually (which more often than not results in course level assessment).

What are the disadvantages of course level assessment? In practice over time, assessment at the course level has several limitations. First, by its very nature course level assessment disrupts the unified fabric of what the institution may have thoughtfully designed as a holistic course of study. Second, because assessment must be considered beyond the individual course or section level, the logistical aspects of assessment of individual components are quite cumbersome. Most frequently, individual tests of math, writing, etc., are required of students at different times and in different locations. Finally, assessment of GE in its components or at the course level is labor intensive and on most campuses lasts only briefly.

The selection of either locally developed or standardized tests of GE is the other fundamental decision in selecting the institution's assessment tools. The standardized means of assessment have the significant disadvantage of "fit" (i.e., appropriateness in relevance to the institution) with the institution's GE program. It has been stated that there are no good standardized tests of GE—only tests that are worse than others. These instruments are reviewed in this volume in the separate resource section by Krotseng and Pike (pp. 58-83). The advantages of using such instruments are that (a) they are readily available, (b) they allow for the comparison of core curriculum with other institutions as well as the comparison of specific criteria, and (c) their relative comprehensiveness concerning the holistic aspect of GE. Ultimately, the greatest limitation is the faculty's perception that these tests do not really reflect the concept of GE practiced at that institution.

The alternatives to standardized tests for assessing GE are locally developed instruments, many of which are discussed in this section. The chief advantage of these locally developed instruments is their ability to focus on the specific components of GE as defined by the institution. Their primary drawbacks relate to the extensive amount of time needed to develop, score, and maintain locally developed instruments; their lack of comparability from institution to institution; and the fact that locally developed instruments rarely extend beyond primary skills in writing and mathematics.

Choosing between GE assessment as a whole or by its various components and between nationally standardized or locally developed instruments is not easy. The assessment tools described in the following section should serve as a selection guide.

General Education Assessment Tools

Assessment tools are the instruments used to measure outcomes. There are many types, ranging from standardized objective tests to subjective personal contacts. Instruments may also be developed locally or nationally depending on various factors. Nevertheless, it is imperative to chose the tool or tools that best measure your institution's specific outcomes (i.e., care should be taken in deciding which tools would provide the most accurate assessment of the institution's outcomes/goals).

There are many tests to chose from nationally, all differing slightly from one another (e.g., resource section page 62). It is important to note that each assessment tool, whether nationally or locally developed, may be employed independently; however, by combining two or more of these tools, a more accurate measurement of institutional outcomes may be achieved. The range of tools are:

- **Portfolio**—The portfolio is a newly rising, locally developed assessment instrument, which is a compilation of an individual's work over a period of time. Portfolios are ideal in evaluating the progression in one area of study from the beginning of study through completion of a program; for example, a student begins an English major in the freshman year at a four-year university, the portfolio is reviewed by the English department faculty annually, and in the fourth year prior to graduation the student is asked to select works from this portfolio and reflect on them. Examples of things contained in the portfolio are short stories, art projects, essays, and the like. It is customary for individual institutions to provide guidelines for portfolio compilation specific to their assessment purposes. The portfolio concentrates on the assessment of overall accomplishments rather than one's ability to succeed on individual examinations (Leavens et al. 1993).
- **Surveys** (i.e., locally developed and nationally normed)—Surveys are batteries administered intermittently during one's educational development to assess outcomes and are the most widely utilized of the assessment tools. Surveys are primarily composed of multiple choice items, but may contain open-ended questions as well. Depending on the specific outcomes one assesses, the number of items varies. It is important to realize the complexity of determining both reliability and validity of locally developed surveys; therefore, nationally normed surveys from which there are many to choose are in certain instances the most appropriate assessment procedures available. Surveys are a preferred means of assessment, as they may be administered to many individuals in a short period of time. Another advantage of the survey is the ability of an institution to retain a core of questions on the survey over a period of years to monitor changes in the attitudes of students, faculty, and alumni. The survey may be administered to populations or samples of populations to obtain generalizable estimates of behavior; for example, 15% of

senior psychology students in PSY 501 completed a test of psychology content knowledge in an attempt to determine the level to which their knowledge of the subject area had reached by their final year of study. Furthermore, institutions use surveys of employers to ascertain the ability of their employees (recent graduates of the institution) to read, write, and do basic mathematics. These surveys also demonstrate the employer's view of recent graduates' characteristics of punctuality, attitude, etc.

- **Interviews**—The interview consists of the assessment of students through question and answer sessions in a personal contact between faculty and student. This method allows elaboration of the details of the student's efforts, explanations of reasoning, etc. A clear representation of student progress may be achieved if this measure is used appropriately. The interview may be conducted with the student's advisor or with a group of department faculty depending on the institution's methods of assessment, time constraints, etc. The presence of more than a single assessor allows for bias to be minimized and the best conclusions to be drawn about an individual.

- **Capstone Course**—The Capstone course is an interdisciplinary seminar course that requires students to utilize digested knowledge over one's course of study and integrate the information drawn from several disciplines through the employment of communication, aesthetic, mathematical, philosophical, scientific, and social skills. The Capstone course is not a means of assessment in itself; rather, student outcomes are assessed by observation of the skills that are demonstrated in the class. The course allows for the availability/access to samples of students' work, which may then be further evaluated. The course is normally required by students in GE programs to be undertaken in the senior year (Leavens et al., 1993; General Education Review Steering Committee, 1991a; General Education Review Steering Committee, 1991b; e.g., Riggs and Worthley, 1992).

- **Standardized Tests**—Standardized tests are composed of a group of objective items and have specific outcomes that have been normed in groups with specific characteristics. Standardized tests may be administered to any number of individuals in the same settings under the same conditions. It is important to note that some standardized tests are specifically designed to provide information about groups rather than individuals, which is one way in which institutions may make broad generalizations about their students (e.g., Educational Testing Service, 1993). Examples of tests used in assessing GE are the American College Testing Program's College Measures Program (ACT COMP), the College Outcomes Survey, the Collegiate Assessment of Academic Proficiency (CAAP), the Academic Profile (AP), and the College Basic Academic Subjects Examination (CBASE). Specific references concerning the acquisition of additional information about each of these instruments are available in the resource section beginning on page 60.

- **Computer-Assisted Testing**—Testing by computer has become a new means of assessment. Individuals are able to sit at a computer while questions are presented in an interactive manner (i.e., tests become custom designed to one's skill level as questions are being answered). A test now available for computer administration is the Computer-Adaptive Placement, Assessment, and Support System (COM-PASS), available through ACT (i.e., ACT Program, P. O. Box 168, Iowa City, IA 52243). The Graduate Records Examination (GRE) is also available for computer administration (i.e., available through the GRE Board, Educational Testing Service, CN 6000, Princeton, NJ 08541-6000). Computerized tests allow a student's true level of competency to be surveyed in the most cost-effective, efficient manner.

Although each assessment tool is capable of determining (at least to some extent) the degree to which intended outcomes have been attained (and in some instances quite accurately), the most appropriate use of these tools is in conjunction with each other. When a number of assessment instruments are combined, more accurate conclusions may be drawn about the achievement of intended outcomes.

Examples of General Education Assessment

Following are examples of the assessment procedures employed at differing institutions around the country. They were chosen for the diversity of the procedures employed. The purpose was to provide the practitioner with strategies of implementation to ease the process of assessing GE (i.e., see what others have done and learn from them).

(a) Clemson University

A study was conducted at Clemson University as the result of a report on Involvement in Learning published by the National Institute of Education in 1984. The report suggested the need for colleges and universities to "explicitly assess the impact they are having on students" (Underwood and Nowaczyk, 1994, p. 1). The trend nationally for requirement of assessment practices was supported by the Southern Association of Colleges and Schools and the South Carolina Commission on Higher Education, Clemson's accrediting agencies' requirements (Underwood and Nowaczyk, 1994).

The first step in the process of implementing outcomes assessment was the establishment of a rationale for such procedures to take place (viz., (a) self-study required by the regional accrediting agency and (b) that mandated by the state for the reporting of institutional effectiveness). As anticipated, the study successfully demonstrated the effects of the GE curriculum on student outcomes from 1984 to the present.

When this study at Clemson was conducted (over an 18-month time period), the university had approximately 16,000 students, primarily composed of South Carolina residents. The GE curricular requirement for undergraduate students was the completion of 38 required semester hours in courses from five areas of concentration (composition and speaking skills, mathematics, science and technology, humanities, and social sciences). Two committees (the Commission on Undergraduate Studies and the University Curriculum Committee) were asked to develop specific GE core course requirements and to evaluate the students in those courses. Since the Commission on Undergraduate Studies and the University Curriculum Committee had substantial time-consuming agendas, which inhibited their ability to devote the needed effort in assessing GE, the University Assessment Committee (composed of a broad array of faculty from across the campus) was formed to meet the two objectives. This committee was able to devote the time necessary for GE assessment at Clemson (Underwood and Nowaczyk, 1992).

The reasons for implementing assessment of GE at the university were (a) the Southern Association of Colleges and Schools (SACS) required self-study (i.e., a study conducted every ten years by SACS institutions for purposes of accreditation) and (b) "the newly legislated state requirements [mandates] to report on institutional effectiveness" in the state (Underwood and Nowaczyk, 1992, p. 7). Since assessment had not been a feature of the university's GE program, the University Assessment Committee set out to install such a pattern (Underwood and Nowaczyk, 1992).

Assessment efforts centered on two tools: (a) a **locally developed alumni survey** administered to both one-year and five-year alumni (this tool focused essentially on graduate employment patterns) and (b) a **nationally developed standardized GE test** (e.g., the matrix form {group results only} of the College BASE test provided by Riverside Publishing). "The judicious use of a commercially available test can get the assessment process going quickly as long as everyone understands that the process and the appropriateness of the test itself will be evaluated" (Underwood and Nowaczyk, 1992, p. 10). This nationally normed test was employed on a trial basis, which did much to gain the approval of faculty. Faculty felt less threatened by the evaluation process as the nationally standardized tool was understood not to immediately affect their faculty status (Underwood and Nowaczyk, 1992). Involvement of the University community (viz., faculty, staff, and students) in the assessment process was imperative to the success of evaluative efforts as cooperation was necessary for gathering useful data (Humphrey, 1994).

Of paramount importance in choosing the most appropriate assessment tools is the relationship between the assessment tools and the expected/intended outcomes. The Riverside College BASE test was selected for its appropriateness with regard to the university's expected/intended outcomes (i.e., goals) and was administered to randomly selected freshman and junior courses to provide for "value-added" measures across academic levels (Underwood and Nowaczyk, 1992, p. 11). In a final effort to assess GE at Clemson, English department faculty reviewed the essays included on the Riverside College BASE test prior to returning the test for scoring. This allowed a cross-referenced assessment both locally by faculty and nationally by the testing agency. The result was that the Riverside publishing company detected very little difference between freshman and junior writing samples, while English department faculty distinguished with a high degree of accuracy the freshman from the junior writing samples through blind scoring (notably, the level of the writing samples were not disclosed prior to faculty scoring). Consequently, alternative means of assessing writing skills are appropriate for Clemson students. The insight to be gained from such a trial effort is that nationally normed tests in most instances are not completely tailored to every institution's GE specific characteristics. Therefore, alternative methods to attain the most accurate results from assessment procedures are necessary if data collection and analysis are to be used at the university for a meaningful purpose.

In conclusion, Clemson University involved its faculty to the maximum extent based on the premise that "no one commercially available test would completely meet the needs" (Underwood and Nowaczyk, 1992, p. 15). Second, the Assessment Committee recognized that ultimately, "the committee responsible for the process must ensure that the process does not end once the results are reported" (Underwood and Nowaczyk, 1992, p. 15). Third, and most important, the results were utilized to make institutional improvements to programs and students outcomes assessment procedures at Clemson University. Assessment is not a means to an end, but must be a continuously employed effort to the betterment of some aim.

(b) The University of Connecticut

Establishment of intended educational outcomes was the first step the University of Connecticut took in the formulation of a GE curriculum for undergraduates. The intended educational outcomes were divided into six achievement areas (science and technology, foreign languages, culture and modern society, philosophy and ethical analysis, social science and comparative analysis, and literature and the arts). The curriculum was formulated to meet the intended educational outcomes in these areas, and the success of this effort was tested by **locally developed testing instruments** created specifically for this purpose. In addition, faculty were surveyed for their opinion of the extent to which GE requirements were met by students. Finally, students were **interviewed** to procure "their views of GE, the requirements, and the courses available to them" (General Education Assessment Office, 1991, p. 1).

The purpose of this exhaustive effort at assessment was ultimately GE program improvement (i.e., improving the curriculum to meet the goals of the institution's GE program), which was decided by the administration at the outset. The University of Connecticut utilized these trial assessment methods ultimately "to determine if the general education curriculum is having a beneficial effect on student learning" (p. 2). Specific use of the results from this project were said to be used for the (a) revision of general education goals, (b) curriculum revisions, and (c) revision of assessment instruments (p. 3).

The University of Connecticut established the GE program with assessment as a forethought. The GE curriculum was instituted in the Fall of 1987, adhering to the university's intended educational outcomes (outlining GE expected outcomes and assessing those criteria are key in developing a sound curriculum). Immediately following were two years of pilot testing the assessment instruments determining the beneficial effect of GE curriculum on student learning. Pilot testing the assessment tools resulted in the revision of the locally developed instruments (i.e., refinement of assessment instruments utilized), and a second implementation of the assessment procedures (General Education Assessment Office, 1991).

The model provided by this institution stresses the tailoring of assessment to the institution by locally developing assessment instruments and, more importantly, the pilot testing of those instruments to improve the quality of results attained from the data. Furthermore, assessment practices were made meaningful as the data collected from the assessment tools were used to make institutional improvements.

(c) Bunker Hill Community College (BHCC)

BHCC began with a GE Steering Committee composed of faculty members from a multitude of disciplines at the institution (i.e., cross section of faculty) who volunteered their efforts to this cause. This committee met weekly to discuss research findings about GE on other campuses and formulated a tentative list of GE intended educational outcomes for BHCC. During the following academic year, the college community examined the intended educational outcomes with other colleagues in an attempt to align them with the purposes of the institution.

The second step for BHCC after the development of GE intended educational outcomes was the development of a GE model (i.e., curriculum development model). Input was obtained from faculty and administrators by the utilization of round table discussions, questionnaires, and brainstorming sessions. Ideas obtained through these methods were distributed across the institution's community, and the GE Steering Committee, after gaining substantial feedback, recommended a curriculum cornerstone (i.e., cluster courses in a specific area coupled with additional courses in certain GE areas). Twenty-one credit hours, divided into areas of English, history, mathematics, behavioral science, science, and humanities, and a capstone course), are to be taken by all students applying to attain a degree. That is, all students take this same GE curriculum (General Education Review Steering Committee, 1991a; General Education Review Steering Committee, 1991b).

The change in the institution was sparked by a need for documenting educational effectiveness at a state level. The GE Steering Committee organized the curriculum in areas, specified the number of hours in each area students must complete, incorporated a capstone course (to incorporate all areas of learning and GE goals by applying these during one holistic course), and formed a model for assessing the attainment of GE goals (General Education Review Steering Committee, 1991a).

The GE Steering Committee concluded that, "a GE model consisting of a core curriculum (12 credits) with prescribed distribution categories (9 credits) best responds to the flexibility and curricular demands of each program of study" (General Education Review Steering Committee, 1991a, p. 16). Each program of study was assessed according to this model in a collaborative effort between the Steering Committee and the departments to ensure the consistency of the intended outcomes across the institution (General Education Review Steering Committee, 1991a).

In conclusion, this institution followed a systematic form of revamping its curriculum by involving the community in the institution's future. In addition, a Capstone Course was added to culminate all GE learning into one encompassing class, which facilitates the ability to assess students' course assignments, which require the combination of several differing skills. Each course has set intended outcomes for students to attain. Once the Capstone course is completed, the Capstone faculty team evaluates the performance by reviewing material completed during this course. There is some speculation as to the usefulness of faculty evaluation procedures in lieu of subjective input that may be received; however, if these faculty, who are responsible for evaluating student outcomes, adhere properly to the objective guidelines of intended educational outcomes, useful data may be gained and applied to institutional improvements.

(d) Ohio University

The assessment in GE at Ohio University differed greatly from the other examples stated. The president led the university on its quest for quality enhancement with the use of the "Institutional Impact Project" (Williford and Moden, 1993, p. 43), which initially stated the need "to provide direction for maintaining high standards of performance for faculty and high expectations for effective teaching and learning…[recommending] the use of student assessment information" (p. 43).

The original intended educational outcomes at the outset of the project were improving the performance of (a) programs and (b) individuals, a simply stated attainable goal. What was accomplished by the development of departmental assessment sub-units (i.e., termed by the authors as planning units) was that academic departments, administration, faculty senate, the University Curriculum Council, the University Advising Council, and alumni were provided with oral and written reports "on the progress of students and an assessment of university programs" for the purposes of making decisions about program and student improvements (p. 44). Furthermore, the university's board of trustees also receives these reports of student outcomes, which in turn "influence [their] decisions (i.e., judgments on academic advising, student retention, evaluation of GE reform, student satisfaction with campus services, etc.) about institutional management, budget approval, and institutional goals" (p. 44). The information gathered by the outcomes assessment process is utilized continuously for purposes of improving both academic programs and student outcomes. These assessment procedures are constantly revised (i.e., edit assessment tools for clarity and practicality in application to the assessment of intended educational outcomes).

The institution assessed GE according to a locally developed and comprehensive instrument designed by members of the University Curriculum Council. Each facet of GE was assessed by this instrument and recommendations for improvements were made in the form of written evaluations. Additional evaluation procedures were added to the process of outcomes assessment in GE (viz., an alumni survey, ACT-COMP test, and GE enrollment patterns). The ACT-COMP has six areas of basic performance information. Beyond this, Ohio University implemented an ad hoc item analysis of this instrument, which allows the institution to acquire information in 22 areas of GE competencies. The primary advantage of this nationally normed instrument is the ability of the institution to track data over years of the GE program and to compare their students' performance in GE with others nationally. The secondary advantage of this instrument is the ability to further evaluate the test on a local level (e.g., faculty evaluation of writing samples) for a more in-depth "fit" (i.e., further evaluating data gathered by the instrument with the specific intended educational outcomes guiding the process) to their institution (i.e., shape the test to suit the expected/intended outcomes). The alumni survey coupled with the ACT-COMP assists in bringing significance to the review and discourse of enrollment patterns.

In conclusion, the assessment patterns at Ohio University are promoted actively by the president and used by many constituencies for improving the institution. People are able not only to read statistical outlines, but also to understand the assessment outcomes by direct involvement in the processes (i.e., professors witness their departmental changes). As a result of such accessible data, external businesses and the general public began to take notice of Ohio University (e.g., the Ohio Board of Regents granted program excellence awards to the institution). Now the state has a legislative mandate that all public colleges and universities in Ohio assess student outcomes. Further excellence in outcomes assessment is a continual process at Ohio University, and a solid model that others may examine to create assessment at their institutions.

(e) Sinclair Community College

The process of implementing assessment at Sinclair Community College began in 1988 with the coordination of an outcomes assessment steering committee chaired by the institution's assessment coordinator (an administrator with assessment expertise to assist in facilitating the process). As suggested by Peter Ewell in a personal contact with the Denny and Strewhar (1994), in order to demonstrate the seriousness of the assessment efforts, the assessment committee must write policies (i.e., expected/intended outcomes) at the forefront, which must in turn be adopted by the institution's board of trustees. The committee followed through with these tasks, which aided in hastening the development of assessment implementation. This was complemented by funding received from the institution to coordinate work with departments on the campus (e.g., involving numerous workshops for the purpose of developing a strong assessment program). However, assessment at Sinclair developed at a slow rate with little success until the assessment committee "returned to the drawing table" so to speak and redefined what GE is exactly and what intended educational outcomes are most appropriate.

Denny and Strewhar's (1994) plan to implement a new outcomes assessment program in 1995, is anticipated to have great success. They plan to make both students and faculty aware of GE and anticipate creating a conscious movement to get the institution "into the [assessment] movement." The key in setting out for success is planning. Points raised in the process of implementing outcomes assessment in the future at Sinclair are as follows: (a) attempt to connect individuals with the whole institution in task and conscious awareness of what the assessment committee is trying to accomplish; (b) involve the faculty and grass roots organizers to lead in the assessment development process as often and as much as possible; (c) give feedback constantly to the institution in small increments; (d) get students' input; (e) discuss and achieve consensus through deliberations (i.e., agree on philosophic assumptions); (f) begin all assessment procedures with regard to the educational values presented by the American Association of Higher Education (AAHE) at the forefront; (g) form interdisciplinary teams and recognize their suggestions; (h) document successes (i.e., the miracles); and, (i) list the outcomes assessment goals as clearly and practically as possible and revise them when needed.

Prior to the "revamping" of outcomes assessment, the assessment process was mostly voluntary with little participation, which rendered the results unable to be generalized. Beyond this, they received resistance from faculty and lacked understanding from students in the entire effort. The assessment committee realized the futility of their effort without a sound base on which to form a strong GE outcomes assessment process, which is why the committee began redefining GE and the intended educational outcomes particular to Sinclair.

Sinclair has been testing pilot assessment procedures to determine what actually works for the institution. Their efforts encompass a wide variety of procedures (e.g., COMP, placement test, externally administered tools, and the like). Ultimately, assessment is in a constant motion whether it be development or refinement of practices. Trial and error are the trademarks of developing successful strong outcomes assessment; and, Sinclair has become well-grounded on this road to success.

GE Assessment in Two-Year Colleges

Assessment of GE in two-year colleges presents two unique characteristics. In the transfer program, designed to parallel the first two years of a four-year degree program, many of the tools detailed earlier are applicable; however, several conditions make the assessment of this area unique. **First**, as students in the transfer program are leaving the institution at the end of two years, the institution's ability to compel them to take seriously any form of assessment occurring near the final term is significantly reduced. This is because in most cases students attentions are focused on the institution to which they are transferring. Motivation of these students is an even greater problem than at four-year institutions, so the two-year colleges' best strategy for the assessment of GE is to embed whatever means or tools are selected within classes typically taken by transfer students in the final term of their second year.

While there are significant problems with assessment of GE at two-year colleges, two particular advantages may exist. First, students transferring into a four-year institution may be required at that institution to take some form of GE assessment; and, the two-year college in many cases can gain access to students' performance on that measure. Second, because of the act of transferring to another institution, two-year colleges can use the performance of students on "follow-up courses" at the four-year college as a means of assessing the success of GE at the two-year campus. That is, the performance of students in writing intensive classes at the four-year institutions may be utilized as the barometer of success of the writing program at the two-year institution. Likewise, performance in mathematics in advanced courses at the four-year institution is a reasonable barometer of the success of the two-year institution in preparing students for this work. In both cases it is necessary to receive course-specific feedback from the four-year institutions regarding transfer students; however, nothing stops such feedback other than the establishment of such cooperative arrangements and the work necessary to provide the information.

Second, one facet of GE frequently overlooked in assessment is the limited amount of GE possible within the occupational/technical programs within the two-year institutions. Usually the amount of GE required of those students in occupational/technical programs consists of 9-12 semester hours covering only the bare essentials of written and verbal communication and mathematics. Nevertheless, the responsibility of the institution for assessing the success of this particular type of GE program remains an issue. Some two-year colleges have found utilization of the assessment processes in the GE transfer programs also appropriate for the occupational-technical programs. At other institutions, assessment of GE programs may be based on opinions of the employers of occupational/technical college students, concerning their employees' (the institution's graduates) ability to read, write, and do mathematics. From whatever source, data focusing upon this, the most limited of all GE programs, should be assembled by the institution.

Conclusion

In retrospect, there are five critical issues regarding assessment of GE that dominate campus activities at either two-year colleges or four-year institutions: (a) Identification of intended educational outcomes, (b) involvement and motivation of the faculty to take part in this essentially interdisciplinary endeavor, (c) deciding whether to approach GE as a whole or through individual assessments of the institution's success in each components (i.e., reading, writing, mathematics, etc.), (d) choosing standardized or locally developed measures, and (e) motivation of students to seriously take part in GE assessment.

There are many different combinations which may be utilized to assess GE. The most important steps are to (a) get commitment to the cause at hand, (b) establish intended educational outcomes which adhere to the institution's mission, (c) involve the institution's community (including students, if possible), (d) choose the most appropriate assessment instruments for your institution, (e) follow through with data collection, (f) use the data, and (g) document the assessment procedures so that others across the nation may learn from both successes and failures of others.

The examples provided by the institutions are meant to be a guide to outcomes assessment at your institution. They are by no means to be used as a script for implementing assessment; however, by learning from colleagues across the nation faced with the cumbersome task of implementing assessment in GE, the process may be made less painful. The learning process is strengthened by this collaboration with colleagues in similar circumstances and mistakes may be halted before they begin by sharing these processes. The Task Group on General Education (1988, p. 52) perhaps depicted the credo best:

> The art of assessment is far from perfect, but it is a feasible art and can stimulate curiosity, foster self-consciousness, and strengthen education....

References

Corbett, H. D., and Wilson, B. L. (1991). *Testing, Reform and Rebellion*. Norwood, NJ: Ablex.

Denny, L., and Strewhar, B. (Speakers). (1994). *A Community College Package for Assessing General Education*. Paper presented at the 9TH Annual AAHE Conference on Assessment in Higher Education. (Cassette Recording No. 94CAHE-70). Valencia, CA: Mobiltape.

Dressel, P. L., and Lorimer, M. F. (1960). *Attitudes of Liberal Arts Faculty Members Toward Liberal and Professional Education* (Monograph). New York: Columbia University, Institute of Higher Education.

Educational Testing Service. (1993). *Tasks in Critical Thinking*. Trenton, NJ: New Jersey Department of Higher Education.

General Education Assessment Office. (1991). *Assessing General Education Outcomes: An Institution-Specific Approach*. (J. H. Watt, project director). Storrs, CT: The University of Connecticut.

General Education Review Steering Committee. (1991a). *General Education: A Curriculum Cornerstone*. Boston: Bunker Hill Community College. (ERIC Document Reproduction Service No. ED 345 774)

General Education Review Steering Committee. (1991b). *General Education: Curriculum*. Boston: Bunker Hill Community College. (ERIC Document Reproduction Service No. ED 345 775)

Humphrey, R. (1994). Institutional Effectiveness: Faculty and Staff Development as a Part of Keeping Abreast of Trends and Meeting the Changing Needs of Higher Education. In Commission on Institutions of Higher Education (ed.), *A Collection of Papers on Self- Study and Institutional Improvement* (pp. 181-201). Chicago, IL: Commission on Institutions of Higher Education of the North Central Association of Colleges and Schools.

Leavens, D., Young, C., Gordon, G., Vorkink, S., Easley, K., and Magruder, J. (1994). General Education: Goals, Design, and Assessment. In Commission on Institutions of Higher Education (ed.), *A Collection of Papers on Self-Study and Institutional Improvement* (pp. 181-201). Chicago, IL: Commission on Institutions of Higher Education of the North Central Association of Colleges and Schools.

Miller, G. E. (1988). *The Meaning of General Education: The Emergence of a Curriculum Paradigm*. New York: Teachers College Press.

Riggs, M. L., and Worthley, J. S. (1992). *Baseline Characteristics of Successful Programs of Student Outcomes Assessment*. (Report No. 143). San Bernadino, CA: California State University. (ERIC Document Reproduction Service No. ED 353 285)

Task Group on General Education. (1988). *A New Vitality for General Education*. Washington, DC: Association of American Colleges.

The Fund for Adult Education. (1957). *The Randall Lectures*. White Plains, NY: Robertson.

Underwood, D. G., and Nowaczyk, R. H. (1992). *Involving Faculty in the Assessment of General Education*. (Paper presented at the Annual Forum of the Association for Institutional Research in Atlanta, GA May 10-13, 1992). Clemson, SC: Clemson.

Underwood, D. G., and Nowaczyk, R. H. (1994). Involving Faculty in the Assessment of General Education: A Case Study. *AIR Professional File, 52*(2), 1-6.

Williford, A. M., and Moden, G. O. (1993). Using Assessment to Enhance Quality. In T. W. Banta (ed.), *Making a Difference*. San Francisco: Jossey-Bass.

Setting and Evaluating Objectives and Outcomes in Nonacademic Units[1]

Donald J. Reichard

From the time the second edition of *The Practitioner's Handbook* was released in 1991 to the present, there have been substantial changes in the manner in which institutional effectiveness in nonacademic units is being accomplished. The myriad of techniques used to analyze institutional effectiveness, including attitudinal surveys, administrative practice or systems indicators derived from annual reports, periodic self-study, outside peer reviewers, standards set by professional groups such as the Council for the Advancement of Standards (CAS), all continue to have relevance. The application of these techniques, however, is taking place within an ever-changing environment.

The overall emphasis of assuring ongoing evaluation consonant with the larger context of institutional effectiveness remains largely the same. However, the techniques used in analyzing institutional effectiveness have been broadened considerably. Now the derivation of a plan for assessing institutional effectiveness also ranges into the areas of benchmarking, management audits, and performance indicators, as well as the realm of Total Quality Management (TQM) and Continuous Quality Improvement (CQI).

The application of benchmarking, performance indicators, management audits, and especially TQM/CQI principles and practices is significantly altering the manner in which objectives and outcomes in nonacademic units are being evaluated. Now, **both** process and outcome are important and must be considered within the new meanings evolving from statewide pressures for an increasing degree of accountability on the part of postsecondary institutions.

The era of "just leave the money on the stoop" as a method of accountability for higher education, if it ever existed, has been replaced by the necessity of demonstrating achievement of outcomes not necessarily chosen by the academy itself (Ashworth, 1994). With an increasing diversity of forces indicating needs for accountability, it should not

---

1. A portion of this resource section has been adapted from "Developing and Implementing a Process for the Review of Nonacademic Units" by M. K. Brown, 1989, *Research in Higher Education*, *30*(1), pp. 89-112. Adapted with the written permission of the publisher.

be surprising that postsecondary institutions have developed hybrid approaches to assessing accountability.

One way of promoting effectiveness in operating units is to subject them to formal reviews based on established criteria. A major portion of this chapter which appeared in the second edition of *A Practitioner's Handbook* defined a model for a formal academic support unit review process employed at the University of Maryland by Marilyn Brown, the chapter's co-author, now deceased. In this third edition a model utilizing the CAS Standards and Guidelines employed within the Student Affairs Division at the University of North Carolina at Greensboro is explicated in a separate Appendix E to this volume. The current chapter also cites a growing body of literature related to performance indicators, total quality management, and benchmarking, not cited in the earlier editions. These orientations and processes may be helpful in setting and evaluating objectives and outcomes in a variety of nonacademic units.

Need for Evaluation

The emphasis of the institutional effectiveness movement to date has been primarily on instructional programs. If an institution of higher education is to be effective in achieving its total mission through its principal activities of instruction, research, and public service, the effectiveness of all its operations must be evaluated. Effective instructional, research, and public service programs may be jeopardized by poorly designed or poorly managed administrative support. Therefore, evaluating the organizational performance of support units becomes important to assure that they are operating effectively in consonance with institutional goals.

Interest in the evaluation of academic, student services, or administrative support units has grown for a variety of reasons. Although many nonacademic units may be small, the cumulative resources required for their continued support may be substantial. The existence of ongoing procedures for academic program review may lead to increased interest in support unit reviews as administrative structures increase in size. Such factors may result, as in Illinois, in requirements by state coordinating boards that administrative units be evaluated regularly (Wilson, 1987).

Regardless of the motivation for undertaking reviews of nonacademic units, the reviews should ultimately be cost-free in the sense that the return should equal the investment (Wergin and Braskamp, 1987, p. 97). Because the goal of evaluation is overall institutional improvement, such evaluations, when devised in accordance with the institutional mission, may lead to new ways of looking at a unit's role within the institution as well as a redefinition of important priorities for the unit.

APPROACHES TO EVALUATING OBJECTIVES AND OUTCOMES

Just as Institutional Effectiveness requires an overall look at a unit's goals and objectives in relation to those of the larger institution, Total Quality Management (TQM)/Continuous Quality Improvement (CQI) and the development of Performance Indicators represent new, holistic processes by which the interrelationships of unit and institutional or system goals may be examined. Although such processes are often complementary, some brief comments upon their similarities and differences may be helpful.

Total Quality Management/Continuous Quality Improvement

Many frameworks for examining effectiveness emphasize the evaluation of outputs in relation to a given set of inputs. TQM/CQI goes somewhat farther in that it also looks at the effectiveness and efficiency of the processes by which inputs are transformed into a set of outputs.

In indicating the commonalities of several performance systems, and several criteria by which such systems might be judged, Tuttle (1994, p. 25) noted:

> First, there should be a direct relationship between the mission and strategy of the organization and what the performance system measures. Second, the measurement system must contain a number of separate indicators that address the critical facets of the mission and strategy. Third, this family of indicators should address a variety of internal, external, financial and nonfinancial, as well as past and future dimensions such as learning and innovation. Fourth, the system should be easy to explain and understand.

TQM provides a set of principles and tools that organizations can use to pursue quality consciously and systematically. The foundations of TQM, as noted by Dooris and Teeter (1994, p. 51), are as follows: "develop a mission and create a vision, focus on the customer, focus on process improvement, use systematic analysis, promote collaboration, and recognize the organization as a system." Systematic collection and analysis of data are needed to learn about and understand processes.

While institutional effectiveness processes may tend to identify a somewhat static set of output indicators, with TQM, indicators may be applied in a somewhat different manner. According to Dooris and Teeter (1994, p. 54):

> Traditional measures often examine inputs and outputs such as admissions, student head counts, degrees awarded, or student-faculty ratios. TQM tends to deal instead with critical processes: teaching and learning, research, scholarship, faculty recruitment and development, or enrollment management. As a result, the information provided by a traditional static measure such as faculty FTE, though still valuable, must be supplemented by more dynamic indicators in TQM. For example, in addition to familiar snapshot measures, TQM must use change, flow, or process-oriented measures of cycle time, customer satisfaction, error rates, or student development. How many minutes are required to process a student refund? How many days does it take to notify applicants of admissions decisions? What percentage of research accounts are lost due to billing errors? What percentage of students are succeeding on standardized licensing examinations? What is the point-of-service satisfaction with student services?

Total Quality Management views administrative organizations in terms of interdependent work processes (Lembcke, 1994). In an enrollment management context, an office such as undergraduate admissions supplies critical data, information, or services for "downstream" operations within separate but interrelated registration, orientation, financial aid, housing, or academic advising units. Because the inputs of "upstream" offices are critical to the operations of related units, closer coordination and understanding of processes in mutually related areas is essential. Thus in order to be of maximum use, performance must be measured not only in terms of the effectiveness of the individual unit, but also in the context of the overall organization.

As described by Heverly (1993, p. 5), TQM is marked less by the inspection of outputs of a process and more by examination of the process itself with an eye toward continuous improvement. For TQM to be successful, a transformation in management is required whereby each unit needs to:

1. Identify its mission and describe how it supports the college mission;
2. Identify its critical processes, identify the suppliers and customers of the process, and develop top-down flow charts of each critical process;
3. Identify quality characteristics for each critical process and develop performance measures to assess these characteristics; and
4. Develop a data collection plan for monitoring the performance of each critical process.

Many paradigms have been suggested for TQM/CQI process management. The Shewhart/Deming Plan-Do-Check-Act (PDCA) Cycle has general applicability at the office (strategic), project(management), and activity (operating) levels for many types of nonacademic units. Within the PDCA cycle, **Planning** includes establishing the measures of success as well as determining the processes to be followed. The **Do** aspect may involve prototyping of the project and the related managerial consultations and considerations necessary for project completion. The **Check** aspect of the cycle assesses the effect of the activity or event with the key criterion being satisfaction of customers and the requisite understandings of who the customers are and what they need. The **Act** aspect reflects the changes in products or behaviors instituted as a result of what has been learned through the check process. An illustrative example of the PDCA cycle as applied to the management of institutional research offices is provided by McLaughlin and Snyder (1993).

A basic tenet of TQM is that most processes contain the data needed to improve them. Thus, by using more dynamic indicators of change, TQM helps to remove the mystery associated with "black box" processes.

Performance Indicators

Performance indicators (PIs) derive their significance from the ability to link outcomes with purposes and processes. PIs are intended to measure how well something is being done. However, Borden and Bottrill (1994, p. 6) caution "beyond this simple and compelling concept lie many complicated issues regarding who defines the goals and criteria for performance, who uses the indicators and for what purposes, and the many technical issues that surround any measurement effort."

To be of maximum utility, indicators should be derived locally at the single campus or departmental level. When indicators come to be aggregated and interpreted at the multi-campus or state levels, meanings and interpretations become less clear. If imposed in a disorganized or haphazard fashion by those who control the purse strings, Borden and Bottrill further caution that indicators may provide both "the best promise and worst nightmare for colleges and universities."

Banta and Borden (1994, p. 96) recommend that indicator systems should (1) have a clear purpose; (2) be coordinated throughout an organization or system (vertical alignment); (3) extend across the entire range of organizational processes; (4) be derived from a variety of coordinated methods; and (5) be used to inform decision making.

Along with the selection of indicators come a number of questions with regard to how the use of indicators may be communicated in order to enhance the informed pursuit of institutional goals across administrative areas. Periodic monitoring of key success indicators as described by Sapp and Temares (1992) and Sapp (1994) suggest ways in which key success indicators may be selected, monitored, and communicated within complex organizations. The process of having a number of individual units identify key success indicators helps to encourage team-building and assure accuracy because individual offices assume ownership of key data elements and added responsibility for improving the overall integrity of the data.

A wide range of issues abound with regard to the selection, linkage among organizational levels, and measurement of performance indicators. In order to be useful, Ewell and Jones (1994) stress that any indicator should suggest specifically what needs to be done in order to improve performance.

Benchmarking

Benchmarking is a method of establishing normative reference points for practices in a given area against which performance can be gauged. Standards for Good Practice against which individual colleges and universities may evaluate themselves may be derived from such processes. In this regard, comparative data in some 35 functional areas has been developed through a major project sponsored by the National Association of College and University Business Officers (1993).

The development and interpretation of benchmarking data is fraught with the difficulties inherent in all data exchange activities. It must be recognized that no institution or individual administrative unit is truly comparable to another and that the various methodologies for determining cost or productivity measures among units are affected greatly by varying patterns of centralized or decentralized administrative structure. Rather than focusing upon end-product efficiency or cost measures, benchmarking may be most helpful when it focuses upon developing understandings of how best practices and processes at other institutions produce desirable benchmark targets or goals.

In a related area, guidelines for facility renewal and adaptation have been developed through the joint efforts of the Society for College and University Planning, the Association of Physical Plant Administrators of Colleges and Universities, the National Association of College and University Business Officers (NACUBO), and the firm of Coopers and Lybrand (Dunn, 1989).

Management Audits

In a time of increasing pressures for public accountability, it should not be surprising that agencies of state government should seek to monitor the efficiency, effectiveness, and overall performance of state-supported colleges and universities. An example in this area is the series of Management Control Audits undertaken by the Office of the Texas State Auditor.

Management control audits are intended to be somewhat similar to assessments conducted by private consulting firms. They follow guidelines for Government Auditing Standards issued by the Comptroller General of the United States and a *Management Audit Methodology* developed by the State of Texas. Such audits seek to "compare a university's policies, procedures, and management systems against established criteria" (Alwin, 1993, p. 48).

The dialogue developed between the agency conducting a management audit and the University participating in the audit may serve to identify criteria of evaluation for specific nonacademic units or functions. Thus, in the process of auditing the performance of the research function at the University of Texas (Alwin, 1993, p. 15), the University suggested several measures including: (1) the percentage of faculty with at least one publication in a refereed journal in the last three years; (2) the percentage of faculty with terminal degrees in their disciplines; (3) the percentage of faculty with external research support; (4) the academic computing capacity; (5) the national statistical rankings of library collections and activities; and (6) the amount of external funding received from intellectual property and technology licensing or communication activities.

Another performance audit conducted in Texas (Alwin 1991, pp. 16-19) suggested guidelines for measuring the performance of information systems. Four primary activities were specified including: (1) Application Development and Maintenance; (2) Operations and Telecommunications; (3) I/S Support for End-users; and (4) Planning and Strategic Consulting. The first three activities were evaluated by a series of performance indicators relating to productivity, quality, user satisfaction, and responsiveness. It was suggested that Planning and Strategic Consulting Activities should be evaluated by goal attainment, revisions to plans, and budget variances.

INSTITUTIONAL EFFECTIVENESS

Within the Institutional Effectiveness paradigm, administrative and educational support units will be expected to provide evidence that their operations support accomplishment of their institution's Expanded Statement of Institutional Purpose by accomplishing their departmental intended objectives. As noted by Nichols (1991, pp. 60-62), in order to accomplish these ends, departments will need to: (a) formulate objectives similar in some ways to those statements of intended student outcomes prepared by academic programs; (b) indicate how those objectives support or link to the institution's Expanded Statement of Institutional Purpose; and (c) demonstrate that their departmental objectives are being accomplished through assessment. The above schema may resemble a management by objectives approach in that departments are asked to identify their objectives and then determine if those objectives are being met. However, it does not resemble a strict MBO approach in that:

1. There is no intention that individuals within nonacademic units establish separate objectives for each person or function. Rather, the professional staff in each unit should work together with the department head to establish a limited number of overarching objectives for the unit as a whole.

2. The objectives established are separate from the institution's personnel evaluation process and resource (funding) request/allocation cycle. Thus, the institutional effectiveness paradigm allows academic and nonacademic units to stretch themselves and to attempt innovative approaches to problem-solving without fear of failure. An institutional effectiveness orientation stresses that departments are not held accountable for failure or success, only for having in place a process for stating objectives, measuring accomplishments, and using the results to improve programming.

3. When possible, statements of administrative objectives should focus upon the results of administrative or educational support operations rather than the processes themselves. MBO applications in higher education tend to focus on "what we will do." Service areas covered by nonacademic units by their nature will also focus upon process considerations. However, objectives should be stated in results-oriented terms, as indicated in *The Departmental Guide and Record Book* (1995). Thus, rather than the Office of the Registrar setting an objective related to improved handling of transcript request, an administrative objective stating that "95% of transcript requests will be processed and mailed within 72 hours of their receipt" should be stated. Similarly: "Rather than the Physical Plant setting as an objective—'Three buildings will be brought into the institution's Energy Management System (EMS),'—the administrative objective set might state: As a result of three buildings being brought within the institution's EMS, $18,000 annually will be avoided in utility expenditures for these buildings.'" (Nichols, 1995, p. 60)

Examples of statements of administrative objectives may be found in Appendix B of *Assessment Case Studies*. These examples also provide descriptions of means of assessment commonly utilized in nonacademic units. Figure 15 on the following page provides a partially complete example of implementation in career services related to a mission statement supporting the Expanded Statement of Institutional Purpose for that unit as required by SACS effective January 1, 1995.

REVIEW OF ASSESSMENT MEANS AVAILABLE FOR RESEARCH AND SERVICE OUTCOMES AND ADMINISTRATIVE OBJECTIVES

Most four-year institutions incorporate references to research and public service in their mission statements and may employ a wide range of resources in setting Research and Public Service outcomes and administrative objectives. One of the most helpful general references is the *Outcomes Measures and Procedures Manual* (Micek, Service, and

Figure 15

Career Services Center

Example of Linkage between Expanded Statement of Institutional Purpose, Departmental/Program Intended Outcomes/Objectives, and Assessment Criteria and Procedures at Our University

Expanded Statement of Institutional Purpose	Departmental/Program Intended Outcomes/Objectives	Assessment Criteria & Procedures
Our University Mission Statement: We also seek to provide a supportive and challenging environment in which students can realize the full potential of their abilities.	1. Of those graduates seeking employment, at least half will have been offered a job prior to leaving the University.	1a. A follow-up survey of Career Services Center registrants will indicate that of those students responding, 40% had received a job offer by October after graduation. 1b. Of those students seeking to be employed after graduation. on the Graduating Student Survey, 50% will indicate that they were already employed or had received a job offer.
Extract from Student Affairs Division Mission Statement: To provide services which assist students in selecting their vocation and making the transition into the world of work.	2. Offer an increasing number of job search strategy work-shops each year that are attended by more students annually.	2a. Records maintained will indicate more job search workshops offered each academic year. 2b. Records maintained will indicate an increase in the number of students attending job strategy workshops each year.
	3. Clients will be pleased with the services received from the Career Services Center.	3a. The level of satisfaction with the Career Services Center expressed by students on the Graduating Student Survey will exceed that for overall student services. 3b. 95% of students completing a point of contact survey at the close of the job search strategy workshop will "agree" or "strongly agree" with the statement "This workshop fulfilled my expectations and provided clear, useful advice in the job search."

Lee, 1975); this document specifies measures that administrators might wish to employ as well as definitions, data sources, and procedures for collecting such measures. Other means of assessing outcomes and setting administrative objectives include direct measures, attitudinal measures, measures derived from standard administrative practice, and data system indicators. Examples from the research and public service areas are used to illustrate how desired outcomes and objectives may be derived from a variety of sources.

Direct Measures

In the area of research services, the identification of outcomes employed in measuring institutional effectiveness may have several sources. First, and most common, is the specification of direct measures of research program activity. Here, the number and dollar amounts of proposals developed, submitted, and funded often serve as the primary reference point. Such data are usually collected routinely as requirements by state and federal agencies for reporting purposes. Such readily available baseline external funding statistics may serve as ideal benchmarks for formulating intended research outcomes. Goals identified in the Expanded Statement of Institutional Purpose may also be stated and analyzed in terms of the sources of restricted revenue (federal, state, or local governments, private gifts and contracts) from which sponsored research moneys were sought and obtained.

Public service/community impact measures that institutions may wish to consider include (a) enrollment levels/community participation in program offerings; (b) the extent to which an institution participates in community affairs or makes its social, cultural, and recreational programs and facilities available to the community; (c) the economic impact of an institution on its local community; and (d) the extent to which an institution, through its industrial and educational enterprises, assists the community in the development and application of new technologies.

Attitudinal Measures

Beyond the usual quantitative outcome indicators, attitudinal indicators gathered primarily through satisfaction surveys of the users are helpful in formulating outcome indicators. The most common focus of such surveys would be feedback regarding the scope of desired services coupled with measures of satisfaction with existing services.

Several types of surveys may be helpful in the assessment of progress in reaching program outcomes and objectives in the sponsored research and community service areas. The first type of attitudinal measure may be a needs survey seeking input from faculty, students, or community clientele about the most-needed services or educational programs.

Once services and programs have been implemented in response to defined needs, user surveys may be quite helpful in assessing the degree of satisfaction and eliciting suggestions for the improvement of existing or expanded programs and services (Gravely and Cochran, 1991). Longitudinal follow-up studies of program participants may be helpful in assessing the long-term effects of an institution's program and service offerings.

All too often, institutions survey only the clientele whom they are currently serving. Efforts must also be made to obtain reactions from persons who express interest in program offerings but do not actually participate in an institution's activities. Such surveys may help identify obstacles to program participation that may be remedied in the future.

Organizational performance or effectiveness requires customer research through the routine monitoring of: (1) customer needs, expectations, and requirements; (2) customer satisfaction or dissatisfaction; or (3) customer loyalty or attrition. While most organizations examine needs and satisfaction with some regularity, the examination of loyalty or attrition is somewhat less common. Lembcke (1994, p. 55) notes further "The purpose of customer loyalty assessment is not necessarily to recover lost customers but to learn how to improve services and products in ways that prevent further attrition. This assessment is particularly useful for understanding the issues that underlie increases in the number of nonreturning students, nonrepeat donors and students defection from residence halls." Services may be outsourced or duplicated internally because downstream systems are dissatisfied with upstream services.

Data System Indicators

In the research and public service areas, as in most areas of institutional activity, the institution's normal operations may provide a range of data system indicators useful in assessing outcomes and progress toward stated administrative objectives. Normal federal data-reporting procedures will yield financial data on research and public service activities via the IPEDS Financial Statistics Report. Often, additional reports required at the state level will also yield standard indicators of the extent of sponsored program or public service activities. The National Science Foundation (NSF) surveys, as well as survey responses to a number of collegiate guides at the graduate and undergraduate levels, may also provide a variety of outcomes indicators.

Administrative Practice

Standard administrative practices such as conducting a management audit or submission of a unit's annual report may also provide suitable objectives for assessment. Information obtained from a management audit may be helpful in formulating outcomes related to an assessment of research services. The primary focus in this regard is on the efficiency of procedures employed in administering contracts and grants. Such procedures are generally designed to assure the orderly commitment of external and internal funds in administering contracts for special projects and programs. Audits may be performed by a team of internal or state auditors or by independent accounting firms.

Virtually every administrative unit will file an annual report with the office to which it reports. Information in these reports may provide a starting point in assessing progress toward goals and objectives. In short, if an office maintains any type of database on a central administrative computer or a microcomputer, it has the capability of transforming its operational data into analytical information suitable for evaluating program and administrative objectives.

Professional Standards

The statement of Research and Public Service outcomes and objectives may flow logically from the Expanded Statement of Institutional Purpose. If it does not, efforts to develop standards or statements of recommended professional practice for research and public service may also serve as a source for establishing administrative objectives. Often the administration of grants and contracts is carried out by an institution's Business Office, whereas assistance in obtaining research funds and services is provided to faculty from an office reporting to the Academic Affairs Office or the Graduate School Office. In the former instance, familiarity with contract and grant procedures developed by the National Association of College and University Business Officers (NACUBO, 1987) may be helpful. In the latter instance, information concerning desired research services and information sources useful in obtaining grants and contracts is available through the activities and information networks of such professional organizations as the National Council of University Research Administrators (NCURA) or the Society of Research Administrators (SRA).

In the area of public service, continuing educators have focused considerable attention on the definition of standards and the formulation of principles of good practice. The Principles of Good Practice for Continuing Education (Council on the Continuing Education Unit, 1984) are designed to serve sponsors, providers, and users of continuing education in collegiate and noncollegiate settings. Development of more current standards for continuing education was preceded by a study of attitudes toward previously existing standards of good practice in a variety of organizational settings (House, 1983). The 18 general principles and 70 statements of good practice in relation to learning needs, learning outcomes, learning experiences, assessment, and administration of continuing education programs may serve as a model for research, public service, or other units of various types.

Educational Support Services

Educational support services are equivalent to "Academic Support Services" in the illustrative Expanded Statement of Institutional Purpose contained in Appendix A of this Handbook. Collier (1978) defines academic support services as "those activities carried out in direct support of one or more of the three primary programs (Instruction, Research, Public Service)" (p. 37). Subprograms or areas of academic support include library services, museums and galleries, educational media services, academic computing support, academic administration and personnel development, and course and curriculum development.

There may not be universal agreement when one attempts to define the administrative areas included under a given functional area. The broader Program Classification Structure (PCS), described by Myers and Topping (1974), helps to define administrative units falling under the primary PCS areas of instruction, research, public service, academic support, student service, and institutional support.

The emergence of new areas such as enrollment management, for which Dolence

(1989) has developed a series of evaluation criteria, complicates attempts to define administrative areas and, at the same time, illustrates the fluid nature of college and university organization. In a related area, Hossler (1991) offers criteria for evaluating student recruitment and retention programs.

Areas such as library services and computing services are frequently structured as independent units. These units in particular must coordinate their objectives with those of the academic units, which in turn should coordinate their plans with the support service units to be sure that intended outcomes requiring substantial increases in resources or services are feasible. For example, the library may have an objective of automating its catalog and providing on-line catalog search service to all departments. If the departments are not aware of this intention and have not requested funds for appropriate equipment in their budgets, this objective will not be achieved fully. Automating the catalog can be achieved by the library without support from other units, but the use of an on-line service by academic units depends on the purchase of equipment out of departmental budgets. Unless academic units allocate funds for equipment, the service will very likely be unused.

The assessment procedures developed by academic support units may differ from those developed by academic units, in that examination of records, logs of activities, and supporting documents for annual reports may play a much larger role. A library can document that its catalog is automated by reporting details of the development procedure and having the catalog available for review. An art museum can document that it has increased its collection in a particular area by listing new acquisitions in a simple report, assuming that dated sales agreements or letters describing donations are on file and assuming that the new acquisitions are available for examination. In summary, academic support units will most often be documenting activities using routine record keeping and reports and will rarely have to use special data collection methods or surveys.

EVALUATION OF NONACADEMIC UNITS

The trend toward self-regulation on the part of individual-based and institution-based professional associations, combined with increased interest in the evaluation of such services and programs on the part of single institutions, has led to the emergence of a growing but somewhat fugitive literature base on the evaluation of noninstructional areas. With regard to self-regulation, the work of the Council for the Advancement of Standards in Higher Education (CAS, 1989) and the Student Services Program Review Project (SSPRP, 1986) have been especially notable.

Council for Advancement of Standards (CAS)

The Council for the Advancement of Standards for Student Services/Development Programs (CAS) was formed in 1979. By 1988, CAS had developed and published sets of evaluation standards and guidelines for evaluating 17 functional work areas in student affairs. This was followed in 1988 by the publishing of self-assessment guides which are the operational versions of the CAS *Standards and Guidelines*. The early work of CAS was carried out over six years through the efforts of 22 CAS professional associations with support and encouragement from the American Council on Education's Advisory Committee on Self-Regulation Initiatives and the Council on Postsecondary Accreditation (COPA).

By 1994, CAS had established standards and guidelines for 19 functional areas of higher education programs and services. Each area addressed by CAS includes a self-assessment guide, along with directions for documenting the assessment, enhancing strengths, and recommending change and improvement.

In the development of the CAS Standards and Guidelines, no particular organizational or administrative structure was presupposed or mandated. Therefore, the standards that emerged apply to all types of postsecondary institutions. General standards were developed for each of the following functional areas: mission, program, leadership and management, organization and administration, human resources, funding, facilities, legal responsibilities, equal opportunity, access and affirmative action, campus and community relations, multicultural programs and services, ethics, and evaluation.

Academic support services for which CAS standards had been developed by 1994 include academic advising, admissions programs, learning assistance programs, and women student programs and services. Student service areas addressed in the CAS Standards and Guidelines include alcohol and other drug programs, campus activities, career planning and placement, college unions, commuter student programs, disabled student services, fraternity and sorority advising, housing and residence life, judicial programs, minority student services, recreational sports, religious programs, and student activities. In the area of institutional support services, CAS standards and guidelines have been developed for student orientation programs and for the evaluation of research and evaluation services.

As regional accrediting organizations have continued to place emphasis on institutional effectiveness in recent years, the CAS Standards and Guidelines have enabled institutions to better assess study, and evaluate their student services and development programs and to improve and utilize them more fully (Mable, 1991).

Internally, CAS Standards and Guidelines may be helpful in a variety of ways. In this regard Bryan and Mullendore (1991) suggest a number of applications and strategies for enhancing the effectiveness and use of CAS standards and guidelines for a variety of purposes including program development, accreditation self-study, staff development, program evaluation, developing comparisons across institutions, developing or enhancing program credibility, gaining acceptance of programs and departments, educating the campus community, improving political maneuverability, and competing for dollars when institutional budgets are limited.

The Division of Student Affairs at the University of North Carolina at Greensboro began using the CAS Standards as the basis for their program evaluation process in 1987. The systematic method utilized and sample evaluation schedule are explained in Appendix E (page 270).

CAS is composed of 27 member organizations with professional constituencies of over 75,000 members. Standards and guidelines are continuing to be updated in many of the above areas. New standards and guidelines are expected to be available for Financial Aid,

International Student Educators, Student Records and Registration Programs, and Student Leadership Programs by 1995. CAS clearinghouse activities are coordinated by the Office of the Vice President for Student Affairs at the University of Maryland. CAS Standards and Guidelines may be obtained from the CAS Secretary, 2108 Mitchell Building, University of Maryland at College Park, College Park, Maryland 20742-5221—(301) 314-8428.

Student Services Program Review Project

The Student Services Program Review Project (SSPRP), developed in California, is of particular interest to the community college sector but has general applicability to all postsecondary institutions. The goal of the project was to develop and pilot test evaluation designs in order to assist colleges in implementing program evaluations for selected campus-based student services programs. Over a three-year period, more than a thousand persons were involved in the development and testing of evaluation designs—including goals, criteria, measures, and methods—that were field based and field produced. The following were the specific objectives (SSPRP, 1986, p. 3):

1. Develop evaluation models;
2. Develop data collection, data analysis, and information-reporting procedures;
3. Pilot test evaluation models and procedures;
4. Widely disseminate models and procedures; and,
5. Develop support materials and services to assist colleges in implementing program evaluations appropriate to their institutions.

The SSPRP developed evaluation designs and procedures for admissions and records, assessment services, career/life planning, counseling, financial aid, job placement, student affairs, and tutorial services.

Rather than focusing on existing generalized program evaluation models and their applicability to administrative settings, Wergin and Braskamp (1987) have discussed issues and strategies for evaluating specific programs. They presented specific criteria and evaluative schema are presented for institutional planning, business affairs, intercollegiate athletic programs, student support services, counseling centers, faculty development programs, and campus computing services. Key questions addressed are as follows:

1. How can institutional researchers and academic administrators authorize and produce information on program effectiveness that is useful for decision making?
2. How are administrators to know how well these administrative and support services are working and what might be done to improve them?

CAMPUS-BASED EVALUATION PLANS FOR NONACADEMIC UNITS

A number of campus-based plans for the evaluation of nonacademic units have emerged in recent years (Brown, 1989; Haberaecker, 1990; Northwestern University, 1989). The Northwestern University review process which was applied to some 93 academic department centers or administrative units from the 1985-86 through 1988-89 academic years was cited as Appendix E of the Second Edition of the *Practitioner's Handbook.*

In this section, we shall note principles and considerations underlying the development of a campus-based evaluation system at the University of Maryland. The considerations discussed by Brown and Reichard (1991, pp. 196-203) in the second edition of *The Practitioner's Handbook* included purpose of evaluation, level of analysis, constituents to be included, external environment, domains of activity to be considered, time frame, type of data to be utilized, and referents. A more detailed description of the University of Maryland process is provided by Brown (1989).

Regardless of the approach taken, the assessment process must not be so labor-intensive and time-consuming that it becomes an end in itself. The Northwestern and College Park evaluation processes cited in the second edition operated on a seven-year cycle with each unit being reviewed only once in seven years. Elements of the process, such as surveys of users, can be performed on a more routine basis. Both processes also include follow-up procedures that assure continued, but less stringent, assessment procedures. The College Park process was conducted in each nonacademic unit using a modified self-study approach.

Self-study is a process familiar to members of most campus communities. It is used in the accreditation review process and in the academic unit review process. Utilization of a modified self-study concept requires the formation of a self-study committee to oversee the evaluation. This committee should comprise representatives of the several constituencies with an interest in the unit. Constituencies to be represented would include senior administrators, unit managers, unit staff, campus users of the unit's services, external suppliers or users, and the unit head (usually a director). This committee, appointed by the senior administrator in charge of the unit, in consultation with the unit director, should oversee the self-study and prepare a report using the institution's framework as a guide.

A study by Brown (1990) reinforced the need to select the members of the oversight committee very carefully. The chair must be viewed as objective and have some stature on campus. He or she must also be interested in the review process. Committee members must be willing to devote considerable time and effort to the process. Selecting users who were critical of the unit to serve on the self-study committee was shown to have a positive effect on the attitude of these constituents.

Upon completion of the self-study, it is often advisable to bring in two or more external consultants to the campus to perform an independent evaluation of the unit. Their report would be incorporated into the report of the self-study committee. The UMCP framework for the review of nonacademic units is based on the seven issues critical for a successful evaluation (Cameron and Whetten, 1983; Goodman and Pennings, 1980; Steers, 1975).

Purpose of Evaluation. Since significant resources in the form of both staff time and money will be invested in this evaluation process, the evaluations should produce results that are useful to everyone involved, especially the senior administrator responsible for the unit and the director of the unit, but also the unit staff and other constituents as well.

Therefore, evaluation will be "utilization focused" (Patton, 1978). By its nature, utilization-focused evaluation is formative, rather than summative, evaluation. The primary purpose of the assessment of academic support units is to collect information that can be used to improve and further develop the unit.

It is also important to recognize that evaluation "is partly a political process" (Patton, 1978, p. 49). Through the generation of information for prediction and control, decision makers use evaluation results to reduce uncertainty. Unit heads could utilize the evaluation process to influence constituencies and use the results of the evaluation to garner additional resources. The stated purpose of this evaluation process is to assess the effectiveness of the units. More to the point, however, is the purpose of the evaluation as viewed by the senior administrator as well as the unit head. The first step in a utilization-focused evaluation is to have the self-study committee discuss the evaluation with these administrators and determine particular issues and/or problems they would like to have explored during review of the unit (Patton, 1978). The evaluation cannot be useful if it does not provide the specific information these administrators need to make decisions and improve the operation of the unit. The primary purpose of the evaluation, then, is to meet the requirements of administrators for information concerning the effectiveness of their unit.

Another purpose of evaluation in any organization is to improve the quality of the organization. This is particularly important in an institution of higher education that is striving to achieve excellence. If a college is to achieve academic excellence, its leaders must also be concerned with the performance and quality of the institution's nonacademic units (Keller, 1983). It is equally important for senior administrators, as well as the college's constituencies, to know whether the resources being expended on nonacademic support are being utilized as effectively and efficiently as possible.

Level of Analysis. The nature of the evaluation process has determined that in the nonacademic area the unit is the level at which the evaluation will be conducted. Goodman and Pennings (1977) support assessment at this level: "It seems strategically advantageous to focus on subunits' characteristics, including their technological and human resources and the social structure and processes that they have developed" (p. 150).

Constituents to Be Included. The perspectives of all identifiable constituents of the unit should be considered in the evaluation. There are two ways of assuring that the perspectives of all constituents are considered in a review: (1) A representative of the constituency can serve as a member of the self-study committee, and (2) constituents can be surveyed.

Summary

Institutions can expect a considerable degree of variance in the technical merit of statements of program intent, outcomes, and objectives. Particularly at the inception of institutional effectiveness operations, such differences are not only acceptable but desirable to the extent that they reflect active involvement by the institution's administrative units. However, this resource section and the examples contained *Assessment Case*

Studies suggest that outcomes/objectives should be linked to the Expanded Statement of Institutional Purpose; should exhibit (explicitly or implicitly) many of the attributes described earlier; and, in most cases, should be measurable.

References: Cited and Recommended

Alwin L. F. (1993). *Mastering A Complex Management Challenge: An Audit Report on Management at the University of Texas at Austin.* SAO Report Number 3-040. Austin: Office of the State Auditor.

Alwin, L. F. (1991). *A Guide to Measure the Performance of Information Systems.* SAO Report Number 1-112. Austin: Office of the State Auditor.

Ashworth, K. H. (1994). Performance-Based Funding in Higher Education: The Texas Case Study. *Change, 26,*(6), 8-15.

Banta. T. W., and Borden, V. M. H. (1994). Performance Indicators for Accountability and Improvement (pp. 95-105). Using Performance Measures to Guide Strategic Decision Making. *New Directions for Institutional Research*, no. 82. San Francisco: Jossey-Bass.

Borden, V. M. H., and Bottrill, K. V. (1994). Performance Indicators: History, Definitions, and Methods (pp. 5-21). Using Performance Indicators to Guide Strategic Decision Making. *New Directions for Institutional Research*, no. 82. San Francisco: Jossey-Bass.

Brewer, G. D. (1983). Assessing Outcomes and Effects. In K. S. Cameron and D. S. Whetton (eds.), *Organizational Effectiveness: A Comparison of Multiple Models.* New York: Academic Press.

Brown, M. K. (1989). Developing and Implementing a Process for the Review of Nonacademic Units. *Research in Higher Education, 30*(1), 89-112.

Brown, M. K., and Reichard, D. J. (1991). Setting and Evaluating Objectives in Nonacademic Units (pp. 188-208). In J. O. Nichols (ed.), *A Practitioner's Handbook for Institutional Effectiveness and Student Outcomes Assessment Implementation.* New York: Agathon Press.

Bryan, W. B., and Mullendore, R. H. (1991). Operationalizing CAS Standards for Program Evaluation and Planning. In Bryan, W. B., Winston, R. B., and Miller, T. K. (eds.)., Using Professional Standards in Student Affairs (pp. 29-44). *New Directions for Student Services*, no. 53. San Francisco: Jossey-Bass.

Bryan, W. B., Winston, R. B., and Miller, T. K. (eds.). (1991). Using Professional Standards in Student Affairs. *New Directions for Student Services*, no. 53. San Francisco: Jossey- Bass.

Cameron, K. S. (1981). Domains of Organizational Effectiveness in Colleges and Universities. *Academy of Management Journal, 24*, 25-47.

Cameron, K. S., and Whetton, D. S. (1983). *Organizational Effectiveness: A Comparison of Multiple Models.* New York: Academic Press.

Collier, D. V. (1978). *Program Classification Structure.* (Technical Report No. 106). Boulder, CO: National Center for Higher Education Management Systems (NCHEMS) at Western Interstate Commission for Higher Education.

Council for the Advancement of Standards for Student Services/Development Programs. (1989). *CAS Standards and Guidelines for Student Service/Development Programs.* College Park, MD: Council on the Continuing Education Unit.

Dolence, M. G. (1989). Evaluation Criteria for an Enrollment Management Program. *Planning for Higher Education. 218*(1), 1-3.

Dooris, M. J., and Teeter. D. J. (1994). Total Quality Management Perspective on Assessing Institutional Performance. In Borden, V. M. H. and Banta, T. W. (eds.), Using Performance Indicators to Guide Strategic Decision Making (pp. 51-62). *New Directions for Institutional Research*, no. 82. San Francisco: Jossey-Bass.

Dunn, J. A. Jr. (1989). *Planning Guidelines for Facility Renewal and Adaptation.* Ann Arbor, MI: Society for College and University Planning.

Ewell, P. T., and Jones D. P. (1994). Data, Indicators, and the National Center for Higher Education Management Systems. In Borden, V. M. H. and Banta, T. W. (eds.), Using Performance Indicators to Guide

Strategic Decision Making (pp.23-35). *New Directions for Institutional Research*, no. 82. San Francisco: Jossey-Bass.

Fincher, C. (1978). Importance of Criteria for Institutional Goals. In R. H. Fenske (ed.), Using Goals in Research and Planning (pp. 1-15). *New Directions for Institutional Research*, no. 19. San Francisco: Jossey-Bass.

Goldman, B. A., and Mitchell, D. F. (1995). *Directory of Unpublished Experimental Mental Measures: Volume V*. Washington, DC: American Psychological Association.

Goodman, P. S., and Pennings, J. M. (1977). *New Perspectives on Organizational Effectiveness*. San Francisco: Jossey-Bass.

Goodman, P. S., and Pennings, J. M. (1980). Critical Issues in Assessing Organizational Effectiveness. In E. E. Lawler, D. A. Nadler, and C. Cammann (eds.), *Organizational Assessment: Perspectives on the Management of Organizational Behavior*. New York: Wiley

Gravely, A. R. and Cochran, T. R. (1991), *The Use of Perceptual Data in the Assessment of Administrative Offices*. Paper presented at the 31st Annual Forum of the Association for Institutional Research, San Francisco, CA.

Haberaecker, H. J. (1990). *Developing Interinstitutional Comparisons of Nonacademic Units for Use in the Review Process*. Paper presented at the 1990 Association for Institutional Research Forum, Louisville, KY.

Hage, J. (1980). *Theories of Organization*. New York: Wiley.

Hannan, M. T., and Freeman, J. (1977). Obstacles to Comparative Studies. In P. S. Goodman, J. M. Pennings, and Associates (eds.), *New Perspectives on Organizational Effectiveness*. San Francisco: Jossey-Bass.

Harris, J. (1985). Assessing Outcomes in Higher Education. In C. Adelman (ed.), *Assessment in American Higher Education: Issues and Contexts*. Washington, DC: U.S. Department of Education.

Heverly, M. A. (1993). Using Total Quality to Better Manage an Institutional Research Office. *AIR Professional File*, No. 46. Tallahassee: The Association for Institutional Research.

Hossler, D. (1991). Evaluating Student Retention and Recruitment Programs. *New Directions for Institutional Research*, no. 70. San Francisco: Jossey-Bass.

House, R. M. (1983). *Standards of Practice in Continuing Education: A Status Study*. Silver Springs, MD: Council on the Continuing Education Unit.

Keller, G. (1983). *Academic Strategy*. Baltimore, MD: Johns Hopkins University Press.

Lembcke, B. A. (1994). Organizational Performance Measures: The Vital Signs of TQM Investments. In D. Seymour (ed), Total Quality Management on Campus (pp.45-59), *New Directions for Higher Education*, no. 88. San Francisco: Jossey-Bass.

Mable, P. (1991). Professional Standards: An Introduction and Historical Perspective. In Bryan, W. A., Winston, R. B., and Miller, T. K. Using Professional Standards in Student Affairs (pp. 5-18). *New Directions for Student Services*, no. 53. San Francisco: Jossey-Bass.

McLaughlin, G. W., and Snyder, J. K. (1993). Plan-Do-Check-Act and the Management of Institutional Research. *AIR Professional*, File no. 48. Tallahassee: The Association for Institutional Research.

Micek, S. S., Service, A. L., and Lee, Y. S. (1975). *Outcome Measures and Procedures Manual: Field Edition*. (Technical Report No. 70). Boulder, CO: NCHEMS at Western Interstate Commission for Higher Education.

Miles, R. H. (1980). *Macro Organizational Behavior*. Santa Monica, CA: Goodyear.

Miller, R. I. (1980). Appraising Institutional Performance. In P. Jedamus, M. W. Peterson, and Associates (eds.), *Improving Academic Management* (pp. 406-431). San Francisco: Jossey-Bass.

Miller, T. K. (1991). Using Standards in Professional Preparation. In Bryan, W. A., Winston, R. B., and Miller, T. K. (eds.), Using Professional Standards in Student Affairs (pp.45-62). *New Directions for Student Services*, no. 53. San Francisco: Jossey-Bass.

Moore, K. M. (1986). Assessment of Institutional Effectiveness. In J. Losak (ed.), Applying Institutional Research in Decision Making (pp. 49-60). *New Directions for Community Colleges*, no. 56. San Francisco: Jossey-Bass.

Myers, E. M., and Topping, J. R. (1974). *Information Exchange Procedures Activity Structure.* (Technical Report No. 63). Boulder, CO: NCHEMS.

National Association of College and University Business Officers. (1993). *NACUBO Benchmarking Project.* Washington, DC: Author.

National Laboratory for Higher Education. (1974). *Developing Measurable Objectives.* Durham, NC: Author.

Nichols, J. O. (1995). *The Departmental Guide and Record Book for Student Outcomes and Institutional Effectiveness.* New York: Agathon Press.

Northwestern University. (1989). *Academic and Administrative Review Procedures.* Evanston, IL: Office of the Vice President for Administration and Planning.

Pace, C. R. (1983). *College Student Experiences.* Los Angeles: Higher Education Research Institute, UCLA.

Patton, M. Q. (1978). *Utilization-Focused Evaluation.* Beverly Hills, CA: Sage.

Perrow, C. (1961). The Analysis of Goals in Complex Organizations. *American Sociological Review*, 26(December), 854-866.

Pratt, L. K., and Reichard, D. J. (1983). Assessing Institutional Goals. In N. P. Uhl (ed.), Using Research for Institutional Planning (pp. 53-66). *New Directions for Institutional Research*, no. 37. San Francisco: Jossey-Bass.

Resource Manual on Institutional Effectiveness. (1989). Atlanta, GA: Commission on Colleges of the Southern Association of Colleges and Schools.

Sapp, M. M. (1994). Setting Up a Key Success Index Report: A How-To Manual. *AIR Professional File*, no. 51. Tallahassee: The Association for Institutional Research.

Sapp, M. M., and Temares, M. L. (1992, March). A Monthly Checkup: Key Success Indices Track Health of the University of Miami. *NACUBO Business Officer*, 25, 24-31.

Scott, R. A. (1984). Determining the Effectiveness of Campus Services. *New Directions for Institutional Research*, no. 41. San Francisco: Jossey-Bass.

Seymour, D. (ed.). (1994). Total Quality Management on Campus. *New Directions for Higher Education*, no. 88. San Francisco: Jossey-Bass.

Steers, R. M. (1975). Problems in the Measurement of Organizational Effectiveness. *Administrative Science Quarterly*, 20, 546-556.

Student Services Program Review Project (SSPRP). (1986). *They Said it Couldn't Be Done.* Santa Ana, CA: Author (ERIC ED 280 518).

Tuttle, T. C. (1994). Is Total Quality Worth the Effort? How do We Know? In D. Seymour (ed.), Total Quality Management on Campus (pp.21-32). *New Directions for Higher Education*, no. 88. San Francisco: Jossey-Bass.

Wergin, J. F., and Braskamp, L. A. (eds.). (1987). Evaluating Administrative Services and Programs. *New Directions for Institutional Research*, no. 56. San Francisco: Jossey-Bass.

Wilson, R. F. (1987). A Perspective on Evaluating Administrative Units in Higher Education. In J. F. Wergin and L. A. Braskamp (eds.), Evaluating Administrative Services and Programs (pp. 3-13). *New Directions for Institutional Research*, no. 56. San Francisco: Jossey-Bass.

Assessment and Continuous Quality Improvement

Eliot S. Elfner

The assessment movement has become part of most higher education institutions because of the many reasons already presented in this book. Another philosophy recently being addressed is that of Continuous Quality Improvement (CQI), also referred to as Total Quality Management (TQM) in the industrial arena. This section presents the CQI movement, and relates its philosophy to the assessment movement. The first topic is the origins of quality improvement and its adaptation to higher education. The second focus of this discussion provides a definition of quality in higher education. With this foundation, this section lists the basic components of CQI in a higher education environment. Then, the CQI parallel to the assessment paradigm is presented.

The centrality of mission, the dependence on the strategic planning phase of management, the emphasis of formative processes, and the reliance on faculty involvement are all common to both CQI and Assessment. It seems clear that assessment and CQI are complementary activities. Each benefits from the support of the other. This section is a discussion of these issues, leading to the above conclusion.

Introduction to CQI in Higher Education

The original concept of CQI is often attributed to the late W. Edwards Deming. Dr. Deming was a student of mathematics and physics, and became interested in the application of statistical process control concepts early in his career. Other early practitioners of CQI included Philip B. Crosby and Joseph M. Juran. These proponents of CQI developed a rich body of knowledge, primarily in the context of industrial applications. More recently, two widely distributed video documentaries, narrated by Lloyd Dobyns, have presented the case for quality: *If Japan Can, Why Can't We*, (1980), and *Quality or Else* (1990). Both served to expose a wide audience to the concepts and principles of CQI.

A related book appeared in 1982 when Tom Peters and Robert Waterman published *In Search of Excellence*. Through the presentation of several case studies, Peters and Waterman illustrated the characteristics necessary for organizations to achieve excellence. Their approach is parallel to those presented by the CQI authors.

A transition of the CQI movement to higher education began in the mid-1980's. Alexander Astin, who had published widely in the assessment literature, addressed the phenomenon of excellence in the context of higher education in 1985. Also in 1985, Volume I of *Higher Education: Handbook of Theory and Research*, edited by John C. Smart, contained two relevant chapters: "Program Quality in Higher Education: A Review and Critique of Literature and Research," by Conrad and Blackburn; and "The Quest for Excellence: Underlying Policy Issues," by Morgan and Mitchell. Both chapters address the issues of quality in the context of higher education. These early presentations led to interest among numerous writers in the higher education literature.

Several champions of quality in higher education have emerged recently. Ted Marchese, Vice President of American Association of Higher Education (AAHE), began writing editorials on CQI in *Change* in 1990, and has continued to promote the CQI movement in higher education ever since. Dan Seymour, a quality consultant, wrote *On Q: Causing Quality in Higher Education* in 1991. Lawrence A. Sherr and Deborah J. Teeter edited the Fall 1991 issue of *New Directions for Institutional Research* subtitled *Total Quality in Higher Education*. It contained seven articles and three appendices directed toward the implementation of CQI in higher education. A subsequent issue of *New Directions for Institutional Research*, edited by Deb Teeter and G. Gregory Lozier and published in the summer of 1993, provided 24 case studies and comments on the application of CQI to higher education.

Two books, one by Robert Cornesky in 1990, and one by Cornesky and Samuel McCool, in 1992, integrate the teachings of Deming with the issues of implementing CQI in higher education. In 1989, Xerox initiated "The Total Quality Forum" with The Procter and Gamble Company, American Express Company, Ford Motor Company, IBM Corporation, and Motorola, Inc., all of which are notable players in the CQI movement among major corporations. This Forum had as one of its purposes the exposure of the concepts and principles of CQI to university leaders. This Forum has continued annually through 1992.

Two more publications illustrate the application of CQI in the university setting. John W. Harris and Mark Baggett of Samford University in Birmingham, Alabama, prepared a manual describing the efforts of that university to define and implement CQI there. It contains 17 commentaries on the progress made at Samford University. The work by E. Grady Bogue and Robert L. Saunders (1992) is among the more conceptual approaches thus far. After first defining quality in higher education, they present a section describing the several means of testing for quality in higher education. The final section is concerned with enhancing quality.

Increasingly, colleges and universities that have developed and implemented CQI in their environments are sharing their experiences. Many of the publications mentioned above present discussions of cases involving one or more institutions. As an example, the Summer 1993 issues of *New Directions for Institutional Research* described above presents information from 15 institutions. They include small private schools, two-year institutions, comprehensive four-year universities, and doctoral-granting institutions. The conferences discussed above also increasingly present sessions by representatives of CQI institutions. It is now possible to find in nearly every region of the country an institution that has begun wrestling with the issues surrounding the implementation of CQI. Most are very willing to share their experiences with others.

The last impetus for CQI in higher education discussed here comes from the accreditation agencies. Both regional and program accreditation are beginning to address the issues behind CQI in their evaluation of institutions seeking to achieve or continue accreditation. The Southern Association uses the terminology of Institutional Effectiveness to address the continuous improvement responsibility of accreditation. The North Central Association includes a prescription for using assessment of student outcomes to improve the institution. It also calls for the "strengthening" of the education processes of its member institutions, implying a continuous improvement prescription in all facets of an institution's operations. In 1992, the American Association of Collegiate Schools of Business (AACSB) implemented revised accreditation standards derived specifically from the tenets of TQM.

While the accrediting bodies are careful to avoid the CQI terminology in their criteria and prescriptions, they indeed do impose the concepts and principles of CQI on their member institutions. As they continue to address the concerns of accreditation and accountability, we can expect to see more direct references to the concepts and principles of CQI in their literature.

The review of the development of CQI literature in higher education provides us with an understanding of the relative importance placed on CQI. The original work of Deming and his contemporaries serve as the foundation. The first few tentative approaches to implement CQI in higher education generated a broad-ranging set of questions about the benefits and costs of implementing CQI in this new environment. The growth in literature and learning opportunities lends credence to the idea that CQI will become widely applied in the ongoing activities of colleges and universities. This conclusion leads to a number of important questions. How might one define quality in higher education? What is a CQI system? What are its components? And how do they relate to each other?

How Does One Define Quality in Higher Education?

The term "quality" has been the subject of discussions in many environments. Pirsig's discussion in *Zen and the Art of Motorcycle Maintenance* suggested its complexity when he wrote "obviously some things are better than others…but what's the 'betterness?'…so round and round you go, spinning mental wheels and nowhere finding anywhere to get traction. What the hell is quality? What is it?" (Pirsig, 1974, p. 184).

The traditional dictionary definition of the term quality suggests quality is excellence in character. It has to do with the properties or characteristics associated with an entity. We have an intuitive feeling for what quality is, but it becomes difficult to describe. Typically we understand quality to be the degree of goodness or excellence associated with an entity. One having high quality has much "goodness" and "excellence" associated with it.

In higher education, what is "good" or "excellent" is often subject to differing points of view. Quality in higher education is not a simply defined concept. A number of definitions of quality in higher education have been suggested. Astin (1985) notes that there are four traditional views of quality in higher education: (a) excellence as reputation, (b) excellence as resources, (c) excellence as outcomes, and (d) excellence as content. To these he adds a fifth perspective: excellence as "talent development." He suggests institutions of high quality are those that have the greatest impact on students. His is a value added approach to student knowledge and development.

Mayhew, Ford, and Hubbard (1990) define quality as learning through words, numbers, and abstract concepts to understand, cope with, and positively influence the environment in which one finds ones self. This definition implies a value orientation in the learning process, suggesting that students should have a positive influence on their environment. Bogue and Saunders reinforce the values component with support from Goodland, Soder, and Sirotnik in *The Moral Dimensions of Teaching* (1990), and from Bronowski in *Science and Human Values* (1956). The several definitions of quality each impose different constraints on teachers and administrators in colleges and universities. Any single definition restricts the opportunities for diverse institutions to pursue varying visions. Regional accrediting agencies, in recognition of this, accept diverse mission and purpose statements when evaluating their institutions. This approach provides a bridge to a definition of quality that seems congruent with both the several perspectives discussed above and the requirements for accreditation. In fact, Bogue and Saunders present their definition in just such a fashion: "Quality is conformance to mission specification and goal achievement—within publicly accepted standards of accountability and integrity" (1992, p. 20).

But, what are the components of a CQI System? In addition to defining the concept of quality, we need to develop an understanding of what a quality system is. Industrial models describe a package that is labeled Total Quality Management (TQM). These have been adopted to higher education as Continuous Quality Improvement (CQI). Marchese (1993) provides a succinct definition of Total Quality Improvement (TQI). It encompasses a large body of ideas focused on continuous improvement of all organizational processes that are important to those served by the institution. He describes a TQI environment as one where there is a collective sense of responsibility, the people listen to those they serve, and they have a preference for data, an ethic for continuous improvement, and a determination to develop to the fullest the talents of every learner; they also acknowledge they are professionally accountable to one another and to those they serve. This provides an ambitious aspiration for an institution implementing CQI.

There are five necessary components for CQI:

1. A Statement of Commitment to Excellence in the Mission;
2. Attention to the Service Provider/Receiver Chain;
3. A Passionate Commitment to Continuous Improvement;
4. The Development and Use of Quality Improvement Teams; and,
5. A Systematic Approach to Data Based Decision Making.

Figure 16 depicts them and illustrates that their integration leads to the creation of a Continuous Quality Improvement Culture for the institution.

First, and fundamental to the process, is that an institution must adopt a philosophy and culture of excellence in its mission and purpose statements. This is a process that requires a common vision by everyone in the institution. Deming's concern for constancy of purpose illustrates the need to express commitment to CQI in a widely accepted institutional mission of excellence. While top level commitment and leadership is required, it alone is not sufficient to successfully implement CQI. The commitment of middle and lower level personnel is important too, but again not sufficient. Until everyone associated with the institution is aware of and supports CQI, efforts to achieve other components of the quality culture will be unsuccessful.

FIGURE 16

CONTINUOUS QUALITY IMPROVEMENT
CREATING A CQI CULTURE

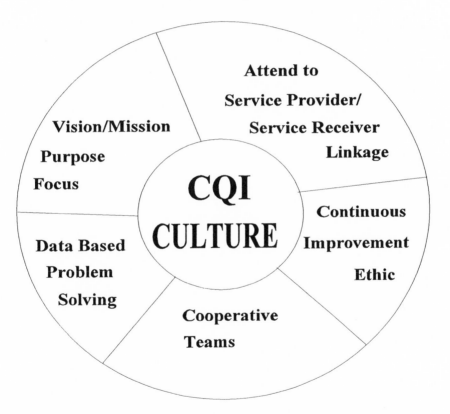

Secondly, a subtle but very important component of CQI is implied in the above discussion. The concept of "everyone associated with the institution" is far reaching and inclusive. The CQI environment extends not only to direct employees at all levels but also to those who provide resources to the institution, including suppliers who provide equipment and material used in the delivery of education; donors who provide resources in support of additional programs, housing, or other activities; high schools that send their graduates to the institution; and the people in the local communities where the institution offer its programs.

By implication, "everyone associated with the institution" also included those whom the institution serves. Traditionally TQM and CQI are devoted to the **customer**, and **customer satisfaction and delight** define education. For the purposes of CQI in higher education, Marchese's phrase recognizing that colleges and universities exist to provide service to others makes an important point: that the customer focus of TQM/CQI is incorporated by attending to those whom we serve. Rather than being confused about who is "the customer" in higher education, we recognize that anyone receiving the services from an institution is considered a "customer," and that the central focus of TQM/CQI is accommodation. It is important to acknowledge that those we serve have a large voice in determining the level of quality we provide.

Finally we must become aware of the references to both internal and external linkages among service receivers and service providers. There is the obvious link to those who deal services across the institution's boundaries. This view of linkages must also include the internal providers and receivers of services. Some of the people within the institution provide services to others within the institution, just as others receive services from colleagues within the institution. For example, a faculty member teaching a course is providing a service to students in that course (they may be considered external service receivers). But if that course is a prerequisite to another course taught by a colleague, the colleague also becomes a receiver of services and exists internal to the institutional borders. Thus the service provider/receiver linkages that are central to the CQI culture include both internal and external linkages.

Another central component of CQI systems is the imbedded cultural ethic of continuous improvement. By this we mean that institutional processes are never seen as complete, but rather as continuously evolving. The problems addressed in a CQI environment require a focus on processes, not people. CQI is based on the assumption that quality problems are largely a result of the processes in place; they are not due to mistakes by the people in the system. Course development by teachers, curriculum development and implementation, registering students, financial aid processes, etc., are all perceived by a CQI community as potential improvement processes. This does not imply that current processes are inappropriate or even inadequate, but rather that the processes can always be improved. "Even if it ain't broke, it CAN be improved" embodies this perspective.

The entire culture of CQI environments must also be committed to cooperative team approaches in striving for continuous improvement. This imperative is based on the presumption that while those with an intimate understanding of problems with the processes may be most able to propose solutions, they need the resources and expertise of others to implement solutions. Therefore, the intimate knowledge of the problems by operatives, and the resources and expertise of others with opportunity to assist are brought together in teams to address the quality problems that exist in the system. Training in CQI tools and analytical methods will be part of team training efforts. The training imperative requires a major commitment of time, attitude, and effort of people.

Finally, in a CQI environment, problem solving is based on a systematic approach, that involves gathering, organizing, interpreting, and using data and information. This involves a preference on the part of problem solving teams for data based decision making. It requires that intuitive decisions be tested against data.

These central components of CQI systems are integrated into a cultural whole. Successful implementation of all five components will lead to the institutional culture being driven by the prescriptions of CQI. Attention to suppliers helps the institution assure quality of resources; attention paid to those served assures that necessary outcomes are achieved. The devotion to continuous improvement of all institutional processes, by the use of data based, team oriented problem solving involves a wide representation of the institution's constituents.

CQI Parallels with Assessment

Institutional Mission. Probably the most obvious, and most important, parallel between the assessment or institutional effectiveness paradigm and CQI is that the basis of both is in the institutional strategic planning effort and mission statement. This requires an extensive effort to define the distinctive character of the institution, and to state that character in student outcomes terms. Other goals and objectives of the institution must also be incorporated in this mission statement. In order to determine whether or not the institution is successful, a clear statement of the vision, mission, and purpose must be made.

Strategic Planning. The institutional effectiveness paradigm prescribes a clear statement of purpose. Once developed, it must be incorporated into the strategic planning process of the institution. This is the foundation of strategic planning. Likewise, as an institution develops its vision/mission/purpose statement, it must undertake the steps to implement CQI. After completing the initial consideration of CQI, an institution must incorporate an explicit affirmation of the CQI philosophy within the context of its mission. Both assessment and CQI rely on the clear expression of a strong mission statement for an institution as a central component of the strategic planning process.

The institutional effectiveness paradigm requires the clear presentation of desired outcomes for the institution. The basics of the CQI process also require the clear presentation of desired outcomes. But CQI goes even further, requiring what Deming calls "Constancy of Purpose." Not only must there be a clear presentation of the institutional mission and purpose. Additionally, everyone involved with the organization must know, understand, and overtly work toward their attainment. This tenet of CQI is a basic part of the CQI culture.

Likewise, the institutional effectiveness paradigm prescribes the inclusion of assessment in the institutional strategic planning activities. Both the development and use of assessment results are important to the long-range planning process of an institution. External scanning and the assessment of institutional capabilities are both traditional strategic planning activities. To that end, the CQI process prescribes the gathering of information from institutional constituencies as a co-equal component of the long range strategic planning. This is part of the "customer" focus of CQI implemented at the front end of the planning process for an institution.

In summary, both the institutional effectiveness paradigm, and the CQI process focus attention on the institutional mission. Both require the development and approval of a clear and comprehensive statement of the institution's vision/mission/purpose across the various institutional constituencies. Included in this statement must be an explicit call for quality improvement as the central operating philosophy of the institution. All stakeholders in the institution are bound to uphold this vision/mission/purpose statement, which includes the commitment to continuous quality improvement as a foundation of the strategic planning process.

Formative Nature. Inherent in the understanding of CQI is the necessity to use the data and information collected for the purpose of improving the institution's processes. The institutional effectiveness paradigm's motivation is to provide evidence that the institution is satisfactorily accomplishing its purposes. This, of course, is primarily a summative process. But it also requires that the results also be used to feed back information so that problems can be diagnosed and analyzed. This is decidedly formative in approach.

A major concern about adapting the institutional effectiveness paradigm into the CQI activities of an institution is that of assessing the final results of the educational process —what is termed as endpoint inspection in the jargon of CQI. While this provides information about the degree to which the institution have attained its objectives, it seldom provides information about how to improve the process. And CQI is about processes, not end results. Thus, it is important to understand that the assessment activities conducted by an institution also be directed at the process indicators related to the desired outcomes, not just the final outcomes indicating the degree to which the goal or objective has been realized.

Fortunately, the institutional effectiveness paradigm is also clearly organized for the purpose of formatively providing feedback. It prescribes the feedback of results to the people in charge of the programs that were designed to result in certain outcomes. Assessment of results without feedback would lead to a lack of credibility about the measurement processes used to obtain the results. Likewise the relevancy of the measures used comes into question. Therefore, the involvement by appropriate participants in both the development and feedback of the assessment data is prescribed as central to the institutional effectiveness paradigm. Even accrediting agencies, the public's consumer protection agencies for higher education, require explicit plans for assessment leading to improvement, in addition to the summative information about how successful the institutions are.

Emphasis on Involvement and Teams. The institutional effectiveness paradigm prescribes the early and central involvement of the institution's faculty. They are pivotal in the development of what is important to measure, and what devices are used to measure them. A group of faculty working together on assessment activities can reach agreement both about what is important to measure relative to goals and objectives and how to go about measuring them. Without the acceptance of the faculty, the likelihood that any particular measures will meaningfully direct a formative effort is minimal.

Similarly, a central tenet of the CQI process is that teams of people are more effective addressing and solving quality problems than are individuals. Adapted to higher education, such a team approach holds much promise. Because most institutions of higher education employ one form or another of institutional governance, people are actively involved in committee work. This experience, though often viewed as inefficient, provides a natural opportunity to implement the team activities of CQI. Most academic committees already are focused on the problems that interfere with quality, so implementing a formal process of continuous quality improvement is congruent with institutional governance processes. With the proper training in CQI philosophy, techniques, and tools, the regular governance process and committee structure of higher education institutions can support the implementation of CQI.

Likewise, the institutional effectiveness paradigm is regularly implemented through a committee structure, usually with an assessment coordinating committee heading the process. Both CQI and assessment are excellent opportunities for applying the teaming process. Both require training and involvement of the faculty and staff to address particular issues. To the extent that assessment concentrates on process-oriented outcomes, the assessment and CQI coordinating committees could best be integrated into a single operating group working to help one another. Because both assessment and CQI rely on teaming and groups, this aspect is seen to be the most congruent activity shared by both processes.

Summary

The above discussion reviewed several activities that can be used to integrate CQI and the institutional effectiveness paradigm. The institutional mission is central to assessment, and becomes the strategic focus of a CQI organization. CQI is by definition a formative process designed to focus the institution's activities on constantly improving itself and its processes. Assessment, while often invoked on a summative, accountability basis, is clearly aimed at using the information about outcomes for feedback and improvement. This improvement focus demonstrates a clear similarity between assessment and CQI. Finally, both assessment and CQI prescribe group activities and teams to develop and analyze the assessment results and the CQI problems facing an institution. It seems clear that assessment and CQI are complementary activities. Each benefits from the support of the other. A best case scenario would formally include the assessment team as a quality circle for the CQI process.

References: Cited and Recommended

Astin, A. W. (1985). *Achieving Educational Excellence: A Critical Assessment of Priorities and Practices in Higher Education.* San Francisco: Jossey-Bass.

Bogue, G. W., and Saunders, R. L. (1992). *The Evidence for Quality: Strengthening the Tests of Academic and Administrative Effectiveness.* San Francisco: Jossey-Bass.

Bronowski, J. (1956). *Science and Human Values.* New York: Harper Collins.

Conrad, C. F., and Blackburn, R. T. (1985). Program Quality in Higher Education: A Review and Critique of Literature and Research. In Smart, J. C. (ed.), *Higher Education: Handbook of Theory and Research,* Vol. I. New York: Agathon.

Corneski, R. A., et al. (1990). *Using Deming to Improve Quality in Colleges and Universities.* Madison, WI: Magna.

Corneski, R. A., and McCool S. A. (1992). *Total Quality Improvement Guide for Institutions of Higher Education.* Madison, WI: Magna.

Dobyns, Lloyd, and Frank, R. (June 24, 1980). *If Japan Can, Why Can't We?* (video) New York: NBC News.

Dobyns, Lloyd, and Crawford-Madison, C. (October 13, 20, 27, 1990). *Quality or Else* (video) New York: PBS-WNET TV.

Goodland, J., Soder, R., and Sirotnik, K. (eds.). (1990). *The Moral Dimensions of Teaching.* San Francisco: Jossey-Bass.

Harris, J. W., and Baggett, J. M. (1992). *Quality Quest in the Academic Process.* Methuen, MA: GOAL/QPC.

Marchese, T. J. (June 1990). Cost and Quality. *Change, 22*(3), 4.

Mayhew, L., Ford, P., and Hubbard, D. (1990). *The Quest for Quality: The Challenge for Undergraduate Education in the 1990's.* San Francisco: Jossey-Bass.

Morgan, A. W., and Mitchell, B. L. (1985). The Quest for Excellence: Underlying Policy Issues. In J. C. Smart (ed.), *Higher Education: Handbook of Theory and Research,* Vol I. New York: Agathon Press.

Palmer, P. J. (June, 1993). *Assessment, CQI, and Undergraduate Improvement.* Keynote Address, 8th annual assessment conference and first continuous quality improvement conference. Chicago: American Association for Higher Education.

Peters, T. J., and Waterman, R. H., Jr. (1982). *In Search of Excellence: Lessons from America's Best Run Companies.* New York: Harper and Row.

Pirsig, R. (1974). *Zen and the Art of Motorcycle Maintenance.* New York: Morrow.

Seymour, D. T. (1991). *On Q: Causing Quality in Higher Education.* New York: ACE/Macmillan.

Sherr, L. A., and Teeter, D. J. (1991). Total Quality Management in Higher Education. *New Directions for Institutional Research, 18*(3), San Francisco: Jossey-Bass.

Teeter, D. J., and Lozier, G. G. (eds.). (1993). Pursuit of Quality in Higher Education: Case Studies in Total Quality Management. *New Directions for Institutional Research, 15*(78), San Francisco: Jossey-Bass.

CHAPTER FIVE

Initial Implementation

Following preparation first at the institutional and, subsequently, departmental level, the institution should be ready for initial operational implementation of institutional effectiveness at the beginning of the third period (shown on Figure 17). By that time the institution should have in place the following key elements developed during the first two phases of implementation:

1. **Expanded Statement of Institutional Purpose**—developed during the first year or period of implementation preparation;
2. **Statements of Intended Educational, Research, and Service Outcomes as well as Statements of Administrative Objectives**—prepared during the second year or period by each department/program and linked to the expanded statement of purpose; and,
3. **Assessment Plan**—designed in close coordination with departmental/program statements of intended outcomes/objectives during the second phase.

With these three important components serving as the foundation, the institution is ready to begin operational institutional effectiveness implementation; however, a modest amount of institutional remotivation may be necessary to refocus the institution's attention on the task immediately at hand.

At the beginning of the third phase, the institution should reflect on what has been accomplished regarding institutional effectiveness, then current implementation activities, and the ultimate value of complete implementation. This process could be accomplished by distribution of a well-prepared document covering these points; however, it probably would best be accomplished through either a single campus-wide convocation or through multiple smaller meetings highlighting these points as the document is distributed. The purpose of this activity, whether written or covered in meetings, preferably both, is to rekindle the enthusiasm and energy with which implementation activities commenced earlier and to demonstrate the CEO's continued high level of interest in the subject. Regardless of the success earlier preparatory activities have enjoyed, the best and most successful implementation effort will begin to "wilt" after several years of steady work. It is essential that an implementation "pep rally," in one form or another, be held as actual operational implementation begins in order to revitalize those taking part in the implementation process.

As shown on Figure 17, implementation during this third year continues on both the

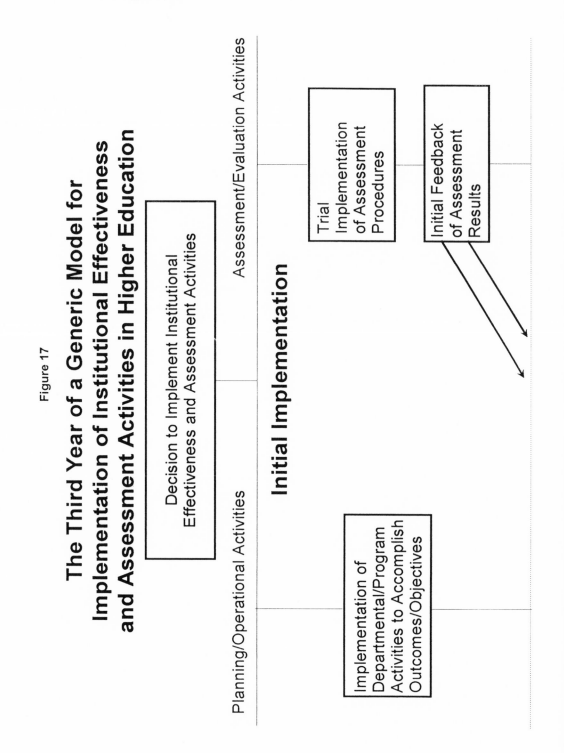

Figure 17

The Third Year of a Generic Model for Implementation of Institutional Effectiveness and Assessment Activities in Higher Education

planning/operational and assessment/evaluation tracks. However, the bulk of developmental or new work is focused in "Trial Implementation of Assessment Procedures," while the institution's academic and administrative departments conduct relatively normal operations designed to accomplish their intended outcomes/objectives. A separate resource section describing the unique aspects of implementation in the two-year college is found beginning on page 225.

Planning/Operational Activities

Following the considerable amount of departmental/program effort required to establish statements of intended outcomes or objectives just concluded, the degree of involvement by academic and administrative department/program personnel at this time may seem to some like a respite from previous preparatory activities directed toward implementation. In fact, the only activity scheduled on the planning/operational activities track during the third period is "Implementation of Departmental/Program Activities to Accomplish Outcomes/Objectives." Stated differently, academic and administrative departments are not required to do anything except their functional tasks (teaching, research, public service, student registration, maintenance of fiscal records, etc.) and assist in the "Trial Implementation of Assessment Procedures" later during the third year of implementation.

Superficially, this appears to be a relatively easy year for the academic and administrative departments/programs within the institution; however, in reality, many departments/programs will be implementing new or substantially revised curricular patterns or services growing from development of their statements of intended outcomes or objectives.

The very act of specifying their intended outcomes or objectives earlier will lead many departments to consider and then implement improved educational or service activities during the third year. An academic department may have determined that, in order for its degree program graduates to accomplish a particular cognitive outcome, a new course will be required. A research-oriented department may have concluded that to reach its level of intended grant commitment by external agencies, a shift or change in grant application procedures is necessary. In order to accomplish specified objectives regarding student residential life, administrators and staff in student affairs may have determined it necessary to modify greatly the social programs taking place at the institution. In all of these examples the central point is similar: Even as operational implementation of institutional effectiveness is begun and before the implementation of any formal assessment, many of the institution's departments/programs will begin to benefit from their natural response to the challenge of setting intended outcomes or objectives and then seeking to conduct departmental/program operations so as to accomplish those ends.

Within these departmental efforts toward accomplishment of their intended outcomes or objectives, some units may wish to conduct informal or departmental mid-year mini-assessments of their progress. However, in those units in which substantial changes have taken place in operations, it may well take several years for the full impact of their revised operations to become evident through assessment.

Assessment/Evaluation Activities

Clearly, the bulk of the activity during this initial year of operational implementation of institutional effectiveness will be involved with initiation of assessment procedures and feedback mechanisms.

Both the second period of implementation and the first half of this third year will undoubtedly be filled with the design of and planning for assessment, but it is in the later half of the third phase of implementation that "Trial Implementation of Assessment Procedures" will take place. Assuming that implementation roughly parallels academic years, trial implementation and feedback would take place between March and August of the third year. This period of time should be evenly divided between assessment activities conducted primarily during the months of March, April, and May, and results processing and feedback during June, July, and August.

The assessment-and-feedback cycle should be initiated by the end of the academic year and be completed before the next academic year begins. These timing restraints mean that the majority of the work in this area will take place as faculty and students, who might otherwise be engaged in supporting these activities, are preparing to leave the campus or have actually departed for the summer. Hence, institutions should seriously consider employment of several faculty members (perhaps one from each college or school) and a number of students during the trial implementation summer to assist in processing the data received and preparing the necessary feedback for presentation to the faculty and staff at the beginning of the next academic year.

What activities can be expected in the "Trial Implementation of Assessment Procedures"? The "Trial Implementation of Assessment Procedures" will result in a considerable amount of effort in at least four major areas of endeavor: (a) standardized cognitive testing, (b) administration of attitudinal surveys, (c) information drawn from institutional databases and other institutional data sources, and (d) departmental reports of assessment means implemented within the department.

Standardized Cognitive Testing

Undoubtedly, the fulfillment of a number of statements of intended educational outcomes will be assessed through students' performance on standardized cognitive tests. Hence, a considerable increase in the number of students taking such examinations can be anticipated. The procedures implemented regarding such testing should ensure that students have ample opportunity to take such tests and that students applying for graduation in a particular program register to take the appropriate test. Three basic questions will emerge concerning increased student participation in cognitive testing:

1. Who pays for such standardized examinations?
2. Should achievement of a specific score be required for graduation?
3. How can the institution motivate students to take such examinations seriously if a "passing" score is not required for graduation?

The answer to the first two of these logical inquiries relates to the primary purpose for the administration of the standardized examinations—assessment of institutional effectiveness. Although performance on such examinations will reflect on individual students, the primary intent is to assess the effectiveness of the institution's educational programs, not its students. Hence, either asking students to pay directly for taking standardized tests or setting a passing score for students to attain before graduation is inconsistent with the primary purpose of administration. However, this statement should not be construed as opposition to increasing the general student activity fee or tuition sufficiently to cover assessment-related costs.

Assuming that students are not required to achieve a specific score or pay directly for taking such standardized tests, how are institutions going to get students to take such examinations seriously? The answer is that each institution must seek and encourage voluntary compliance by specifically explaining to students why their taking the examination is important to continued institutional improvement. Institutions may further seek voluntary compliance by describing to students the potential benefit of having such standardized examination results on file when they graduate. Some institutions, having failed to gain student commitment intrinsically, suggest extrinsic motivational means, such as altering the sequence of preregistration or distribution of student parking permits to reward students who achieve certain scores on standardized cognitive measures routinely administered at the end of their second year in attendance. Among the case study institutions, the most effective means for motivating students to take seriously the assessment effort was to imbed the means of assessment within a class. The students were hence motivated to do their best on the standardized test for the sake of their grade in the class and the means of assessment was subsequently utilized by the departmental faculty as a whole for program assessment purposes.

Attitudinal Surveys

Also taking place during this period of time will be distribution to and return of attitudinal surveys by those students completing educational programs at the institution. These instruments, designed and pilot tested earlier in the implementation process, are best distributed and collected during the student's administrative processing for graduation. Some institutions may find it useful to distribute the survey when students obtain their application for graduation and to collect the completed questionnaire when a diploma fee is paid.

Other attitudinal surveys such as those of alumni, students leaving the institution prior to graduation, or employers are less constrained within the March-to-May time frame. In order to spread the workload of the trial assessment procedures implementation over the entire period of time, institutions should consider distribution of attitudinal surveys to such recipients during the period prior to March to avoid scheduling this activity concurrently with other assessment procedures more directly tied to the last half of the year.

Information Drawn from Institutional Data Systems

As the academic year draws to a close, data concerning student achievements, retention, and other subjects should be drawn from the institution's data system (as well as the data systems of other institutions) to support the assessment process. Data drawn from other institutions' data systems will be necessary to ascertain the success of students transferring from two-year colleges to four-year institutions and later to gauge the success in graduate school of baccalaureate program graduates.

Departmental Reports

During May and June, the institution's academic departments can be expected to be administering various cognitive and performance measures that they have designed both for assessment of the extent to which their intended programmatic outcomes have been achieved and, potentially, as requirements for student graduation. Although such means of assessment must be administered at the departmental level, there should also be institutional responsibility and effort to ensure that such activities are actually undertaken by the responsible departments and that the results are forwarded to a central point for compilation with other assessment results relating to the program.

Assembly and Processing of Assessment Results

During the early part to midsummer of the third phase of implementation, the institution should be literally awash in assessment-related data. Student scores for standardized cognitive tests taken earlier should be arriving. The results of attitudinal surveys (particularly the graduating student survey) will become available. Data drawn from institutional sources and other databases should have been processed. Departmental assessment results should be available. How should this flood of data be organized and refined into useful assessment information for the departments/programs and the institution?

The key to organizing this variety of assessment data is the establishment of a centralized agency (office, department, etc.) to which all such data are forwarded for compilation. Within that agency (staffed by both its own permanent employees and temporary faculty and students), separate folders or files for each department/program establishing intended departmental outcomes or objectives should be established. The folder should contain a copy of the departmental statements of intention (including their proposed means for assessment) and all of the trial assessment implementation results relating to that department/program. During the early part of the summer, it will be necessary that an outcome-by-outcome (or objective-by-objective) comparison of the proposed means of assessment with the results in the folder, and for one reason or another, which means of assessment were not accomplished. The comparison and subsequent follow-up will determine which data are missing from the folder but available within the institution and which means of assessment were, for one reason or another, not accomplished. By the end of June all assessment data available should have been collected and filed in the appropriate folder by department/program prior to analysis and preparation of feedback to the departments.

Initial Feedback of Results

Once the results of the trial assessment procedure implementation are received and filed, analysis of the results and preparation of feedback should commence. Analysis of such results will always remain a matter of subjective judgment at the departmental/program level, and only limited centralized analysis of results need, or indeed should, be provided to the department. On the other hand, centralized organization of the information to focus on departmental statements of intentions, summarization of individual student results into departmental/program averages, or interpretation of departmental/program results in light of institutional or national normative data may greatly enhance a department's willingness and ability to analyze and apply the results of the trial assessment procedures toward improvement in operations and results.

Although little direct analysis of results needs to be provided to the departmental/program level, a general need exists at the institutional level for insight into the extent to which the institution is accomplishing its Expanded Statement of Institutional Purpose. If the statement of purpose portrays the institution as a selective entity whose graduates should excel academically, but the trial assessment results indicate that its students are consistently exhibiting cognitive learning levels that might be expected of graduates at a substantially less selective institution, the institution should seriously consider adjusting its Expanded Statement of Institutional Purpose. Those individuals responsible at the institutional level for analysis and departmental/program information preparation will undoubtedly form general opinions concerning the extent to which departmental/program statements of intentions are being realized. Through these generalizations (subject to confirmation by individual department personnel), a basic understanding of the extent to which intentions expressed in the Expanded Statement of Institutional Purpose are being accomplished can be established.

The means for and timing of the feedback of assessment results to the departmental/program level are crucial to their use for improvement of the institution. During design of the assessment process, considerable thought should have been given to the data processing needed to obtain the desired data layouts and tables regarding each means of assessment. Following assembly of the various assessment results relating to each department/program by intended outcome/objective, a relatively standardized set of data presentation formats—designed earlier—for the results of each assessment means (cognitive test, attitudinal survey, etc.) should be completed.

There is no intention to homogenize departmental/program data analysis or presentation by use of standardized information formats. Rather, the intention is to devote considerable time and expertise to design a professionally developed set of data formats that can be quickly and efficiently adapted to each outcome/objective and assessment means. The use of such formats also precludes the expenditure of an inordinate amount of time summarizing the data for each outcome/objective by an individual (faculty or student) very possibly not trained in data analysis or presentation techniques.

To the maximum extent feasible, feedback of the assessment results should be part of a face-to-face report presented by a representative of the assessment team to the department/program. Such a presentation not only explains the results more clearly and provides an opportunity for the answering of questions, but also enhances the professional and collegial image of the assessment team and stimulates greater use of the results within the department/program. The use of faculty employed during the summer to support the assessment effort in feedback seminars in their college/school should be given serious consideration.

Without much doubt, the most appropriate time to present assessment feedback results is when the institution begins its next academic year. At that time all of the faculty will be present, and the tradition of starting anew will facilitate review of past accomplishments, revision of statements of departmental/program intentions, or adjustment of operational activities to better accomplish current intentions.

Unfortunately, taking advantage of the beginning of the academic year as the period for assessment feedback across the institution means that a great deal of information must be conveyed in a short period. For this task to be accomplished, sets of feedback presentation data must be prepared before the beginning of the academic year, and for several weeks those involved with presenting departmental/program assessment seminars must conduct several such seminars each day. Regardless of the effort involved, there is no more crucial portion of the assessment process than successful feedback of the results.

Expectations for Initial Implementation

What is reasonable to expect during this third year from the institution's initial operational implementation of institutional effectiveness, and particularly its assessment plan? Anything less than near total chaos should be considered a substantial success. It must be borne in mind that what should be taking place is perhaps the most pervasive and comprehensive change in the institution's means of doing business in many years and that this initial implementation is simply going to be a bit bumpy.

On many campuses incomplete implementation may be the rule rather than the exception. However, during this initial implementation, evidence of a good-faith effort to implement the assessment plan is as important, if not more so, than the comprehensiveness or precision of this initial implementation, which should be viewed as a pilot test of the assessment and feedback procedures designed.

As the third phase or period of implementation of institutional effectiveness (and the first year of operational implementation) draws to a close, the institution should accentuate the positive through press releases concerning the most successful aspects of the "Trial Assessment Procedures Implementation." It should also emphasize concrete examples of the benefits that the campus and students can expect to gain through "Initiation of the Annual Institutional Assessment Cycle" during the fourth period of implementation. In addition, the institution should treat generously those who have contributed most to successful implementation as an incentive to others to act in a similar manner as the annual cycle is implemented in the following year.

Implementing Institutional Effectiveness at Two-year Colleges

Harriott Calhoun

The term **two-year college** is applied to colleges that differ among themselves as much as they differ from other segments of higher education. The category includes technical colleges, technical community colleges, comprehensive community colleges, junior colleges, two-year campuses of university systems, and other colleges that, regardless of their names, fulfill some combination of the functions that are generally associated with two-year community colleges.

Although the institutional effectiveness paradigm and the implementation plan presented in this Handbook are applicable for all types and sizes of institutions, there are some factors of particular concern to two-year institutions in demonstrating institutional effectiveness. First, many two-year colleges (particularly comprehensive community colleges) have broad and diverse missions that include providing the traditional freshman- and sophomore-level college course work, career/vocational programs, job training/retraining, developmental education, continuing education programs, and a variety of individual and community enrichment activities.

A second factor is a student population that is increasingly diverse in terms of age, race, socioeconomic background, academic preparation, and purpose for enrollment. Additionally, two-year college students tend to use the curricula and services of the college for pursuing their educational objectives in their own time frames. They are most often commuters who attend part-time, for a variety of purposes, for one term or over a very extended period of time. Palmer (1990, p. 23) has described two-year college students as having "ad hoc attendance and course-taking patterns that often do not follow established curricular paths." Clifford Adelman (1992, p. v) has concluded that community college students "engage in learning on their own terms and in their own time."

These factors and others provide unique problems both in defining appropriate indicators of institutional effectiveness and in collecting appropriate data for assessing effectiveness. The institutional effectiveness assessment model adopted by two-year institutions must address this diversity in institutional purpose, student population, and student purpose for enrollment.

Expanded Statement of Institutional Purpose

Since the purposes of two-year colleges are often misconstrued by the public and by other segments of postsecondary education, it is critical for each college to articulate clearly what kind of institution it is and what it is trying to accomplish. A carefully worded statement of purpose is essential, both for communication with those outside the institution and as a practical first step in assessing institutional effectiveness.

The Expanded Statement of Institutional Purpose for Your Community College, provided in Appendix B, is not intended as an expression of what all two-year colleges should be, but rather illustrates an effectively worded statement of purpose for one hypothetical community college. Some elements of the purpose for Your Community College may be inappropriate for a technical college or a traditional junior college. Also, a particular college may give more weight or attention to some functions than others, depending on the needs of its constituents and the programs provided within the service area by other agencies and institutions. Whatever the particular functions of the institution, detailed design at the departmental level must clearly relate institutional effectiveness measures to the college's Expanded Statement of Institutional Purpose.

Detailed Design at the Departmental Level/Identification of Intended Student Outcomes and Administrative Objectives

As on any campus, winning the commitment and support of faculty and administrative personnel at the department/unit level is one of the most difficult tasks in implementing institutional effectiveness. At two-year colleges, developing outcomes or objectives and the strategies for assessing their achievement involves additional tasks for people who have heavy work loads and may feel considerable skepticism about the benefits of such a substantial undertaking. The president and chief academic officer must demonstrate their commitment by providing resources and release time to the extent that institutional constraints permit. To ensure a process that will ultimately strengthen the institution, commitment by the leadership must be as strong a motivator as are external requirements from an accrediting agency, a governing board, or a coordinating board.

The following general suggestions are offered:

1. Focus on the total institution so that all functions are addressed (credit instruction, continuing education, training for business and industry, support services, etc.).
2. Add minimally to the already heavy work load by stressing those things that are essential and that will facilitate decisions that the institution is prepared to make.
3. Be sensitive to the implications of assessment. Insensitivity in the reporting of some measures can be harmful to minority and nontraditional students who are already underrepresented in higher education. Internally, results of assessment should be seen as formative, not punitive.
4. Allow for flexibility, because "responsiveness" is part of the distinctiveness of the two-year colleges.
5. Identify responsibility at the department/unit level and coordinate centrally at the institutional level to ensure that attention to institutional effectiveness efforts is not lost in the pressure to carry out the process functions of the institution.
6. Involve the total campus community in the process. Faculty, administrators, professional staff, and students must experience involvement if the results are to be meaningful.

Each academic and administrative unit of the college should identify appropriate outcomes or objectives carefully linked to the Expanded Statement of Institutional Purpose and the means through which their results will be assessed. Some community colleges have expressed instructional outcomes in the form of competencies that students will possess at the completion of a course or an educational program. Specific competencies may be developed for special functions within the curriculum, such as general education or developmental education, as well as for each degree and certificate program.

Assessment/Evaluation

Since two-year colleges face some special problems in assessing institutional effectiveness because of broad diversity in institutional purpose, in student population, and in student intent/purpose for enrollment, accurate assessment requires multiple and realistic measures that address these issues. Consequently, some definitions and effectiveness measures that are appropriate for four-year colleges may be inappropriate for two-year colleges.

Student tracking presents particular difficulties at two-year colleges because of the large number of students who move rapidly in and out of the institution and the extended period of time usually required by nontraditional students for program completion. Further, students enrolling in one or two courses for personal enrichment, specific job skills, or transfer will require different assessment measures than those who intend to obtain an associate degree. Kreider and Walleri (1988) persuasively make the case that two-year colleges should "seize the agenda" in assessment by utilizing a student-success approach that is tied to student intentions.

As a prerequisite to any tracking efforts, students should be identified as to their educational intent/purpose for enrollment. To ensure data collection on student intent, Prince George's Community College, Maryland, has required two pertinent questions in their computerized registration process (Clagett, 1989). One question asks for the student's immediate educational goal (to obtain a degree, to obtain a certificate, or to take courses only), and the other asks for the student's primary reason for attending the college (prepare for new job/career, update skills for current job/career, prepare for transfer, explore academic or occupational areas, or pursue personal enrichment).

Jefferson State Community College, Alabama, requests the purpose for enrollment on the application for admission and affirms/changes the student's purpose as part of the advising process prior to each registration. Students are asked to select one of the following purposes: (1) to obtain an Associate Transfer degree—AA or AS; (2) to obtain an Associate Career degree—AAS; (3) to obtain a certificate; (4) to take a few courses before transfer; (5) to take courses for self-improvement or personal enrichment; (6) to take job-related courses; or (7) no definite purpose in mind.

Because of the centrality of student intent to any assessment of institutional effectiveness, each institution should identify the appropriate question(s) and establish procedures that capture this information at initial enrollment and verify it in subsequent terms of enrollment. Even the graduation rate, which is a rather straightforward calculation at some types of institutions, cannot be calculated appropriately at two-year colleges without knowing which students entered the institution with the intention of obtaining the associate degree.

Generally speaking, transactional and historical student files that make up the typical student information system are not adequate to answer key questions about two-year college students' enrollment patterns, performance while enrolled, and performance in employment and education after leaving the college. A cohort-based, longitudinal tracking system, that is independent of the transactional student records system and is both comprehensive and flexible, will assist a college in responding to external accountability requirements such as those in the "Student-Right-to-Know" legislation and in answering its own questions about the diverse student population that it serves.

The following suggestions are offered in establishing a longitudinal, cohort-based, student tracking system:

1. Include all students who are new to the college during the term that the cohort is established;
2. Establish data elements that will identify appropriate sub-sets of the cohort such as full-time/part-time, first-time any college/transfer, purpose for enrollment, degree intent, etc.;
3. Establish new cohorts at regular intervals, such as each fall term;
4. Track each cohort for five to seven years (or whatever is a sufficient period to determine the fate of 90% of the students in the cohort); and,
5. Include data elements for each student on attributes, enrollment and progress at the college, and follow-up after exit from the college.

Assessing Instruction and Instructional Outcomes

Developmental Education

Offering students preparatory courses prior to their entering mainstream undergraduate programming is a function frequently found at a two-year college. These courses are known as remedial, transitional, or developmental in nature, and provide students the opportunity to acquire those academic skills which for one reason or another they have not earlier acquired as a preparation for entry into postsecondary education. Two aspects of assessment of this type of instruction are unique. First, assessment of developmental education effectiveness can be done "in-house" by the use of success in "mainstream" courses as a measure of the success of earlier developmental programming. This one of only two occasions in which grading practices may be utilized as a means of assessment. Second, the highly unstructured and relatively customized instructional programming utilized in many developmental education programs suggests utilization of standardized testing at program completion more so than most other areas. A partially complete example of Developmental Education implementation is shown as Figure 18.

Figure 18

Developmental Education

Example of Linkage between Expanded Statement of Institutional Purpose, Departmental/Program Intended Outcomes/Objectives, and Assessment Criteria and Procedures at Your Community College

Expanded Statement of Institutional Purpose

Mission Statement:

Your Community College operates in the belief that all individuals should be:
1. ....
2. Afforded equal opportunity to acquire a complete education experience.
3. ....
4. ....

Goal Statements:

D. Assist students in overcoming deficiencies and acquiring skills fundamental to further academic and career achievement.

Departmental/Program Intended Outcomes/Objectives

1. Students completing the remedial program in mathematics will be prepared to succeed in introductory college level mathematics classes.

2. Students' ability to read will substantially improve each semester that they are enrolled in the developmental reading program.

3. Students completing the developmental writing program will succeed in the introductory college level composition course (English 101).

Assessment Criteria & Procedures

1a. Seventy-five percent of those students completing remedial mathematics (Math 100) will score 41 or more on the Intermediate Algebra ACT Asset Test administered at the end of the class as a final examination.

1b. Seventy-five percent of those students completing remedial math (Math 100) will achieve a "C" or better in their introductory college level mathematics classes.

2a. Eighty percent of the students tested on the Nelson-Denny reading test at the beginning of each semester as reading at the 3rd through the 9th grade equivalent and attending a minimum of forty hours of reading instruction during the semester will progress at least three levels by the close of the term.

2b. Eighty percent of the students tested on the Nelson-Denny reading test as reading at the 10th grade equivalent or higher at the beginning of the semester and attending a minimum of forty hours of reading instruction during the semester will progress at least one equivalent level by the close of the term.

3a. Seventy-five percent of the students completing developmental writing (English 100) will achieve a grade of "C" or better on the final essay in English 101.

Course Performance

Student performance in individual courses is a fundamental learning outcome and is particularly important for colleges where a large portion of students enroll for the purpose of taking only one or a few selected courses. Faculty do the assessing and should individually or collectively determine the criteria. Regular analysis of course grade distribution is useful for determining high-risk courses where special strategies of instruction or tutorial/learning assistance programs are needed.

General Education

Many two-year colleges have designated a core curriculum of general education for every degree or certificate, with the largest number of general education units required for the AA/AS degrees and significantly fewer for the AAS (Associate in Applied Science). Certificate programs may require no more than one course in English composition and one in mathematics. Although the use of a nationally normed, standardized test may seem attractive as a measure of general knowledge at the end of a degree program, relatively few published tests are available and their appropriateness for two-year-college graduates, particularly those obtaining the AAS, has been questioned.

Two-year colleges may find a criterion-referenced examination more appropriate and useful than a norm-referenced test. An advantage to using a criterion-referenced test is that the performance of completers of any particular program, as measured against the established criteria, can be evaluated in terms of the degree to which the curriculum of that program addresses each of the specified criteria.

Assuming that an appropriate test is identified, the institution must also determine which students should take the test and motivate those students to participate. For those two-year-college students who are simultaneously coping with job, family, and school responsibilities, a lengthy test as a condition for graduation may be a strong disincentive to graduation.

The Institutional Matrix Form of College BASE (a criterion-referenced achievement examination described on page 66) is appealing in part because it requires only 40 minutes of testing time. Using a matrix sampling design, the entire test battery (covering English, mathematics, science, and social studies; three cross-disciplinary reasoning skills; and a writing sample) is distributed among the students being tested. If sufficient numbers of students are tested, institutional data may be reported for subgroups that have varying requirements in general education, such as those receiving the AA, AS, and AAS degrees that have varying requirements in general education. One should note that the Institutional Matrix Form of College BASE yields aggregate data appropriate for institutional program review but does not produce individual student scores (*Presenting College BASE*, 1989).

An additional or alternative approach to assessing the outcomes of general education utilizes institutionally developed measures that are incorporated into the exit examinations of required general education courses. Departmentally approved final examinations in specified courses can be assessed once for purposes of assigning student grades and a second time to determine institutional-level results that are useful in program review.

A measure sometimes overlooked is students' self-assessment of the contribution of general education to their development. Johnson County Community College, Kansas, has incorporated this measure into several routine student follow-up surveys (see Seybert, 1990a, 1990b).

Assessment in the Major

Two-year colleges often have certificate or applied degree programs that directly prepare students to take licensure or certification examinations. These examinations are nationally or regionally normed and can serve as an important measure of program effectiveness. The following examples illustrate the type of reports available:

The *National Council Licensure Examination for Registered Nurses* (NCLEX-RN), published by the National Council of State Boards of Nursing (625 North Michigan Avenue, Suite 1544,Chicago, Illinois 60611) is a criterion-referenced test for which results are reported as pass/fail. Summary reports include number of candidates writing the exam for the first time, number repeating the exam, and percentage of each category passing, for the institution and for other member (accredited) programs within the institution's state jurisdiction. An institution may also subscribe to *NCLEX Summary Profiles* (CTB/McGraw-Hill, 2500 Garden Road, Monterey, California 93940), which reports examination performance of the institution's graduates in the context of several theoretical/curriculum categories and gives the program's rank (based on examination results) within its jurisdiction and among all member jurisdictions.

The institutional reports from some certification boards provide scaled scores and subtest scores as well as pass/fail rates. The *Medical Laboratory Technician Examination* is a national certification examination given by the Board of Registry of the American Society of Clinical Pathologists (ASCP, P.O. Box 12270, Chicago, Illinois 60612-0270). The *Program Performance Summary*, provided by ASCP to each institution whose graduates take the examination, includes five parts: (1) individual student scaled scores; (2) program and national scaled score comparisons; (3) national distribution of examinee scaled scores; (4) national distribution of program scaled scores; and (5) program and national subtest and item p-score comparisons.

The *Summary Report to Educational Programs: Certification Examination in Radiologic Technology* (American Registry of Radiologic Technologists, 1255 Northland Drive, Mendota Heights, Minnesota 55120) reports the average scaled score for the total test and content sections within the test for each administration of the examination. Both institutional and national data are provided that enable program faculty to compare a given score to the scores obtained by other examinees and to interpret individual and group scores in terms of the degree of mastery of the material. The conference of Funeral Service Examining Boards (15 Third Street N.E., Washington, Indiana 47501) provides the institution with individual student scores for its program graduates and a national mean score for comparison.

In fields where no certification is required, a capstone course or end-of-sequence examination is an appropriate indicator of student learning in the major field. Institutions might consider developing a test locally or analyzing a commercially produced standardized test to determine its appropriateness for a particular program. Institutions with vocational programs might review the Student Occupational Competency Achievement Test (SOCAT), which is available for 65 programs from the National Occupational Competency Testing Institute.

In addition to SOCAT, institutions may wish to consider the Engineering Technician and Technologist Certification Programs conducted by the National Society for Engineering Technologies (NICET) sponsored by the National Society for Engineers. Those students passing the examinations are certified nationally. However, examinations are offered in less than ten engineering technologies fields and students must travel to central testing site in each state to take the examination.

Surveys of career program graduates and their employers provide another source of data on program outcomes. Routinely included are questions on the relationship of employment to the major, salary/wages earned, and evaluation of preparation for employment. A partially completed example of implementation in an occupationally technical program is shown in Figure 19.

Transfer Data

Academic education for those preparing for transfer to baccalaureate-granting institutions is one of the functions for many, though not all, two-year institutions. Among those for which it is a specified function, assessment of transfer effectiveness poses difficult conceptual and methodological problems. Among these is determination of whatever the institution offers "one" or "many" transfer programs. For most institutions, the answer is that they offer one transfer program; however, institutions transferring large numbers (500+) of students annually may wish to establish separate programs for the "education transfer," "liberal arts transfer," "engineering transfer," etc. The most common indicators of transfer effectiveness include: (1) transferability of courses, which involves course articulation with the receiving institutions; (2) rate of transfer, which is calculated in various ways; (3) student success after transfer, which is often measured by GPA and persistence to graduation; (4) and student satisfaction with preparation for transfer, which is obtained in routine student follow-up surveys.

The "transfer rate" is the measure that has recently drawn the most public attention and is probably the most difficult for institutions to obtain accurately. Entirely different rates are derived, depending on the definitions and algorithms used. Once definitions are established, institutions must have the pertinent data and the ability to access it so that the pool of potential transfer students can be identified, and they must receive complete and comparative data from the institutions to which their students transfer (Bers, Seybert, & Friedel, 1990).

Defining the denominator used in calculating transfer rates is basically a question of identifying those who are expected to transfer. Although some measures of transfer effectiveness presume that all students should/could/might transfer, this presumption is naive and inappropriate when one considers the missions of two-year colleges and the characteristics, behaviors, and purposes for enrollment of their students.

Figure 19

Your Community College
Automotive Technology Program

Example of Linkage between
Expanded Statement of Institutional Purpose,
Departmental/Program Intended Outcomes/Objectives,
and Assessment Criteria and Procedures

Expanded Statement of Institutional Purpose

Mission Statement:

Your Community College is an open-admission, community-based, comprehensive college designed to provide inexpensive, quality educational opportunities (college transfer, career/technical and continuing education) to residents of a five-county service area in the central portion of the Magnolia State.

Goal Statements:

Serve persons of all ages in preparing for job entry and careers in a variety of fields.

a. Recipients of an Associate of Applied Science (AAS) degree will be well prepared for first or entry-level positions in a career field.

b. College AAS degree programs will be focused on career-related opportunities for graduates in the five-county area.

c. The majority of AAS graduates will find employment in the five-county area.

Departmental/Program Intended Outcomes/Objectives

1. Graduates of the Automotive Technology Program will be successfully employed in the field.

2. Graduates of the Automotive Technology Program will be technically proficient.

3. Employers of the Automotive Technology Program graduates in the five-county service area will be pleased with the education received by their employees

Assessment Criteria & Procedures

1a. Fifty percent of the graduates of the Automotive Technology Program will report employment in the field on the Graduating Student Survey administered at the time of program completion.

1b. Eighty percent of the graduates of the Automotive Technology Program will report employment in the field on the Recent Alumni Survey distributed one year after graduation.

2a. At the close of their final term, 90% of the graduates will be able to identify and correct within a given period of time all of the mechanical problems in five test cars that have been "prepared" for the students by Automotive Technology Program faculty.

3a. Eighty percent of the automotive respondents to an Employer Survey conducted every 3 years by the college will respond that they would be pleased to employ future graduates of the Automotive Technology Program.

3b. Fifty percent of automotive employers registered with the College Placement Service will make at least one offer to a graduate of the Automotive Technology program each year.

The most restrictive definition would hold that the denominator should be based on the graduates who receive the transfer degree (AA or AS), as these are the students for whom the institution is accountable in preparing them for transfer. In reality, however, these are not the only students who transfer (Calhoun, 1985; Clagett, 1989). Many students transfer without completing their associate degree and should perhaps be included in the pool used to determine the transfer rate. One approach is to include in the denominator all those who express the intent to transfer and achieve at least 12 semester hours of transferable credits.

The numerator in the calculation of transfer rate is most often defined as attendance at a senior institution. Cohen (1990) adds a time factor to his definition by specifying that the transfer student must "take one or more classes at the university within four years" (of initial enrollment at the community college). Given the extended time frame usual for nontraditional students, this would seem to be a low minimum.

Varying data definitions and reporting methods used by receiving institutions and undercounting due to institutions that do not report back to the sending institutions are major problems in establishing the numerator. Routine, statewide cooperative efforts among both public and private institutions are necessary if two-year colleges are to answer even the most basic questions about how many students transfer and how well they perform after transfer. Initiatives are in place or being developed in several states to establish a state data base from which institutions can obtain information on subsequent enrollment of their former students at other institutions within the state. From such statewide data systems, as well as understood institutions, it is possible to obtain student specific information concerning grades in "follow on" courses at the four-year college which may be utilized as a means of assessment for both the transfer function and general education programs of the two-year college. A partially completed example of implementation in a college and transfer program is shown as Figure 20.

Program Review

Many two-year colleges assess a broad range of institutional functions under the rubric of program review. These include credit and noncredit instruction, developmental studies, student services, administrative services, and support services. In addition to the usual productivity and quality measures that can be derived from existing institutional data systems, two-year colleges make extensive use of student follow-up surveys, "user" surveys, and advisory committees as important elements in program development and evaluation. For example, some institutions evaluate all courses and customized programs offered for business and industry by surveying both program participants and company managers. Two examples of comprehensive educational program review are found in the *Manual for Evaluating Occupational/Technical Programs* (J. Sargent Reynolds Community College, revised ed., 1990) and in *Instructional Program Evaluation: Procedures, Instructions, Formats* (Jefferson State Community College, 1993).

Figure 20

Your Community College Transfer Program

Example of Linkage between
Expanded Statement of Institutional Purpose,
Departmental/Program Intended Outcomes/Objectives,
and Assessment Criteria and Procedures

Expanded Statement of Institutional Purpose	Departmental/Program Intended Outcomes/Objectives	Assessment Criteria & Procedures
Mission Statement: Your Community College is an open-admission, community-based, comprehensive college designed to provide inexpensive, quality educational opportunities (college transfer, career/technical and continuing education) to residents of a five-county service area in the central portion of the Magnolia State.	1. Students transferring will find courses taken at Your Community College fully accepted as the prerequisites for junior and senior level courses at four-year colleges.	1a. Ninety percent of those students responding to a follow-up survey one year after transfer to a four-year institution will respond that all their Your Community College courses were accepted as prerequisites for junior and senior level courses. 1b. Each year one of the college's six academic departments will contact their counterparts at the three four-year institutions to whom most College students transfer and all of the courses designed by the department to support the transfer of students will be found to be fully accepted as prerequisites by the four-year institution contacted.
Goal Statements: Serve traditional students seeking the first two years of instruction leading to a bachelor's degree. a. Recipients of the Associate of Arts (AA) or the Associate of Science (AS) degree will be readily accepted at all public universities in the Magnolia State. b. Graduates with the AA/AS degree will complete their bachelor's degrees at almost the same rate and in about as much time as students completing their entire degree at four-year institutions in the state. c. Courses offered at the College as a foundation or prerequisite for courses at four-year colleges will be fully accepted for	2. After one year of adjustment to the four-year college, the grades of students transferring from Your Community College will be similar to those of students who initially enrolled at four-year colleges. 3. Students completing the two-year course of study leading toward transfer to a four-year college as a full-time student will complete their baccalaureate degree at almost the same rate as those students originally enrolling at the four-year college.	2a. Analysis of data received by Your Community College concerning the grades of students transferring to its primary three four-year colleges will indicate that the difference each semester between the average of such transfer students' GPA's and that of students originally enrolling at the four-year college is statistically insignificant one year after the transfer students' enrollment at the four-year college. 3a. Analysis of data received from each of Your Community Colleges' three primary transfer student destinations will indicate that the difference in the average number of semesters to baccalaureate degree completion of full-time transfer students from Your Community College and students originally enrolling at each four-year college is statistically insignificant.

Summary

Although two-year colleges confront the same basic issues that are addressed by other segments of higher education in attempting to provide quality educational programs and assessing their effectiveness, the special mission of these institutions in serving their communities and the diverse and transient nature of their student populations present unique problems. Two-year colleges have historically emphasized the teaching function, and they have taken the lead for the last three decades in educating nontraditional students. Losak (1986) has said of community college students, "Stopping out of college is more prevalent, part-time enrollment is increasing, and most students have objectives that are not synonymous with earning a baccalaureate degree within four years." More recently, Adelman (1992) has said that community college students use the college for a variety of "occasional" roles and has likened this to the way people use other normative institutions in our society.

Because two-year institutions are often misunderstood by the general public and by other segments of higher education, these colleges must be assertive in developing appropriate measures for assessing effectiveness. The nature of these institutions and the educational goals of their students require quite different definitions of success than those appropriate for other colleges and universities.

Resources are always limited. At two-year colleges, faculty have heavy teaching loads, administrators carry out multiple job functions, and support staff is at a minimum. A meaningful program of assessment of institutional effectiveness must make effective use of time and personnel, which are basic resources. The following suggestions are offered:

1. Use existing data as much as possible;
2. Incorporate assessment procedures into routine operations of the functional units;
3. Coordinate surveying efforts;
4. Use a cycle of assessment so that everything is assessed within a three-year to five-year period;
5. Develop definitions (for transfer rate, graduation rate, student success, etc.) that are appropriate to the mission of the college;
6. Collect only information that will be used; and,
7. Establish baseline information and set targets so that expectations of results are realistic.

Assessment is not new to two-year colleges. Not only assessment for placement but also advisory committees and student follow-up studies for program development and evaluation have been employed for decades. Once institutions recognize and utilize the assessment measures that are already in place, many may find that only a few additional measures are needed. Institutions that assess themselves with appropriate and realistic measures not only have information vital for improvement, but also the means with which to demonstrate institutional effectiveness to others.

NOTE: Appreciation is extended to the following members of the Association for Institutional Research who sent material and assisted in identifying the special issues involved in institutional assessment at two-year colleges: Bob Alexander, North Hennepin Community College (C.C.), MN; D. L. Anderson, Mississippi Gulf Coast C.C., MS; Felix Acquino, Dallas County C.C. District, TX; Richard Bailey, San Jacinto College District, TX; Trudy Bers, Oakton C.C., IL; Kathleen Bigby, Centre for Curriculum & Professional Development, British Columbia Council of College and Institute Principals, Vancouver, BC; Randy Braswell, Gordan College, GA; Craig Clagett, Prince George's C.C., MD; Thomas Hawk, C.C. of Philadelphia, PA; Lucy Hinson, Greenville Tech. College, SC; Laurel M. Kilbeck, Cuyahoga C.C.,OH; Arthur Kramer, Passaic County C.C., NJ; Mark Oromaner, Hudson County C.C., NJ; John Quinley, Central Piedmont C.C., NC; K. Rajasekhara, Dundalk C.C., MD; Estelle Resnik, Cumberland County College, NJ; Jeffrey Seybert, Johnson County C.C., KS; Jeffrey Stuckman, Florida C.C. at Jacksonville, FL; Janice Van Dyke, State Tech. Institute at Memphis, TN; Dan Walleri, Mt. Hood C.C., OR; and Faith Willis, Bruns-wick College, GA. Appreciation is also extended to James W. Firnberg, President of Our Lady of the Lake College of Nursing and Allied Health, LA, and to Cathryn A. McDonald, Tammie Brown Rickey, and Ellen F. Peak, my colleagues at Jefferson State Community College, AL, who offered suggestions on this section.

References: Cited and Recommended

Adelman, C. (1992). *The Way We Are: The Community College as American Thermometer*. Washington, DC: U. S. Government Printing Office.

Bers, T. H., Seybert, J. A., & Friedel, J. (1990). *Measuring the Effectiveness of the Transfer Function*. A paper presented at the Institute for Institutional Effectiveness and Student Success in the Community College, Toronto.

Calhoun, H. D. (1985). *The Transfer Process*. Office of Institutional Research Report, Jefferson State Community College, Birmingham, AL.

Clagett, C. A. (1989). Student Goal Analysis for Accountability and Marketing. *Community College Review, 16*(4), 38-41.

Cohen, A. M. (1990). Counting the Transfers: Pick a Number. *The Community, Technical, and Junior College Times, 2*(9), 2, 8.

Ewell, P. T., & Jones, D. P. (1991). *Assessing and Reporting Student Progress: A Response to the New Accountability*. Denver: State Higher Education Executive Officers.

Instructional Program Evaluation: Procedures, Instructions, Formats. (1993). Birmingham, AL: Jefferson State Community College.

Kreider, P. E., & Walleri, R. D. (1988). Seizing the Agenda: Institutional Effectiveness and Student Outcomes for Community Colleges. *Community College Review, 16*(2), 44-50.

Lenth, C. S., & Russell, A. B. (1991). *Statewide Student Data Systems and Capabilities to Report Postsecondary Graduation Rates*. Denver: State Higher Education Executive Officers.

Losak, J. (1986). What Constitutes Student Success in the Community College? *Community College Journal for Research and Planning, 5*(2).

Manual for Evaluating Occupational/Technical Programs. (1990). Richmond, VA: J. Sargent Reynolds Community College.

Palmer, J. (1990). *Accountability through Student Tracking: A Review of the Literature*. Washington, DC: The American Association of Community and Junior Colleges.

Palmer, J. (1990, June/July). Is Vocationalism to Blame? *Community, Technical, and Junior College Journal, 60*(6), 21-23, 25.

Presenting College BASE. (1989). Chicago, IL: Riverside.

Seybert, J. A. (1990a). *A Transfer Study*. Overland Park, KS: Office of Institutional Research, Johnson County Community College.

Seybert, J. A. (1990b). *Assessment of Institutional Effectiveness at Johnson County Community College*. Overland Park, KS: Office of Institutional Research, Johnson County Community College.

Walleri, R. D. (1990). Tracking and Follow-Up for Community College Students: Institutional and Statewide Initiatives. *Community/Junior College Quarterly of Research and Practice, 14*(1), 21-34.

CHAPTER SIX

Establishment of the Annual Institutional Effectiveness Cycle

The work of the three previous years or periods will have resulted in substantive planning/operational and assessment/evaluation accomplishments. Among the planning/operational accomplishments will be "Establishment of an Expanded Statement of Institutional Purpose"; "Identification of Intended Educational, Research, and Public Service Outcomes"; "Establishment of Administrative Objectives"; and "Implementation of Departmental/Program Activities to Accomplish Outcomes/Objectives Identified" (see Figure 3, p. 18). Assessment/evaluation activities during the first three years can best be summarized as the design and initial implementation of a comprehensive program of evaluation and assessment of the extent to which institutional intentions—expressed in the expanded statement of purpose—are being fulfilled through departmental/program achievements.

Just as the third year of implementation draws to a close, feedback from the initial implementation of assessment/evaluation activities will be forwarded to the institutional level as well as to the department/program level. The receipt, consideration, and ultimate use of this information initiate the series of events that will be repeated each year and that become the basis for practical implementation of the Institutional Effectiveness Paradigm shown in Figure 1 (see page 8) and further illustrated in Figure 21 as the **Annual Institutional Effectiveness Cycle** (AIEC). This cycle constitutes the strong "feedback" or "continuous quality improvement" loop sought by most regional accrediting associations in their requirements.

The establishment of the Annual Institutional Effectiveness Cycle is of paramount importance on the campus. Institutions tend to operate on an annual cycle of events conditioned by the academic year and the annual budgetary process. If implementation of institutional effectiveness is to become part of the institution's normal or routine method of doing business, then it must become a part of the yearly sequence of events expected at the institution.

Initiation of the Annual Institutional Effectiveness Cycle must be based on the accomplishments (planning/operational and assessment/evaluation) made during the first three periods of implementation. The AIEC turns what probably had been on some campuses episodic and discontinuous efforts toward assessment for educational improvement into an ongoing program of institutional improvement. Although immediate movement by a cam-

236

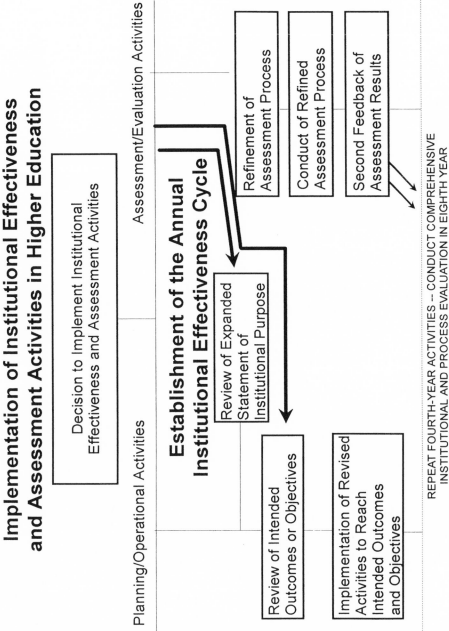

Figure 21

The Final Year of a Generic Model for Implementation of Institutional Effectiveness and Assessment Activities in Higher Education

Planning/Operational Activities   Assessment/Evaluation Activities

Decision to Implement Institutional Effectiveness and Assessment Activities

Establishment of the Annual Institutional Effectiveness Cycle

Review of Expanded Statement of Institutional Purpose

Review of Intended Outcomes or Objectives

Implementation of Revised Activities to Reach Intended Outcomes and Objectives

Refinement of Assessment Process

Conduct of Refined Assessment Process

Second Feedback of Assessment Results

REPEAT FOURTH-YEAR ACTIVITIES -- CONDUCT COMPREHENSIVE INSTITUTIONAL AND PROCESS EVALUATION IN EIGHTH YEAR pus to implement the AIEC is an attractive course of action, it is simply unreasonable to expect that an institution can divert sufficient resources (time of current employees and additional out-of-pocket expenditures) in a single year to accomplish effectively all of the necessary tasks among the planning/operational and assessment/evaluation activities described earlier. Even if sufficient resources were provided, the campus-wide political ramifications of such an effort could easily preclude its success. In order to consider institutional effectiveness annually and to integrate it into the routine of campus operations, these accomplishments must be firmly established so that they can be **reviewed**, **adjusted**, and **evaluated** as part of the Annual Institutional Effectiveness Cycle.

On many campuses excellent programs of educational assessment or evaluation have flourished. Unfortunately, few of these programs have been comprehensive or long-lived. There are many explanations for the limited scope and relatively short life of many of these programs. Too often the most common explanations relate to the establishment of such programs in response to the interests of an individual, who may subsequently change positions, or the requirements of a professional or regional accrediting body, whose periodic reviews, once completed, are quickly forgotten. Establishment of the Annual Institutional Effectiveness Cycle replaces transient personnel and external motivation with the systematic review and improvement of educational and administrative operations as part of the ongoing institutional process.

As the institution approaches implementation of the Annual Institutional Effectiveness Cycle in the fourth year of implementation activities, a certain amount of remotivation must again take place. Although the institution's reward systems should have demonstrated not only the need for, but also the wisdom of, departmental program implementation during the first three years, a summary type of document regarding current status (accomplishments during the past three years) and components of the Annual Institutional Effectiveness Cycle to be undertaken in the coming year should be prepared and widely distributed. The role of the CEO in solid support of institutional effectiveness implementation should be visible to all as he or she leads the review of the Expanded Statement of Institutional Purpose and administers his or her office's objectives. The components of the Annual Institutional Effectiveness Cycle are as shown in Figure 21 and described in the following paragraphs.

Planning/Operational Activities and the Annual Institutional Effectiveness Cycle

The primary planning/operational activities conducted each year as part of the Annual Institutional Effectiveness Cycle relate to the review and, if needed, revision of institutional and departmental statements of intentions. At both levels, these actions are initiated at the earliest part of the annual cycle (July through August) by receipt of assessment results from the previous year's cycle.

At the institutional level, activity is centered around review and refinement of the Expanded Statement of Institutional Purpose. Based on analysis of the results of the previous year's assessment activities (as generalized and focused at the institutional level), a decision should be reached annually regarding the appropriateness of the then current Expanded Statement of Institutional Purpose and its goals statements in particular. Should analysis of the assessment results emanating from the previous year indicate substantially less accomplishment than intended, then a value judgment must be made concerning either adjustment downward of institutional expectations or renewal of efforts to accomplish the original institutional aspirations. Although the decision to renew efforts may be more politically palatable and defensible over the short run, the institution's intentions eventually should be roughly aligned with its accomplishments as revealed through assessment results reported annually.

Review of the Expanded Statement of Institutional Purpose should be conducted relatively quickly and with input from external data sources. Each year, the review should be conducted within the first several weeks of the AIEC by a relatively small representative group headed by the institution's CEO. There is no reason to replicate the effort that went into establishing the Expanded Statement of Institutional Purpose. Rather, the focus should be on review and adjustment of the statement based on assessment results and, at those institutions practicing strategic planning, information concerning environmental fit, or the relationship of the institution to its external environment.

The result of review and adjustment of the Expanded Statement of Institutional Purpose will be the establishment of such a statement appropriate for the then current Annual Institutional Effectiveness Cycle. This statement should be distributed widely on the campus within the first several weeks of the cycle as the basis for further activities.

At the departmental/program level, the Annual Institutional Effectiveness Cycle is initiated based on receipt of the previous year's assessment results and the current cycle's Expanded Statement of Institutional Purpose. Each department/program is initially called on to compare the results of the previous year's assessment with the intended outcomes or objectives for that period. Undoubtedly, assessment results will reveal outcomes or objectives that are being overrealized as well as ones that are not being completely achieved or for which the results are inconclusive.

In the case of overrealization, departments/programs will probably adjust their statements of intended outcomes or objectives upward to match their accomplishments. In the case of those intended outcomes or objectives whose assessment results indicate that they are not being met, departments/programs should determine whether to lower their expectations or revise their procedures or activities designed to accomplish their intentions. It is vitally important—particularly in the institution's academic departments—that consideration of the previous year's assessment results and the adjustment of departmental statements of intentions (as just described) be undertaken by the department/program as a whole, with emphasis on input from all faculty or professional staff involved and their ultimate identification with the decision reached (see the "Closing the Loop" section in this chapter).

An important part of this departmental/program consideration of the previous year's assessment results is the evaluation of those results themselves. Particularly in those cases in which assessment results appear incomplete or contradictory regarding an intended outcome or objective, departments should review carefully the adequacy, validity, and completeness of the assessment results provided. The results of this review should be reported to those individuals responsible for conducting the institution's assessment/evaluation activities so that the problems identified can be corrected in the following AIEC.

In addition to reviewing the results of assessment related to its departmental/program intentions, each unit should carefully review the then current Expanded Statement of Institutional Purpose and compare it with the previous year's purpose statement. Such a review may provide the basis and impetus for revision of departmental/program statements of intentions, which must be linked to the current institutional statement of intentions.

The results of departmental/program review, as well as any revisions, will be a current set of intended outcomes or objectives for this Annual Institutional Effectiveness Cycle. This set of departmental/program statements should be finalized by the very early fall semester each year. As future iterations of the AIEC take place, progressively fewer adjustments to such statements should be expected.

The balance of the planning/operational activities (roughly September through July) will focus on departmental/program activities designed to accomplish the refined departmental/program statements of intended outcomes or objectives. Departments should bear in mind that it may take several iterations of the Annual Institutional Effectiveness Cycle for changes in departmental policies, actions, curricula, and so forth, to be reflected fully in assessment results.

In summary, planning/operational activities during the Annual Institutional Effectiveness Cycle are loaded into the first several months of each cycle with review and use of assessment results to "Close the Loop" and revision, if needed, of institutional and departmental/program statements of intention. The balance of the year is devoted to normal institutional and departmental operations aimed toward accomplishment of the statement of purpose and of intended outcomes/objectives.

Assessment/Evaluation Activities in the Annual Institutional Effectiveness Cycle

Each year the assessment/evaluation activities associated with the Annual Institutional Effectiveness Cycle comprise three actions: (a) review of the previous year's assessment activities and "Refinement of Assessment Process," (b) "Conduct of Refined Assessment Procedures," and (c) the "Feedback of Assessment Results" to the departmental/program and institutional levels as the basis for the next year's cycle (see Figure 21, page 237).

Although the bulk of actual assessment/evaluation work each year will take place in the last four to five months of the annual cycle, a critical review of the previous year's assessment/evaluation activities and plans for refinement of such procedures should take place within the first several months of each year's cycle. Information concerning the previous year's assessment/evaluation activities will come from the departments/programs being serviced and from those individuals coordinating the assessment/evaluation program. As part of the feedback mechanism, departments/programs should be submitting reports concerning both gaps in assessment/evaluation coverage of their statements of intentions and seemingly contradictory results that require further technical review. Additionally, those charged with coordinating and conducting the assessment/evaluation activities will, doubtlessly, have compiled a list of problems encountered during the previous year which they do not wish to repeat. Typically, this problem list will be fairly extensive in the initial AIEC iterations but will be shortened with successive refinements of the procedures.

In addition to a review of recent assessment/evaluation efforts, assessment procedures will need to be updated in light of both campus and external changes. On campus, those charged with coordination of assessment/evaluation activities will need to ensure that changes to departmental/program statements of intentions are incorporated into the assessment plan and that adequate coverage is provided. Additionally, changes in and additions to assessment/evaluation technology (standardized testing instruments, licensure examinations, survey instruments and techniques, etc.) should be considered for incorporation into the institution's refined assessment/evaluation procedures.

The results of the review and updating of institutional assessment/evaluation procedures should be a refined assessment/evaluation plan for implementation during the second half of the Annual Institutional Effectiveness Cycle. During early iterations of the cycle, implementation of the assessment/evaluation plan can be expected to focus on smoothing implementation mechanics, filling gaps in coverage of assessment/evaluation procedures, and increasing the efficiency of the process.

With any operation as large and complex as the process of implementing assessment/evaluation activities on a campus, there are bound to be a substantial number of "bumps," "stumbles," and apparent failures in initial implementation. There will be simply too many unforeseen and uncontrollable variables for which to plan initially. Once the process has been implemented on a trial basis, these problems will surface and will take several iterations to reduce to a manageable level—although a comprehensive institutional assessment/evaluation program inevitably involves a degree of discomfort no matter how well done.

Likewise, initial implementation of the assessment/evaluation plan can be expected to leave considerable gaps in coverage of departmental/program intentions. These gaps will exist for numerous reasons, and over the years most will be filled by one or more assessment/evaluation techniques.

Once active implementation begins, increased efficiency in conducting the assessment/evaluation process may be realized. A considerable portion of the initial year's implementation time will result from the inherent inefficiency in starting most processes. As the years progress, expenditures for assessment/evaluation should remain relatively constant; however, efficiency gained in implementation should be expected to offset (partially or completely) cost escalations and expansion of the process to fill gaps. The final assessment/evaluation activity conducted each year as a portion of the Annual Institutional Effectiveness Cycle is the provision of assessment/evaluation results—otherwise known as feedback—which acts as the stimulus for the next year's cycle. Although this activity will transpire in the last several weeks of the cycle just ending, review of reactions by the departments/programs to the feedback techniques used in the previous year should be gathered early in the next year's cycle results.

Two important improvements in early feedback procedures should be possible in succeeding years. First, by accumulation of results over several years, the limited number, or *N*, of results concerning certain programs should be mitigated and greater confidence established in the combined results of several years. Second, refinements in techniques should lead to increased utilization of graphic and narrative forms of feedback and the gradual de-emphasizing of tabular data presentation.

"Closing the Loop"

Earlier editions of *A Practitioner's Handbook* have offered examples of implementation such as those found in Figures 14, 15, 18, 19, and 20 of this edition. These three-column models are now only **partially complete** because of the maturation of the institutional effectiveness or assessment movement to the point that in many cases, the expectation is now not that of being able to show not only what is planned (the three-column model), but that of demonstrating what has been done (the five-column model). The completed examples shown in the following Figures 22-27 extend the previously provided three-column model to the full five-column model showing both results and use of the results where justified to improve programming at the institution. Additionally, a five-column model concerning an Undergraduate Accounting Program is provided.

Institutions within the Southern Association of Colleges and Schools' region are now expected to be able to show the five-column model comprehensively across all programs and administrative departments at the institution. Institutions in other portions of the country are at various stages of expectation; however, in general, require little more comprehensively than the three-column model as of this writing. However, within only several years (1997 at the latest), institutions across the country will be expected to be able to show the full five-column model indicating "Closing the Loop" through the use of the data resulting from assessment activities to bring about changes, where appropriate, in educational and administrative/educational support programming.

These type of changes, if warranted by the assessment results, can be classified primarily as substantive and procedural in nature. Among the substantive changes made, particularly in educational programs, are those that alter **what** is taught to better or more fully cover intended educational outcomes, or **how** we go about teaching to more adequately convey the intended information. Procedural changes, resulting from assessment activities, are primarily those which relate to refinement or a change in the means of assessment utilized or potentially to the criteria for program success identified.

It should be emphasized that all assessment results will not indicate the need for change in educational or administrative programs. On the author's own campus, a very early sampling of assessment reports from a small number of departments indicated that roughly 40% of the program/departments reporting were able to show the use of results to improve programming, while another 40% found no justification for change based upon their assessment results, and the final 20% reported changes in their means of assessment as a result of the first implemental.tion of the process.

In those areas in which assessment results should result in the change of programming, the tendency for faculty to make such changes is directly related to the extent to which they identify their own criteria for success of the program prior to seeing the assessment results. If the faculty answer the question, "How well **ought** our students be doing if our program is a success?" then the tendency for faculty to utilize the data where **discrepancy** between the ideal state (ought) and actual state exist is strong. Without the existence of such a **discrepancy** faculty on only rare occasions identify uses of assessment results to improve programming.

"Closing the Loop" need not result in the provision of voluminous reports. As seen in the examples provided, cursory notes describing simple uses of assessment results to make changes where necessary are sufficient. The key to documentation of the use of results is assignment for the responsibility for that documentation early in the process and maintaining the simplicity of the report required.

While the five-column models displayed are a useful means to depict on a single page the individual institutional effectiveness components and linkage between the individual components, this graphic portrayal is not feasible for replication throughout most institutions. To provide a more narrative (if lengthier) format, while still retaining the clear linkages of the five-column model, the Departmental Record Book forms are offered as Appendix A to *The Departmental Guide and Assessment Record Book*. Permission is granted to photo copy forms A, B, and C, which when completed provide the information contained in the five-column model.

Summary

Shown as Figure 28 is a month-by-month representation of the Annual Institutional Effectiveness Cycle that might be typical of those institutions operating on an "early semester" calendar and a June 30 to July 1 fiscal year. This timing would necessarily need to be modified at those institutions with significantly different academic and fiscal cycles.

The establishment of the Annual Institutional Effectiveness Cycle and the continuing program of institutional study/assessment/evaluation that it represents is the final process-oriented result of the implementation process. However, the final actual result is improved student learning and effectiveness of all our efforts to accomplish that end depicted in Figures 22-27.

Figure 22
Undergraduate English Program

Example of Linkage between Expanded Statement of Institutional Purpose, Departmental/Program Intended Outcomes/Objectives, Results, and Use of Results at Our University

Expanded Statement of Institutional Purpose	Departmental/Program Intended Outcomes/Objectives	Assessment Criteria & Procedures	Assessment Results	Use of Results
Mission Statement: The principal focus of Our University's curricular program is undergraduate education in the liberal arts and sciences combined with a number of directly career related and preprofessional fields.	1. Students completing the baccalaureate program in English will compare very favorably in their knowledge of literature with those students completing a similar program nationally.	1a. The average score of the graduates of the baccalaureate program in English on the "Literature in English" MFAT subject test (which they will be required to take shortly before graduation) will be at or near the 50th percentile compared to national results.	1a. MFAT score for this year's graduates (18) found to be at 37th percentile primarily due to the 23rd percentile score on "American Literature" scale.	1a. Course offerings in "American Literature" are being reviewed for consistency with MFAT technical description and items.
		1b. Ninety percent of the English baccalaureate program will "agree" or "strongly agree" with the statement "In the field of literature I feel as well prepared as the majority of individuals nationwide who have completed a similar degree during the past year."	1b. Ninety-three percent responded "agree" or "strongly agree."	1b. No change required.
Goal Statements: Each graduate of Our University will be treated as an individual, and all graduates of baccalaureate-level programs at the University will have developed a depth of understanding in their major field and been afforded the opportunity to prepare for a career or profession following graduation.	2. Graduates will be able to critique a brief draft essay, pointing out the grammatical, spelling, and punctuation errors, and offering appropriate suggestions for correction of the deficiencies.	2a. As part of a departmental comprehensive examination administered during the students' final semester prior to graduation, they will critique a short draft essay; identify grammatical, spelling, and punctuation errors; and offer suggestions for correction of the deficiencies. Eighty percent of the program's graduates will identify and offer suggestions for remediation of 90% of the errors in the draft essay.	2a. Ninety-two percent of graduates identified 87% of errors. However, grammatical conventions regarding capitalization were not consistently applied.	2a. Faculty use of commonly accepted conventions regarding capitalization in reviewing upper division papers is being emphasized.
	3. Students completing the baccalaureate program will be capable of writing a brief journal article and having it published.	3a. All graduates of the baccalaureate level program in English will prepare a journal article for submission and forward it to the English department.	3a. Article received from all (18) graduates.	3a. No action required.
		3b. Eighty percent of those journal articles submitted will be judged acceptable for publication by a jury of English department faculty from an institution comparable to Our University.	3b. Fifty-five percent of articles reviewed were found acceptable for publication.	3b. English 407 (advanced writing) is being modified to include journal article exercises.
		3c. Twenty percent of those articles submitted will be published in student or other publications.	3c. Thirty percent of articles were published.	3c. No action required.

Figure 23

Accounting Degree Program

Example of Linkage between Expanded Statement of
Institutional Purpose, Departmental/Program Intended
Outcomes/Objectives, Assessment Criteria and Procedures,
Results, and Use of Results at Our University

Expanded Statement of Institutional Purpose	Departmental/Program Intended Outcomes/Objectives	Assessment Criteria & Procedures	Assessment Results	Use of Results
Mission Statement: The principal focus of Our University's curricular program is undergraduate education in the liberal arts and sciences, combined with a number of directly career related and preprofessional fields.	1. Students completing the baccalaureate program in accounting will be well prepared for their first position in the field.	1a. Eighty percent of those taking the CPA exam each year and indicating an accounting degree from Our University will pass three of four parts on the exam.	1a. Seventy percent of those taking the CPA exam passed all four parts. Ninety percent passed three of four parts. Seventy-five percent passed the auditing portion.	1a. Method of teaching auditing being revised by faculty.
		1b. Eighty-five percent of the graduates of the accounting baccalaureate program will "agree" or "strongly agree" with the statement "I am well prepared for my first position" contained in Our University's Graduating Student Questionnaire.	1b. Ninety responded "agree" or "strongly agree."	1b. No action required.
		1c. Employers of accounting program graduates hired through the Our University Placement Service will indicate on a survey forwarded to them by the Placement Service one year after employment of the graduate, an average rating of 7.5 or more (on a scale of 1-10) in response to the question "How well was your employee prepared for their position by Our University?"	1c. Average ranking of 8.3 was recorded, but bimodel frequency distribution encountered.	1c. Follow-up telephone interview being conducted with all employers rating 6.0 or lower.
Goal Statements: All graduates of baccalaureate programs will have developed a depth of understanding in their major field and been afforded the opportunity to prepare for a career following graduation.	2. Baccalaureate graduates of the accounting program will find ready employment in the field.	2a. Ninety percent of accounting graduates registered with the placement service each fall will have received a job offer by the close of spring semester each year.	2a. Ninety-five percent received a job offer or currently employed.	2a. No action required.
		2b. Sixty percent of students completing the accounting degree program will indicate that they are currently employed or have accepted a job offer in their response to the Our University Graduating Student Questionnaire.	2b. Eighty percent indicated receipt of job offer.	2b. Criterion being raised to 80%.
		2c. Eighty percent of the accounting program graduates responding to the Our University Recent Alumni survey will indicate that they are employed in a "directly career related" position.	2c. Ninety percent indicated employment	2c. No action required.
	3. Graduates will be experienced in the use of microcomputers for accounting procedures.	3a. Baccalaureate accounting program graduates will be required to complete successfully (as judged by a jury of faculty from the department) a major accounting project utilizing microcomputer applications during one of several classes in their last semester at the university.	3a. Sixty percent of graduates' projects were judged acceptable on first review by faculty panel.	3a. More microcomputer applications are being integrated into core of Accounting classes.
		3b. Seventy-five percent of accounting graduates will "agree" or "strongly agree" with the statement "I feel very comfortable in an automated accounting environment" on the Our University Graduating Student Questionnaire.	3b. Eighty percent indicated "agree" or "strongly agree."	3b. No action required.

Figure 24

Career Services Center

Example of Linkage between Expanded Statement of Institutional Purpose, Departmental/Program Intended Outcomes/Objectives, Assessment Criteria and Procedures, Results, and Use of Results at Our University

Expanded Statement of Institutional Purpose	Departmental/Program Intended Outcomes/Objectives	Assessment Criteria & Procedures	Assessment Results	Use of Results
Our University Mission Statement: We also seek to provide a supportive and challenging environment in which students can realize the full potential of their abilities.	1. Of those graduates seeking employment, at least half will have been offered a job prior to leaving the University.	1a. A follow-up survey of Career Services Center registrants will indicate that of those students responding, 40% had received a job offer by October after graduation.	1a. 43% of those responding indicated receipt of a job offer.	1a. No action required.
		1b. Of those students seeking to be employed after graduation, on the Graduating Student Survey, 50% will indicate that they were already employed or had received a job offer.	1b. 32% indicated employment or receipt of a job offer.	1b. Efforts to encourage student registration with Career Services Center increased. A computer job listing program was placed on-line for student access.
	2. Offer an increasing number of job search strategy workshops each year that are attended by more students annually.	2a. Records maintained will indicate more job search workshops offered each academic year.	2a. Records indicate the offering of three more job strategy workshops this past academic year than during the previous academic year.	2a. No action required.
		2b. Records maintained will indicate an increase in the number of students attending job strategy workshops each year.	2b. Attendance at job search strategy workshops declined by 7% this past academic year.	2b. Increase articles concerning career issues in student newspaper. Development of a career information peer group to provide information to fraternities and sororities.
Extract from Student Affairs Division Mission Statement: To provide services which assist students in selecting their vocation and making the transition into the world of work.	3. Clients will be pleased with the services received from the Career Services Center.	3a. The level of satisfaction with the Career Services Center expressed by students on the Graduating Student Survey will exceed that for overall student services.	3a. This past academic year, graduating students rated overall student services 3.2 on a satisfaction scale from 1-5 and the Career Center 3.4.	3a. No action required.
		3b. 95% of students completing a point of contact survey at the close of the job search strategy workshop will "agree" or "strongly agree" with the statement "This workshop fulfilled my expectations and provided clear, useful advice in the job search."	3b. 83% of past academic year respondents "agreed" or "strongly agreed." Workshops presented by one employee rated only 63% on average.	3b. Solicited feedback regarding presentation improvement from career information peer group. One presenter rehearsed and videotaped to improve presentation.

Figure 25

Developmental Education

Example of Linkage between Expanded Statement of Institutional Purpose,
Departmental/Program Intended Outcomes/Objectives, Assessment Criteria and
Procedures, Results, and Use of Results at Your Community College

Expanded Statement of Institutional Purpose	Departmental/Program Intended Outcomes/Objectives	Assessment Criteria & Procedures	Assessment Results	Use of Results
Mission Statement: Your Community College operates in the belief that all individuals should be: 1.... 2. Afforded equal opportunity to acquire a complete education experience. 3.... 4....	1. Students completing the remedial program in mathematics will be prepared to succeed in introductory college level mathematics classes.	1a. Seventy-five percent of those students completing remedial mathematics (Math 100) will score 41 or more on the Intermediate Algebra ACT Asset Test administered at the end of the class as a final examination. 1b. Seventy-five percent of those students completing remedial math (Math 100) will achieve a "C" or better in their introductory college level mathematics classes.	1a. Eighty percent of those students completing remedial mathematics (Math 100) scored 41 or more on the Intermediate Algebra ACT Asset Test during the past academic year. 1b. Ninety percent of the students completing remedial math (Math 100) achieved a grade of "C" or better in Technical Mathematics (Math 105), but only sixty percent scored "C" or better in College Algebra (Math 101).	1a. No action required. 1b. Separate sections of Math 100 emphasizing Algebra or Technical Mathematics are being scheduled.
Goal Statements: D. Assist students in overcoming deficiencies and acquiring skills fundamental to further academic and career achievement.	2. Students' ability to read will substantially improve each semester that they are enrolled in the developmental reading program.	2a. Eighty percent of the students tested on the Nelson–Denny reading test at the beginning of each semester as reading at the 3rd through the 9th grade equivalent and attending a minimum of forty hours of reading instruction during the semester will progress at least three levels by the close of the term. 2b. Eighty percent of the students tested on the Nelson–Denny reading test as reading at the 10th grade equivalent or higher at the beginning of the semester and attending a minimum forty hours of reading instruction during the semester will progress at least one equivalent level by the close of the term.	2a. Ninety-three percent of students tested at the 3rd through 9th grade equivalency at the beginning of the semester and attending at least forty hours of instruction were found to have progressed a minimum of three levels by the end of the term. 2b. Eighty-one percent of students tested at the 10th grade equivalent or higher reading level at the beginning of the semester during the past academic year were found to have increased by one or more reading levels by the end of the term.	2a. No action required. 2b. No action required.
	3. Students completing the developmental writing program will succeed in the introductory college level composition course (English 101).	3a. Seventy-five percent of the students completing developmental writing (English 100) will achieve a grade of "C" or better on the final essay in English 101.	3a. Eighty-three percent of students previously taking developmental writing achieved a grade of "C" or better on the final essay in English 101 this past year. However, they were noted for more problems with spelling than most students.	3a. Upon review, it was determined that the final examination essay in English 101 was handwritten under timed circumstances; whereas, all writing in English 100 was accomplished on word processors (with spell check) in an untimed circumstance. An additional unit in spelling is being added to English 100. Also, several timed handwritten exercises are being included.

Figure 26

Your Community College
Automotive Technology Program

Example of Linkage between
Expanded Statement of Institutional Purpose,
Departmental/Program Intended Outcomes/Objectives,
Assessment Criteria and Procedures, Results, and Use of Results

Expanded Statement of Institutional Purpose	Departmental/Program Intended Outcomes/Objectives	Assessment Criteria & Procedures	Assessment Results	Use of Results
Mission Statement: Your Community College is an open-admission, community-based, comprehensive college designed to provide inexpensive, quality educational opportunities (college transfer, career/technical and continuing education) to residents of a five-county service area in the central portion of the Magnolia State.	1. Graduates of the Automotive Technology Program will be successfully employed in the field.	1a. Fifty percent of the graduates of the Automotive Technology Program will report employment in the field on the Graduating Student Survey administered at the time of program completion. 1b. Eighty percent of the graduates of the Automotive Technology Program will report employment in the field on the Recent Alumni Survey distributed one year after graduation.	1a. Seventy percent reported employment. 1b. Eighty percent reported employment.	1a. No action necessary. 1b. No action necessary.
Goal Statements: Serve persons of all ages in preparing for job entry and careers in a variety of fields. a. Recipients of an Associate of Applied Science (AAS) degree will be well prepared for first or entry-level positions in a career field. b. College AAS degree programs will be focused on career-related opportunities for graduates in the five-county area. c. The majority of AAS graduates will find employment in the five-county area.	2. Graduates of the Automotive Technology Program will be technically proficient.	2a. At the close of their final term, 90% of the graduates will be able to identify and correct within a given period of time all of the mechanical problems in five test cars that have been "prepared" for the students by Automotive Technology Program faculty. 2b. Eighty percent of Automotive Technology Program graduates will pass the National Automotive Test.	2a. Eighty percent success rate. Most failures could not find problem in electrical system. 2b. Eighty-three percent pass rate on National Automotive Test - Weakness in items regarding hydraulic theory.	2a. Expanded Electrical Trouble Shooting Component of AT 202 Automotive Electrical Systems. 2b. Modified means of teaching hydraulic theory in AT 102 Basic Auto Systems.
	3. Employers of the Automotive Technology Program graduates in the five-county service area will be pleased with the education received by their employees.	3a. Eighty percent of the automotive respondents to an Employer Survey conducted every 3 years by the college will respond that they would be pleased to employ future graduates of the Automotive Technology Program. 3b. Fifty percent of automotive employers registered with the College Placement Service will make at least one offer to a graduate of the Automotive Technology program each year.	3a. Ninety percent reported willingness to employ, but only 50% of body shops. 3b. Eighty percent of employers registered had made a job offer.	3a. Added body shop representative to Advisory Committee and are reviewing curriculum to determine if separate program is needed. 3b. No action necessary.

Figure 27

**Your Community College
Transfer Program**

Example of Linkage between
Expanded Statement of Institutional Purpose,
Departmental/Program Intended Outcomes/Objectives,
Assessment Criteria and Procedures, Results, and Use of Results

Expanded Statement of Institutional Purpose	Departmental/Program Intended Outcomes/Objectives	Assessment Criteria & Procedures	Assessment Results	Use of Results
Mission Statement: Your Community College is an open-admission, community-based, comprehensive college designed to provide inexpensive, quality educational opportunities (college transfer, career/technical and continuing education) to residents of a five-county service area in the central portion of the Magnolia State. **Goal Statements:** Serve traditional students seeking the first two years of instruction leading to a bachelor's degree. a. Recipients of the Associate of Arts (AA) or the Associate of Science (AS) degree will be readily accepted at all public universities in the Magnolia State. b Graduates with the AA/AS degree will complete their bachelor's degrees at almost the same rate and in about as much time as students completing their entire degree at four-year institutions in the state. . Courses offered at the College as a undation or prerequisite for courses at ur-year colleges will be fully accepted · that purpose.	1. Students transferring will find courses taken at Your Community College fully accepted as the prerequisites for junior and senior level courses at four-year colleges. 2. After one year of adjustment to the four-year college, the grades of students transferring from Your Community College will be similar to those of students who initially enrolled at four-year colleges. 3. Students completing the two-year course of study leading toward transfer to a four-year college as a full-time student will complete their baccalaureate degree at almost the same rate as those students originally enrolling at the four-year college.	1a. Ninety percent of those students responding to a follow-up survey one year after transfer to a four-year institution will respond that all their Your Community College courses were accepted as prerequisites for junior and senior level courses. 1b. Each year one of the college's six academic departments will contact their counterparts at the three four-year institutions to whom most College students transfer and all of the courses designed by the department to support the transfer of students will be found to be fully accepted as prerequisites by the four-year institution contacted. 2a. Analysis of data received by Your Community College concerning the grades of students transferring to its primary three four-year colleges will indicate that the difference each semester between the average of such transfer students' GPA's and that of students originally enrolling at the four-year college is statistically insignificant one year after the transfer students' enrollment at the four-year college. 3a. Analysis of data received from each of Your Community Colleges' three primary transfer student destinations will indicate that the difference in the average number of semesters to baccalaureate degree completion of full-time transfer students from Your Community College and students originally enrolling at each four-year college is statistically insignificant.	1a. Ninety-five percent of responding students reported acceptance. 1b. Problem noted in change of introductory accounting course to microcomputer assisted at two of three primary transfer institutions. 2a. Overall GPA of Your Community College transfers found to be slightly (not significant) less than native students, but significantly less in math classes. 3a. Degree completion time of Your Community College transfer students found to be virtually identical to native students.	1a. No action necessary. 1b. Expansion of microcomputer utilization in introductory accounting problems at Your Community College is underway. 2a. Math 107 (college algebra) is being strengthened to better relate with calculus at four-year institutions. 3a. No change necessary.

Figure 28

Annual Institutional Effectiveness Cycle
Applied to an Academic Year Sequence
(Early Semester)

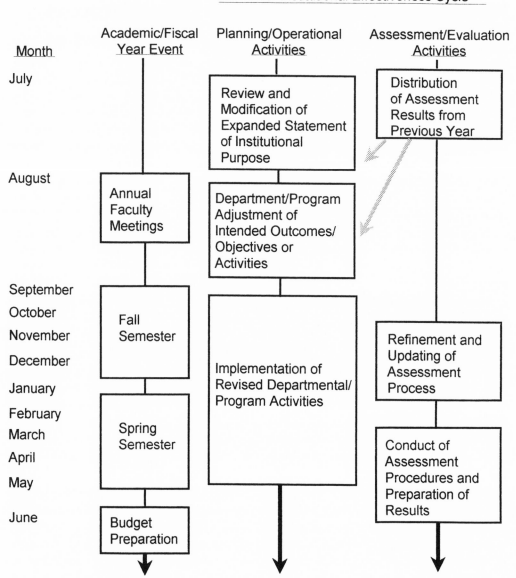

Annual Institutional Effectiveness Cycle

Month	Academic/Fiscal Year Event	Planning/Operational Activities	Assessment/Evaluation Activities
July		Review and Modification of Expanded Statement of Institutional Purpose	Distribution of Assessment Results from Previous Year
August	Annual Faculty Meetings	Department/Program Adjustment of Intended Outcomes/ Objectives or Activities	
September October November December January	Fall Semester	Implementation of Revised Departmental/ Program Activities	Refinement and Updating of Assessment Process
February March April May	Spring Semester		Conduct of Assessment Procedures and Preparation of Results
June	Budget Preparation		

Maintaining Institutional Effectiveness Operations Over an Extended Period of Time

The initial work to implement institutional effectiveness on a campus may have appeared to be an almost "insurmountable opportunity," as Pogo might say, but the maintenance of institutional effectiveness operations over an extended period of time represents an even greater challenge. Assuming that an institution has put into place the Annual Institutional Effectiveness Cycle described in the previous chapter and that it wishes to continue such operations, there are further developmental phases that can be expected and forces that will affect successful continuation.

During the fourth through approximately the seventh year of implementation, the campus should repeat the Annual Institutional Effectiveness Cycle. In addition to the smoothing-out process inherent in the cycle, several other adjustments should take place during this period.

First, each year minor adjustments should be made in the Expanded Statement of Institutional Purpose in reaction to the generalized assessment findings of the previous cycle and changes in the institution's external environment. Additionally, relatively substantial changes should take place in departmental/program statements of intentions during the first several years of cycle implementation as a result of the detailed assessment/evaluation results provided. If either institutional or departmental/program statements of intention remain static from year to year, institutional effectiveness is not being taken seriously and will ultimately be discontinued at the institution as a pointless exercise.

During the fourth through the seventh year of implementation, a task almost as important as institutional adjustments of statements of intentions is the gradual expansion of the assessment plan to address service gaps in initial coverage and utilize assessment/evaluation methods developed; without doubt, gaps in coverage and inconsistent results will emerge from the assessment/evaluation activities undertaken during the first several years of implementation of the Annual Institutional Effectiveness Cycle. As problems are resolved, major adjustments in and expansion of assessment/evaluation activities as well as implementation of newly developed means of assessment should occur each year.

Finally, during the period of Annual Institutional Effectiveness Cycle implementation in years four through seven of implementation, substantive improvement can be expected in feedback procedures and in the extent to which departments/programs understand and use the results to "Close the Loop." Part of this improvement in communication and understanding of the results can be attributed to both increasing familiarity with the assessment/evaluation results provided to departments/programs each year and the improvement in feedback mechanisms.

Comprehensive Review of Institutional Effectiveness Operations

The basic philosophy behind institutional effectiveness is that of stating an institution's intentions, conducting activities, and assessing/evaluating the extent to which the institution's intentions have been accomplished. This same philosophy must also guide institutional effectiveness operations themselves. In approximately the eighth year of implementation (after four complete repetitions of the AIEC), a thorough assessment of institutional effectiveness operations should take place.

Such a comprehensive assessment should probably have both procedural and substantive components. Each of the components (activities) during the Annual Institutional Effectiveness Cycle should be reviewed regarding its internal merits and the manner in which that element is functioning as a portion of the annual cycle. From the substantive perspective, the institution should conduct a thorough review and updating of its Expanded Statement of Institutional Purpose as well as its departmental/programmatic statements of intended educational outcomes/administrative objectives. Although adjustments and refinements to these statements should be expected annually, these actions cannot take the place of a periodically conducted thoughtful and extended reconsideration of the institution's and departments'/programs' basic purposes or intentions and the means utilized to ascertain the degree of accomplishments of those intentions.

The comprehensive review of institutional effectiveness operations envisioned should take the better portion of a year. Hence, it is suggested that the Annual Institutional Effectiveness Cycle be discontinued during the year in which the comprehensive review takes place and resumed the following year, using the changes suggested from the review.

Forces Impeding Continuation of Institutional Effectiveness Operations

A number of natural and understandable forces that impede long-term continuation of institutional effectiveness operations on a campus can be expected to come into play. These same forces tend to thwart long-term continuation of all except absolutely essential (registration, budgeting, etc.) activities.

The first of these forces is what can be characterized as institutional exhaustion or loss of interest. Frankly, institutional effectiveness operations are not absolutely essential to maintaining an institution (registering students, holding classes, conducting research, etc.)—only to leading an institution toward accomplishment of its stated intentions. After the period of additional effort required to implement the Annual Institutional Effectiveness Cycle, many individuals will tend to consider the matter accomplished and want to return to maintaining the institution in the manner in which it had been functioning earlier.

Naturally complementing this tendency toward regression to previous methods of operations may well be the departure from the institution of those individuals most responsible for institutional effectiveness implementation. Normal personnel turbulence during the period of time between initial implementation and comprehensive review of the process will result in the loss of a number of personnel instrumental in institutional effectiveness implementation and personally identified with such operations. There is also some likelihood that a disproportionately heavy share of turnover among faculty and key staff will be among those most responsible for institutional effectiveness implementation as their progressive ideas and actions are recognized and they are selected for positions of greater responsibility. Such action may leave those less supportive of institutional effectiveness to greet the replacements for those more supportive. It should be observed that these replacements will probably not be personally identified with institutional effectiveness to the extent that their predecessors were and that these replacements may well be less enthusiastic about continuation of institutional effectiveness operations as they seek to make their own mark on the institution.

Both institutional exhaustion and personnel turnover can be described as passive impediments to continued institutional effectiveness operations. Some members of the campus community, however, may actively resist continuation. This active resistance is likely to arise from individuals who are philosophically opposed to institutional effectiveness or whose personal interests are not best met by the process. Even following successful implementation of the Annual Institutional Effectiveness Cycle, some members of the campus community will remain unalterably opposed philosophically to institutional effectiveness because they do not believe the results of the educational process are assessable. On the other (more pragmatic) hand, some individuals will continue to see their own personal ends as better served through a less objective (and frequently more political) decision-making process. These people will oppose continuation on grounds more publicly acceptable than vested self-interest, but with that single aim in mind. Active opposition to continuation of institutional effectiveness operations can be expected to increase from both of these groups as the proponents of institutional effectiveness depart, their less committed replacements arrive, and institutional commitment becomes less apparent.

Marshaling Forces to Encourage Continuation of Institutional Effectiveness Operations

Without the long-term existence on a campus of a "true believer" in institutional effectiveness or a senior member of the administrative staff closely identified with the concept, there is an excellent chance that institutional effectiveness operations will gradually diminish. There must be an individual to champion the cause of continuation, and that person must have the active and visible support of the CEO. If such a person exists and is supported by the CEO, he or she can call into play a number of forces that will facilitate continuation of institutional effectiveness operations.

From a philosophical standpoint, proponents of institutional effectiveness can argue the intrinsic value of the process and support this assertion with examples of institutional and departmental/program improvements that have been brought about through institutional effectiveness. This is potentially one of the strongest inducements toward continued support by a substantial segment of the campus community, but this argument will have little impact on those actively opposed to continuation.

Another strong motivation toward continued implementation of institutional effectiveness operations may be external pressure in the form of regional and professional accreditation requirements. With implementation of the current national movement toward increased emphasis on assessment of student learning outcomes as part of accreditation requirements, institutions will be required to document their activities in institutional effectiveness and outcomes assessment by an increasing number of accrediting bodies. Such activities are obviously not easily initiated in a short period of time, and institutions desiring to have their various professional and specific regional accreditations reaffirmed will find it far easier to continue their existing institutional effectiveness operations than to reinitiate such operations in response to the demands of various external accrediting bodies.

For public institutions external pressure from accrediting agencies may not be the only form of pressure being exerted from beyond the campus. The vast majority of central governing boards and state legislatures are currently requiring information regarding institutional practices concerning outcomes assessment or institutional effectiveness. Thus, pressure from the agencies that provide funding to public institutions can be a significant factor in the continuation of institutional effectiveness operations.

Both the intrinsic value of institutional effectiveness and potential external pressure should serve to foster continuation of institutional effectiveness operations, but the best motivation to that end is the incorporation of these operations into the recurring annual series of events at the institution. Just as naturally as fall semester registration is expected to take place in the last week of August, review of the Expanded Statement of Institutional Purpose and departmental/program statements of intentions should be anticipated during the first three weeks in August. Just as operational budgets are expected to become effective July 1 each year on most campuses, assessment findings or results should arrive in the institution's departments during the last week in July. Before students take part in graduation exercises each spring, they are expected to have completed cognitive or performance testing in their major and to have returned their graduating student questionnaire. Institutional effectiveness operations should become the norm or expectation, and breaking that momentum should become just as difficult as was breaking the inertia of institutional resistance when such operations were initiated.

Despite significant forces operating to impede long-term continuation of institutional effectiveness operations, sufficient incentives, motivation, and means exist to support successful long-term institutional effectiveness practices for the welfare of the institution and those whom it would serve.

Note: For additional information regarding any of the procedures described in
this publication, address inquiries to
James O. Nichols, Box 6471, University, MS 38677

Our University Statement of Institutional Mission

Our University is an independent, nonsectarian, coeducational institution, in the tradition of the liberal arts and sciences. Seeking to be faithful to the ideals of its heritage, Our University is committed, in all of its policies and practices, to the unrestricted and rigorous pursuit of truth, to the centrality of values in human life, and to a respect for differing points of view.

Our mission is to provide an outstanding education for a relatively small number of talented and highly motivated students from a diversity of geographic, ethnic, and socioeconomic backgrounds. To achieve this end, we recruit and retain outstanding faculty members who are dedicated to the art of teaching and advising; to the search for and dissemination of truth through scholarship, research, and creative endeavor; and to service to the university and the larger community. We also seek to provide a supportive and challenging environment in which students can realize the full potential of their abilities and come to understand their responsibility of service in the human community.

The principal focus of Our University's curricular programs is undergraduate education in the liberal arts and sciences, combined with a number of directly career related and preprofessional fields. Relations between the liberal arts and the career related and preprofessional fields are carefully nurtured to provide mutually reinforcing intellectual experiences for students and faculty. Our University also offers master's and doctoral degree programs in selected professional areas that will prepare individuals for positions of leadership in their chosen careers. In addition, recognizing its responsibility to the larger community, Our University provides a variety of carefully selected programs of continuing education and cultural enrichment. Finally, Our University recognizes its responsibility in maintaining a position of excellence and leadership in research.

In its recruitment and retention of members of the University community, Our University, consistent with its academic and institutional heritage, maintains an openness to all qualified persons.

OUR UNIVERSITY STATEMENT OF INSTITUTIONAL GOALS

I. Introduction

- The "Statement of Institutional Mission" on the preceding page expresses a vision of what our institution intends to be and do. The purpose of the present document is to set forth specific goals for each major area of the university for the next 5 years, with the conviction that the achievement of these goals will lead to the fulfillment of Our University's stated mission.

- It must be recognized that such achievement is contingent upon a number of circumstances, including the availability of adequate financial and other resources. Indeed, decisions regarding essentially academic matters must sometimes be based, at least in part, on factors that are themselves not specifically academic in nature. What immediately follows in this introduction, therefore, is a summary of certain economic assumptions (i.e., matters over which the university has little or no control), planning parameters, and implications that are presupposed in the following sections of the document.

A. *Economic Assumptions*

1. Inflation will remain approximately at 3% to 4% over the next 5 years.
2. Financial support to private institutions and students by state and federal agencies will tend to be reduced in the next 5 years.
3. The annual income from the current unrestricted endowment sources will remain relatively fixed over the next 5 years.

B. *Planning Parameters*

1. The student-faculty ratio (FTE students to FTE faculty) will stabilize at 13 to 1 by 1998-99.
2. The Education and General (E & G) Budget (the basic operating budget) will increase between 7% and 8% each year in the next 5 years and will reach approximately $50 million in the 1998-99 academic year.
3. Annual giving will increase moderately between now and 1997.
4. Adequate fiscal reserves should be created or enlarged to allow for the timely renovation of campus buildings and other facilities.
5. Annual tuition rate increases will be approximately 7% in each of the next 5 years.

C. *Implications*

1. By the 1998-99 academic year, the total number of undergraduate students will stabilize at approximately 4,000.
2. The number of entering freshmen will increase by approximately 30 per year and will reach a class size of approximately 1,200 by the 1998-99 academic year.
3. Efforts will be made to increase the number of applications for admission each year so that we obtain 3,200 applications from highly qualified students by 1998-99.

4. The proportion of the undergraduate students who attend on a full-time basis will increase by approximately 1% per year for the next 5 years.

5. The six year attrition rate will be reduced by .5% per year for each of the next 5 years.

6. The increasing number of undergraduate students will create the need for a new residence hall in the 1997-98 academic year.

7. To accommodate more undergraduate students, funds should be dedicated to development of more playing/athletic fields.

8. To accommodate the needs of our changing student body, we will need to renovate/add to the University Center.

II. ACADEMIC AFFAIRS

• The goal of Our University is to be one of the leading independent liberal arts and sciences universities in the nation, as measured by the quality of its faculty, the strength of its curriculum and academic programs, the effectiveness of its support services, the excellence of its graduates, and the accomplishment of its intended outcomes. Significant steps already have been taken toward achievement of this goal through continued offering of both liberal arts programs designed to impart a depth of understanding in the major field and preprofessional programs preparing the graduate for employment upon graduation. Although the following goals do not represent the totality of intellectual and administrative activity within academic affairs, they do represent focal points for action in the near future.

A. *Curriculum and Academic Programs*

• Our University is committed to offering all students a distinctive and challenging academic foundation in liberal studies in order to enhance their communication and analytic skills; to provide an understanding of their intellectual and cultural heritage; and to assist them in the development of self-awareness, responsible leadership, and the capacity to make reasoned, moral judgments. Our University will continue to offer the range of disciplines basic to a liberal education and will maintain a balance in the undergraduate curriculum among the humanities, fine arts, behavioral sciences, natural sciences, and selected preprofessional programs. The following goals are of high priority:

1. Study the university's general education program to determine whether revisions are desirable.

2. Initiate more varied forms of instruction for entering students, such as freshman seminars.

3. Establish a process to identify systematically those academic programs that should be targeted for qualitative enhancement and/or numerical growth. The principal criteria to be employed in making these judgments should be centrality to our mission, quality of the existing program, demand, cost-effectiveness, and comparative advantage in offering the program.

4. Encourage new academic program initiatives, particularly of an interdisciplinary nature, that reflect emerging intellectual perspectives and that are appropriate to the mission of Our University.

5. Encourage the development of new minors and areas of concentration that complement existing degree programs and are responsive to student interests and societal needs.

6. Be responsive to the continuing education needs of local business and industry in areas in which Our University is academically strong.

B. *Graduate and Research Programs*

• Although the primary academic thrust of Our University will continue to be its undergraduate program of instruction, graduate education and research will play an increasing role in support of the institution and its attraction and retention of outstanding students and faculty. Within this secondary academic role, Our University will seek during the next 5 years to:

1. Develop a limited number of additional graduate-level programs in areas in which the institution maintains a strong undergraduate program, sufficient student demand is evidenced, and local or regional demand for graduates is identified.

2. Review current graduate programs to determine the academic and economic feasibility of their continuation.

3. Increase the level of organized or sponsored research expenditures by 5% per year for the next 5 years.

4. Focus the development of proposals for externally funded or organized research on subjects directly related to local/regional industries or those subjects of particular interest to foundations with which Our University has enjoyed a continuing relationship.

C. *Continuing Education/Public Service*

• While maintaining primary commitments to teaching and research, Our University is also committed to helping to meet the continuing education and cultural enrichment needs of our surrounding community. In the next 5 years Our University's goals are to:

1. Offer noncredit instruction targeted to meet the continuing education needs of Our University's faculty, staff, and surrounding community. Such programs should not duplicate the efforts of two- and four-year postsecondary institutions within a 25-mile radius of Our University.

2. Provide cultural enrichment opportunities for the university and surrounding community through an artist/lecture/concert series.

3. Offer in-service specialized short courses and seminars for local business and industry.

D. *Faculty*

- Persons who combine a love of teaching with a continuing curiosity and a passion for learning, scholarship, research, and creativity are the most important resources of the university. Excellent teaching and advising are essential to the fulfillment of the mission of Our University, as is the conduct of both basic and applied research that contributes to the advancement of knowledge and to the consideration of important societal problems. Various steps have already been taken to develop and maintain an excellent faculty, and the following goals are particularly important:

    1. Maintain salaries at highly competitive levels in order to attract a diverse faculty noted for its teaching excellence, scholarly achievements, and dedication to the highest standards of professional activity.
    2. Continue to emphasize research and scholarly activity through research assistants' support, travel funds, library materials, adequate access to computer facilities, and other forms of faculty development such as academic leaves and summer stipends.
    3. Continue to develop the emphasis placed on advising and working directly with individual students.

E. *Students*

- Our University will remain an institution of modest size with a total enrollment of no more than 4,000 students. In the recruitment of all students, emphasis is placed on potential for the very highest in academic achievement; leadership, special talents, and abilities; and diversity in geographic origin, ethnicity, and socioeconomic status. Appropriate scholarships and need-based financial aid programs will be administered to facilitate recruitment and retention of these students, continuing the significant advances made in the 1980s.

    1. Our University seeks to make it possible for each student to experience the academic and cultural diversity of the university, and the following academic goals for the composition of the student body directly address this commitment:
        a. Continue to increase the number of academically talented students attending Our University, achieve by 1999 an average SAT score for entering freshmen of 1200, and maintain this level as a minimum throughout the rest of the planning period.
        b. Continue to increase the number of out-of-state students attending Our University, so that this group will comprise 50% of the student body by 1999, and maintain this percentage as a minimum for the rest of the planning period.
        c. Give increased emphasis to recruitment of minority students (Hispanic, Black, Asian, and Native American) and increase their representation in the overall student population.
        d. Strive to have an equal number of men and women in the student body.

2. Each graduate of Our University will be treated as an individual, and all graduates of baccalaureate-level programs at the university will have developed a depth of understanding in their major field and been afforded the opportunity to prepare for a career or profession following graduation. Additionally, they will be able to

a. Express themselves clearly, correctly, and succinctly in writing.

b. Make an effective verbal presentation of their ideas concerning a topic.

c. Read and offer an analysis of periodical literature concerning a topic of interest.

d. Complete accurately basic mathematical calculations.

e. Demonstrate a sufficient level of computer literacy.

f. Utilize basic scholarly modes of inquiry.

F. *Academic Support Services*

- Services in direct support of academic programs must be both effective and efficient in the accomplishment of their assigned activities. Our University will strive for excellence in the following goals:

1. Continue to increase library acquisitions so that the number of bound volumes will reach 650,000 by 1998.

2. Improve the quality of library materials supporting instruction by acquiring the most advanced audiovisual equipment and by judiciously purchasing periodicals applicable to a liberal arts and sciences curriculum, as well as the limited number of graduate programs offered.

3. Increase accessibility of computer facilities at the university for both students and faculty through expansion of microcomputer laboratories and enhancement of computer support.

4. Develop more systematic data concerning the outcomes of each student's educational experiences.

5. Plan and modify the existing classroom and laboratory space to meet the evolving needs of the new curriculum.

III. STUDENT AFFAIRS

- The function of the Student Affairs Office is to establish an environment at Our University that supports and encourages students in their academic progress and to assist those students in their personal and social development. Student Affairs prepares Our University graduates for adult life by teaching them to appreciate quality, to develop values, to accept responsibility for their decisions and actions, and to know how and when to compromise.

- To accomplish this mission, the following specific goals must receive continuing and expanded attention:

A. *Environment*

1. Provide a comfortable and secure living environment in the residence halls.

2. Encourage development of appropriate attitudes and conduct for a communal academic environment.
3. Expand and encourage supplemental cultural and intellectual enrichment opportunities outside the classroom.
4. Explore the possibility of offering more options in housing.
5. Provide opportunities in an informal atmosphere for interaction of faculty with students outside the classroom.
6. Include in the University Center, which is being redesigned, a bookstore offering excellent academic support materials and current literature, as well as appropriate notions, supplies, and services needed by students, faculty, and staff.
7. Provide a variety of options for nutritional meals in comfortable and attractive settings for resident as well as commuting students, faculty, staff, and guests.

B. *Development*
1. Offer opportunities for self-evaluation and self-knowledge through administration and interpretation of standardized tests.
2. Provide comprehensive career planning for all students and career counseling for seniors and graduate students, prepare students to conduct effective job searches, and coordinate employment interviews on the campus.

IV. FISCAL AFFAIRS
- The purpose of the university's Fiscal Affairs operations is to provide an environment that enables faculty, staff, and students to concentrate on their appropriate tasks, which are essentially educational.
- Fiscal Affairs has two major areas of responsibility: (1) the management of, and accounting for, financial resources (the handling of funds, endowments, investments, and expenditures for salaries and wages); and (2) the operation of support services (physical plant, purchasing, security, personnel, and other areas). These two essential areas provide a base upon which the institution can accomplish its mission.

A. *Financial Resources*
1. To achieve expansion and growth in financial assets, Our University will
   a. Manage the budget prudently.
   b. Encourage and assist its faculty in seeking university-administered grants and contracts from external sources.
   c. Price its auxiliary enterprise services so that they are self-sustaining and do not draw from other resources of the institution.
2. In allocating funds for its academic and economic needs, the university will emphasize the following goals:
   a. Maintaining a level of salaries that will attract and retain competent professionals.

b. Providing adequate funding for scholarships to attract exceptional students.

c. Purchasing and replacing equipment in support of the instruction and research needs of the university.

d. Building adequate plant-fund reserves in order to protect against deferred maintenance.

B. *Support Services*

1. To achieve maximum utilization of its resources, our University will

a. Use its personnel, equipment, structures, and funds efficiently and effectively to provide a safe and comfortable environment for all faculty, staff, and students.

b. Fund support services at a level that provides for the most efficient operation consistent with a scholarly environment.

2. In personnel matters, the university will

a. Improve communications between support services and all employees to ensure that applicable fiscal and personnel procedures are understood.

b. Maintain a vigorous affirmative action program that will include specific goals and a systematic review of procedures and progress.

V. UNIVERSITY RELATIONS AND DEVELOPMENT

• The University Relations and Development function manages the closely related areas of fund raising, alumni activities, and public relations. Most of the activities and programs take place for the ultimate purpose of increasing gift income for the university and attracting qualified students and faculty to the university.

• Within this context, the University Relations and Development function has established the following integrated goals:

A. *Fund Raising*

1. Build a permanent university endowment of $150 million to $155 million by 1999.

2. Achieve a level of annual giving (unrestricted annual fund) of at least $750,000 per year by 1999.

3. Achieve 35% participation among alumni in the annual giving program.

B. *Alumni Activities*

1. Have 5% of all alumni return to campus for various programs such as Alumni Weekend, Alumni College, class reunions, etc.

2. Develop an active national alumni association with chapters in all cities where 100 or more alumni reside.

C. *Public Relations*

1. Achieve a national image of the university as a high-quality, selective-admissions liberal arts and sciences institution that is among the best of its type in the nation.

2. Maintain a positive relationship with the community in which the institution is located.

APPENDIX B

Your Community College Mission

Your Community College is an open-admission, community-based comprehensive college designed to provide inexpensive, quality educational opportunities to residents of a five-county service area in the central portion of the Magnolia State. The college was formed early in 1971 by the joint action of the Smith, Lawrence, Karnes, Neuceuss, and Willow county governments and recognized by the legislature and the State Board of Community Colleges later in that year. The college replaced a former branch of Magnolia State University and has developed an educational mission characterized by diversification, growth, and community orientation.

Your Community College operates in the belief that all individuals should be

a. Treated with dignity and respect,
b. Afforded equal opportunity to acquire a complete educational experience,
c. Given an opportunity to discover and develop their special aptitudes and insights,
d. Provided an opportunity to equip themselves for a fulfilling life and responsible citizenship in a world characterized by change.

Finally, the college functions as an integral part of the five-county area that it serves and has a responsibility to provide educational and cultural leadership to this constituency.

Institutional Goals

Your Community College seeks to:

A. Serve students in the first 2 years of instruction leading to a bachelor's degree.
   1. Recipients of the Associate of Arts (AA) or Associate of Science (AS) degree will be readily accepted at all public universities in the Magnolia State.
   2. The majority of graduates with the AA or AS degree attending four-year institutions on a full-time basis will complete their bachelor's degrees within 3 years of enrollment at the four-year institution.
   3. Courses offered at the college as a foundation or prerequisite for courses at public four-year colleges will be fully accepted for that purpose.
B. Serve persons of all ages in preparing for job entry and careers in a variety of fields.
   1. Recipients of an Associate of Applied Science (AAS) degree will be well prepared for their first or entry-level position in a career field.
   2. The great majority of AAS graduates will find employment in the five-county service area.
   3. College AAS programs will be focused on career-related opportunities for graduates in the five-county area.

C. Insure that all recipients of an associate (AA/AS or AAS) degree will be able to
   1. Express their thoughts clearly and correctly in writing.
   2. Read and understand literature and current event articles commonly found in the print media.
   3. Perform the basic mathematical calculations required to function in society.
D. Assist students in overcoming deficiencies and acquiring skills fundamental to further academic and career achievement.
   1. Prior to entry into AA/AS or AAS degree programs, all students will hold a high school diploma or GED certificate.
   2. The college will provide a noncredit college preparatory curriculum for students seeking to receive their GED certificate.
   3. Students completing noncredit occupational/technical training programs will be offered assistance with obtaining their GED certificate if they have not completed high school.
E. Provide a broad range of student services, including counseling, career planning, placement, and financial assistance.
   1. Counseling and career planning services will support both transfer (AA/AS) and career/technical (AAS) students.
   2. Placement services will be oriented toward the support of career/technical (AAS) graduates and focused in the five-county area.
   3. Every effort possible will be pursued to provide financial assistance for those in need of such support to attend the college.
F. Serve constituents who need additional training for advancement in their current field or retraining for employment in new fields.
   1. Continuing career education classes will be offered annually at night in each field in which the college offers an AAS.
   2. In conjunction with Magnolia State University, continuing professional education opportunities will be offered in business and other professional areas.
   3. Opportunities for retraining will be made available to all citizens of the five counties and be intensified, should economic circumstances warrant.
G. Provide educational programs to meet the needs of employers in the five-county area.
H. Serve persons who want to take special classes and workshops, as well as regular credit classes for personal development or cultural enrichment.
I. Cooperate with community agencies in community development activities.

Expanded Statement of Institutional Purpose—University of Mississippi, Oxford Campus

The University of Mississippi Statement of Academic Focus and Goals for the 1990s contained in the following pages constitute the central core values that will guide the University's actions during the balance of the 1990s. These statements provide the over-arching framework of institutional aspirations, concepts, and ideals upon which the University's plans and expected results are to be based and against which its accomplishments must ultimately be judged or assessed.

The following Statement of Academic Purpose for the University is intended to serve as the foundation for University decision making concerning its academic offerings, the basis for its existence. It identifies the "core" or "essential" areas of academic endeavor in which the University will be engaged throughout the balance of this century.

Statement of Academic Focus for the 1990s

The University of Mississippi is the oldest public institution of higher learning in the state. Its fundamental purpose is the creation and dissemination of knowledge. Through-out its long history the University has enhanced the educational, economic, and cultural foundations of the state, region, and nation. As a comprehensive, doctoral-degree grant-ing institution, the University offers a broad range of undergraduate and graduate pro-grams as well as opportunities for continuing study.

While recognizing that its primary role is to serve the state of Mississippi, the Univer-sity educates students to assume leadership roles in both the state and nation through its nationally recognized programs of undergraduate, graduate, and professional study. Its teaching, research, and service missions are characterized by equal access and equal opportunity to all who qualify. Within this framework, the University will focus its resources on:

1. **Science and Humanities**. The University will continue its traditional leadership in the Liberal Arts by emphasizing existing programs of strength in the sciences and humanities and programs that sustain nationally important centers of research and service.

2. **Health**. The University will continue to provide the professional education of those who deliver and administer human health services and those who perform research aimed at improving the efficiency, effectiveness, quality, and availability of healthcare.

3. **Legal Education**. The University will continue to provide the initial and continuing professional education of those who formulate, interpret, and practice law.
4. **Business Development and Economic Growth**. The University recognizes that economic growth and business development are essential to the future of Mississippi in the increasingly integrated world economy. The University will enhance the development of entrepreneurial, financial, managerial, and information processing activities through existing preprofessional, professional, and public service programs.
5. **Communications and Related Technologies**. The University recognizes that communications technology will be one of the most important growth areas of the next century. The University will continue developing programs that sustain the communication and telecommunication industries. The area of focus crosses disciplinary boundaries and incorporates expertise from specialties such as foreign languages, journalism, engineering, computing, and distance learning.

University of Mississippi Oxford Campus—Goals for the 1990s

Goal 1. The University will improve undergraduate education, especially in lower-division courses.

Goal 2. The University will concentrate graduate education and research in areas of strength consistent with the Focus Areas.

Goal 3. The University will increase employee compensation to the Southern University Group (SUG) average in order to attract and retain a highly qualified faculty and staff.

Goal 4. The University will improve educational support services (library, computer networking, database availability, instructional support, etc.) to increase access to information and communication on the campus.

Goal 5. The University will disseminate its expertise and knowledge to nonacademic communities throughout the state of Mississippi and the Midsouth region.

Goal 6. The University will continue to develop leadership and to instill in its students a sense of justice, moral courage, and tolerance for the views of others.

Goal 7. The University will maintain efficient and effective administrative services to support the University's instructional, research, and public service programs.

Goal 8. The University will increase faculty and staff involvement in University planning.

Goal 9. The University will increase its efforts to secure support from federal, state, and private sources.

Outline of Twelve-Month Sequence of Events for Preparation of Expanded Statement of Institutional Purpose

I. Doing the Homework (September through December)

A. Appoint Broad-Based Constituent Group—The group should be composed of faculty (probably the majority), administrators, student leaders, and representatives of the governing board. The purpose of the group is to serve as the overall steering committee that will review and discuss important issues related to the mission or purpose of the institution. This group may become somewhat large due to the need to involve various constituencies; however, most of the work done will be accomplished by several staff members appointed to support the work of the representative group.

B. Review Current Statement of Purpose—The current statement of purpose should be reviewed for several reasons. First, it represents the official policy of the institution as of the beginning of the process. Second, from a political standpoint, it may be that this existing statement cannot be entirely discarded due to legal ramifications or other circumstances and will need to be incorporated into the ESIP or circumvented.

C. Gather Input from Constituents—The attempt to involve the greater campus community in consideration of the ESIP should involve a broad canvassing of faculty, administrators, student leaders, and the governing board members for their opinions concerning the future development of the institution. The Institutional Goals Inventory from the Educational Testing Service has proven to be a useful tool for this purpose and is a relatively easy way to gain maximum participation with minimum effort and cost.

D. Determine External Opportunities and Constraints—The term **environmental scanning** conjures up massive efforts by a substantial staff to describe every detail of the environment in which the institution operates. On the contrary, an abbreviated environmental scan can not only be a valuable source of relatively easily obtained information but also provide an opportunity for participation by faculty experts in the different areas. It is possible to conduct an abbreviated environmental scan within 2 to 3 months and to present to the institution a summary of the political, economic, educational, and social issues forming the context within which it operated.

E. Consider Analysis of Internal Strengths/Weaknesses—It is highly unlikely (though possible) that the institution has the "intestinal fortitude" necessary to identify its weaknesses on paper. In most instances, institutions can go about the task of identifying those areas widely regarded on the campus as strengths. In this case, areas not identified as strengths should be considered as either generally acceptable or as weaknesses of the institution.

II. **Conducting Meaningful Deliberations (January through April)**
  A. Establish Issues to Be Addressed
    1. Identify Key Issues/Topics—The product of "Doing the Homework" should suggest a number of issues or topics (clientele, programs, research, etc.) that need to be addressed in the ESIP. It is important both to identify these topics as early as possible and to leave time for further topics to be developed during this second portion of the process.
    2. Determine Relative Priorities—Some of the topics identified initially will obviously be of greater importance to the institution than others. As early as possible, these topics should be identified and sequenced for consideration, leaving several periods of time open for consideration of topics developed during this second phase.
  B. Follow the Sequence of Deliberations
    1. Schedule Meetings with Topics—The number of topics identified will determine, to a great extent, the number and frequency of meetings to be scheduled. It is important, however, that these meetings be scheduled in advance so that members will know what topic is to be considered at which meetings and, accordingly, can arrange their calendars well in advance.
    2. Assign Responsibilities for the Drafting Component of Mission and Goals Statements—Each topic to be discussed should have a "floor manager" appointed to consider the information provided during the "Doing the Homework" phase and to frame initial components of the ESIP consideration by the group.
    3. Target Draft Completion by March 31—Preparation of the draft ESIP in the 3 months from January 1 to March 31 will doubtlessly require a number of meetings to discuss the topics identified and the original draft of the ESIP. The staff members supporting the broad-based constituent group can be expected to bear primary responsibility for logistical aspects of the completion of the initial draft.
  C. Distribute Draft ESIP on Campus for Review/Comment and Hold Open Meeting—During early April, the draft ESIP prepared should be widely distributed on the campus for comment and review by faculty, administrators, student leaders, and members of the governing board. An open meeting will need to be held, at which widely differing viewpoints will no doubt be aired.
  D. Complete Revised Draft of ESIP by the End of April—By the end of April, a revised ESIP should be forwarded to the chief executive officer for his or her review and potential modification.

III. Seek Approval and Complete Publication (May through August)

A. Have Final Review/Modification by Chief Executive Officer—The constituent groups' proposed ESIP should not come as a surprise to the CEO, since he or she should have been kept informed of progress throughout their deliberations. The CEO should have the authority to adjust and refine the statement presented to him or her; however, major or substantive changes of the proposed ESIP should be discussed with the broad-based constituent group prior to forwarding them to the governing board.

B. Gain Approval of Governing Board—Ultimately, the governing board of the institution should approve the ESIP. Chief executive officers who have accomplished this indicate that it is not among the most "comfortable" experiences they have "enjoyed." As members of the governing board, many for the first time, they are asked to play a meaningful role in charting the course of the future of their institution. However, following discussion, modification, and approval of the ESIP, the governing board should be more supportive of the CEO's implementation of the concepts contained as representative of their collective will.

C. Publish Statement in Catalog—At least the mission component of the ESIP should be published in the college catalog. In addition, the complete ESIP should be widely disseminated on the campus so that faculty, administrators, and student leaders are knowledgeable concerning the directions for future growth of the institution.

D. Present Document to the Institution as the Basis for Institutional Effectiveness Implementation/Self-Study—Finally, the ESIP should be presented to the faculty at the beginning of the following academic year as the basis for implementation of outcomes assessment, institutional effectiveness, and, in many cases, the self-study process.

Executive Summary of the Program Review Process of the Division of Student Affairs at The University of North Carolina at Greensboro

Background

The initial evaluation process for individual student affairs programs and services began in 1987 and involved two components. First, mission, goals, and objectives for each office were prepared in preparation for a SACS reaccreditation visit (see Example 1). This took place over an eighteen-month period. Each year since that time, staff members in each student affairs office review the mission and develop goals and objectives for the coming academic year as part of the ongoing program planning. These are then reviewed at the end of the next academic year to assess the"actual results" received for teach of the "expected results." Any changes that need to be made are then noted for program planning in the following year (see Example 2). This produces a cyclical evaluation program which is in keeping with the spirit of the SACS Institutional Effectiveness Criteria.

Second, a process was put in place whereby each office would have a systematic program evaluation. A decision was made to review each program and service using the CAS Standards (1986) (or similar professional standards where none are provided by CAS) as the baseline. This enabled the Student Affairs Division to meet the SACS Criteria 5.5 (of evaluating our programs), as well as criteria in 3.1 related to Institutional Effectiveness (The institution must evaluate its effectiveness and use the results in broad-based continuous planning and evaluation process). This would require an ongoing program in place prior to a reaccreditation visit.

Summary of Process and Schedule

CAS Reviews were used to review each office in relation to nationally accepted criteria for student services. An overall schedule for all areas in the Division was established, allowing more time for completing review of more complex operations, i.e. resident life, student activities (see Example 3). The initial CAS Review process which was implemented consisted of several components:

1. The Vice Chancellor would meet with the Director of the office to be reviewed and the Director of Student Affairs Research and Evaluation who coordinated the review process. During this discussion, a decision would be made regarding the

person who would chair the review committee. Other committee members would be selected from faculty, staff and students who were in some way related to that office. For example, the committee which reviewed Judicial Services included the Director of Campus Security, a faculty member whose area of expertise was higher education law, a student affairs staff member who served on many student hearing panels, and a student from the student government's Attorney General's Office.

2. While the review committee was being appointed, each employee in the office under review anonymously completed the CAS Self-Assessment Guide (1988). These responses were then compiled into one report which could be used by the review committee.

3. Prior to the initial meeting of the review committee, a copy of the CAS Standards for the office under review, the office's annual report, and any other supporting documents were sent to the committee members. The initial meeting of the review committee was a time for the Vice Chancellor to formally charge the committee and for the Director of the office under review to provide overview information. The committee would also discuss the need for additional resources they felt they would need to proceed with their task. Often this would include some type of assessment data which the Director of Student Affairs Research and Evaluation would need to collect. Usually this included a user satisfaction survey.

4. The review committees proceeded in a variety of ways depending on the nature of the office user population and services. Some interviewed employees in the office under review, talked with students, faculty, and other staff members, and called other campuses to inquire about that program or service on that campus. Most completed their reviews within one semester. The entire process was completed within one academic year.

5. Once the report was submitted to the Vice Chancellor's office, the appropriate supervisor would have six weeks to respond to any recommendations made by the committee. Follow-up reports were provided on an "as needed" basis. Recommendations which required major budgetary considerations were addressed in the yearly budget cycle.

6. The CAS review of each student affairs office was scheduled to take place once every four years. The initial review was designed to be a comparison of the program and procedures currently in use against those outlined in the Standards. Areas where the office was not meeting the standard were noted and suggestions for improvement were offered.

7. The second time an office was to be reviewed, there was a slight modification in this process. There was still an external review committee. However, the office under review completed a self-study using the CAS Standards prior to the appointment of this committee. The resulting report was used by the review committee for completing the program evaluation.

The CAS review process as it was implemented proved to be very helpful for getting all staff members to begin thinking about assessment in a structured manner. The outcome of the reviews resulted in observable changes and improvements in many of the program areas and this added to employee support for the process. It is important to guard against conducting evaluations and then NOT using the results in some meaningful way. If you make that mistake, people will cease to view the process as a way to make improvements.

Dr. Diane L. Cooper
Assistant Professor–Human Development and Psychological Counseling
Student Development Program
Appalachian State University
Boone, NC 28608

References: Cited

Council for the Advancement of Standards for Student Services/Development Programs. (1986). *CAS Standards and Guidelines for Student Service/Development Programs.* Washington DC: Author.

Council for the Advancement of Standards for Student Services/Development Programs. (1988). *CAS Self Assessment Guide.* Washington DC: Author.

Example 1
Example of Goals and Objectives

Career Services Mission Statement

The primary mission of the Career Services Center is to aid students in the development, assessment, effective initiation, and implementation of career development plans. Career planning is a developmental and lifelong process that must be fostered during the entire time the student is involved with The University of North Carolina at Greensboro (UNCG). Placement services reflect accountability of the University to establish employer relationships and services that aid students, current graduates, and alumni in obtaining viable employment. The Career Services Center promotes awareness in the University of careers and trends in the world of work.

A. Goal: To assist students in securing major-appropriate, postgraduate employment by providing on campus recruiting and placement services.

a. Objective: The office will facilitate the entry of graduates into their chosen careers.

Expected Results: Develop a campus placement service that is used by more than half of the institution's graduates and that produces appropriate job placement for at least 75% of the graduates who use it.

Assessment Procedures: Survey graduating students on an annual basis to ask if they have used the placement service (and if not, why not) and if they perceive that they have obtained appropriate placement through that service.

Administration of Assessment Procedures: Questions about the use of the placement service and the outcomes of placement will be included in a survey administered to graduating students by the student services division.

Use of Assessment Findings: If fewer than half of the graduates are using the placement service, the service should be promoted more effectively through presentations to student groups and distribution of descriptive printed materials to all students. If aspects of the service are criticized, or if placement rates are lower than expected, explicit plans for improvement will be designed by the staff during the annual summer retreat.

Example 2
Follow-up to Goals and Objectives

Beginning of YEAR 1

A. Goal: To assist students in securing major-appropriate, postgraduate employment by providing on campus recruiting and placement services.

a. Objectives: The office will facilitate the entry of graduates into their chosen careers.

Expected Results: Develop a campus placement service that is used by at least 40% of the institution's graduates and that produces appropriate job placement for at least 50% of the graduates who use it.

End of YEAR 1

Actual Results: We had 36% of the students eligible for graduation this year actually use our job placement services. Our employer follow-up surveys showed that 60% of the students using our placement services received job offers. We will need to survey our recent graduates to get the actual number of accepted offers.

Changes to be implemented due to results: We seem to be doing a fairly good job of getting students in to use our services yet would like to see the percentage of users increase. We will explore better marketing ideas to use in the coming academic year.

Example 3
Sample Time Line for Initial CAS Review

August	•	Appoint Review Committee
	•	Staff of office under review given the CAS Self-Assessment Guide to complete
September	•	Initial meeting of the review committee—talk with office Director, discuss data needs
	•	Collect and compile information from the staff self-assessment—distribute to committee
October	•	Design assessment projects related to data needs
	•	Review committee begins to take each part of the Standards and collects information which indicates the level of compliance with each 'must'and 'should' statement
December	•	Data requested is provided to the committee
	•	Committee meets to discuss findings—outline of next step completed
February	•	Committee completes draft of report
April	•	Final report provided to office supervisor
June	•	Response to report provided to the office under review and the review committee by the Vice Chancellor.

Index

Academic advising 46, 167-168, 198
Academic freedom 157
Academic Profile test 66
Academic support services 10, 186-204, 260
Access to data 158
Accreditation
  agencies 2-7, 9, 11, 24, 126, 140, 149, 163,
    198, 212, 224, 254
  common components 7
  process 7-11, 81
  regional 5-6, 198
  requirements 7
ACT (see American College Testing Service)
Administrative objectives, non-academic units
    10, 18-19, 24, 140-143, 186-204, 232, 252
Administrative practice 16-17, 41, 195
Adult Learner Needs Assessment 44-45
Alumni follow-up, surveys 28, 44-48, 54,
    91-92, 95-98, 112, 118-119, 135, 154, 166,
    167, 219
  Alumni Outcomes Survey 45
  Alumni Survey 45
Alverno College 78, 81, 99-100, 153
American Assembly of Collegiate Schools of
    Business (AACSB) 72, 120, 207
American Association for Higher Education
    166, 182
American Chemical Society 73
American College Testing Service (ACT)
    44-48, 50, 62-64, 176-177, 181
  assessment 62-64
  profile 46-47, 66
American Council on Education (ACE) 4-5,
    61, 67, 110, 198
American Institute of Certified Public
    Accountants (AICPA) 72-73
  Achievement Test for Accounting 72
American Registry of Radiologic
    Technologists 229
American Society of Clinical Pathologists
    (ASCP) 229
  Program Performance Summary 229
Annual Institutional Effectiveness Cycle
    (AIEC) 19, 136, 236-253
  closing the loop 242-243
  evaluation 240-242

initial implementation assumptions 23
  maintaining 251-254
  planning 238-240
  second year 138
Assessment
  academic/educational support systems
    18-19, 196-198, 260
  activities 27-28
  administrative objectives 10, 18-19, 22-24,
    140-143, 186-204, 224-225, 252-253
  affective outcomes 166-168
  behavioral change and performance 86-106,
    132-133, 164, 168-169
  campus-based 199-201
  classroom 101
  cognitive assessment 60-85, 75-78,
    132-133, 218
  connection to teaching and learning
    101-102, 157-172
  data systems 28, 115-119, 195
  departmental level 3, 9-10, 18-19, 138-156,
    157-171, 186-204, 217, 251
  general knowledge 62-69
  major field 69-75, 229-230
  multiple procedures 151-152
  logistical support 154-155
  objectives and outcomes 186-204
  planning 34-35, 123-138, 211, 215, 217,
    224-225, 143
  product and performance 98
  psychomotor 168-169
  related information 107-122
  research outcomes 192-199
  specialized knowledge 69-75
  strategies 92
  two-year colleges 180, 183-184, 223-236
Assessment center 99-100
Assessment planning (see Assessment,
    planning)
Association of College and University
    Business Officers (NACUBO) 190
Astin, A. W. 205-207
Attitudinal measures 17, 27-28, 43-58, 194-
    195, 219

Atwell, R. 5
Austin Peay State University 164

Banta, T. A. 2, 4
Benchmarking 187, 190, 194
Bunker Hill Community College 180-181
Butler University 79

Capstone courses 176, 180
Chief Executive Officer (CEO) ix, 1-2, 16- 17, 140, 146, 153, 238-239, 253, 268-269
Classification of Instructional Programs (CIP) 111
Clemson University 177-179
Closing the loop 3, 19, 239-240, 242-243
Cognitive instruments (see also Assessment, cognitive assessment) 60-86, 164-166, 168, 218-219
College Base (CBASE) 66-67, 176, 178, 228
College Entrance Examination Board (CEEB) 65-66, 71
College environment 98
College Level Academic Skills Project (CLASP) 67
College-Level Examination Program (CLEP) 62, 65, 71
  general chemistry 71
College Outcomes Survey 45
College of William and Mary 79
College Outcome Measures Program (COMP) 63-65, 68, 176, 181
College Student Experiences Questionnaire (CSEQ) 98, 166
College Student Needs Assessment Survey 44
Collegiate Assessment of Academic Proficiency (CAAP) 62, 64, 176
Commercially available instruments 28, 44- 50, 53, 62-74
Community Colleges (see Assessment, two-year colleges; Two-year colleges)
Comprehensive Alumni Assessment Survey (CAAS) 48
Computer-assisted testing 176-177
Connecticut, University of 179
Consultants and advisors 15, 23, 25, 50-51, 201
Continuous Quality Improvement (CQI) x, xii, 19, 142, 186-189, 205-214, 236
  administrative support 191
  benchmarking 190
  defining quality 207-211
    educational support 191
    higher education 205
    management audits 191
    parallels 211-213
    performance indicators 189-190
    program review 232
    strategic planning 211
    teams 213
    terminology 207
Cooperative Institutional Research Program (CIRP) 44, 50
Coopers & Lybrand 190
Costs 11, 13-17, 20, 28, 39, 51, 53, 75, 92- 93, 103, 110, 124, 154-155, 186, 198, 241, 249
Council for the Advancement of Standards (CAS) 197-199, 270-272, 275
Council on Postsecondary accreditation (COPA) 5-7, 198

Data systems 28, 107-122
  comparing successive test scores and inventory results 117
  cross sectional 112-113
  determine course enrollment patters 117
  longitudinal 113
  operational support systems 108-110
  retention and graduation rates calculation 116
  supporting outcomes assessment 114
Demming, W.E. 205
Departmental level (see also Assessment, departmental level)
  leadership 138-140
  responsibility 14-16, 20
  support 10
Direct measures 98-99, 163, 194
Dundalk Community College 79

Economic assumptions 256
Educational Assessment Series (EAS) 65
Educational Testing Service (ETS) 27, 44, 49-50, 65-66, 70-72, 78, 80-81, 132, 176-177, 267
El-Khawas, E. 62, 110
Entrance examination 27
  Entering Student Survey 46
Equal Employment Opportunity Commission (EEOC) 111
Erwin Scale of Intellectual Development 76

Evaluation/Survey Service (ESS) 44
Evergreen State College 169
Ewell. P. 51-52, 57, 68, 74, 115, 153, 158, 182, 190
Executive summary 270
Expanded Statement of Institutional Purpose (ESIP)/Mission 3, 7-10, 17-19, 23-24, 27-28, 30-31, 61, 89-90, 94, 108, 123, 191, 194, 196, 236
  aligning with instructional objectives 160-161, 202
  at two-year colleges 223-225
  CAS 198
  components 31
  CQI 208, 211
  development of 30-42
  example 265-269
  formative statements 9-10
  initial implementation of 215-222, 251
  linkage to results 146-149
  logistical support of 154-156
  planning/operational activities 140-142
  progressive revision 152, 238-240, 254
  revision of standards 152
  TQM/CQI 189
  two-year institutions 223-224
Experimental design 95
Faculty input 20, 33, 35-36, 49-50, 110, 124-125, 151, 157-159
  resistance 21
Fund for Adult Education 172
Funding (see Cost)
General education 45, 164, 172-185, 228-229, 257
  approaches 174-175
  examples 177-183
  surveys 175-176
  tools 175-177
  two-year institutions 183-184
Georgia, University System of 68
Goals 5, 24, 33, 90, 100-102, 113, 142, 147-148, 154, 159, 187
  administrative statements 110, 256-261, 263-264
  common questions 37
  description 38
  developing 36-41

  example 266, 274
  ingredients 38-39
  national 87
  of cognitive assessment 60
Governing and coordinating boards (steering committees) 34-35, 41, 67-68, 97, 163, 177-178, 180-181, 186, 224, 229
Government 4-6, 107
Graduate Program Self-Assessment Service 49, 166
Graduate Record Examination (GRE) 62, 65, 177
  general test 62, 71
  general chemistry 71
  psychology 71
Graduating Student Examination 27-28
Graduating Writing Assessment Requirement (GWAR) 68
Grants 16
Higher Education General Information Survey (HEGIS) 111, 163
Indiana University of Pennsylvania 74
Initial implementation 215-236
Initial feedback of results 221-222
Institutional effectiveness and outcomes assessment (see also Outcomes assessment) 3, 5-6, 225-226
  assessment activities 218
  assessment in the major 229-230
  components 7
  coordinator 13-14
  course performance 228
  data reports 220
  definition 6
  developmental education 226
  differences 6
  establishment of annual cycle 236-253
  expectations 222
  foundation 23-29
  general education 228-229
  implementation model 13-22, 223
  implementation problems 20-21
  movement 4-6
  paradigm 7, 11, 14, 60, 111, 123, 190-192, 211-213, 223, 236
  program review 232
  results 220-222

transfer data 230-232
Institutional Goals Inventory (IGI) 49
Institutional Performance Survey (IPS) 48
Integrated Postsecondary Educational Data
    Support Systems (IPEDS) 111, 163
Interviews 77, 167, 176

Jefferson State Community College xii, 225
Johnson County Community College 229

Kean College 78
Kenyon College 79
King's College 74

Laws 33, 97-98, 111-120
Licensure 27, 126, 219
Locally developed surveys (see Surveys,
    locally developed)

Maintaining institutional effectiveness over
    time 251-254
  impeding forces 252-253
  marshaling forces 253-254
  operations review 252
Major Field Achievement Test (MFAT)
    bucnology 70-71
Management audits 191
Maryland, University of 187, 199-200
Measure of Epistemological Reflection 76
Medical Laboratory Technician Examination
    229
Miami University 78
Mission (see Expanded Statement of
    Institutional Purpose)
Mississippi, University of xii-xv, 242, 265-
    266

National Association of Secondary School
    Principals 100
National Center for Higher Education
    (NCHEMS) 44, 47-50, 128
National commissions/committees 4
National Council for the Accreditation of
    Teacher Education (NCATE) 126
National Council Licensure Examination for
    Registered Nurses (NCLEX-RN) 229
National Council of State Boards of Nursing
    229
National Institute of Education 4
National Laboratory for Higher Education 149
National Policy Board (NPB) 5-7
National Society for Engineering
    Technologies (NICET) 230

Technologist Certification Programs 230
National Society of Engineers 230
National Teacher Examination (NTE) 73
New Jersey College Basic Skills Placement
    Test (NJCBSPT) 68
North Carolina, University of, at Greensboro
    xiii, 187, 198, 270-273
North Central Association of Colleges and
    Schools (NCA) 125, 207
Northeastern Missouri State University 81,
    153
Northwestern University 199, 200

Office of Civil Rights (OCR) 111
Office of Vocational and Adult Education
    (OVAE) 111
Ohio University 181-182
Oregon System of Higher Education 87
Our University 31-34, 142, 149, 152, 161,
    255-262
Outcomes assessment 3, 6, 9, 28-29, 49,
    164-166
  departmental 129, 142
  evaluation 162-164
  how 13, 19-20
  linkage to results 146-148
  setting 157-162

Performance indicators 28, 187, 189-191
Pirsig, T. J. 207
Plan-Do-Check-Act (PDCA) cycle 189
Planning parameters 256
Portfolio assessment 78-81, 86, 152, 169-170,
    175
Portland Community College 87
Prince George's Community College 225
Professional standards 196
Program of Self-Assessment Service (PSAS)
    49, 166
Project for Area Concentration Achievement
    Testing 164

Reflective Judgment Interview 76-77
Reporting systems 111-112, 119-120
    111-112

Saint John's 69
Samford University 206
San Diego State University 80
Sinclair Community College 182-183
Society for College and University Planning
    190

Southern Association of Colleges and Schools (SACS) xii, 6, 146-147, 149-150, 177-178, 207, 242, 270
State Postsecondary Review Entity (SPRE) 5, 62
State University System of New York at Fredonia (SUNY-Fredonia) 79
Statement of intended outcomes
Strategic planning (see Assessment, planning)
Student Achievement Test (SAT) 62-64
Student compliance 219, 228
Student Follow-Up Survey 95-96
Student Information Form (SIF) 50
Student Instructional Report (SIR) 49-50
Student Occupational Competency Achievements Test (SOCAT) 74, 132, 230
Student Opinion Survey 46
Student Outcomes Information Service (SOIS) 47-48
Student Services Program Review Project 197, 199
Student tracking 93-94, 97, 225
Summary Report to Educational Programs: Certification Examination in Radiologic Technology 229
Survey of Academic Advising 46
Survey of Current Activities and Plans 46
Survey of Postsecondary Plans 47
Survey populations 54
Surveys
    attitudinal 43-59, 86-87, 128, 194-195, 219
    characteristics 53-54
    commercial 44-50
    locally developed 51-54, 56, 75-76, 128, 133, 174-175, 179, 184
    populations 54-55

suggestions 56-57
Swarthmore College 69
Teaching systems 93-94
Tennessee, University of, at Knoxville 74, 81, 153
Tennessee Technological University 63
Test of Thematic Analysis 77
Texas, University of 191
Total Quality Forum 206
Total Quality Improvement (TQI) (see Continuous Quality Improvement--CQI)
Total Quality Management (TQM) (see Continuous Quality Improvement--CQI)
Tracking 47, 114, 183
Two-year colleges 183-184, 223-236
    assessment instruments 226-230
    linkage with four-year institutions 97
    statement of purpose 223-224
    transfer data 159, 219-220, 230
Unit of analysis 91
University relations and development 262
Use of Results 55
    documentation 133
Utilization of assessment results 109, 147, 158, 251
Virginia, University of 78
Washington State Board for Community College Education 97
Watson-Glaser Critical Thinking Appraisal 77
Wingspread 5
Withdrawing/Nonreturning Student Survey 47
Writing 68, 78-79, 98, 163, 168, 183, 228
Your Community College 224, 263-264